How Did We Get Here?

Library of Congress Cataloging-in-Publication Data

A CIP record for this book is available from the Library of Congress
http://www.loc.gov

ISBN: 978-1-64802-963-9 (Paperback)
       978-1-64802-964-6 (Hardcover)
       978-1-64802-965-3 (E-Book)

How Did We Get Here?

The Decay of the Teaching Profession

edited by

Henry Tran
University of South Carolina

Douglas A. Smith
Iowa State University

INFORMATION AGE PUBLISHING, INC.
Charlotte, NC • www.infoagepub.com

CONTENTS

PART I

HOW DID WE GET HERE: THE HISTORICAL AND RACIAL CONTEXT OF THE TEACHING PROFESSION'S DECAY

PART I

HOW DID WE GET HERE:
THE HISTORICAL AND RACIAL CONTEXT OF THE
TEACHING PROFESSION'S DECAY

CHAPTER 1

AN INTRODUCTION TO THE CURRENT STATUS OF THE TEACHING PROFESSION

The Case of South Carolina

Henry Tran
University of South Carolina

Douglas A. Smith
Iowa State University

A sea of approximately 10,000 people, dressed in "emergency" red, convened at the state capital in downtown Columbia, South Carolina, on the sunny Wednesday morning of May 1, 2019 (Bowers, 2019b). This statewide teacher walkout was assembled to call for the improvement of teachers' working conditions and the learning environments of their students. The number of participants far surpassed the prior night's estimation of 4,000 to 5,000. The crowd comprised of teachers from across South Carolina who walked out of their classrooms, as well as students, parents, university

How Did We Get Here?, pages 3–16
Copyright © 2022 by Information Age Publishing
www.infoagepub.com
All rights of reproduction in any form reserved.

faculty, and other community members who rallied with teachers in solidarity. A teacher advocacy organization, SC for Ed, had organized and coordinated the #alloutMay1 teacher rally as a "day of reflection" for the state to bring attention to issues related to low salaries, increasing health care premiums, inadequate school funding, lack of mental health counselors in schools, unfavorable work conditions (such as the lack of guaranteed work break and protected classroom planning time during the school day), and an overall lack of respect for those in the education profession.

According to former educator and current State Senator Mike Fanning, this historic march was the largest demonstration of teacher activism ever in the state, despite only approximately a week and a half official notice for the convening. Seven districts, serving a total of 123,000 students (1/6th of the public presecondary students in the state), canceled school on the day to brace themselves for the massive protest and teacher absences including rural, urban, and suburban serving districts and a public charter school (Bowers, 2019a; Bowers 2019b). Many of the districts that remained open relied on substitutes to fill their teaching void, although not all of the substitutes used were trained teachers (some, e.g., included district office staff who stepped in for classroom coverage).

The protest was, in some ways, reminiscent of the Charleston hospital strike of 1969, where another group of mostly women workers rallied for the improvement of pay and working conditions. Specifically, according to the South Carolina Encyclopedia (Hopkins, 2016), that strike involved more than 400 Black nurses against Medical College Hospital and the Charleston County Hospital. Due to a culture of disrespect shown to Black hospital workers by their White counterparts, the pay gap between the two employee groups, and a generally hostile work environment. After 12 nurses were fired for protesting their employers' refusal to recognize their union and negotiate in good faith, over 5,000 people marched against the deplorable working conditions. Amid the struggle, the city of Charleston was declared to be in a state of emergency, where 500 National Guardsmen worked in conjunction with hundreds of police officers to enforce a curfew that was sustained for months. Scores of arrests were made in the process. Ultimately, the hospital agreed to some of the strikers' demands, including rehiring the fired workers, raising pay, and establishing a formal grievance procedure. To bring it back full circle, Louise Brown, a participant in the nursing strike, spoke in front of the Statehouse at the teacher walkout in 2019 (Bowers, 2020).

Undergirding both the nurses' strike in 1969 and the teachers' protest 50 years later was a history of patriarchal systems that resulted in the lack of respect in the respective professions and the exploitation of women in these labor markets. However, it is important to note that teachers in colonial America were predominately male when education was primarily reserved for the wealthy elite. But, by the turn of the 20th century, it became a predominately female occupation following the rise of compulsory education state laws in the latter half of the 19th century. Boyle (2004) described the change from a male-dominated to a female-dominated profession as stemming from a combination of shifting career options for men and women, societies' changing perceptions of women in the workforce, changes in the preferred personal characteristics of teachers, and changes in the social status of teachers in America. Reviewing changes from colonial to modern times, Boyle explained that teaching in early America was considered a temporary position that one would take on their way to their "real" career. As the need for teachers grew in America during the 1800s, women were increasingly looked upon to fill this need given the perception of their nurturing dispositions and the low pay provided to teachers relative to more traditionally masculine higher-paying labor and mechanical jobs. To make matters worse is the historical belief that remains today, that teachers should sacrifice for their students and that if they are motivated by money, they are in the wrong profession. This belief further justifies the marginalization of teacher concerns and needs that serve as barriers to self-advocacy.

A statewide teacher walkout in North Carolina occurred in conjunction with the walkout in South Carolina, representing the 8th and 9th large-scale teacher activism walkouts within the prior 3 months (Camera, 2019). Much of the momentum of the statewide walkouts across the nation were ignited by West Virginia's 9-day teacher and service personnel strike that started on February 22, 2018, and ended with a 5% pay raise for all teachers and state employees. Shortly after, states like Oklahoma (9-day strike) and Arizona (6-day strike) followed suit to combat the austerity facing education finance and gain funding increases in the process. The nationwide strikes that occurred in 2018 were the largest since the 1980s (Campbell, 2019), and the geographic patterns of the initiating states of the educator labor movement earned it the nickname: "The Red State Revolt" (Blanc, 2019; Jamieson & Waldron, 2018).

It is not a coincidence that most teacher strikes originated from conservative "right-to-work" states (i.e., states that prohibited mandatory joining of unions or payment of union dues). Hansen (2018), a labor economist and director of the Brookings Institution's Brown Center on Education Policy, identified four characteristics common to the initial striking states that include (a) low average teaching salaries relative to the rest of the nation, (b) reductions in inflation-adjusted teacher salaries and (c) in per-pupil spending since the Great Recession, and (d) a state determined salary schedule. In addition, these states, like South Carolina, often reduced school funding while providing tax cuts that benefit businesses and individuals at the highest tiers of economic classifications. The espoused rationale behind these cuts was often to motivate increased spending by those who receive the cuts to improve the economy (e.g., employers who benefit from tax cuts might provide their employees with higher wages through trickle down economics), but this seldom occurred. Overall, the cuts resulted in fewer resources to fund schools, hurting teacher salaries and negatively impacting working conditions, such as failing to provide sufficient and updated classroom resources, as well as ballooning class sizes (which has unenforced cap limits since 2010; Bowers, 2019a). These states often had the lowest-paid teachers in the country, where the state-mandated minimum teacher salary schedule has not kept up with inflation since 2003 (Bowers, 2019a). These conditions, coupled with an "accountability" environment that significantly reduces (and some would say removed) the teacher voice in decisions involving their classrooms, have created an unfavorable work environment that simultaneously deters potential teachers from entry into the teaching profession, but also promotes turnover and attrition from teachers that are in the classrooms.

Perhaps uncoincidentally, the deterioration of the teacher working conditions existed concurrently alongside a decline in school academic performance. U.S. News & World Report annually ranks states by education quality based on college readiness (ACT/SAT), high school graduation rate, National Assessment of Education Progress (NAEP) math scores, NAEP reading scores, preschool enrollment, educational attainment rates, college graduation rates, college debt, and college tuition costs. Consistently hovering towards the bottom of the nation, South Carolina ranked 43rd in 2019, 48th in 2018, and dead last (50th) in 2017 (U.S. News & World Report, 2017, 2018, 2019). The issues are cyclical, as poor educational outcomes deter teacher employment in the state. Relatedly, a 2019 Wallet Hub article evaluated 49 key indicators of family-friendliness to rank all 50 states from best to worst for raising a family. In this report, South Carolina ranked 43rd overall and ranked consistently between 38th and 42nd across the major categories of family fun, health and safety, education and child care, affordability, and socioeconomics (McCann, 2019).

The declining revenue for school funding in South Carolina was exacerbated by over 100 sales tax exemptions that include (but are not limited to) shipping containers, computers used by data centers, purchases made by motion picture production companies in connection with the film or production, material for missile production, and 70% of the gross proceed of portable toilets (South Carolina Department of Revenue, 2019). These exemptions reflected the non-education priorities of the state, with the corporate tax exemption alone being estimated to have cost South Carolina over $318 million a year in lost revenue (Goodjobsfirst.org, 2018). Beyond the sales tax exemptions, South Carolina public education funding was also hurt by a major homeowner school operating tax exemption known as Act

388 (Tran, 2018). Act 388, first passed in 2006, added a 100% exemption for owner-occupied residential property from tax millage for school operations. This act effectively eliminated homeowners directly from school funding. Part of Act 388 included a tradeoff clause to increase the state sales tax by a penny, among other tax reforms, with a promise to send money to school districts to offset the lost revenue from the homeowner exemption. However, in reality, education funding has worsened in South Carolina since Act 388 was passed in 2006 due to the swapping of a relatively stable property tax for a relatively unstable sales tax that dramatically declined during the Great Recession, just a year after implementation of the act (see Chapter 4 by Tran et al. and Chapter 5 by Martínez & Tran, this volume, for more details).

Furthermore, the state has consistently underfunded school districts, as can be seen, reflected in the gap between the estimated base student cost per the state funding formula to the actual state appropriation approved by the state legislature. In the 31 years since 1989, the appropriated base student cost equaled or exceeded the estimated base student cost only 11 times, the last time being 2008–2009 (Tran, 2018). The 2019–2020 estimated state base student cost was $3,095 per pupil, while the appropriated base cost was $2,489 per pupil (a $606 difference). These constellations of funding and political events have negatively affected resources for educators and their students. At the same time, an accountability environment in education has scrutinized the profession to the point where the profession has earned the perception of a generally unfavorable working career (see Chapter 9 by Jackson Smith & Sauls, this volume).

Case in point, from 2000 to 2017, teacher salaries in South Carolina dropped 6%, adjusting for inflation (National Center for Educational Statistics, n.d.), exceeding the national average of 1.6%. Chapter 7 (with Tran & Jackson) delves deeper into the topic of South Carolina teacher pay, highlighting the increasing economic disincentive to teach. Low pay has real-life implications for those who tough it out in the field. Low teacher pay has prompted many teachers to work two or three jobs to make ends meet (e.g., pay rent, mortgage, student loans), and their stories are increasingly receiving media attention (Bowers, 2019c). One South Carolina factory notably employed over 650 teachers, who worked their second shift to as late as 11:00 p.m. after they fulfilled their teaching duties in the first half of their day (Chuck, 2019). Many of the teachers moonlight on the weekends to earn additional pay. However, these extra additional responsibilities elevate the exhaustion of the already overworked educators. Nationally, a market research firm found that most teachers (59%) reported working a second job to secure a livable wage (IPSOS, 2018).

Concurrently, in an era of increasing standardization and alignment of curriculum and instructional approaches with standardized-based assessment, teacher autonomy and professionalization have been reduced in many districts (Phi Delta Kappa, 2018). Teacher expertise is often not acknowledged, and teachers are often not recognized as professionals. At the same time, more expectations, responsibilities, and accountability have been placed on educators' shoulders. To make matters worse, education funding cuts necessitate most teachers to dip into their personal funds to provide classroom resources to enhance the learning opportunities of their students.

Results from the U.S. Department of Education's nationally representative survey of teachers suggest that 94% of public-school teachers spent their own non-reimbursable money on classroom material in 2014–2015 (National Center for Education Statistics, 2018). In South Carolina, the average amount spent was $433. For teachers who teach schools from economically impoverished backgrounds, these funds may go towards daily necessities such as food and clothes, in addition to classroom material. The legality of the additional, ever-expanding, uncompensated work duties, coupled with the pressure of teachers to spend their own money on resources, has been called into question (see *Burgess v. Cherokee County School District*). Uncoincidentally, crippling teacher shortages have been on the rise in many states (Garcia & Weiss, 2019), but especially in South Carolina for reasons that will be explored much deeper in this book.

Bowers et al. (2018) described the South Carolina public education system as displaying a "legacy of apathy and low expectations that threatens the state's newfound prosperity" (para. 1). They describe how the state legislature has ignored its funding mandates on education (e.g., expanded kindergarten, new school buses, teacher pay increases), allowing students to underperform, school buildings to crumble, and teachers to abandon the profession. Consequently, teacher staffing problems in the state have been described as reaching "crisis" levels as the leaky ships of districts continue to see teachers hemorrhaging out of their classrooms (Chuck, 2019).

The declining status and respectability of the teaching profession contribute to the teaching shortage as it influences many college students to refrain from considering education as a career in the state and across the nation at large (Tran & Smith, 2019). In fact, according to a report from Phi Delta Kappa (2018) entitled *Teaching: Respect with Dwindling Appeal,* the majority of parents in the United States do not want their children to pursue a career in education, and the children themselves do not want to become educators as the pay is not equivalent to those with similar degrees, the profession does not garnish respect, and the work demands are high. In a televised interview with Fox Carolina on January 24, 2019 (Fox Carolina News, 2019), Superintendent of Greenville County Schools, Burke Royster, echoed this sentiment by stating, "We've got to raise teacher pay to an amount that it is an attractive profession, attractive career option for students when they are looking at going to college."

Attracting talented people into the teaching profession is important for many reasons, not the least of which is the fact that South Carolina districts lose more teachers than the state prepares each year. The Center for Educator Recruitment, Retention, and Advancement (CERRA) reported a growing gap between the number of teachers who were no longer teaching in the state (5,341 in 2018–2019) and the number of graduates from in-state teacher education programs (1,642 in 2018–2019). This gap amounts to a shortfall of 3,699 teachers that must be replaced through means other than the traditional route of in-state teacher preparation programs (Figure 1.1).

One mechanism that districts have used to fill teacher vacancies in the face of rising departures and fewer in-state prepared teachers has been through hiring international teachers. While hiring international teachers provides immediate relief, they are a short-term stopgap measure that is only a band-aid fix. The intent of the U.S. Department of State's H-1B visa program is aimed at temporarily employing foreign workers in specialty occupations. H-1B visas are for 3 years, extendable to 6 years. Likewise, districts seeking to hire foreign teachers on H-1B visas often incur added costs to assist prospective teachers with the visa process. When it comes to the international teacher program itself, its purpose is for cultural exchange

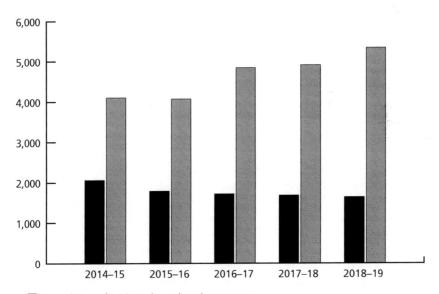

■ Completers of a SC teacher education program

▨ Teachers who left their positions and are no longer teaching in any SC public school

Figure 1.1 South Carolina educators leaving teaching vs. new teacher education program graduates.

to bring diversity exposure to students who are unlikely to receive them. The program was not meant to address teacher shortages. Nonetheless, as districts in South Carolina experience teacher shortages, they have increasingly turned to international teachers as a source of remedy. CERRA (2019) reports that nearly 400 international teachers were employed in South Carolina public schools in 2018–2019, a dramatic four-fold employment escalation from the approximately 100 international teachers working in 2013–2014.

In 2018–2019, South Carolina school districts relied on 643 alternatively certified teachers to fill vacancies. These included 408 new teachers prepared through South Carolina's Program of Alternative Certification for Educators (PACE), 111 through South Carolina's Career and Technology Education (CATE) Work-Based Certification Program, 24 through the American Board, 24 through Teachers for Tomorrow, 23 through District-based Alternative Certification Programs, and 53 through Teach for America. Critics of alternative certifications have argued that it represents a dumbing down of the entry standards to address teacher shortage concerns and that this tradeoff has severe teacher quality implications for students in the classrooms (Darling-Hammond et al., 2005; Lasko-Kerr & Berliner, 2003).

Months of conversations, public input, and hearings on teacher working conditions precipitated the Palmetto state teacher walkout (#alloutMay1), but progress was sluggish and often ground to a halt. For example, the week before the event, an education overhaul bill had stalled in the Senate, delaying any changes to the system until at least the following year (Bowers, 2019b). Similarly, although initially the state of South Carolina was found guilty of failing to provide a "minimally adequate education" for students of the state in the almost three-decade-long *Abbeville v. South Carolina* school funding lawsuit initiated by the state's poorest and most rural school districts, upon turnover and replacement of some of the state supreme court justices, the case was ultimately dismissed with little substantive change in the underlying conditions for the plaintiff districts (Tran, 2018). As will be highlighted in Chapter 4 by Tran, Aziz, and Reinhardt, the disparity between the economically impoverished plaintiff districts and the non-plaintiff districts in the state grew over time.

The protests in South Carolina differed from some of the earlier strikes around the nation in several ways. For example, whereas the work stoppages in Oklahoma, Arizona, and West Virginia spanned several days, in South Carolina, the walkout only happened for 1 day. Furthermore, in South Carolina, the walkout was "not an official strike, like those that have swept through school districts across the country in the last year. Instead, teachers used a personal day to protest in their state capitols" (Weiner, 2019, para. 2). Teachers that did not have sufficient personal days had to request unpaid days off from their districts, which meant they lost earnings for participating in their activism engagement. Overall, the "day of reflection" that occurred in South Carolina was much less aggressive than the teacher activism that had occurred in many of the other states in the wave of teacher strikes that happened before. This "soft strike" can be attributed to the political sentiment against unionization and collective bargaining rights that permeated the state.

Some criticized the nationwide teacher walkouts as political, described as part of a leftist socialist plot to push a progressive agenda instead of truly being interested in public education concerns. For example, the son of the president of the United States, Donald Trump Jr., criticized teacher activists as "these loser teachers that are trying to sell you on socialism from birth" (Wolf, 2019, para. 3). Others pitted the teachers' self-advocacy against the students. For example, 2 days before the statewide walkout, South Carolina's State Superintendent Molly Spearman released a statement stating she "will not be joining those teachers who decide to walk out on their classrooms. Instead, I will be walking into the classroom of an absent teacher to serve as a substitute. I am not doing this to help facilitate the walkout, but rather to do all I can to ensure as many students as possible receive the instruction they deserve" (Spearman, 2019, para. 2). Governor Henry McMaster similarly argued "teachers leaving their classrooms sends the wrong message to students" (Bowers, 2019b, para. 32).

Districts also varied in their responses to the walkout. Some districts, like Chester County, closed the district on May 1 and released statements supporting the movement (Bennett, 2019). Whereas Charleston County board member Todd Garrett described the walkout as teachers "using kids as political stunts... Particularly in a year when we've missed six days [due to weather], this is wrong. It's wrong for the kids, it's wrong for their working parents, and it's wrong for the taxpayers to have to foot the bill for political activism" (Bowers, 2019a, para. 39). Berkeley County School District similarly released a statement emphasizing concerns for the walkout's impact on the children but later apologized after receiving a poor reception from the local community and teachers regarding the statement.

THE ALL OUT MAY 1ST RALLY

The #alloutMay1 rally was scheduled to begin on May 1, 2019, at 9:00 a.m. outside the South Carolina Department of Education. Teachers, students, and supporters held descriptive signs that created awareness for the conditions facing schools. For example, one student held a sign that said, "My father is a teacher and I qualify for Medicaid," alluding to the low pay teachers earn in the state. Similarly, on the same topic of pay, other signs included "8 years experience, 1 master's degree = $9 [in teachers account] until payday" and "Funding for this poster was provided by my other 2 jobs." Some signage spoke to broader issues. For example, one read, "No student in S.C. is minimal," referencing the often criticized the underwhelming "Minimally Adequate" education standard established in *Abbeville v. South Carolina* for the state (Tran, 2018), which some view as reflective of the philosophy of how education is treated in the state.

At 9:45 a.m. the march progressed to and around the State House, where speakers and protesters assembled outside the steps of the State House to unify their voices to encourage change in classrooms and schools across the state. The vast majority of teachers and their supporters were cloaked in the unifying color of red as they took their stand for education and rocked the state to awaken them from business-as-usual apathy typically directed towards teachers' work concerns. The teacher activism movement in South Carolina borrowed from many successful strategies in Arizona, including reliance on social media, donning red attire as the color for solidarity for the cause, and adopting the "forEd" moniker at the tail end of SC for Ed. Many of these ideas have been attributed to teacher and education organizer Noah Karvelis and Arizona Education Association (teacher's union) President Joe Thomas (Karvelis, 2019).

In addition to signs and colors, the protesting teachers and their supporters sent verbal messages to lawmakers to prioritize education. Beyond chanting "S.C. for E.D.!" they also responded to the state superintendent's lack of support for the cause by repeatedly vocalizing "Where is Molly?!" and "Do your job!" in choral unison. Speakers at the State House steps included politicians, teachers, students, and other supporters. Mike Burgress, a River Bluff high school teacher, called the event "The world's largest faculty meeting." State Representative Russell Ott publicly acknowledged that those who attended today's rally might be shamed and criticized for being selfish, but he reminded the teachers that they are not making it all about themselves, but that this march is for the students (Schechter et al., 2019). Many teachers did experience the outward rebuke of some influential stakeholders and politicians.

One of the speakers was former South Carolina teacher Sariah McCall, who recently shared a highly publicized resignation letter to Charleston County School District detailing the horrendous working environment and conditions that led to her departure from teaching altogether. The publicly shared letter was accompanied by a vivid description of her nearly 17-hour daily routine that began with classroom teaching, meeting attendance, working lunch duties, lesson planning and preparation, bus or hall duty, and concluding with grading and paperwork, with almost no break in between. In her letter, she described the hard decision to leave the profession because although she loved her work and the students, she noted, "I cannot set myself on fire to keep someone else warm." She further explained,

The systemic abuse and neglect of educators and other public service workers in the state of South Carolina should have its citizens so enraged. The unrealistic demands and all-consuming nature of the profession are not sustainable. I am still a human being. There was no time to be a functioning human being and give this job all the attention and love it deserves. This career with its never-ending list of "extra duties and responsibilities" that we are not given the resources for completing. I cannot let a career dictate and demand all of me for another minute, and I will not be bullied into continuing to do so out of misguided guilt for possibly neglecting the children. It is unrealistic to expect this much from people. We're teachers, but we're still people.

I have compared the systematic expectations of the profession to the list of signs of abuse provided by the Domestic Abuse Hotline. If you replace "he" with "public education," it would almost match perfectly with what we are all going through across America. If I were to say that my partner is putting me through all of this abuse and mistreatment, people would be putting me in a shelter and insisting that I leave him. But because this is my calling and I must sacrifice myself for the sake of the children, then it's really not that big of a deal. Because if I really love my job and I really love the kids, then I should be willing to do whatever it takes and make whatever sacrifices I need to in order to give them everything they need. Do more with less time, funding, and resources. Take more of the blame, guilt, and responsibility. Be ready to sacrifice your personal life, mental health, and physical safety. Don't be a complainer. After all, if you only work 7–3 for 180 days of the year, then what could there possibly be to complain about? If only it were that easy. In the hardest act of selfishness I have ever been faced with, I must put myself over the demands of helping raise other people's children. I won't be in an abusive relationship with public education any longer. I will model to my current and past students what self-respect, setting hard boundaries, and standing your ground for what's right looks like in action. (McCall from Strauss, 2019, para. 10)

While there have been slight teacher pay raises over the years, they have been minimal and insufficient to overcome inadequate teacher salaries. This is a recurring pattern in South Carolina. Instead of sustained efforts to address entrenched problems, South Carolina has often relied on stopgap measures. Education decisions in the state often operate in reaction to politics. That is, South Carolina addresses hot button topics with a crisis-driven mentality to develop a hodgepodge patchwork of fixes that ultimately do not address the underlying root cause of the problems (Bowers et al., 2018).

Teachers in South Carolina have been quiet for a long time. They have waited and hoped for things to improve for education in the state but have come to the epiphany that they have to stand up for themselves and demand change if there is the hope of real progress. Fewer than 25% of the legislature have children attending public schools (Bowers et al., 2018), which could likely be an uphill battle. People are unlikely to advocate and support education initiatives if they do not understand their needs. On May

1, the All Out protest for education rocked South Carolina's state capitol as a crescendo of outrage chanted and demanded change. However, no matter how successful, a 1-day event cannot eradicate the harmful effect of decades of teacher bashing and educational neglect. One goal of the teacher rally was to increase the general public's awareness concerning the state of affairs of the underinvestment and the substandard working conditions in education. This book continues that work by exploring the factors and events that have led to the need for the massive teacher demonstration in the first place. Many events have happened since the walkout and to some, it has become a distant memory. However, we believe the momentum must be sustained and hope that this book can contribute to that effort.

REFERENCES

Blanc, E. (2019). *Red state revolt: The Teachers' strike wave and working-class politics.* Verso Books.

Bennett, Z. (2019, April 16). *May 1 teacher walkout could spark change and repercussions.* Carolina News & Reporter. https://carolinanewsandreporter.cic.sc.edu/may-1-teacher-walkout-could-spark-both-change-and-repercussions/

Bowers, P. (2019a, April 30). Got questions about South Carolina teachers' May 1 protest? We got answers. *Post and Courier.* https://www.postandcourier.com/news/got-questions-about-south-carolina-teachers-may-1-protest-weve-got-answers/article_473223a4-6b4f-11e9-928c-ff6de43fca28.html

Bowers, P. (2019b, May 1). 10,000 South Carolina teachers, supporters march on the statehouse. *Post and Courier.* www.postandcourier.com/news/south-carolina-teachers-supporters-march-on-the-statehouse/article_4507e9da-6a8a-11e9-b66c-7b128dfe6021.html

Bowers, P. (2019c, April 7). Meet the South Carolina teachers working 2nd and 3rd jobs to pay the bills. *Post and Courier.* https://www.postandcourier.com/news/meet-the-south-carolina-teachers-working-nd-and-rd-jobs/article_71aabe38-4f08-11e9-b0f3-ab6226458c0e.html

Bowers, P. (2000, September 14). 10,000 South Carolina teachers, supporters march on the Statehouse. *Post and Courier.* https://www.postandcourier.com/news/10-000-south-carolina-teachers-supporters-march-on-the-statehouse/article_4507e9da-6a8a-11e9-b66c-7b128dfe6021.html

Bowers, P., Smith, G., Adcox, S. J. B., & Moore, T. (2018). Minimally adequate part one. How South Carolina's 'minimally adequate' education system fails too many students. *The Post and Courier.* https://data.postandcourier.com/saga/minimally-adequate/page/1

Boyle, E. (2004). *The feminization of teaching in America.* Massachusetts Institute of Technology. https://static1.squarespace.com/static/571136450442627fff34d2f5/t/5988af33a803bbf89aea5913/1502129971611/2004Boyle.pdf

Camera, L. (2019, May 1). Teachers in North and South Carolina protest low pay. *U.S. News & World Report.* https://www.usnews.com/news/education

-news/articles/2019-05-01/teachers-in-north-carolina-and-south-carolina
-walk-out-to-protest-low-pay

Campbell, A. F. (2019, February 13). *A record number of U.S. workers went on strike in 2018*. Vox. https://www.vox.com/policy-and-politics/2019/2/13/18223211/worker-teacher-strikes-2018-record

Center for Educator Recruitment, Retention, & Advancement. (2019). *South Carolina annual educator supply & demand report (2018–19 school year)*. https://www.che.sc.gov/CHE_Docs/academicaffairs/2019_January/2b.pdf

Chuck, E. (2019, July 11). *School by day, assembly line by night: How teachers in South Carolina make ends meet*. NBC News. https://www.nbcnews.com/news/us-news/school-day-assembly-line-night-how-teachers-south-carolina-make-n1026381

Darling-Hammond, L., Holtzman, D. J. H., Gatlin, S. J., & Heilig, J. V. (2005). Does teacher preparation matter? Evidence about teacher certification, teach for America, and teacher effectiveness. *Education Policy Analysis Archives, 13*(42), 1–34.

Fox Carolina News. (2019, January 24). *South Carolina facing teacher shortage* [Video]. https://www.youtube.com/watch?v=MTfYus2uRKk

Garcia, E., & Weiss, E. (2019). The teacher shortage is real, large and growing, and worse than we thought. *Economic Policy Institute*. https://www.epi.org/files/pdf/163651.pdf

Goodjobsfirst.org. (2018). *The new math on school finance. Adding up the first-ever disclosure of corporate tax abatements' cost to public education*. https://www.goodjobsfirst.org/sites/default/files/docs/pdfs/newmath3.pdf

Hansen, M. (2018, April 13). *Which states might experience the next wave of teacher strikes?* Brookings. https://www.brookings.edu/blog/brown-center-chalkboard/2018/04/13/which-states-might-experience-the-next-wave-of-teacher-strikes/

Hopkins, G. W. (2016). *Charleston hospital workers' strike*. South Carolina Encyclopedia. http://www.scencyclopedia.org/sce/entries/charleston-hospital-workers-strike/

IPSOS. (2018). *Teachers relying on second jobs, debt to make ends meet*. https://www.ipsos.com/sites/default/files/ct/news/documents/2018-05/node-410846-411026.zip

Jamieson, D., & Waldron, T. (2018, April 7). *The red-state teacher revolt has been brewing for decades*. HuffPost. https://www.huffpost.com/entry/americas-growing-teacher-strikes-were-decades-in-the-making_n_5ac8f468e4b0337ad1e8979c

Karvelis, N. (2019). You need rank and file to win: How Arizona teachers built a movement. *Rethinking Schools, 33*(2). https://www.rethinkingschools.org/articles/you-need-rank-and-file-to-win-how-arizona-teachers-built-a-movement?fbclid=IwAR3twjr8glS0a1kAvFQ408Kn6aeb1FxWAWyXWne0sq7PebhecDrZCVoP1pU

Lasko-Kerr, I., & Berliner, D. C. (2003). In harm's way: How undercertified teachers hurt their students. *Educational Leadership, 60*(8), 34–39.

McCann, A. (2019, January 7). *Best and worst states to raise a family*. https://web.archive.org/web/20190712140313/https://wallethub.com/edu/best-states-to-raise-a-family/31065/

National Center for Education Statistics. (2018). *Public school teacher spending on school supplies* (NCES 2018-097). U.S. Department of Education. https://files.eric.ed.gov/fulltext/ED583062.pdf

Phi Delta Kappa. (2018). *Teaching: Respect but dwindling appeal.* https://www.jstor.org/stable/26552430

Schechter, M., Barton, M., Cueto, I., & Marchant, B. (2019, May 1). 10,000 SC teachers march to state house May 1. *The State.* https://www.thestate.com/news/politics-government/article229863299.html

South Carolina Department of Revenue. (2019). *Chapter 9: Exemptions.* https://dor.sc.gov/resources-site/lawandpolicy/Documents/SandU_9.pdf

Spearman, M. (2019, April 29). *Statement from State Superintendent Molly Spearman on May 1st teacher walkout.* South Carolina Department of Education. https://ed.sc.gov/newsroom/news-releases/statement-from-state-superintendent-molly-spearman-on-may-1-teacher-walkout/

Strauss, V. (2019, April 16). Why this South Carolina teacher quit mid-year: 'The unrealistic demands and all consuming nature of the profession are not sustainable.' *The Washington Post.* https://www.washingtonpost.com/education/2019/04/16/why-this-south-carolina-teacher-quit-mid-year-the-unrealistic-demands-all-consuming-nature-profession-are-not-sustainable/

Tran, H. (2018). *Taking the mystery out of South Carolina school finance* (2nd ed.). ICPEL Publications.

Tran, H., & Smith, D. (2019). Insufficient money and inadequate respect: What obstructs the recruitment of college students to teach in hard-to-staff schools. *Journal of Educational Administration, 57*(2), 152–166.

U.S. News & World Report. (2017). *Best states 2017: Ranking performance throughout all 50 states.* https://media.beam.usnews.com/b5/c5/ecf250de4930b201f74063d5150e/171206-best-states-overall-rankings-2017.pdf

U.S. News & World Report. (2018). *Best states 2018: Ranking performance throughout all 50 states.* https://media.beam.usnews.com/ba/b2/c75f31c94080b1d8a17931bcddd0/171206-best-states-overall-rankings-2018.pdf

U.S. News & World Report. (2019). *Best states 2019: Ranking performance throughout all 50 states.* https://media.beam.usnews.com/69/4f/9ec3a3e94c4080b146d64d27288a/190508-best-states-overall-rankings-2019.pdf

Weiner, S. (2019, May 2). *North and South Carolina teachers are protesting again.* Splinter News. https://splinternews.com/north-and-south-carolina-teachers-are-protesting-again-1834463664

Wolf, Z. B. (2019, February 23). *Why teacher strikes are touching every part of America.* CNN. https://www.cnn.com/2019/02/23/politics/teacher-strikes-politics/index.html

CHAPTER 2

RADICALIZING THE SCHOOLHOUSE

The Overlooked Civil Rights Agenda of Black Educators in South Carolina Since Reconstruction

Jon N. Hale
University of Illinois at Urbana–Champaign

Christopher Getowicz
University of Illinois at Urbana–Champaign

Like Black teachers across the southern United States, Black educators in South Carolina shaped the field of education by demanding education as a fundamental civil right. Their work demonstrates the political nature of teaching and the educational landscape. Teachers continue a historical tradition of sowing seeds of resistance that transform education and society. Since their founding in the post-Reconstruction era, Black teacher's associations like the Palmetto Education Association in South Carolina utilized their

How Did We Get Here?, pages 17–41
Copyright © 2022 by Information Age Publishing
www.infoagepub.com
All rights of reproduction in any form reserved.

organizations to improve educational opportunities, demand salary equalization, improve working conditions, and ultimately the right to work during the era of desegregation. The history of the Palmetto Education Association and other Black teacher associations contextualizes the current lack of diversity in the teacher workforce while concomitantly demonstrating the political possibilities of Black teachers in the era of Black Lives Matter.

Black teachers in South Carolina played a major role in the Civil Rights Movement that demanded quality education as a fundamental right. The Palmetto Education Association and other teacher associations were a critical part of the struggle for African American education rights, beginning in the wake of Reconstruction and continuing throughout the rise of the Civil Rights Movement and the *Brown v. Board of Education* (1954) decision. Black teacher associations continued to play a crucial role in the wake of the *Brown* ruling during the desegregation of public schools in the south through the 1970s. This chapter builds upon the studies of Black southern teacher associations organized in the era of segregation by Vanessa Siddle-Walker (2009a, 2009b, 2013, 2017). It is situated in the historical context of Black educator activism across the South during the Civil Rights Movement (Alridge, 2008, 2019; Baker, 2011; Charron, 2009; Fairclough, 1999, 2007; Hale, 2018, 2019; Hale & Blanton, 2021; Jelks, 2012).

Further, it is predicated on the fact that much of the Black teaching profession in South Carolina, like the South, was a workforce stratified by labor divisions meaning that most teachers in segregated classrooms were women (Dixon, 2003; Hunter, 1997; James-Gallaway & Harris, 2021; Johnson, 2000; Jones, 1985; Loder-Jackson, 2012; Shaw, 1996). This is an attempt to delineate an arrangement of rights that informed the collective agency of Black educators in South Carolina during the nascent stages of the Civil Rights Movement in the 1920s through the era of desegregation in the 1970s. This treatise is premised on notions of professionalization posited by D'Amico (2020), Hale (2018, 2019), Perillo (2012), and Urban (2000) to illustrate how the professional work of educators produced a form of activism not typically identified within the traditional historical narrative of the Civil Rights Movement. While popular political discourse dismisses notions of teacher professionalism, issues like improving the working conditions of teachers in segregated schools, creating culturally relevant curricula, attending institutions of higher learning for professional development, making demands for equal salaries, and protecting the due process of embattled Black educators during desegregation, all underscore the political work of Black educators as civil rights activists.

Black educators inextricably linked their professional work to protecting and expanding education as a right within the context of institutionalized *de jure* segregation throughout the south, particularly after the *Plessy v. Ferguson* (1896) decision. Despite court-mandated White supremacy and the ongoing maintenance of a segregated and unequal education system, Black educators in South Carolina, like their peers across the South, exposed the contradictions of segregation as an infringement on the constitutional right to education as avowed by Article XI of the 1895 state constitution. As these contradictions of White supremacy increasingly infringed upon the constitutionally protected education rights of Black residents of South Carolina, teachers organized professional associations to defend their rights, professionalizing their craft and implementing progressive instruction in the segregated schools and classrooms they served.

This organizational undertaking helped establish a foundation to challenge institutional discrimination. Teacher associations and political allies, such as the National Association for the Advancement of Colored People (NAACP), collaborated to demand salary equalization, for example, and positioned themselves as serious political actors in the Civil Rights Movement during the 1930s and 1940s. Moreover, Black teachers moved to protect their right to work during the late 1960s and early 1970s, when public school desegregation and the merging of Black and White teacher associations threatened the opportunities of Black educators, who were deemed disposable in an integrated educational arrangement by White leaders and policymakers (Hale, 2019; Hale & Blanton, 2021; Murphy, 1990; Urban, 2000; West, 1980). Faced with endemic unemployment, Black educators adamantly struggled for their right to work in desegregated public schools, which inserted an economic imperative into the education platform of a civil rights agenda that narrowly focused on desegregation.

The constellation of activism and political organizing undertaken by Black teachers in South Carolina and across the South constitute an assertion of their rights and the right to education in the earliest stages of the Civil Rights Movement and throughout the era that followed the *Brown* ruling. By focusing attention on the work of Black educators in South Carolina and across the south, two misconceptions of educational history can be revised. A significant part of the historiography around teacher activism focuses on urban, northern, and largely White spaces. This vantage point, by implication, overlooks the specific work of African American teachers in the South. As Murphy (1990), Perillo (2012), Urban (1982, 2000), and others have noted, local teacher unions in Chicago, Detroit, New York, Philadelphia, Minneapolis, and Toledo, among other locations, formed the origins of the National Education Association (NEA), the American Federation of Teachers (AFT), and the city-wide teacher strikes that birthed such organizations (Gaffney, 2007; Karpinski, 2008; Lichtenstein, 2002; Lyons, 2008; McCartin, 2008; Mirel, 1984; Tyack et al., 1984; Wesley, 1957). Emphasis on the histories of the AFT or NEA privilege a northern and urban perspective that does not center the racialized dynamics of professional teacher associations in the segregated South.

Additionally, the history of Black teacher organizations in South Carolina and the South more generally can expand the understanding of civil rights history, illustrating how Black teachers infused their politics in the educational aspirations of the civil rights agenda. Under the threats posed by anti-union politics, White supremacy, and sexism, Black teacher associations across the South were left to organize in separate and segregated organizations. Doing so asserted a political agenda that both protested segregation and promoted civil rights from the onset. Over the first half of the 20th century, these Black educators would shape the vision of the Civil Rights Movement and project a broad democratic vision well beyond that of their White or Northern peers.

The history of Black education associations, like the Palmetto Education Association, demonstrates the important contributions made by their organizers to the groundwork of the Civil Rights Movement, revising narratives of passive or apolitical teachers. Further, this history of teacher organizing disrupts a narrative that schools or classrooms are apolitical spaces. By studying how Black educators organized throughout the early 20th century in places like South Carolina, it becomes clear that they saw their work as both political and inherently tied to the struggle for civil rights. These undertakings affirm the need for ongoing work by teachers to contest education inequalities, asserting that education is a right and that Black lives matter.

BLACK EDUCATORS AS CIVIL RIGHTS ACTIVISTS

During Reconstruction, Black political power articulated an understanding of freedom and citizenship that necessitated education as a right. Black teacher associations emerged out of the Reconstruction era alongside growing public education institutions, as envisioned by free African Americans in the South. W. E. B. Du Bois (1935) observed that "public education for all at public expense, in the South, was a Negro idea" (p. 638). Despite this, White politicians and legislatures, reclaiming political power in the post Reconstruction era, insisted on discriminatory educational policies that produced separate and unequal educational opportunities. The backlash against Reconstruction and the reassertion of White supremacy, along with the limitations placed on the equal protection clause of the Fourteenth Amendment by *Plessy v. Ferguson* (1896), ensured that a system of *de jure* segregation under Jim Crow would define education for decades to follow (Bolton, 2005; Bullock, 1967; Dittmer, 1994; Foner, 1988; McMillen, 1989; Powers, 1994; Williams, 2005).

As legal protections were rolled back and federal oversight of the South ended, White supremacy reasserted itself economically and politically over African Americans in the South. Separate and unequal education took form in this context. Access and opportunity for African American education were constrained under these circumstances. For example, Whites used "tax shifting" to tax African Americans through alternative methods. Used since Reconstruction, elected White officials benefited themselves and other elites and their children and forced African Americans to bear the burden of a dual tax system to fund their own separate educational opportunities (Anderson, 1988; McMillen, 1989). Over time, such arrangements began to demonstrate materially the falsehood of the myth of "separate but equal" in places like South Carolina, where the numbers and qualities of schools became a quantifiable measure of inequality (Solomon, 1955). The result of this dramatic reclamation of power by White elites was that African Americans in South Carolina and across the southern United States were cast into a role of responsibility for their own educational opportunities. As Whites benefited themselves through controlling legal and tax codes as "legitimate" taxpayers through a process that Camille Walsh (2018) termed "racial taxation," Black communities were forced to assume a material and financial burden to ensure even a basic level of education (Anderson, 1988; Black, 2021; McMillen, 1989).

The assertion of education rights and the onus of protection of those rights fell squarely on the shoulders of Black educators and the professional organizations they formed (Anderson, 1988; Bolton, 2005; Bullock, 1967; Foner, 1988; Hale, 2018; Hale & Blanton, 2021; Hale & Cooper, 2015; Lynch, 1913; Span, 2009; Williams, 2005). White educators of the mid-19th century were already organizing professionally in the United States under the banners of the National Teacher Association (NTA) in 1857. The organization proclaimed its intention "to promote the educational welfare of our country [and] to advance the dignity, respectability, and usefulness of their calling" (NTA, 1857). However, the NTA was exclusively a White organization, and African American educators were marginalized as it formed. Additionally, Black educators in the South remained on the sidelines of the NTA, which privileged teachers in the northeast and the midwestern United States. Left on their own by White, northern, and urban-focused educators, southern Black teachers began organizing locally in their own home communities. In South Carolina, this took the form of the Palmetto Education Association, established in 1900 (Picott, 1975; Potts, 1978; Siddle-Walker, 2009a, 2009b; Thompson, 1973). This happened at a time when Black education associations were sprouting up in states across the South, including Tennessee, North Carolina, and Alabama (ASTA, 1939; Fairclough, 2007; Murray, 1984; Perry, 1975; Pierson, 2014). These associations would come together collectively in 1907 as the National Association of Teachers in Colored Schools (NATCS), later renamed the American Teachers Association (ATA) in 1937 (Perry, 1975).

The founding of the Palmetto Education Association was the direct result of exclusion from White education associations in South Carolina. Its aims and objectives were focused on improving Black education in segregated South Carolina public schools. These efforts aimed broadly "to promote public interest in the cause of education" and "to elevate the standards of the teaching profession and improve the Negro race educationally" (Potts, 1978, p. 44). Professionalism and an emphasis on teacher quality were central tenants of many Black education organizers. This was described by F. O. Alexander (1935), who wrote that "one very serious weakness in the educational programs...is the lack of efficient teachers." She went on to call for a higher standard for teacher education, higher salaries, improved school conditions, and "a change in attitude and policies of many administrators and school officials" (p. 57). In addition to these professional demands made by South Carolina teachers and their peers in the South, their interest was also deeply invested in what Dr. G. W. Trenholm, the influential president of the Alabama State Teachers Association, called "the child's natural right." Throughout the era of Jim Crow, Black educators in South Carolina and across the South remained steadfastly committed to education as a right for the children of their communities (ASTA, n.d.; Perry, 1975; Trenholm, G. W., 1975; Trenholm, H. C., 1956).

Within the context of strict racial segregation in South Carolina and the South, defending education as a right and making professional demands to improve the professional environment of teachers was in and of itself a claim to civil rights. As stated in the constitution of the NATCS, the "objects, aims, and purposes [of the association] shall be to assist in raising the standard and promoting the interests of the teaching profession, and in advancing the cause of education" (National Association of Teachers in Colored Schools, 1929). The professionalization of teaching or "promoting the interests of the teaching profession" included adopting higher teacher training standards, professional development requirements, and stronger credential standards (D'Amico, 2011; Hale & Blanton, 2021; Perillo, 2012; Urban, 1989). Black educators, therefore, simultaneously called for professionalization amid their demands for and defense of the right to an education. The concomitant efforts to protect education as a right and demand professionalization defined the essence of Black teacher's labor within a civil rights context throughout the first decades of education associations, such as the Palmetto Education Association. Organizing for greater professional standards in the context of Jim Crow directly inserted the aims of teacher professionalism into a civil rights agenda, which is concurrently exposed in challenges to White supremacy through the demands for content and curriculum-affirming values of Black history and culture in schools.

Determining the curriculum in Black schools was a politically potent weapon in the fight to combat White supremacy, particularly as many of its most harmful effects were perpetuated through stereotypes, misinformation, and a complete dismissal of Black history and culture in public schools. Black southern teacher associations were directly combatting these racist ideological currents by the 1920s. In doing so, they were on the frontlines of the struggle to oppose White supremacist ideologies in school textbooks when, for example, they challenged the use of texts written with a pro-Confederacy orientation (Fairclough, 2007). In other cases, Black teacher associations actively sought to incorporate the achievement of Black history and culture into the curriculum by emulating the work of Carter G. Woodson and incorporating into the curriculum the literature published through his organization, the Association for the Study of Negro Life and History (Fairclough, 2007; Woodson, 1926). These efforts were expressed broadly by the NATCS in 1925, when its findings committee released a report in which it wrote, "We earnestly recommend the increased study of Negro History in our schools" (Perry, 1975, pp. 199–201). By advocating for and asserting the right to Black history and culture in their education, Black teachers challenged White supremacist ideology and advocated for a curriculum that affirmed the value of African American history and culture. In doing so, they took the lead in efforts to control what they taught in their classrooms, asserting that academic content and instruction were their professional prerogative.

Black women in South Carolina and across the South played a critical role as political activists, though often overlooked. Since emancipation and the Reconstruction era, Black women have built education as a critical pillar of their communities. Educators like Mamie Fields and Septima Clark in South Carolina committed personal finances, time, and other forms of capital to Black children and the schools that served them. They later invigorated local NAACP chapters to bolster the quality of education they labored to provide. Through community leadership and social and political networks, Black women were critical to the sustenance of a liberatory education (Baker, 2006; Charron, 2009; Littlefield, 2012; Robnet, 1996).

Gendered divisions of labor have "feminized" the teaching profession, mirrored in Black communities in South Carolina and across the South where Black women have occupied a central role in the historical struggles demanding education as a right (Jones, 1985; Shaw, 1996). The history of Black education in the South tends to overlook the intersections of race and gender, privileging White paternalism and philanthropy, or overemphasizing the role of men. To correct some of these oversights in the history of the Civil Rights Movement, scholars are examining the role of women as political activists in the struggles for education rights and racial justice (Collier-Thomas & Franklin, 2001; Crawford et al., 1993; Johnson, 2000; Kirk, 2009; Olson, 2001). Scholarship has begun to emerge showing that Black women have consistently demonstrated a politically conscious and culturally relevant pedagogy in their classrooms, grounded in an intersectional orientation around race, gender, and class (Dixson, 2003; James-Galloway & Harris, 2021; Ramsey, 2012). Thus, it is necessary to acknowledge the disproportionate number of Black women who taught in places like South Carolina and that their work as teachers was regularly intertwined with the activism of the Civil Rights Movement.

Black women have historically embraced teaching associations and other professional organizations as a matter of political and economic interest (Jones, 1985; Shaw, 1996). As a consequence of gendered labor stratification, Black women and girls often acquired higher degrees of literacy, which helped them prioritize education among their families and communities (Jones, 1985). By the early 20th century, women nationally outnumbered men as teachers by a ratio of 5 to 1, and in the South, three-quarters of the Black teaching force was comprised of women (Jones, 1985; Kirk, 2009). This disproportionate contribution of women to the profession represents a critical foundation for any account of Black teacher activism in South Carolina. The study of Black teacher activism in South Carolina and the South demonstrates how women were present and participated in generations of political struggle. Black women educators like Septima Clark and Viola Louis Duvall or longtime South Carolina NAACP leader Modjeska Monteith Simkins highlight the importance of an intersectional awareness in studying Black teachers' political activism (Cunningham, 2021; Kirk, 2009). The role of women in collective struggles, like those of teachers from the Elloree Training School, demonstrates the prominent political role they undertook in South Carolina throughout the Civil Rights Movement (Cunningham, 2021). Historically, the contribution of Black educators to the Civil Rights Movement must account for the role of women in the struggle.

TEACHER EDUCATION AND THE
CIVIL RIGHTS MOVEMENT

Teacher preparation was perhaps the most important aspect of the professionalization of Black teachers in a civil rights context. Many Black educators earned degrees in higher education from premier universities across the nation. As Siddle Walker (2009a) has noted, many Black educators were graduates of elite, predominately White institutions (PWI's), such as the University of Chicago, Columbia, Harvard, Cornell, and New York University, often completing advanced degrees in the process. Many other Black teachers studied at historically Black colleges and universities (HBCUs), such as Morehouse College, Fisk University, and Howard University. Black educators demonstrated a great sense of urgency in attaining high-quality education throughout the early 20th century and the era of Jim Crow. Undertaking rigorous study in the fields such as biology, chemistry, mathematics, or physics at prestigious institutions, Black teachers completed the rigorous requirements of a collegiate education at a time when just over one-half of all Americans attended high schools. To be sure, Black teachers were among the most progressively educated professionals in the communities they served (Baker, 2011; Burke High School, 1959; Cecelski, 1994; Fairclough, 2007; Jordan-Taylor, 2011; Siddle-Walker, 1996). These achievements would provide the historical foundation for the rise of Black educational attainment in higher education institutions in the years immediately following the Second World War (Freeman, 1976). Politically, intellectually, and socially, Black teachers represented a form of leadership in their communities, characterized by upward middle-class mobility, and armed with faith that their work as educators was a political act that could benefit a broader community uplift.

Teacher education in the 1920s and 1930s fostered an intellectual environment rooted in northern, urban Progressive Era educators, such as William H. Kilpatrick, John Dewey, and George Counts. Their work fostered critical insights and left a lasting impact on future Black educators. In addition to these White progressive theorists who often dismissed race, Black public intellectuals, scholars, and educators such as W. E. B. Du Bois, Benjamin Mays, Septima Clark, R. R. Moton, and John Hope helped contend that race is at the center of educational discourse (Alridge, 2008a, 2008b; Baker, 2011; Charron, 2009; Du Bois, 1935; Jelks, 2012). Intellectuals including Kilpatrick, Counts, Mays, and Dewey regarded teachers as critical social and political actors and situated schools as logical sites to facilitate progressive changes in society. As one of the most radical of those scholars, George Counts, who authored *Dare the School Build a New Social Order?* in 1932, advanced the idea that "resources must be dedicated to the promotion of the welfare of the great masses of the people" (Counts, 1932/1969, p. 43; see also, Cremin, 1964; Gutek, 1971, 1984). The influence of this intellectual environment on Black educators of the era was an educational outlook firmly rooted in critical thought, progressive democratic principles, and a serious outlook on the social and political world surrounding schools.

Black educators also pursued educational opportunities and growth in segregated Black colleges and universities during Jim Crow. These spaces were also steeped in the principles of progressive education and offered opportunities to apply such principles to the lives and experiences of Black educators studying in those spaces. For example, Howard University offered a course in "The Courts and Racial Integration in Education," which is indicative of how Black educators applied the insights of progressive education into their lives and experiences. There, English teacher Lois Simms of Burke High School in Charleston, South Carolina, took this course as part of her graduate education. As part of her master's thesis studies, she researched discrepancies in education funding between Black and White schools in South Carolina, revealing how discriminatory policies and practices shaped her professional life and the educational experiences of her students (Drago, 1990; Richardson & Jones, 2009; Simms, 1954, 1995). The adoption and application of critical analyses bare the ideological outlook of many young Black teachers going to work, educating students in segregated schools.

Once in their classrooms, Black educators in places like South Carolina applied and renegotiated progressivism, fusing rigorous academic standards with the ideals of participatory democratic citizenship. Teachers utilizing Black history and literature in their lesson plans, course work, and educational philosophies, helped nurture critical thinking and participatory values in their students (Cuban, 1993, pp. 115–146; Hale, 2018). Black teachers in Charleston, South Carolina, exemplify these tendencies. Mr. Eugene Hunt, a colleague of Lois Simms, who also taught English at Burke High School, presented his students with notions of democratic equality and the avenues to substantive change in American government through the writings and speeches of Thomas Jefferson and Franklin Delano Roosevelt (Hunt, 1945–1980; Hunt, n.d.). For her part, Lois Simms similarly emphasized a rigorous course of study for her students, teaching canonical literature, including Charles Dickens, Ralph Waldo Emerson, and Mark Twain (Mrs. Lois Simms, personal communication, December 5, 2011; Simms, 1954, 1995). In the eyes of Mr. Hunt, Mrs. Simms, and their peers who fostered high academic standards and enriching educational experiences for their classes, their students had an equal right to flourish. Their work set out to critically challenge the White supremacist ideology and assert Black political, intellectual, and educational rights.

By the 1930s, Black educators across the segregated South distinguished themselves with upward mobility into the Black middle class and an assertion of education as a right. Precarious as their middle-class status remained, as the Great Depression wore on, their status as community, civil rights, and labor leaders set them apart. With the arrival of the Second World War, their demands evolved beyond the scope of professionalization and the assertion of limited educational opportunities, as defined by state laws alone. The 1940s marked an evolutionary turn in the demands for both civil rights and education rights by Black teachers. At this critical turn, Black teachers in South Carolina and across the South staked important positions in the civil rights upheaval to come.

EQUAL PAY AND THE EQUALIZATION CAMPAIGNS OF BLACK TEACHER ASSOCIATIONS

Black teachers in South Carolina joined their peers across the South when they shifted their efforts toward demanding equal pay to White teachers during and immediately following the Second World War. These claims were situated in a broader effort by the NAACP during the 1930s and 1940s to uphold the "separate but equal" doctrine of *Plessy*. In asserting these rights, teachers would be at the forefront of African American labor activism for the equalization campaigns of an era that abetted the rise of the Civil Rights Movement. Their longstanding role as recognized and respected community leaders and advocates for educational, labor, and civil rights, ensured that Black educators were critically positioned as agitators in the rising tide of the popular mass movement for civil rights (Fairclough, 1999; Kluger, 2004; Sullivan, 2009; Tushnet, 1987). Black teachers' leading role in the Civil Rights Movement during the post-war years would figure prominently in the years preceding the political shift of the *Brown* decision, ultimately disrupting and obscuring their organizational roles and capacities.

The demand for equal pay between Black and White educators was taken up across the South between the 1930s and 1940s. The political energies animating the campaign for equal salaries among Black teachers rose to prominence due to the 1938 case of Norfolk, Virginia teacher Aline E. Black, who ultimately lost her job in the effort (Wilkerson, 1960). Educator and editor of *The Journal of Negro Education*, Charles H. Thompson (1936), helped foster the movement for equalization by highlighting the efforts of such a campaign undertaken in states of Maryland and Virginia in the 1930s. The first legal victory in the efforts was in the 1939 case of *Mills v. Board of Education* in Maryland, quickly followed by a favorable ruling for Black educators in *Alston v. School Board of Norfolk* in 1940 (Baker, 1995). In South Carolina, the Palmetto State Teachers Association was part of the ongoing work of the NAACP to equalize salaries (Charron, 2009; Potts, 1978). Burke High School teacher Viola Louise Duvall filed suit in *Duvall et al. v. J. F. Seignous* (1943), demanding equal pay with the support of the NAACP, only to have the state of South Carolina respond by constructing a discriminating pay system based on a test-based merit system (Baker, 2006; Charron, 2009; Cunningham, 2018; Drago, 1990; Simms, 1995). These efforts towards equalization were mirrored across southern states and varied in outcome and success as they collided with a roadblock conjured by test specialist Ben D. Wood and the obstruction of his allegedly race-neutral National Teacher Exam (NTE; Baker, 1995; Cunningham 2018). The result was the adoption of so-called objective testing merits to maintain racially unequal salaries. The result for most teachers who had taken up activism to fight for equal salary rights was the sacrifice of their careers.

White officials in South Carolina and across the South almost uniformly responded to the demand for equal salary with contempt and hostility. Teachers who challenged White authorities for equal pay almost always did so at the expense of their jobs. In South Carolina, Palmetto State Teachers Association president J. T. W. Mims was denied contract renewal for supporting the equalization campaign. Punitive measures from White officials resulted in hardship for former president of the Palmetto Teachers Association, J. R. McCain, and rank-and-file teacher Septima Clark, who were denied renewal of teaching contracts (Charron, 2009; Potts, 1978). This was the primary threat that precariously loomed for those individual teachers who engaged in activism to assert their rights. For those teachers who did sacrifice their teaching positions in support of the equalization campaign, critical resources from the teacher associations and the community often served as a safety net. In this way, teachers' associations helped foster an environment where Black teachers could engage in political activism that served their collective interest in civil rights.

However, White officials and politicians did not limit themselves to isolated or individual retribution for such undertakings. The equalization campaign was also met by a broader attack in the context of the post-war Red Scare. For example, the NAACP was targeted as a "subversive organization." Such charges came under the red-baiting crusades of southern states wielding the 1947 Labor Management Relations Act's (Taft-Hartley Act) prohibition of Communist affiliation. As such, White officials charged any involvement with the NAACP equated with Communist affiliation. Teachers were suspended and dismissed for political affiliations with organizations such as the NAACP (Carter, 1949; Charron, 2009; Cunningham, 2021; Fairclough, 2007; Gray et al., 1987; Potts, 1978; Turner, 2010; Williamson, 2004). Such charges would continue well beyond *Brown* too. In 1956, South Carolina saw punitive measures taken against Black teachers affiliated with the NAACP confronted by teachers from the Elloree Technical School in court, including *Bryan v. Austin* (1956). Eloree teachers risked their jobs for the struggle to disrupt the anti-NAACP oaths being required for employment, many facing blacklisting for their efforts which ultimately led to the removal of such requirements by 1957 (Cunningham, 2021). Throughout the Civil Rights Movement, South Carolina's Black educators were the target for their activism by racist revanchist attacks cloaked in cold war anti-communist hysteria. Many would pay for their activism with their teaching careers. Even as equal rights under *Plessy* shifted to desegregation, with *Brown*, teachers continued to struggle despite such hostilities.

THE "RIGHT TO WORK" AND TEACHER ASSOCIATION MERGERS DURING DESEGREGATION

Amid the salary equalization campaign, the NAACP shifted its strategy and adopted a direct strategy to take the *Plessy* ruling head-on. This shift in strategy meant an abandonment of teachers and their allies, who were attempting to make gains using the equal standings, as ruled by *Plessy*. In doing so, they transformed their positions in the Civil Rights Movement. The threat to their professional standing and that of Black teacher associations themselves, as posed by desegregation, represented a looming threat in the political turn towards undoing *Plessy*. As the NAACP shifted its strategy, the political landscape transformed with it. Teachers were suddenly no longer in the vanguard of the struggle for civil rights; rather, their struggles to win equalization appeared conservative and antithetical. As a result, they moved from central actors in the struggle for civil rights to the periphery, leaving many feeling frustrated and alienated. Black teachers' positions grew increasingly complicated amid desegregation efforts. Many supported the NAACP push publicly, while others maintained a commitment to pedagogical activism within the hallways of their own school buildings and in the environment of their own classrooms (Baker, 2011; Hale, 2013, 2016, 2018, 2019). Yet, desegregation also threatened to destabilize their careers by putting them in unfavorable competition with White teachers. The consequences of desegregation for Black teachers in South Carolina were particularly devastating. While *Brown* marked a decisive turn in the Civil Rights Movement, the aftermath was not always marked by progress or equal rights.

The *Brown* decision disrupted and destabilized many Black teaching careers. It was not subversive activism or affiliations with the NAACP that resulted in mass layoffs of Black teachers, but the dismantling of segregated schools by White legislatures, policymakers, and school leaders, who reluctantly oversaw desegregation of schools in the wake of *Brown*. In 1954, between 71,000 and 82,000 Black teachers taught over 2 million students across the country. They constituted 8.5% of the national teaching force and a sizable 25% of all southern educators (Bureau of the Census, 1955; Ramsey, 2005; Thompson, 1953; Tillman, 2004). By 1964, their ranks would be slashed by 38,000 in the 17 southern and border states (Anderson, 2006; Fultz, 2006; Madkins, 2011; Ramsey, 2005; Tillman, 2004). Tillman (2004) estimated that over 39,000 Black educators were dismissed by 1972, constituting a loss of 46% of the Black teaching force within the first 2 decades after the *Brown* decision. Fultz (2004) found that in the six southern states that reported information to the Office of Health, Education, and Welfare, 23% of Black teachers exited the profession between 1968 and 1970 alone. By 1970, Black educators made up approximately 2% of all teachers in the United States, and only 7% in the south, at a time when overall growth in public education saw the system nearly double in size nationally to accommodate the baby boomer cohort (Bureau of the Census, 1970). Even the more conservative estimates acknowledge the devastating loss of Black educators, triggered by desegregation in the 2 decades following the *Brown* decision (Fultz, 2004; Hale, 2019; King, 1993; Siddle-Walker, 2009a, 2009b).

It was not simply that Black teachers were discharged, but that hiring practices reinforced the exclusionary character of the education force in the decades after *Brown*. According to the Office of Civil Rights, six White teachers were hired for every one Black teacher throughout the 1970s (Tillman, 2004). As *Brown* unfolded, desegregation of public schools effectively meant expulsion and exclusion of Black teachers. Institutional discrimination is best demonstrated by the "objective" tests that merited or disqualified teacher placement and pay across the South. According to Baker (2006), the National Teacher Examination adopted by South Carolina was used to limit Black educators' opportunities in desegregating schools, mercilessly eliminating over 40% of the Black teaching force by 1970. The increased dependence on these allegedly "color blind" and "objective" merit-based tests to certify teachers directly contributed to the exclusion of Black teachers and their drastic decrease in employment in the decades following *Brown* (Baker et al., 2014; Daniel, 2004; Hale, 2019).

Similar push out occurred in the Black educational leadership of schools. Fultz (2004) found that in nearly 500 school districts across the South in 1970, 34 of the districts dismissed Black principals, while 194 districts demoted at least 386 Black principals. Similarly, Tillman (2004) found that 90% of Black high school principals lost their jobs in 13 southern states and the border states in the 1970s. In South Carolina, reports detailing hiring practices exposed that hired White teachers at a staggeringly disproportionate rate than their Black peers, that dozens of teachers had contract renewals denied, and that administrators were being demoted and dismissed in the late 1960s (Cunningham, 2021; Hooker, 1970; U.S. Office of Education, 1972). These disruptions of Black leadership coincided with dramatic changes in Black higher educational and employment pursuits. The Civil Rights Act of 1964 opened opportunities via the prohibitions placed on discrimination hiring and promotion policies (Freeman, 1976). This shift in higher education is apparent from 1971, when 14,000 Black students majored in education, to the mere 4,300 who did so in 1991 (King, 1993). These dramatic changes in professional tracts and development have resulted in a lasting absence of Black educational leadership and professionals.

Yet contrary to the popular narratives of the Civil Rights Movement historiography, Black teachers' struggles did not end with the *Brown* court ruling and the onset of desegregation. At the 1963 annual convention of the NEA in Detroit, "Resolution 12" urged its members to adopt "the principles of desegregation as it applies to professional membership in organizations affiliated with NEA" (NEA, 1963). It continued, stating that "state and local associations where racial membership restrictions are still in effect to establish consultative committees to facilitate their removal" (Murphy, 1990; NEA, 1963). The implications for Black teachers would mean merging their professional associations with their White colleagues. Like the desegregation of schools, met with massive White resistance across the South, the desegregation and merging of southern teacher associations would take years and would not begin to take hold until well into the 1970s (Gilmore, 2017; Murray, 1984; NEA, 1965; Picott, 1975; Ridley, 1952; Robinson, 1967; Thompson, 1973).

These mergers were contested as Black teachers' associations asserted their right to work in desegregating schools. The shift toward a right to work from a right to equal pay marked a political transition and demonstrated the continued struggle for Black educators' rights beyond the *Brown* decision. In South Carolina, Black teachers were wary of merging with what had always been hostile White teacher associations and consistently found themselves demoted or their positions eliminated (Cunningham, 2021). The Palmetto Education Association organized the Commission to Professional Rights and Responsibilities in South Carolina. In doing so, it asserted its intention to "defend members of the teaching profession, schools, and the cause of education against unjust attack [and] to investigate controversies involving teachers and schools justly, fearlessly, and in the public interest" (Potts, 1978, pp. 200–201; see also, American Friends Service Committee, 1970; Gilmore, 2017). The undertaking of the Palmetto Education Association mirrored efforts across the NEA in the era of desegregation, when state affiliates across the South created "Professional Rights and Responsibilities" committees and subcommittees on the "Human Rights of Educators," to hear the cases of dismissed teachers (NEA, 1966b). Additional support came from the American Teachers Association (ATA), representing 75,000 private and public schools in 36 states in 1965, which identified the defense of Black teachers from discharge as a central issue during the years of school desegregation (Perry, 1975; see telegram, p. 299). The ATA passed its own resolution, echoing the Palmetto Education Association, calling upon "the educational profession, its administrators and other leaders to make certain that high professional ethics and the best professional practice without regard to race, are following in the employment of principals for school in the south" (Potts, 1978, pp. 200–201).

These coordinated efforts to support Black teachers were significant in southern districts like South Carolina, where teachers were not granted tenure and worked on annual contracts requiring regular renewal. Educational employment opportunities were marred by an increasingly color-blind meritocracy of educational policies, such as the National Teacher Exam. White administrations and leadership hardly demonstrated any interest in or commitment to racial equity in opportunity, or advancement in the desegregation era, leaving job prospects for Black teachers in a precarious state. The adoption of a framework of the right to work by the Palmetto Educators Association, NEA, and the ATA, signified efforts by both teachers and the organizations representing them to grapple with the dramatic shift of the struggle for education rights and the dismal prospects faced by teachers in South Carolina and across the south in the post-*Brown* era.

The NEA and its affiliates also engaged in a broader ideological struggle in the desegregation years. As Black educators asserted their rights to continue working with students of color in desegregating schools, they and organizations representing them, such as the NEA, worked to incorporate culturally relevant curriculums into desegregating classrooms. While supporting the right of Black educators to work, who were exiled by desegregation, the NEA also supported the publication of multicultural teaching materials, maintained a formal affiliation with the Association for the Study of Afro-American Life and History, and established the NEA Center for Human Relations (Karpinski, 2008; Perry, 1975; Urban, 2000). While the NEA worked toward desegregation of teacher associations, a backlash would emerge appropriating the "right to work" as an anti-union slogan. Adopting a race-neutral rhetoric, a conservative White opposition would challenge desegregation, the right of Black educators to teach, and the protection of labor by unions (Crespino, 2007; Delmont, 2016; Kruse, 2005; Lassiter, 2006; Lassiter & Crespino, 2010; Lichtenstein, 2002; Lichtenstein & Tandy Shermer, 2012; McGirr, 2001). The result of this backlash has been devastating, aiding in the ushering in of a "post-racial" era that has seen the teaching workforce in South Carolina hemorrhage Black teachers, wages and livelihood, and quality public education as a right.

* * *

The history of Black teacher associations in South Carolina and across the South demonstrates the contested and altering terrain of education rights. Beginning with the demand for the right to an education in the 1880s, Black teachers continued through the decades of the first half of the 20th century to demand access to educational resources and equal wages in the decades leading up to the *Brown v. Board of Education* decision. With the revolutionary changes brought about with demands for integration and the NAACP legal victory in *Brown*, Black teachers in South Carolina and across the South continued to assert their rights in the struggle against displacement, demotion, and dismissal in the era of desegregations.

The history of the Palmetto Education Association and its fellow Black teacher associations across the South challenges the narrative of the Civil Rights Movement, both by demonstrating teachers as active participants and acting on behalf of the particular interest in education rights (Gilmore, 2017; Hale, 2018, 2019). Despite the historical oversight of Black teachers, their impact on education in South Carolina cannot be overlooked, and their distinguished undertakings cannot be dismissed. Despite a complex association with the desegregation movement, Black teachers and their organizational undertakings, through teachers' associations like PEA, press the historical record on what constituted activism in the Civil Rights

Movement. Less visible than sit-ins and other nonviolent direct action undertaken by activists, Black teachers nonetheless demonstrated a lasting pedagogical and intellectual contribution to the Civil Rights Movement and its activism. In the segregated classrooms of segregated schools, Black educators fostered intellectual and pedagogical environments that shaped the tone of the activism that emerged across South Carolina and the South. Further, through implementing curriculum, extracurricular activities, and culturally relevant education, Black educators nurtured a community of critical resistance for their youth to take on a more visible leadership in the fight against White supremacy.

By examining Black educators' struggles in South Carolina for employment in the wake of desegregation, a context for education today comes into a sharper definition. While the public education system predominately serves students of color, over 80% of their teachers are White (NCES, 2012–2013; U.S. Department of Education, 2016). The significance of the absence of educators of colors in this system is imbued with a different meaning when examined with the historical context of the PEA and Black teacher association struggles. As desegregation unfolded, Black teachers were excluded from the opportunities to continue as educators in integrating schools. This did not go uncontested, but demands for inclusion in ongoing education for students of color in the post-*Brown* era have been too easily overlooked or mistaken as resistance to desegregation. The needs of a diverse student population in schools today demands a reflection on the expulsion of a once more diverse teaching force, and a reevaluation of narratives of failure, in the context of professional marginalization. As students of color continue to struggle for an education in the punitive school-prison nexus and the rising for-profit school industry, the stakes remain high. The history of Black teacher activism demonstrates that this moment was neither inevitable nor did it arrive uncontested. Teachers and students continue to prove the potential to be integral to political struggles for education and human rights.

REFERENCES

Alabama State Teachers Association. (n.d). *Proposed constitution for the Alabama State Teachers Association.* Zelda S. Evans, ASTA Collection (Box 13, Folder 31), ASU, Montgomery, AL.

Alabama State Teachers Association. (1930–1931). *A year book on Negro education in Alabama in 1930–1931.* ASTA Collection, "articles, news clippings, pamphlets, certificates" (Box 15, Folder 52), Alabama State University archives (ASU), Montgomery, AL.

Alabama State Teachers Association. (1939). *ASTA report of the Constitution Committee.* (Box 13, Folder 39), ASU, Montgomery, AL.

Alexander, F. O. (1935). Better trained teachers. *Mississippi Educational Journal: A Monthly Magazine for Teachers in Colored Schools, 6,* 57. Mississippi Department of Archives and History, Jackson, MS.

Alridge, D. P. (2008). *The educational thought of W. E. B. Du Bois: An intellectual history.* Teachers College Press.

Alridge, D. P. (2019). *Teachers in the movement.* https://teachersinthemovement.com/meet-the-team/derrick-p-alridge

Alston v. School Board of City of Norfolk 112 F.2d 992. (1940). https://law.justia .com/cases/federal/appellate-courts/F2/112/992/1498702/

American Friends Service Committee. (1970). *Your schools: Newsletter of South Carolina community relations program.* NEA Records, "Dual Association Merger–South Carolina," Gelman Library (Box 0519, Folder 5), Washington, DC.

American Teachers Association. (1975). ATA telegram of June 12, 1965. In T. D. Perry (Ed.), *History of the American Teachers Association* (pp. 299–300). National Education Association.

Anderson, J. (1988). *The education of Blacks in the South, 1860–1935.* University of North Carolina Press.

Anderson, J. (2006). A tale of two Browns: Constitutional equality and unequal education. *Yearbook of the National Society for the Study of Education, 108*(14), 30–32.

Baker, S. (1995). The National Teacher Examination and the NAACP's legal campaign to equalize teachers' salaries in the South, 1936–63. *History of Education Quarterly, 35*(1), 49–64.

Baker, R. S. (2006). *Paradoxes of desegregation: African American struggles for educational equity in Charleston, South Carolina, 1926–1972.* University of South Carolina Press.

Baker, R. S. (2011). Pedagogies of protest: African American teachers and the history of the Civil Rights Movement, 1940–1963. *Teachers College Record, 113*(12), 2777–2803.

Baker, S., Myers, A., & Vasquez, B. (2014). Desegregation, accountability, and equality: North Carolina and the nation, 1971–2002. *Education Policy Analysis Archives, 22*(117), 1–25.

Bates, G. N. (1949). *Community in which I live.* Gladys Noel Bates Papers, "Speeches and papers, 1948, 1968, 1991-1992" (Box 3), MDAH, Jackson, MS.

Black, D. (2020). *Schoolhouse burning: Public education and the assault on American democracy.* Public Affairs.

Bolton, C. (2005). *The hardest deal of all: The battle over school integration in Mississippi, 1870–1980.* University Press of Mississippi.

Brown v. Board of Education, 347 U.S. 483 (1954). https://supreme.justia.com/cases/federal/us/347/483/

Bryan v. Austin, 148 F. Supp 563 (1957). https://law.justia.com/cases/federal/district-courts/FSupp/148/563/1875071/

Bullock, H. A. (1967). *A history of Negro education in the South.* Harvard University Press.

Bureau of the Census. (1955). *Statistical abstract of the United States.* U.S. Government Printing Office.

Bureau of the Census. (1970). *Statistical abstract of the United States.* U.S. Government Printing Office.

Burke High School. (1959). *The 1959 Bulldog* (Burke High School yearbook). Lois A. Simms Papers, Avery Research Center (Box 2, Folder 23), Charleston, SC.

Carter, R. L. (1949, April 19). [Letter to A. L. Johnson]. Gladys Noel Bates Papers (Box 2, "Scrapbook, 1948-1960"), MDAH, Jackson, MS.

Cecelski, D. S. (1994). *Along freedom road: Hyde County, North Carolina and the fate of Black schools in the South.* University of North Carolina Press.

Charron, K. M. (2009). *Freedom's teacher: The life of Septima Clark.* University of North Carolina Press.

Civil Rights Act of 1964, Pub. L. 88-352, 78 Stat. 241 (1964). https://www.govinfo.gov/content/pkg/STATUTE-78/pdf/STATUTE-78-Pg241.pdf#page=12

Collier-Thomas, B., & Franklin, V. P. (2001). *Sisters in the struggle: African American women in the civil rights-Black Power movement.* New York University Press.

Counts, G. S. (1969). *Dare the school build a new social order?* Arno. (Originally published in 1932)

Crawford, V. L., Rouse, J. A., & Woods, C. (1993). *Women in the Civil Rights Movement: Trailblazers and torchbearers, 1941–1965.* Indiana University Press.

Cremin, L. A. (1964). *The transformation of the school: Progressivism in American education, 1876–1957.* Vintage.

Crespino, J. (2007). *In search of another country: Mississippi and the conservative counter-revolution.* Princeton University Press.

Cuban, L. (1993). *How teachers taught: Constancy and change in American classrooms 1890–1990* (2nd ed.). Teachers College Press.

Cunningham, C. (2018). *"I hope they fire me:" Black teachers in the fight for equal education, 1910–1970.* Order No. 10789308, University of South Carolina. https://www.proquest.com/dissertations-theses/i-hope-they-fire-me-black-teachers-fight-equal/docview/2071383532/se-2?accountid=14553.

Cunningham, C. J. (n.d.). *Meaning of education.* "Compositions, 1932–1933; n.d.," Charles J. Cunningham Papers (Box 1, Folder 4), MDAH, Jackson, MS.

Cunningham C. J. (2021) "Hell is Popping Here in South Carolina": Orangeburg County Black teachers and their community in the immediate post-Brown era. *History of Education Quarterly, 61*(S1), 36–62.

Cunningham, C. J. (1933). Education for a changing civilization; Mankind at the cross-roads; Meaning of a liberal education, "class papers/notes 1933" Charles J. Cunningham Papers (Box 1, Folder 3), MDAH, Jackson, MS.

D'Amico, D. (2011). *Claiming profession: The dynamic struggle for teacher professionalism in the twentieth century* [Doctoral dissertation]. New York University, New York.

D'Amico Pawlewicz, D. (2020). *Blaming teachers: Professionalization policies and the failure of reform in American history.* Rutgers University Press.

Daniel, P. (2004). Accountability and desegregation: *Brown* and its legacy. *The Journal of Negro Education, 73*(3), 255–267.

Delmont, M. (2016) *Why busing failed: Race, media, and the national resistance to school desegregation.* University of California Press.

Dittmer, J. (1994). *Local people: The struggle for civil rights in Mississippi.* University of Illinois Press.

Drago, E. L. (1990). *Initiative, paternalism, and race relations: Charleston's Avery Normal Institute.* University of Georgia Press

Du Bois, W. E. B. (1935). Does the Negro need separate schools? *The Journal of Negro Education, 4*(3), 328–335.

Du Bois, W. E. B. (1998). *Black reconstruction in America, 1860–1880.* Free Press. (Original work published 1935)

Fairclough, A. (1999). *Race & democracy: The civil rights struggle in Louisiana, 1915–1972.* University of Georgia Press.

Fairclough, A. (2007). *A class of their own: Black teachers in the segregated South.* Belknap.

Fantini, M., Gittell, M., & Magat, R. (1970). *Community control and the urban school.* Praeger.

Foner, E. (1988). *Reconstruction: America's unfinished revolution, 1863–1877.* Harper.

Franklin v. County School Board of Giles County, 242 F. Supp. 371 (1965).

Freeman, R. B. (1976). *Black elite: The new market for highly educated Black Americans.* McGraw-Hill.

Fultz, M. (2004). The displacement of Black educators post-Brown: An overview and analysis. *History of Education Quarterly, 44*(1), 11–45.

Gaffney, D. (2007). *Teachers united: The rise of New York state united teachers.* State University of New York Press.

Gilmore, A. T. (2017). *A more perfect union: The merger of the South Carolina Educational Association and the Palmetto Education Association.* The National Education Association.

Gray, J. A., Reed, J. L., & Walton, N. W. (1987). *History of the Alabama State Teachers Association.* National Education Association.

Gutek, G. L. (1971). *The educational theory of George S. Counts.* Ohio State University Press.

Hale, J. N. (2013). 'The fight was instilled in us': High school student activism and the Civil Rights Movement in Charleston, South Carolina. *The South Carolina Historical Magazine, 114*(1), 4–28.

Hale, J. N. (2016). *The freedom schools: Student activists in the Mississippi Civil Rights Movement.* Columbia University Press.

Hale, J. N. (2018). "The development of power is the main business of the school": The agency of southern Black teacher associations from Jim Crow through desegregation. *The Journal of Nego Education, 87*(4), 444–459.

Hale, J. N. (2019). On race, teacher activism and the right to work: Historicizing the 'Red for Ed' movement in the American South. *West Virginia Law Review, 121*(3), 851–882.

Hale, J., & Cooper, C. (2018). Lowcountry, high standards: The struggle for quality education in Charleston, South Carolina. In V. Showers Johnson, G. Graml, & P. W. Williams (Eds.), *Deferred dreams, defiant struggles: Critical perspectives on Blackness, belonging and civil rights* (pp. 154–174). Liverpool University Press.

Hale, J. N., & Blanton, K. (2021). The civil rights agenda of Black educators in the South and its implication for the "Red for Ed" reform movement. In D. D'Amico Pawlewicz (Ed.), *Walkout: Teacher militancy, activism, and school reform* (pp. 25–43). Information Age Publishing.

Hatch, R. C. (1938). Minutes of the meeting of the executive committee, August 13, 1938. "ASTA minutes," ASTA Papers (Box 13, Folder 40), ASU, Montgomery, AL.

Hooker, R. W. (1970). *Displacement of Black teachers in the eleven southern states, special report race.* Relations Information Center.

Hunt, E. C. (n.d.). Vita Sheet, Eugene Hunt Collection, Vita. Avery Research Center (Box 1, Folder 1), Charleston, SC.

Hunt, E. C. (1945–1980). Burke High School teaching materials. Eugene Hunt Collection, Avery Research Center (Box 3, Folder 2), Charleston, SC.

Hunter, T. W. (1997). *To 'joy my freedom: Southern Black women's lives and labor after the Civil War.* Harvard University Press.

James-Galloway A. D., & Harris, T. (2021). We been relevant: Culturally relevant pedagogy and Black women teachers in segregated schools. *Educational Studies, 57*(2), 124–141. https://doi.org/10.1080/00131946.2021.1878179

Jannik, C. (1996, December 23). [Interview by G. N. Bates]. The University of Southern Mississippi Center for Oral History and Cultural Heritage, Hattiesburg, MS.

Jelks, R. (2012). *Benjamin Elijah Hays: Schoolmaster of the movement.* University of North Carolina Press.

Johnson, A. L. (1948a, January 14). [Letter to Mr. A. J. Noel]. Gladys Noel Bates Papers (Box 2, "Scrapbook, 1948–1960"), MDAH, Jackson, MS.

Johnson A. L. (1948b, February 23). [Letter to James A. Burns]. Gladys Noel Bates Papers (Box 2, "Scrapbook, 1948–1960"), MDAH, Jackson, MS.

Johnson, K. A. (2000). *Uplifting the women and the race: The Educational philosophies and social activism of Anna Julia Cooper and Nannie Helen Burroughs.* Taylor and Francis.

Johnson, V. S., Graml, G., & Lessane, P. W. (Eds.). (2018). *Deferred dreams, defiant struggles: Critical perspectives on Blackness, belonging and civil rights.* Liverpool University Press.

Jones, J. (1985). *Labor of love, labor of sorrow: Black women, work and the family, from slavery to the present.* Vintage.

Jordan-Taylor, D. (2011). *'I'm not Autherine Lucy': The circular migration of southern Black professionals who completed graduate school in the North during Jim Crow, 1945–1970* [Doctoral dissertation]. University of Washington, Seattle, WA.

Karpinski, C. (2008). *A visible company of professionals: African Americans and the National Education Association during the Civil Rights Movement.* Peter Lang.

Kilpatrick, W. H. (1937). *Education for a changing civilization: Three lectures delivered on the Luther Laflin Kellogg foundation at Rutgers University, 1926.* Macmillan.

King, S. H. (1993). The limited presence of African-American teachers. *Review of Educational Research, 63*(2), 115–149.

Kirk, J. A. (2009). The NAACP campaign for teachers' salary equalization: African American women educators and the early civil rights struggle. *The Journal of African American History, 94*(4), 529–552.

Kluger, R. (2004). *Simple justice: The history of Brown v. Board of Education and Black America's struggle for equality.* Vintage.

Kruse, K. (2005). *White flight: Atlanta and the making of modern conservatism.* Princeton University Press.

Labor Management Relations Act of 1947 29 U.S.C. § 141-197 (Taft-Hartley Act).

Lassiter, M. D. (2006). *The silent majority: Suburban politics in the Sunbelt South.* Princeton University Press.

Lassiter, M. D., & Crespino, J. (2010). *The myth of southern exceptionalism.* Oxford University Press.

Lichtenstein, N. (2002). *State of the Union: A century of American labor.* Princeton University Press.

Lichtenstein, N., & Tandy Shermer, E. (2012). *The right and labor in America: Politics, ideology, and imagination.* University of Pennsylvania Press.

Littlefield, V. W. (2012). Ruby Forsythe and Fannie Phelps Adams: Teaching for confrontation during Jim Crow. In M. J. Spruill, V. W. Littlefield, & J. M. Johnson (Eds.), *South Carolina women: Their lives and times* (pp. 17–34). University of Georgia Press.

Loder-Jackson, T. L. (2012). Hope and despair: Southern Black women educators across pre- and post-civil rights cohorts theorizing about their activism. *Educational Studies, 48*(3), 266–295.

Lynch, J. R. (1913). *The facts of reconstruction.* Neale.

Lyons, J. (2008). *Teachers and reform: Chicago public education, 1929–1970.* University of Illinois Press.

Madkins, T. C. (2011). The Black teacher shortage: A literature review of historical and contemporary trends. *The Journal of Negro Education, 80*(3), 417–427.

McCartin, J. A. (2008). Turnabout years: Public sector unionism and the fiscal crisis. In F. Schulman & J. Zelizer (Eds.), *Rightward bound: Making America conservative in the 1970s* (pp. 210–226). Harvard University Press.

McGirr, L. (2001). *Suburban warriors: The origins of the new American right.* Princeton University Press.

McMillen, N. R. (1989). *Dark journey: Black Mississippians in the age of Jim Crow.* University of Illinois Press.

Mills v. Board of Trustees of Anne Arundel County 30 F. Supp 245 (1939). https://law.justia.com/cases/federal/district-courts/FSupp/30/245/1378476/

Mirel, J. (1984). The politics of educational retrenchment in Detroit, 1929–1935. *History of Education Quarterly, 24*(3), 323–358.

Mississippi Educational Journal: A Monthly Magazine for Teachers in Colored Schools, 18, 74–76 (1934). MDAH, Jackson, MS.

Mississippi Educational Journal: A Monthly Magazine for Teachers in Colored Schools, 11, 1. (1934, October). MDAH, Jackson, MS.

Mississippi Teachers Association. (1935). Proposed constitution and bylaws. *Mississippi Educational Journal: A Monthly Magazine for Teachers in Colored Schools, 11*(6), 106. MDAH, Jackson, MS.

Murphy, M. (1990). *Blackboard union: The AFT & the NEA 1900–1980.* Cornell University Press.

Murray, P. (1984). *History of the North Carolina Teachers Association.* National Education Association.

National Association for the Advancement of Colored People. (1953). *Youth Division, November 16, 1953* [Press release]. NAACP papers, Series 19, Part C, Reel 1.

National Association of Teachers in Colored Schools. (1929). Constitution and by-laws–The National Association of Teachers in colored schools. *The Bulletin* vol. IX VII, The Bulletin, National Education Association Collection, Gelman Library (Box 3044, File 10), Washington, DC.

National Center for Education Statistics. (2012–2013). *Characteristics of public and private elementary and secondary school teachers in the United States.* Department of Education.

National Education Association. (n.d.). *Equal opportunity for all: The NEA's fight for Civil Rights.* NEA Records, Special Historical Facts, Gelman Library (Box 3004, Folder 10), Washington, DC.

National Education Association. (1963). Resolution 12–Desegregation in the public schools. NEA Papers, "Meeting, Seattle, WA," Gelman Library (Box 1274, Folder 15), Washington, DC

National Education Association. (1965). *Resolution of unification.* NEA Records, "Merger 1960-1977," Gelman Library (Box 1275, Folder 3), Washington, DC.

National Education Association. (1966b). *Committee on Professional Rights and Responsibilities.* NEA Records, "Meeting–1966," Gelman Library (Box 1275, Folder 1), Washington, DC.

National Education Association. (1969). Merger dates of eleven southern states, NEA Papers, "Dual Association Mergers–Resolutions," Gelman Library (Box 0519, Folder 1), Washington, DC.

National Teachers Association. (1857). *Proceedings of convention for organization.* NEA Records, Gelman Library (Box 3000, Folder "The Athenaeum: The Birthplace of NEA), Washington, DC.

Nelson, B. (2001). *Divided we stand: American workers and the struggle for Black equality.* Princeton University Press.

Olson, L. (2001). *Freedom's daughters: The unsung heroines of the Civil Rights Movement from 1830–1970.* Simon & Schuster.

Perillo, J. (2012). *Uncivil rights: Teachers, unions, and race in the battle of school equity.* University of Chicago Press.

Perry, T. D. (1975). *History of the American Teachers Association.* National Education Association.

Picott, J. R. (1975). *History of the Virginia Teachers Association.* National Education Association.

Pierson, S. G. (2014). *Laboratory of learning: HBCU laboratory schools and Alabama State College Lab High in the era of Jim Crow.* Peter Lang.

Plessy v. Ferguson, 163 U.S. 537 (1896). https://supreme.justia.com/cases/federal/us/163/537/

Potts, J. F., Sr. (1978). *A history of the Palmetto Education Association.* National Education Association.

Powers, B. E. (1994). *Black Charlestonians: A social history, 1822–1885.* University of Arkansas Press.

Ramsey, S. (2005). We will be ready whenever they are: African American teachers' responses to the Brown decision and public school integration in Nashville, Tennessee, 1954–1966. *The Journal of African American History, 90*(1–2), 29–51.

Ramsey, S. (2012). Caring is activism: Black Southern womanist teachers theorizing and the careers of Kathleen Crosby and Bertha Maxwell-Roddey, 1946–1986. *Educational Studies, 48*(3), 244–265.

Richardson, J. M., & Jones, M. D. (2009). *Education for liberation: The American Missionary Association and African Americans, 1890 to the Civil Rights Movement.* University of Alabama Press.

Ridley, W. (1952, December). Joint action toward unity, Palmetto State Teachers Association. *PSTA Journal,* 4–5.

Robinson, G. (1967, April 19). [Letter to Irvamae Applegate]. NEA Records, "Dual Association Merger–South Carolina," Gelman Library (Box 0519, Folder 4), Washington, DC.

Robnett, B. (1996, May). African-American women in the Civil Rights Movement, 1954–1965: Gender, leadership, and micromobilization. *American Journal of Sociology, 101*(6), 1661–1693.

Shaw, S. (1996). *What a woman ought to be and to do: Black professional women workers during the Jim Crow Era.* University of Chicago Press.

Siddle-Walker, V. (1996). *Their highest potential: An African American school community in the segregated South.* University of North Carolina Press.

Siddle-Walker, V. (2009a). *Hello professor: A Black principal and professional leadership in the segregated South.* University of North Carolina Press.

Siddle-Walker, V. (2009b). Second-class integration: A historical perspective for a contemporary agenda. *Harvard Educational Review, 79*(2), 269–284.

Siddle-Walker, V. (2013). Tolerated tokenism, or the injustice in justice: Black teacher associations and their forgotten struggle for educational justice, 1921–1954. *Equity & Excellence in Education, 46*(1), 64–80.

Siddle-Walker, V. (2017). *The lost education of Horace Tate: Uncovering the hidden heroes who fought for justice in schools.* The New Press.

Simms, L. A. (1954). *A comparative study of provisions for the education of Negro and White pupils in the public schools of South Carolina.* Lois A. Simms Papers, Biographical Records: Academic Work, Howard University, Avery Research Center (Box 1, Folder 12), Charleston, SC.

Simms, L. A. (1956–1960). Assignments for English II and III, Lois A. Simms Papers, Plan Books for English and History, 1956-1957 and 1959-1960, Avery Research Center, (Box 2, Folder 20), Charleston, SC.

Simms, L. A. (1995). *A chalk and chalkboard career in Carolina.* Vantage.

Solomon, W. E. (1955, Summer). Desegregation in public education in South Carolina. The desegregation decision–One year afterward (Summer, 1955). *The Journal of Negro Education, 24*(3), 327–332.

Sullivan, P. (2009). *Lift every voice: The NAACP and the making of the Civil Rights Movement.* The New Press.

Thompson, C. D. (1973). *The history of the Mississippi Teachers Association.* NEA Teachers Rights.

Thompson, C. H. (1932). Editorial comment: Is there an oversupply of Negro teachers? *The Journal of Negro Education, 1*(3/4), 343–346.

Thompson, C. H. (1936). Editorial comment: Discrimination in Negro teachers' salaries in Maryland. *The Journal of Negro Education, 5*(4), 539–542.

Thompson, C. H. (1953). Editorial comment: The Negro teacher and desegregation of the public schools. *The Journal of Negro Education, 22*(2), 95–101.

Tillman, L. C. (2004). (Un)intended consequences? The impact of the *Brown v. Board of Education* decision on the employment status of Black educators. *Education and Urban Society, 36*(3), 280–303.

Trenholm, G. W. (1975). Status of Negro education in Alabama. In T. D. Perry (Ed.), *History of the American Teachers Association* (pp. 57–66). National Education Association.

Trenholm, H. C. (1956). Foreword, 1956 ASTA Yearbook, ASTA collection, ASU, Montgomery, AL.

Turner, J. A. (2010). *Sitting in and speaking out: Student movement in the American South, 1960–1970.* The University of Georgia Press.

Tushnet, M. V. (1987). *The NAACP's legal strategy against segregated education, 1925–1950.* The University of North Carolina Press.

Tyack, D., Lowe, R., & Hansot, E. (1984). *Public schools in hard times: The Great Depression and recent years.* Harvard University Press.

United States Department of Education. (2016). *The state of racial diversity in the educator workforce.* Department of Education.

Urban, W. J. (1982). *Why teachers organized.* Wayne State University Press.

Urban, W. J. (1989). Teacher activism. In D. Warren (Ed.), *American teachers: Histories of a profession at work* (pp. 194–195). Macmillan.

Urban, W. J. (2000). *Gender, race and the National Education Association: Professionalism and its limitations.* Routledge.

U.S. Office of Education. (1972). *Displacement of Black educators in desegregating schools.* Government Printing Office.

Viola Louise Duvall, et al. v. J. F. Seignous 1943 Case No.: 1082.

Walsh, C. (2018). *Racial taxation: Schools, segregation, and taxpayer citizenship, 1869–1973.* University of North Carolina Press.

Walters, W. A. (1947). Why limit the study of the Negro. *Mississippi Educational Journal: A Monthly Magazine for Teachers in Colored Schools, 18,* 88–89.

Wesley, E. B. (1957). *NEA: The first hundred years: The building of the teaching profession.* Harper.

West, A. M. (1980). *The National Education Association: The power base for education.* The Free Press.

Wilkerson, D. (1960). The Negro School Movement in Virginia: From "equalization" to "integration." *The Journal of Negro Education, 29*(1), 17–29. https://doi.org/10.2307/2293542

Williams, H. A. (2005). *Self-taught: African American education in slavery and freedom.* University of North Carolina Press.

Williamson, J. (2004). 'This has been quite a year for heads falling:' Institutional autonomy in the civil rights era. *History of Education Quarterly, 44*(4), 554–576.

Woodson, C. G. (1926). Negro history week. *Mississippi Educational Journal: A Monthly Magazine for Teachers in Colored Schools, 18,* 57.

CHAPTER 3

ONE STEP FORWARD, TWO STEPS BACK

How Districts' Responses to Desegregation Harmed Black Educators and Students in South Carolina

Vann Holden
University of South Carolina

Henry Tran
University of South Carolina

According to Walker E. Solomon, the executive secretary of the Palmetto Education Association—a professional organization that once represented South Carolina's Black teachers, there were 7,500 Black educators in the state in 1956 (Solomon, 1956). That number rose to approximately 8,301 in the 1963–1964 school year (South Carolina State Department of Education, 1963–1964). The state's general population increased from 2,382,594 in 1960 to 5,084,127 in 2018, and the number of Black South Carolinians

How Did We Get Here?, pages 43–56
Copyright © 2022 by Information Age Publishing
www.infoagepub.com
All rights of reproduction in any form reserved.

similarly increased from 829,291 to 1,377,798 during the same period (U.S. Census Bureau, 1960a, 2018). However, the total number of Black teachers in the state declined from 8,301 in 1963–1964 to 7,722 in 2017–2018 (South Carolina State Department of Education, 1963–1964; South Carolina Department of Education, 2018). Based on our data review of the School Directory of South Carolina, Black teachers made up approximately 38% of the state's teachers in the 1963–1964 school year. However, during the 2017–2018 school year, that percentage was just 15.18% (South Carolina Department of Education, 2018).

While several factors contribute to the current underrepresentation of Black teachers in South Carolina's teaching force, at least part of the imbalance is rooted in the discriminatory influence of districts' decisions and policies during segregation and desegregation. The problem is also profoundly connected to racism in our state's policy development and implementation. The purpose of this chapter is to introduce how both historical and modern-day racism and policies impact today's educators.

The chapter begins with an overview of South Carolina's response to desegregation orders. We then examine how the resulting desegregation policies impacted Black principals, teachers, and students in the state. While the focus is on South Carolina, the events in the state are representative of trends in the South during this period, and regional information is included to add additional context and detail. The desegregation plan of one South Carolina district was examined as part of this research, and the findings are included in this chapter to provide detail on how these patterns were manifested at the local level.

BACKGROUND

In 1954, the United States Supreme Court ruled that separate is inherently unequal in the historic *Brown v. Board of Education of Topeka* case. Consequently, the court ordered the racial desegregation of the school system. White supremacist beliefs were deeply rooted in the state of South Carolina, and this led to active resistance to the court orders. Given that almost half of the White families in the state owned slaves before the Civil War, the "notion that so many Black people would mingle as equals was simply unfathomable" to many Whites (Hawes et al., 2018, para. 59).

In the early 1950s, U.S. Senator Strom Thurmond helped write what would later become known as the Southern Manifesto to rally other senators and politicians to ally and resist court-ordered desegregation (Aucoin, 1996). In 1956, South Carolina's compulsory school attendance law was repealed to circumvent desegregation so that no child would be required to attend an integrated school (Baker, 2006). Governor James Byrnes attempted to delay desegregation by developing policies that claimed to equalize the dual school system. These activities ended with more "equalization" money directed to White schools than Black schools (Dobrasko, 2005).

Charleston County was the first school district in South Carolina to desegregate, with 11 Black students enrolling in previously all-White schools in 1963 (Baker, 2006; Brown et al., 2015). Even a decade removed from *Brown v. Board*, districts continued to delay and make minimal steps towards desegregation. The tide turned when then-Governor Robert E. McNair recommended the reinstatement of the compulsory education law in 1967 (Mickey, 2015). In 1970, the courts ordered the immediate desegregation of Darlington and Greenville County schools (Burton & Reece, 2008). Governor McNair refused to stand in the way of court orders, close the schools, or repeal the newly reinstated compulsory school attendance law (Burton & Reece, 2008). Nearly 2 decades after the landmark *Brown v. Board* ruling, South Carolina's school districts finally began to dismantle de jure systems that prevented Black children from attending schools with White children. In response, many White families pulled their children out of the state's public schools to enroll in all-White private education institutions (Ladson-Billings, 2007).

THE IMPACT OF DESEGREGATION ON BLACK EDUCATORS

Though the integration of the schools held the promise of equitable facilities, curricula, access, and opportunities, the implementation of desegregation policies often had lasting negative consequences on Black educators (i.e., principals and teachers) and students. This perspective is counter to the dominant narrative that suggests rosier outcomes of desegregation, such as reduced racial isolation in schools, growth of cross-cultural understanding between students from different racial backgrounds, improved equitable resource distribution, and progress in learning outcome equity resulting from the *Brown vs. Board* ruling in 1954 (Frankenberg, 2006; Hochschild & Scovronick, 2003; Linn & Welner, 2007). A more nuanced understanding of what happened to Black teachers in the South before and after the desegregation ruling is warranted to understand the discrepancy.

Black teachers in the era of segregated schools were educated professionals. They attended conferences, were members of professional organizations, and worked together to improve practices. Segregated Black schools have been characterized as having excellent, supportive teachers with high expectations and principals that were strong leaders in the school and community (Siddle Walker, 2000). Moreover, research has shown that Black students improve academic outcomes (Egalite et al., 2015), receive higher expectations (Gershenson et al., 2016), and are more likely to complete high school and attend college (Gershenson et al., 2018) when paired with Black teachers. Yet when Southern states and school districts begrudgingly moved to desegregate their schools, one of their first courses of action was to dismiss Black educators from their positions. A longitudinal analysis spanning from 1970 to 2000, Oakley et al. (2009) found that mandated desegregation court orders had significantly drained the pool of Black teachers in the South. With the Black educators removed, Black students were left without critical adult allies, influences, voices, and guidance at school. The Black community was harmed by the dismissal of the educators who had been a strong and influential segment of the community for decades (Ethridge, 1979; Hooker, 1970).

THE REMOVAL OF BLACK PRINCIPALS

The desegregation efforts hurt Black teachers and Black principals, although the latter story is seldom told. Black principals were leaders of the Black community during the era of segregation. They coordinated their schools' instructional programs, professional development, and fundraising activities (Siddle Walker, 2000). In addition to their responsibilities within the school, the principals also provided social, emotional, and financial support to their communities and were active in the local churches. As J. C. James noted, Black principals were role models for Black students (James, 1970).

As segregated Black schools were closed or reconfigured during desegregation, Black principals lost their positions despite their importance to Black students, schools, and communities (Ethridge, 1979; Floyd, 1973; Fultz, 2004; Hooker, 1970). The pathways to principal displacement varied. Demotion of Black principals to teaching or non-principal positions was a common outcome (Floyd, 1973; Fultz, 2004). Some lost their principal positions at high schools and became junior high or elementary schools principals. Others were promoted to district office positions with meaningful-sounding titles but little substantive influence. One Black educator remarked that such positions were akin to being "assistant to the superintendent in charge of light bulbs and erasers" (Hooker, 1970, p. 4).

The drop in the number of Black principals heavily coincided with the desegregation of schools. Fultz (2004) shared that the number of Black high school principals in South Carolina in 1970 was just 33, down from 144 in 1965 when the movement towards desegregation was still relatively stagnant. Floyd (1973) found a similar change, with 142 Black high school principals in the state in 1963–1964 and just 46 in 1972–1973. Floyd also noted that there were no Black high school principals in 22 of the state's 46 counties in 1972–1973. Samuel Ethridge, a longtime official with the National Education

Association, estimated that the state should have had 424 Black principals in 1972 but was 150 short of that number (Ethridge, 1979).

Beyond the importance of their representation, the Black principal was also a crucial figure in the hiring and developing Black teachers. D'Amico et al. (2017) suggest that Black teachers continue to be more likely to be hired by Black principals. Therefore, the removal of Black principals during desegregation was one practice that had a rippling domino effect, resulting in far-reaching consequences for Black teachers.

THE REMOVAL OF BLACK TEACHERS

During desegregation, state laws, district policies, and school-level practices also resulted in extensive, lasting harm done to Black educators. The state repealed the teacher tenure law in 1955, making it easier to dismiss educators (Fultz, 2004). In 1956, new state law prohibited government employees from being members of the National Association for the Advancement of Colored People (NAACP) and required employees to state their membership in the civil rights organization publicly (Baker, 2006). Cunningham's (2021) research on Elloree Training School in South Carolina provides details on how this policy devastated the ranks of Black educators. The year the law went into effect, the Elloree teachers' new contracts asked them to state whether or not they were members of the NAACP or wanted to teach in integrated settings. When 21 of the school's 31 teachers declined to answer either question, the district refused to rehire them.

Baker (2006) reported that Septima Clark and Henry Hutchinson of Charleston were fired from their teaching positions because of their membership in the NAACP and work to advance the cause of integration. Teachers and community members not only risked their jobs in taking these stances, but they also faced hardships when White business owners refused to sell them essential goods. They endured constant threats from organizations and hate groups like the Ku Klux Klan. These threats often resulted in physical harm. For example, the KKK kidnapped principal Reverend E. E. Richburg of Orangeburg County in 1955 (Cunningham, 2018). However, that ordeal did not stop him from openly declaring his membership in the NAACP, stating in response to the law, "I hope they fire me" (Cunningham, 2018, p. 18).

The state also employed new test and certification requirements to remove Black educators. South Carolina was among the first states to adopt the National Teacher Examination (NTE) from Educational Testing Service to determine teacher certification (Baker, 2006). This test was developed from and tailored to White middle-class views and values on education (Oakley et al., 2009). Hooker reported (1970) that South Carolina districts used the test to fire Black teachers who earned below a specific score on the NTE regardless of their years of experience or effectiveness in the classroom. In Clover, Black teachers who did not reach a specific score on the NTE were fired and replaced with White teachers. In what could be considered an attempt to continue segregation-era practices of denying equal pay to Black teachers, the state also tied the NTE scores to teacher salary (Baker, 2006).

Black teachers who were not fired immediately due to the new laws and policies were displaced in other ways. Experienced teachers were transferred to grade levels and subjects they had not previously taught and then fired for incompetence when they did not perform well (Fultz, 2004; Hooker, 1970). Some lost their permanent classrooms and became floaters, while others were forced into support roles. In some instances, positions were tied to grants and federal funds and would be eliminated when the money ran out. In Edgefield, a Black varsity football coach was demoted to an assistant coach position with the junior varsity team, and three additional White coaches were hired to assist the varsity team (Hooker, 1970).

White policymakers, school board members, and school leaders decided to displace Black educators on their perceptions that Black educators lacked preparation and were ineffective (Hooker, 1970). However, Siddle Walker (2000) and Fultz (2004) note that Black and White teachers in the Southern states had relatively equal preparation for their teaching positions. In addition, teacher-preparation programs at Black institutions of higher education were often focal points for those colleges and universities, with teaching positions seen as attractive options for young Black professionals after graduation (Fultz, 2004).

Successful outcomes from lawsuits and protested firings provide further evidence to suggest that Black educators were being dismissed for reasons other than their abilities as teachers and leaders (Hooker, 1970). E. B. Palmer made this argument, serving as the North Carolina Teachers Association leader, the state's Black teacher organization, and later serving in a leadership position in the state's integrated teacher association, the North Carolina Association of Educators. In these roles, Palmer stated that he helped fight 19 court cases over the dismissal of Black educators, with many of the firings due to allegations of incompetence against the teachers. However, Palmer noted that Black educators won 18 of the 19 cases, indicating that the dismissal decisions and charges of incompetence were not based on the teachers' effectiveness.

Like Black principals, the number of Black teachers significantly dropped as district desegregation plans were implemented. Based on data collected by the Department of Health, Education, and Welfare's Office for Civil Rights, Hooker (1970) and Fultz (2004) report that the number of Black teachers in 108 districts across six southern states fell from a total of 9,015 in the districts to 8,092 between 1968 and 1970. All of the districts in the report opted for voluntary desegregation plans. Furthermore, the report reveals another factor contributing to the declining numbers of Black teachers during desegregation. From the start to the end of that period, 4,907 teachers in those districts were no longer in their employment positions, of which 1,133 were Black. While 5,196 teachers were hired during that time, only 743 were Black. These statistics suggest an issue in the underrepresentation of Black educators in the wake of desegregation. Black teachers were being forced out of the profession by racially discriminatory policies and practices, all while new positions were being created. White teachers disproportionately filled both types of vacancies. Ethridge (1979) estimates that Black educators lost 39,386 teaching positions in the southern states by 1974.

HOW DESEGREGATION PLANS IMPACTED THE EMPLOYMENT OF BLACK EDUCATORS IN SCHOOL DISTRICT FIVE OF LEXINGTON AND RICHLAND COUNTIES

An in-depth analysis of one South Carolina school district's desegregation plan details how these broader trends played out at the local district level. School District Five of Lexington and Richland Counties (School District Five) is located a few miles northwest of Columbia, South Carolina, and serves students from the Irmo, Dutch Fork, and Chapin communities. Data for this research on School District Five was collected from school board meeting minutes and recorded correspondence between district leaders and the Department of Health, Education, and Welfare. These documents were obtained from the school district and state archives.

School District Five implemented its "freedom-of-choice" desegregation plan in the 1965–1966 academic year. Black teachers made up 28.2% of the district's full-time classroom teacher positions at that time. The district implemented a full desegregation plan during the 1968–1969 school year. This plan converted the segregated Black school, Richlex, into a junior high school for Black and White students and sent the district's Black students to the district's primarily White schools. By 1972–1973, Black teachers represented just 5.6% of the district's full-time classroom teachers.

These percentages only tell part of the story about teacher displacement in School District Five. The district employed 22 Black teachers in 1965–1966, and the district in 1972–1973 employed only 13. The district added 155 new teaching positions during that same period, growing from 78 full-time classroom teachers to 233. Though the district received applications from 45 Black candidates seeking teaching positions in 1971–1972, only one of the 67 new hires was Black. The hiring trend continued the following year as only one of the district's 68 new hires was Black. Of the 233 teachers in the 1972–1973 academic year, 220 were White. The district's refusal to hire Black teachers during this period of rapid expansion played a pivotal role in the makeup of the faculty.

Of the 14 Richlex teachers who remained with the district in 1968–1969, only seven taught the same grade level or subject that they taught the year before at Richlex. The 14 teachers were reassigned to six different schools when the district desegregated. Mrs. Vernetta Riley, the guidance counselor at Richlex, remained a guidance counselor in the district.

The changes to teachers' teaching assignments and the makeup of the district's faculty coincided with the district's decision to displace Mr. Robert Lee Floyd, the principal of the previously segregated, all-Black Richlex School. At the same time, the district converted Richlex into a junior high school for Black and White students. Black students in the community had attended a school on that site since 1918, founded on land donated by the neighboring St. Peter Baptist Church. In its decision to repurpose Richlex, the board also decided that the school would need to be renamed and renovated before serving White students. A few years later, the school would again be repurposed, this time as Dutch Fork Elementary School (DFES). Richlex alumni and current DFES principal Julius Scott keep the memory of the school alive through reunions and celebrations of the school's history.

Though not within the scope of this chapter or book, it is worth pausing to consider how the closure and repurposing of Black schools like Richlex impacted Black communities and students. Various studies point to the central role that segregated Black schools held in their communities (Horsford, 2009; Siddle Walker, 1996), but many of their academic, artistic, and athletic histories were erased by White school boards as districts desegregated. Wilson High School in Florence, Burke High School in Charleston, and C.A. Johnson High School in Columbia are among the few once-segregated Black high schools in South Carolina that continue to serve as high schools in their communities today.

HOW DESEGREGATION DECISIONS IMPACTED
BLACK CHILDREN IN SOUTH CAROLINA

The losses caused by the desegregation era's decisions to displace Black teachers and principals were not just felt by Black educators. Black children entered hostile, desegregated environments without role models, protectors, and advocates. They suffered physical and emotional abuse and lacked support as they attempted to cope with the racism they experienced daily.

An advisory specialist to School District Five during its desegregation process noted in the professional development plan, "Most of the teachers of the district have had little or no experience in working with children of a race other than their own and, therefore, do not fully appreciate and understand the differences that exist between persons of varied cultural, social, economic, and educational backgrounds, and the impact of these factors upon attitudes toward, and achievement in educational institutions" (Ramsey, n.d., p. 3). By 1973, the overwhelming number of these teachers were White, so Black students suffered the consequences of this lack of experience, appreciation, and understanding.

The Lowcountry Digital History Initiative chronicled the experiences of South Carolina students on the frontlines of desegregation in the "Somebody Had to Do It" project (Brown et al., 2015). Theodore Adams of Orangeburg recalled the constant threats of violence made towards himself and the other Black students and the fear and anxiety from doing something that had not been done before. He discussed tacks being placed in his chairs, social ostracization, and being denied extracurricular activities. Adams noted the lack of support from White teachers or administrators in addressing or helping him with the challenging situations he faced. Millicent Brown of Charleston described the social isolation she experienced during the school day and the difficulty she found fitting in with any specific community in or out of school.

Marion Orr and Hanes Walton Jr. (2004) documented similar experiences of children in nearby cities such as Athens and Savannah, Georgia. Ulysses O. Bryant Jr. was hit, kicked, and pushed by White students at Savannah High. On one occasion, a White student spat in his food. Sage Brown noted that White students who attempted to help or be friendly to the Black students desegregating Groves High were punished by their friends. Like Bryant, Brown also noted physical violence and racial slurs directed towards Black students (Orr & Walton, 2004). Bonnie Hampton Travis and Maxie Foster shared similar stories from the Athens schools (Orr & Walton, 2004). A key theme that emerges from Orr and Walton's research is the lack of support for Black students from teachers and administrators concerning how to navigate the racially tense climate.

Even after the first wave of students desegregated South Carolina's schools, racist acts continued to create an unsafe and threatening environment for Black students. In Lamar, South Carolina, White parents and community members attacked and overturned buses that had transported Black students to the newly desegregated schools ("School Buses Overturned in Disturbance at Lamar," 1970). Six students were on the buses. One of the six, David Lunn, recalled the terror of being on the bus and calling out to his friends to see if they were alive during the carnage (McCray, 2019).

Oral histories and interviews with the students who desegregated schools show how the traumatic events changed their lives. These experiences, coupled with the lack of Black educators to protect and advocate for them during this period, were harmful to the Black students who lived through them. The consequences of these historical events are still felt in our classrooms and schools today. The displacement of Black educators harmed Black students and communities, and the wrongs done to these students had second and third-generation effects. Hudson and Holmes (2006) noted that between 1975 and 1985, the number of Black students majoring in education declined by 66%. The dramatic drop in Black education majors contributed to a decline in the number of Black educators entering the profession in the generation after desegregation and undoubtedly has ramifications on the number of Black educators in our schools today.

CONCLUSION

The segregated school systems created inequalities and needed to be dismantled. Desegregation-era policymakers, however, sabotaged the promise of the court's decision. Instead of considering how to provide an integrated experience that would benefit all students, White leaders created policies that met the minimum requirements of the law and preserved the status and advantages of their students, teachers, and communities. Meanwhile, Black educators and students were significantly impacted by the dismissal and non-hiring of Black educators, and these negative impacts have had long-lasting intergenerational effects.

During this period, many scholars have attempted to calculate the number of teaching positions taken from or denied to Black educators in the southern and border states. As noted earlier, some put the number close to 40,000 (Ethridge, 1979). Researchers have attempted to quantify the damage done to the Black community due to the mishandling of the desegregation policies. Ethridge (1979) estimated that these displacement practices cost Black educators $240,564,911 in salaries alone during the 1970–1971 school year. This measure does not account for the long-term costs of the emotional and psychological trauma Black students endured as they desegregated White schools.

Indeed, the full consequences of the discriminatory desegregation policy implementations may never be known due to various factors. Intentionally poor record-keeping by districts to obfuscate discriminatory practices is one barrier to understanding the scope of the problem. However, the analysis is further complicated by questions that have not yet been answered: How many young Black men and women decided against careers in education after their experiences during desegregation? How many potential educators have we lost in subsequent generations because of the lack of representation among our educators? To what extent did the "historical impact of desegregation on Black teachers ... [create] a legacy in the broader field of primary and secondary education that has posed both explicit and implicit barriers to increasing teacher diversity" (Oakley et al., 2009, p. 10)? Perhaps the state would be faring much better with its current teacher shortage dilemmas if we had simply retained and hired the experienced and qualified Black educators of the 1950s and 1960s and sustained a culture of inclusion as opposed to exclusion.

We must also reflect on the additional costs of forcing Black educators from our ranks. Generations of Black educators and potential educators were denied a voice in curriculum, instruction, assessment, and accountability decisions. State standards, textbooks, and resources are selected by teachers, parents, and curriculum leaders, but are these chosen by groups who represent all students and communities of South Carolina or just those with power? Everyday teaching practices are shaped by conversations and collaboration among teachers. We should consider whether or not lessons and activities developed by homogenous groups of educators can meet the needs of students in heterogeneous classrooms. The state assessments and accountability measures reflect the values of the communities and leaders that make them, and it is worth reflecting on what they might look like if the policymakers and educators who developed them were representative of all South Carolinians and not just the privileged few.

One can imagine that the current practices in our schools, districts, and state would be noticeably different if Black teachers and leaders were allowed to fully participate in or lead these discussions over the last half-century. We might also wonder in what immeasurable ways students would have benefited from an educational system shaped in part by people who understood their values, beliefs, and experiences.

With court-ordered desegregation lifted from school districts nationwide, schools have become increasingly segregated again (Reardon et al., 2012). The prevalence of resegregation in our schools and districts rising in the last few decades has resulted in a movement towards racial isolation that is once again being accompanied by an unequal distribution of resources (Darling-Hammond, 2007; Horsford, 2011; Orfield & Lee, 2004). Eventually, the courts, the legislature, or the people themselves will have to confront this issue and decide how we as a state will ensure that public education in South Carolina meets the needs of all students regardless of their race or zip code. When that time comes, we must revisit the lessons from our last failed attempt at desegregation. Policymakers of that era designed and implemented policies that merely fulfilled basic legal requirements instead of addressing the needs and desires of our students and communities. As a state and as a society, we have suffered for it.

How will we ensure that our policies appreciate and understand all South Carolinians when our time comes? How will our policies address the needs of all students? How will we give a voice to those that were previously silenced? How will we make sure that our children and grandchildren aren't sitting around a table 100 years after *Brown* trying to figure out how we can finally integrate our schools and ensure our teachers represent our state and students?

REFERENCES

Aucoin, B. J. (1996). The Southern manifesto and Southern opposition to desegregation. *The Arkansas Historical Quarterly, 55*(2), 173–193.

Baker, R. S. (2006). *Paradoxes of desegregation: African Americans struggles for educational equity in Charleston, South Carolina, 1926–1972.* University of South Carolina Press.

Brown, M., Hale, J., Cooper, C. (2015). *Somebody had to do it: First children in school desegregation.* Lowcountry Digital History Initiative. https://ldhi.library.cofc.edu/exhibits/show/somebody_had_to_do_it

Burton, V., & Reece, L. (2008). The palmetto revolution: School desegregation in South Carolina. In B. J. Daugherity & C. C. Bolton (Eds.), *With all deliberate speed: Implementing Brown v. Board of Education* (pp. 59–92). University of Arkansas Press.

Cunningham, C. (2018). *"I hope they fire me:" Black teachers in the fight for equal education, 1910–1970* [Doctoral dissertation, University of South Carolina]. University of South Carolina. https://scholarcommons.sc.edu/etd/4683/

Cunningham, C. (2021). "Hell is popping here in South Carolina": Orangeburg county black teachers and their community in the immediate post-Brown era. *History of Education Quarterly, 61*(1), 35–62. https://doi.org/10.1017/heq.2020.66

D'Amico, D., Pawlewicz, R. J., Earley, P. M., & McGeehan, A. P. (2017). Where are all the Black teachers? Discrimination in the teacher labor market. *Harvard Educational Review, 87*(1), 26–49.

Darling-Hammond, L. (2007). Race, inequality and educational accountability: The irony of "No Child Left Behind." *Race Ethnicity and Education, 10*(3), 245–260. https://doi.org/10.1080/13613320701503207

Dobrasko, R. (2005). *Upholding 'separate but equal:' South Carolina's school equalization program: 1951–1955* [Master's thesis, University of South Carolina]. http://www.scequalizationschools.org/uploads/1/1/7/0/11700188/hist_799_thesis_final_draft.pdf

Egalite, A. J., Kisida, B., & Winters, M. A. (2015). Representation in the classroom: The effect of own-race teachers on student achievement. *Economics of Education Review, 45*, 44–52.

Ethridge, S. (1979). Impact of the 1954 Brown vs. Topeka Board of Education decision on Black educators. *Negro Educational Review, 30*(4), 217–232.

Floyd, J. (1973). *A study of displaced Black high school principals in the state of South Carolina: 1963–1973* [Unpublished doctoral dissertation]. Northwestern University.

Frankenberg, E. (2006). *The segregation of American teachers.* The Civil Rights Project at Harvard University. https://escholarship.org/uc/item/0jm194w5

Fultz, M. (2004). The displacement of Black educators post-Brown: An overview and analysis. *History of Education Quarterly, 44*(1), 11–45.

Gershenson, S., Hart, C., Hyman, J., Lindsay, C., & Papageorge, N. W. (2018). *The long-run impacts of same-race teachers* (No. w25254). National Bureau of Economic Research.

Gershenson, S., Holt, S. B., & Papageorge, N. W. (2016). Who believes in me? The effect of student–teacher demographic match on teacher expectations. *Economics of Education Review, 52*, 209–224.

Hawes, J. B., Adcox, S., Bowers, P., Moore, T., & Smith, G. (2018). Part 2: Minimally adequate: No accident of history: Echoes of segregation still permeate SC's education system, placing black students in peril. *The Post and Courier.* https://data.postandcourier.com/saga/minimally-adequate/page/2

Hochschild, J. L., & Scovronick, N. (2003). *The American dream and the public schools.* Oxford University Press.

Horsford, S. D. (2011). Vestiges of desegregation: Superintendent perspectives on educational inequality and (dis)integration in the post-civil rights Era. *Urban Education, 46*(1), 34–54. https://doi.org/10.1177/0042085910391596

Hooker, R. (1970). *Displacement of Black Teachers in the eleven southern states.* http://search.ebscohost.com/login.aspx?direct=true&db=epref&AN=AS.B.AFE.HOOKER.DBTESS&site=ehost-live

Horsford, S. D. (2009). From Negro student to Black superintendent: Counternarratives on segregation and desegregation. *The Journal of Negro Education, 78*(2), 172–187. http://www.jstor.org/stable/25608733

Hudson, M. J., & Holmes, B. J. (1994). Missing teachers, impaired communities: The unanticipated consequences of Brown v. Board of education on the African American teaching force at the precollegiate level. *The Journal of Negro Education, 63*(3), 388–393. https://doi.org/10.2307/2967189

James, J. C. (1970). The Black principal: Another vanishing American. *The New Republic, 163*(13), 17–20.

Ladson-Billings, G. (2007). Landing on the wrong note: The price we paid for *Brown. Educational Researcher, 33*(7), 3–13. https://doi.org/10.3102/0013189x033007003

Linn, R. L., & Welner, K. G. (2007). *Race-conscious policies for assigning students to schools: Social science research and the Supreme Court cases.* https://nepc.colorado.edu/sites/default/files/Brief-NAE.pdf

McCray, S. (2019, May 4). Survivors of 1970 racist attack on SC school bus honored. *Florence Morning News.* https://apnews.com/a7ed8d8f6fc64f9a9baff13eb03ae425

Mickey, R. (2015). *Paths out of dixie: The democratization of authoritarian enclaves in America's deep South, 1944–1972* (Vol. 147). Princeton University Press.

Oakley, D., Stowell, J., & Logan, J. (2009). The impact of desegregation on black teachers in the metropolis. *Ethnic Racial Studies, 39*(9), 1–27. https://doi.org/10.1080/01419870902780997

Orfield, G., & Lee, C. (2004). *Brown at 50: King's Dream or Plessy's Nightmare?* The Civil Rights Project at Harvard University.

Orr, M., & Walton, H. (2004). Life on the leading edge of democratic reform: Student perspectives on school desegregation. *PS–Political Science and Politics, 37*(2), 219–224. https://doi.org/10.1017/S1049096504004123

Ramsey, M. (n.d.). *A project to effectively desegregate the public school system of Lexington County School District Number Five in such a manner that the quality of the educational program may be maintained or enhanced.* In School District 5 of Lexington and Richland Counties Records.

Reardon, S. F., Grewal, E. T., Kalogrides, D., & Greenberg, E. (2012). Brown fades: The end of court-ordered school desegregation and the resegregation of American public schools. *Journal of Policy Analysis and Management, 31*(4), 876–904. https://doi.org/10.1002/pam.21649

School Buses Overturned in Disturbance at Lamar. (1970, March 4). *Florence Morning News*, pp. 1A.

Siddle Walker, V. (1996). *Their highest potential: An African American school community in the segregated South.* University of North Carolina Press.

Siddle Walker, V. (2000). Valued segregated schools for African American children in the South, 1935–1969: A review of common themes and characteristics. *Review of Educational Research, 70*(3), 253–285. https://doi.org/10.3102/0034 6543070003253

Solomon, W. E. (1956). The problem of desegregation in South Carolina. *The Journal of Negro Education, 25*(3), 315–323.

South Carolina State Department of Education. (1963–1964). *School directory of South Carolina.*

South Carolina Department of Education. (2018). *Professional certified staff file.*

U.S. Census Bureau. (1960a). *1960 census of population, final population counts for states.* https://www.census.gov/library/publications/1960/dec/population-pc-a1.html

U.S. Census Bureau. (1960b). *General population characteristics.* https://www2.census .gov/library/publications/decennial/1960/population-pc-a2/15611114ch1 .pdf

U.S. Census Bureau. (2018). *Quick facts: South Carolina.* https://www.census.gov/ quickfacts/SC#qf-headnote-a

CHAPTER 4

THE PERENNIAL PROBLEM OF TEACHER RECRUITMENT AND RETENTION FOR PLAINTIFF DISTRICTS IN *ABBEVILLE V. SOUTH CAROLINA*

Henry Tran
University of South Carolina

Mazen Aziz
University of South Carolina

Sara Frakes Reinhardt
University of South Carolina

PROLOGUE

In 1993, almost half ($n = 34$) of South Carolina's school districts at the time initiated a lawsuit against the state for inequitably and inadequately funding their schools. These districts were often neglected and forgotten, being located in the state's most rural and economically impoverished areas along the I-95 corridor and educating large concentrations of students of color. The resulting legacy case, *Abbeville v. South Carolina* (2014), lasted almost 30 years. Although the Supreme Court of South Carolina initially ruled in favor of the plaintiff districts in 2014, the entire lawsuit was ultimately dismissed in 2017, leaving the plaintiffs' districts with no judicial remedy to address their enduring woes.

During the trial, scores of testimonies from educators described their daily work conditions. These conditions consisted of deteriorating infrastructures, unsafe and dangerous facilities, lack of essential educational resources due to high poverty environments, working with students with depleted energy from having up to 12 hour school days (accounting for travel time across great distances on the bus to and from school), as well as severe lack of human capacity. Based on their analysis of the situation, the Supreme Court of South Carolina identified three significant factors that would continue to sustain inequity in the provision of education in the primarily indigent plaintiff rural districts, even if there existed equal financial resources per pupil. These factors included: transportation costs, poverty, and the teacher quality problem (*Abbeville v. South Carolina*, 2014). While this chapter addresses the second and the third issue, given its connection to the book's overall theme, more attention is given to the latter. The court called it the "teacher quality problem," but in reality, staffing supply issues were intricately related and served as a precursor to the lack of quality personnel. The lack of teacher supply often forced districts to employ under qualified instructors and/or substitutes for their classrooms or risk having no teacher at all.

Plaintiff districts struggled to recruit and retain their teachers. This struggle results from low pay and challenging conditions (e.g., working in areas with more low-performing students, old decrepit facilities, limited amenities, and spousal employment opportunities) associated with high poverty rural regions. From a quality perspective, teachers in the plaintiff districts often did not meet governmental education standards, taught out of their certification area, were less likely to hold a continuing contract, more likely serving as a long-term substitute, and had less experience or English fluency than their non-plaintiff counterparts.

At the heart of many of the plaintiff district's staffing problems were inequity and social injustice. This chapter will share results from interviews with five superintendents who were actively leading plaintiff districts during the initial years of the lawsuit. It starts by discussing the challenges and risks they faced in their valiant struggle to improve educational opportunities for their students (Tran et al., 2021). The superintendents then describe the extreme staffing challenges they faced in their local contexts. While districts across the state are increasingly struggling to fill their vacancies, the "teacher shortage crisis" has been the perennial status quo for many of the high-poverty rural plaintiff districts (CERRA, 2020; Correll, 2021).

INTRODUCTION

On May 1, 2019, teachers across South Carolina walked out of the classrooms. Over 10,000 people descended upon the state capitol to protest poor working conditions and inadequate funding for their schools. According to Edweek's 2021 Quality Counts report, South Carolina received an F (57.1%) for school spending, consistent with the state's 2020 rating. This score was determined based on the following criteria: (a) state per-pupil spending amount after adjusting for regional cost differences ($12,100), (b) the percent of students in districts with per-pupil spending at or above the national average (9.3%), and (c) the share of total taxable resources spent on education (4.5%), ranking the state in the lower half in the nation for school finance overall.

Limited public financial support for education in the United States was present even in the beginnings of school funding dating back to the colonial periods (Tran, 2018). In more recent times, South Carolina has not fully funded the state's portion (i.e., base student cost) of the core support program for education (i.e., The Education Finance Act) since 1998 (Tran & Aziz, 2019). While districts across the state suffer in various degrees from the lack of sufficient funding from the state, some districts have long endured its harmful effects, facing resource and staffing issues. The Great Recession in 2007–2009 and the COVID-19 have exacerbated these districts' financial woes.

In 1993, almost half ($n = 34$) of South Carolina's school districts at the time initiated a lawsuit against the state for inequitable and inadequate funding. These districts were primarily located in the state's most rural and economically impoverished areas, with more significant concentrations of children of color, more staffing challenges, a lower tax producing revenue base, as well as a higher concentration of high-poverty and low-achieving students than their non-plaintiff counterparts (Louis, 2016; Tran et al., 2021). The resulting legacy case, *Abbeville vs. South Carolina*, lasted almost 30 years before it reached its conclusion. Although the Supreme Court of South Carolina initially ruled for the plaintiff districts in 2014, declaring that the state has failed even to fund their students to meet the relatively low requirement of providing a "minimum adequate education" to her students, the entire lawsuit was altogether ultimately dismissed in 2017. The dismissal came after two of the justices on the court changed, with replacements appointed by the General Assembly. This dismissal left the plaintiff districts with no judicial recourse to address their pervasive inequities.

After reviewing scores of testimonies from educators describing their workplace conditions, the Supreme Court of South Carolina identified three major factors that would continue to sustain inequity in the provision of education in the primarily indigent plaintiff rural districts, even if there existed equal financial resources per pupil. These factors included: transportation costs, poverty, and the teacher quality problem (*Abbeville v. South Carolina*, 2014). While this chapter addresses both the second and third factors, in connection to the more prominent theme of this book, the latter (i.e., teacher quality problems) will receive greater attention. Insights about teacher staffing challenges will be shared from interviews with five superintendents who were actively leading plaintiff districts during the initial years of the lawsuit. The insight of these leaders is critical to note because, unlike many other school funding and civil rights cases where the parents are the drivers of the lawsuit, in the Abbeville case, education leaders initiated the case against the state. The interviews occurred 1 year after the state Supreme Court dismissed the almost 3-decade-long lawsuit. It began with discussing the challenges and risks the superintendents faced in their valiant struggle for social justice for their students (Tran et al., 2021). Pertinent to the book's theme, the superintendents then describe, in detail, the extreme staffing challenges they faced in their local contexts. While districts across the state are increasingly struggling to fill their vacancies, the teacher shortage crisis has been the perennial status quo for many plaintiff districts. The superintendents then conclude with an overall reflection on the court case and its efforts toward improving social justice for their communities.

CONTEXT

Life is not a fairytale, and sometimes, even when you give your best for a noble purpose, you will not succeed in the end. Such is the story for the plaintiff districts in the legendary court case, *Abbeville v. South Carolina* (2014). This court case was initiated and led by *education leaders* in some of the state's most economically poor rural districts. They sued South Carolina for inequitably and inadequately funding their schools, risking their jobs, the wrath of the state legislature, and their colleagues in their struggle to reform state education policy. They did this hoping to alleviate the struggles of flailing children in rural and underprivileged schools (Truitt, 2009). They enlisted the community's help to fight for the rights of disadvantaged pupils and brought unprecedented attention to their plights.

The court battle prolonged for decades, and the plaintiff districts were initially granted a partial victory in December 2005 at the trial court level. However, both sides of the case were unsatisfied with the outcome, and the case raged on for another decade. After over 2 decades, the plaintiff districts finally received a solid victory in 2014, with the Supreme Court of South Carolina ruling in their favor. Sadly, this victory was short-lived, as the court dismissed the entire lawsuit in November of 2017, 24 years after the claim was filed. The court cited the state's "good faith efforts" and judicial overreach as reasons to dismiss the lawsuit. Critics against this decision assert that this initial argument was rejected in 2014. The only difference now was the appointment of two new justices after two original justices on the bench retired. This change is troublesome as it "note[s] the alarming precedent this sets when new justices simply disregard decisions of earlier judges that have settled law" (Black, 2017; Scoppe, 2017; Tran, 2018, p. 23). Skeptics further point out the inequity of the legislator (as opposed to the people, like in most states) appointing the supreme court judges who would oversee the case for which the state is being sued.

Unfortunately, South Carolina's education system has long-neglected many of the most economically impoverished rural districts in the state and, as a result, the students they educate. Some have argued that the South Carolina education system is dichotomous. The first system attentively focuses on and serves the more populous and growing areas in the state, such as the urban and suburban growth along Interstate 85 in the Upstate, while the other system barely serves the rural and impoverished areas along I-95 (Truitt, 2009). How rural schools are treated in South Carolina is similar to how rurality is treated in education and macro policy. Policymakers and scholars often ignore rurality and focus on education in urban settings. The bias of federal policy and education research towards urban areas has caused generic education to usually refer to urban education (Corbet & White, 2014). When policymakers and researchers consider underrepresented minorities, rural students of color are ignored in preference for their urban counterparts. By ignoring rural students of color, greater marginalization occurs to rural education (Cuervo, 2016). It suggests that somehow these students are treated as less important and deserving of our attention, resources, and support.

SOUTH CAROLINA AND ITS HISTORY OF INJUSTICE

South Carolina is a state with a history of racial segregation and everlasting struggles for civil rights injustice. Case in point, in 1952, *Briggs v. Elliot* desegregated schools in South Carolina. The case began when Harry Briggs and 19 other African American parents pursued equal facilities for their children's schools. *Briggs v. Elliot* began in Clarendon County and was the first of five cases to become *Brown v. Board of Education of Topeka* (1954). The same county is home to the origins of the case of *Abbeville v. South Carolina* (2014). Even though desegregation was abolished with *Briggs v. Elliot*, many Abbeville districts consisted of mostly non-White students (approximately 90% of students Black/Hispanic). These students continue to face unequal educational opportunities relative to their White counterparts in more affluent areas of the state. The existing inequality illuminates the unfulfilled hope of equitable educational opportunities that the *Brown* case sought.

Briggs v. Elliot (1952) was monumental in South Carolina and for the country. It was the first major step towards improving educational equity for students of all backgrounds. While the case resulted in victory for the plaintiffs, it ended negatively for many people involved, including Harry Briggs, who lost his job because of his involvement in the case. Many other supporters of the monumental case lost their homes, jobs, and land (Tran, 2018). When fighting for equity in a historically inequitable context, risks are involved. In our study, these risks represented a theme with education leaders in the *Abbeville v. South Carolina* (2014) case.

Inequality has been prevalent in South Carolina for decades. Segregation and racism in education have been part of the state's history (Tran, 2018) and have continued to overshadow the state. *U.S. News & World Reports* recently ranked South Carolina 44th for the limited educational opportunities. These rankings are based on factors such as test scores, preschool enrollment, school spending, and graduation rates (Ziegler, n.d). Results from the National Assessment of Educational Progress, in particular, show that South Carolina's fourth-grade math and reading scores have declined across time and are ranked in the bottom ten states (National Center for Education Statistics, 2018).

The initial 2014 ruling in favor of the plaintiff districts resulted in questionable progress for the plaintiff districts after the ruling. The lack of progress despite the ruling is particularly alarming given how other states have responded to their school finance lawsuits. In New Jersey's *Robinson v. Cahill* (1973), a compliance deadline was set. It was ruled that if the legislature failed to comply by the given deadline, tax money could not be spent on schools. This ruling, in turn, caused a statewide school system to shut down (Tran, 2018). In *Kentucky's Rose v. Council for Better Education* (1989), the Supreme Court of Kentucky ruled to overhaul Kentucky's education finance system in only 5 years (Truitt, 2009). Unfortunately, in the Abbeville case, not only was there no specific consequence or timeline set, the case was extraordinarily lengthy at almost 3 decades, just to ultimately end with a dismissal.

METHOD

One year after the dismissal of *Abbeville v. South Carolina* (2014), we sought to hear from the districts that were intimately involved in the lawsuit. A diligent effort was undertaken to locate those superintendents by searching school district websites, online records, professional contacts, and calling school districts and educational centers. However, given the elapsed time since the case, finding these former superintendents was not an easy task, especially because many were lost to deaths, retirements, and relocations. Further complicating the search were privacy laws that prevented districts from sharing past employee personal data. Despite these obstacles, we identified and secured agreements to speak with five superintendents who were actively leading plaintiff districts during the initial years of the lawsuit. In-depth multi-hour interviews were conducted with each, two of which were instrumental in initiating the lawsuit at its conception, and the other three were involved in the lawsuit in other substantive capacities (e.g., testifying in court). To the extent possible, we sought to use direct quotes to allow the education leaders to share their stories in their own words. Because of the topic's sensitive nature, the names of the superintendents and their districts were blinded to protect their identities and elicit a deep and honest dialogue. Instead, pseudonyms (Amaru, Frank, Larry, Roland, and Victor) were used for their real names.

THE CHALLENGES FACED BY THE DISTRICTS

As it relates to the challenges and problems faced by the plaintiff districts, the interviews with the superintendents reviewed several common themes that were identified in detail in the paper: "Rage Against the Machine: The Legacy of Education Leaders' Valiant Struggle for Social Justice in *Abbeville v. South Carolina*" (Tran et al., 2021). First, the "Historical Inequities of S.C." theme detailed how the court case results reflect the trend of the ongoing historical inequities of South Carolina. Second, the "Inequitable Education Funding System" theme highlighted the inequitable education funding system, structural segregation, and its economic impact on marginalized communities. And third, the "The Risks Involved with Attempting to Change the Status Quos" theme elucidated how the case brought professional, personal, and communal reputational risks for those who engaged in the lawsuit that ultimately resulted in the districts' perception of "minimal" changes in their conditions after the lawsuit ended.

RACIST HISTORY AND INEQUITABLE FUNDING FORMULA

Several superintendents traced the inequities in resources and the poverty-related academic impact their district faced to the state's racist history and lack of regard for their economically poor rural communities that are heavily comprised of people of color. They identified the state's funding formula as particularly problematic, given its heavy reliance on property taxes, which their communities could not generate much of given their low property wealth. Superintendent Larry recalled how his peers from affluent districts flippantly suggested that the plaintiff districts should just raise taxes if they genuinely needed more money, without any consideration that the plaintiff districts mostly did not have the option available to them to do so given the lack of industry and resources. Superintendent Roland frustratingly delineated, "They don't have the jobs! They don't have the income! You can't tax them but so much," emphasizing their communities' lack of discretionary income to support tax increases (Tran et al., 2021, p. 174).

Moreover, some of the study superintendents voiced severe dissatisfaction with the state's financial investment in battling the plaintiff districts and attributed this to racism, which was the basis of the state's historical foundation. Larry indicated, "[They spent] millions and millions of dollars [to fight us]. And that's all we wanted ... was a few million dollars ... They could have done something good and got praise for it too." He speculates as he struggles to comprehend this obstinacy and lack of empathy for the situation of children, "That's just hate. Hate driven." He further contemplated that, "We might have gotten rid of the iron chains from the Civil War. But we found some damn good ways to keep the financial and philosophical and political chains on those same people."

EDUCATION SEEN AS AN ENTITLEMENT/ MAKING ENEMIES

The superintendents attributed much of the education funding challenges to the mindset of many who view education as an "entitlement," a government "handout," much the same way Medicaid and unemployment benefits often are viewed by some. The plaintiff districts faced many opponents in their quest for social justice. As Superintendent Larry detailed the enemies as

> everyone that had their children in private schools that the state-supported in segregation from the 60s, and we named all these private schools after general-Confederate generals, and we kept electing them as politicians. That's the first hardcore group. The next hardcore group was the [affluent districts who proclaimed], "We don't have enough money so we're going to have to redivide the money and you're not taking it from me in Greenville or Columbia

or Spartanburg or Charleston, the rich areas of the state, to fund people that we think are stupid or ignorant."

Other superintendents corroborated his feelings regarding the sentiment that each district was fighting for itself rather than all fighting collectively to support public education as a whole. From their perspective, the wealthier districts actively resisted the idea of having to redistribute their resources so that the higher poverty districts would receive more funding in a "Robinhood-like manner." As Superintendent Victor recollected, "They sort of view it as 'Hey I've worked up, worked hard, I'm fighting for mine and let them, let somebody else worry about the others' . . . Richer parts of the state are not willing to sacrifice anything for the poor parts of the state . . . it's 'we've got to protect ours.' 'We've got to protect what we have.'"

PROFESSIONAL, PERSONAL, AND REPUTATIONAL RISKS

Consequently, the plaintiff superintendents who engaged in the lawsuits faced many professional, personal, and communal risks to their reputation. The superintendents shared how because of the case, their relationships with colleagues and peers from other districts went from allies to more adversarial, losing partnerships and resource opportunities. They felt their professional mobility was affected by how the affluent districts viewed them in light of their challenge to the system. Their livelihoods and jobs were at risk because they participated in the lawsuit. The superintendents shared how they felt ostracized by their colleagues when attending professional association meetings and noted that those associations would not support the plaintiff districts in efforts not to alienate their wealthier members. Even worse, people lost their jobs because they engaged in the lawsuit.

One particularly tricky situation for the superintendents was that they had to speak to the poor conditions of their schools to advocate for their district and students in the lawsuit. By doing so, many community members felt they were publicly disgraced from the negative publicity because of what Superintendent Roland called the "airing of dirty laundry" in court and the media (Tran et al., 2021, p. 176). Superintendent Frank concurred by explaining:

> When you publicly talk about them to the news people around, they're taking it down. When you get back to your district, everyone knew what you said. So if I go and say the quality of the teaching staff is poor, then I go back, they [the teachers] are mad. (Tran et al., 2021, p. 176)

Nonetheless, the education leaders endured the risks because they believed in what they were fighting for.

The superintendents could influence the state's "adequate" education standard despite facing many political barriers. While undefined before, as a result of the lawsuit, the requirement of South Carolina education was interpreted to mean that students should be provided with appropriate and safe facilities and the opportunity to learn to (a) read, write, and speak English, and knowledge of math and physical science; (b) beginning knowledge of social, economics, and political systems, and history and government processes; and (c) vocational and academic skills (Tran, 2018). Unfortunately, what is normal is determined by dominant groups. This causes condemning labels that create "lifetime losers" (Young, 2006, p. 95). The state's defense attorney, Bobby Stepp, noted that "minimally adequate" means "the least that will do" (Truitt, 2009). Unfortunately, this definition reflects how education is viewed in the state as "minimally adequate." By providing the bare minimum, generations of students will suffer from inadequate education. To make matters worse, the plaintiff districts argued that even this low threshold was not met for them.

THE TEACHER RECRUITMENT AND RETENTION PROBLEM

In the *Abbeville v. South Carolina* (2014) court trial, the Supreme Court of South Carolina identified poor teacher quality as one of three major factors that would continue to sustain inequity in the provision of education in the primarily poor plaintiff rural districts, even if there existed equal financial resources per pupil (*Abbeville County School District v State*, 2014).

While the court called it the "teacher quality problem," this label referred to input quality concerns and rural educator recruitment and retention issues. For the former, the unmet quality metrics included plaintiff teachers often not meeting governmental education standards by teaching out of their certification area, less likely holding a continuing contract, more likely serving as a long-term substitute, and having less experience or English fluency than their non-plaintiff counterparts. For the latter, plaintiff districts struggled to recruit and retain their teachers because of low pay and challenging working conditions (e.g., working in areas with more students who live in poverty, worn out and old facilities, limited amenities, and spousal employment opportunities) associated with the rural high poverty regions. Of course, these issues were related, as the lack of supply reduces the probability of a quality hire. Though inadequate funding and supplies were always an issue, Frank highlighted that staffing problems were the most visible, "[With] no teachers, so how you going to have a school?" There was a consensus among the superintendents that these superficial/surface issues are undergirded by deep-rooted problems revolving around inequity and social justice.

The superintendents concurred with the court by identifying staffing as a major challenge for their district, especially given the lack of resources. Frank succinctly surmised:

> I think the inability to attract and...retain quality personnel, specifically teachers, was the biggest challenge that we faced. And, you know I think money and material resources were part of that equation but not all of that equation. We needed to be able to attract and retain teachers who were effective at teaching children with the greatest needs. To be able to try to attract good quality teachers.

BARRIERS TO RECRUITMENT AND RETENTION

Superintendent Amaru noted several barriers to recruiting teachers, including low pay and lack of amenities,

> The main thing, one was pay. But the other obstacle to recruiting teachers is where's the livelihood for them, you know? In other words, did they have a Walmart to go shop to...do they have the malls? Um...you know were there...available guys? You know, be honest with me, you know, is there any kind of social life available?

Victor elaborated by suggesting that more than just the district working conditions deter potential applicants. It is the lack of infrastructure, homes, and jobs in the community,

> How are we going to attract bright, young, upwardly mobile professionals, when there's no housing here. No affordable housing for a starting teacher who's starting at a salary, below what, just about any other professions going to start at. And I'm convinced of this, until you can change the overall standard of living, if you will, for people within these poor rural communities, it's going to continue to be a challenge attracting the best and the brightest.

Amaru concurred about the lack of housing, stating that it "was a huge problem. You know, I mean, there was no places in my community, basically that teachers could house." He clarified that physically, there was no place for them to live. The community was so unattractive to applicants that he recalled losing applicants upon visiting his schools. Specifically, he shared

> I've had some teachers...recruit them to come, and they agree to come for an interview. And, and they did—I had this happen to me one time, [and the] teacher did come. She got to the community...she called me and told me she was going back. She didn't even come for the interview.

Beyond attraction, Frank acknowledged their staffing plights are also heavily influenced by their inability to retain their teachers,

> And turnover, teacher turnover, yeah absolutely that was a huge issue ... I'm thinking we've had up to at least 37% to 40% of staff vacancies that would, that would be uh, on average I'd say about 35%, because you are always looking to replace 15, 20, to 30 teachers a year sometimes. And that was extremely difficult to do based on the type of location where we were in South Carolina and the type of pay and the type of conditions.

Unfortunately, the superintendents felt the conditions have not improved since they helmed their districts and not only continued to this day but have escalated across time.

THEY LEAVE FOR GREENER PASTURES

Even if high poverty hard-to-staff districts (like the plaintiff districts in the lawsuit) can offer a recruitment incentive that draws in teachers, because of districts' more challenging conditions and lower pay relative to their wealthier counterparts, the teachers often leave for the latter. Superintendent Larry underscored that:

> We got a hundred-year-old facility and the ceiling's leaking, and you got 30 kids in a class, and half of them are not in desks ... you don't want to teach like that. We can't attract outside people in because we can't pay them enough. They are going to go. Beginning teachers make $6,000 more in [the nearby wealthier] county, you know? Where you gonna go if you're young and you got car payments and college loans to pay off?

As a result, Larry concludes that the districts "get stuck surviving" and hiring "survivalists." Superintendent Victor notes that the issue was exacerbated by the fact that the hard-to-staff district invests in the development and growth of new teachers, only to see them take that human capital elsewhere:

> Anytime we tried, as best we could, to develop and build our own, if you will, and we fostered the growth of some folks who showed promise in, at least eight cases out of 10, they got better jobs, higher-paying jobs, in another school district. We would train them, to get them to do what was required, and knew what was required and was learning how to work with people to get that, get that done and [a nearby wealthier district] would call them, and they'd pay them ten thousand dollars more a year than we could pay.

Superintendent Frank agreed,

Money alone didn't level the playing field. Advantaged districts could match or offer more money. We needed a benefit or incentive package for teachers that could not be easily outmatched by the advantaged districts. What they [the advantages districts] did was, any time we tried to do something, they would offset it. So basically, what they did is they took all of our better people. We bring in young new teachers, train them and make them good teachers, and then they, they take, they take them away.

In short, these financially struggling school districts served as a training ground for new teachers. Upon gaining the necessary human capital from the districts, they seek employment elsewhere and take that human capital with them. Frank summarized the teacher staffing challenges from the leadership perspective:

It was a chess game, so you were constantly in this chess game to try to keep people. The problem with the game was that the other districts, the big, the metropolitan, more metropolitan districts, always had a recruiting advantage because of their location and the other amenities that were available to people when they lived there. And they also had more money, they could offer bigger salaries, bigger stipends. So you always have to deal with that.

SHORTCOMINGS TO THE RECRUITMENT
AND RETENTION STRATEGIES EMPLOYED

Because of the general perception of the unattractiveness of the locales of the districts, challenging work conditions, and lack of resources, the districts were limited in the types of strategies they could employ to recruit and retain teachers. Victor candidly shared that "I actually would hire the least, this is horrible to say, I hired the least destructive individual I could find. There were three poor candidates. I didn't like any of them. I picked the least of the ... the one that I thought would do the least amount of damage." Unfortunately, there were many instances where there were no candidates at all.

Several superintendents discussed their use of bonuses attempting to recruit teachers to their districts but noted shortcomings in their efforts. Amaru recalled, "It helped some. Yeah. Then sometimes some people would come and get part of the bonus, and then they'd leave." Frank explained that more financially advantaged districts could match or even exceed any signing bonus they offered.

Districts recruited teachers from out of state (e.g., Pennsylvania, where there was more teacher supply than demand) and across the world through international teacher programs that hired individuals through H1-B visas to fill vacancies. While many districts use these cultural programs to fill their teacher vacancies, they are designed for cultural exchange between diverse teachers and students and not as a stop-gap solution for combatting teacher shortages. The visas themselves are only temporary, which means that teachers "hired" through such means will have to be replaced again in a few years (incurring more replacement costs as a result). Frank exclaimed that although often very hardworking, these teachers often experienced challenges from the rural community. For example, parents would complain that their children could not understand the teachers because of their accents, even when the school faculty and staff noted they could understand the teachers perfectly fine.

The superintendents often also targeted local teachers, because as Frank put it, "there's less probability they will leave than somebody who's driving in." Teachers are more likely to work where they grew up is supported by the "draw of home" literature (Boyd et al., 2005) and is the foundational theory justifying grow-your-own programs.

Frank noted that recommendations were made to the state in request to support them, but

> the state always felt that . . . we just wanted more money and every time, you know, it was always 'let's do a study.' But we didn't need any more studies. We knew what the issues were and had some concept of what they could do to help mitigate these things. But they couldn't get beyond the politics, dragged it out over the years, and they recently dismissed the suit.

THE EXPANDING REACH OF TEACHER SHORTAGES: "NOW THEY FEEL WHAT WE HAVE ALWAYS FELT"

In recent years, South Carolina has been described as being in the midst of a "teacher shortage crisis" (Correll, 2021). Within this environment, districts across the Palmetto state scramble to find teachers from a shrinking pool of candidates to fill an increasing number of vacancies at the start of the school year (CERRA, 2020). However, this status quo has been perennial for many high-poverty rural plaintiff districts. Frank reflects on this issue, declaring,

> The issue here is that the teacher shortage is so acute across the country. At the initial part of the lawsuit, the other districts enjoyed quite an advantage in terms of recruiting and retention of teachers. But as the pool of teachers dwindled over time across the country, I think the quality of teachers, even in some of the other districts, has deteriorated.

Larry concurs by speaking about challenges with the number of applicants and the quality as well,

Your pool of candidates is really small in poor rural areas...and large rural area...and so you have to take what's available a lot of time. The larger, more affluent districts are finally starting to see that now and really, or [feel the] impact [of] that, because of the lack of teachers now.

Roland elaborates,

What they don't realize, what they never realized, and what they may never realize is that we're the rotten barrel. We're the rotten apple in the barrel. If you don't take care of us, we're going to eventually impact the whole damn barrel of Apple's. It's a slow process, but we will, and...they are starting to finally be dragged down to our level. I mean, it always happens. You combine things. If you're not careful, you rise to the lowest level.

AFTERMATH: REFLECTION OF THE CASE

If for nothing else, The *Abbeville* lawsuit shined the spotlight on the darkness of and often neglected circumstances of the students and educators in the plaintiff districts and their communities. One of the more notable moments of media attention was the production and distribution of the documentary, *The Corridor of Shame: The Neglect of South Carolina's Rural Schools was released mid-litigation* in April 2005 (Ferillo, 2005). The documentary highlighted the case and the plight these districts faced. The images depicted in the documentary showed the world the conditions of the schools in the plaintiff districts, including dilapidated buildings that included collapsing ceilings and infrastructures, rusty sinks, and crumbling portables, as well as rattlesnakes in the children's restrooms. Students and educators spoke about a lack of classroom resources and dangers to their safety when they must be housed in such facilities.

While well-intentioned, the documentary and its popularization cemented the label "Corridor of Shame" for the communities along the I-95 corridor where the plaintiff districts reside. This label was perceived to be very pejorative and insulting to the region's people. As Larry exacerbated, "That was a PR misstep...they should have called it the corridor of need. We're not ashamed. We're working like hell. Corridor of shame, that's an insult" (Tran et al., 2021, p. 178). Frank concurred and noted that the label hurt their efforts to recruit industry into the region. Roland admits that the branding disgraced the region's people, but it did motivate some communities to pass referendums that they may not otherwise have done before the public embarrassment.

In 2007, the spotlight magnified in the region when President Barack Obama visited the over century-old building of J. V. Martin Middle School (located in Dillon county) as part of his initial presidential campaign run.

The then-president hopeful had learned about the school and its challenges because of the *Corridor of Shame* (Ferillo, 2005) documentary. Recognizing the vast inequalities that existed between schools in different regions, President Obama noted, "I think this school exemplifies some of the enormous problems that we're having just in terms of getting enough resources to educate our kids" and that "the school itself has become a barrier to education" (Kuenzie, 2007, paras. 4 & 7). Because of the presidential attention, some changes occurred for the school. For example, the aging campus was replaced with a new building, millions of dollars in a developmental grant and bond backing were provided, and perhaps uncoincidentally, student test scores have risen (Richard, 2016), yet many of their challenges remained. While the federal attention was beneficial, ultimately, the state plays a much more significant role in education funding as they are ultimately responsible for providing education (Tran, 2018).

Furthermore, many other schools from other plaintiff districts did not receive the same attention and benefited from the presidential spotlight. They still looked to the lawsuit for change. Unfortunately for the plaintiff districts, the result of that struggle was the court vacating the entire lawsuit. The initial plaintiff superintendents, as predicted, were devastated by the case's dismissal. Larry appeared especially hurt by the loss, stating, "We disserviced so many of our students, by not just having a little bit of funding, to give them a chance, and I wonder how many we turned off." He also expressed his sorrow for his colleagues who began this trip but never saw the lawsuit's end because they lost their jobs in the court battle or passed away while waiting for its resolution.

The Supreme Court of South Carolina ultimately dropped the plaintiff's lawsuit. Even though almost 3 decades had passed, the majority of the study's initial plaintiff superintendents thought that the circumstances of the schools in the plaintiff districts had not improved or that if there had been improvement, it was "limited" given what was characterized as a lack of continuous effort to address the concerns. Victor explains:

> I'll use the court's terminology "minimally." Basically, there's been some minimal improvements. There have been some minimal incremental things that have been done by our state to improve funding for poorer schools...but nothing of a systematic substantive change." (Tran et al., 2021, p. 177)

Frank concurred, "The state threw out a few dollars here and there, a year or two, but they never involved themselves in a sustained effort to try to improve the conditions in the district based on what the court ordered." Contemplating the lack of improvement in his previous district's conditions, he said, "The state never had the political will to try to mitigate the situation in these rural districts." Frank regrettably adds that his old district continues to struggle to this day. Some respondents believed that inequalities have worsened (a claim that, as shared later, does have statistical evidence to support).

Superintendent Larry put it plainly, "The quality of education shouldn't be determined by where you're born. But we all know that it is in South Carolina and it still is to this day, no question about it" (Tran et al., 2021, p. 175). The lack of infrastructure and economy is exacerbated by the out-migration occurring from high potential students who graduate and leave their rural communities because they do not see any opportunities for them at home. The brain drain of human capital reinforces a vicious cycle that maintains the status quo and undermines community sustainability (Tran et al., 2021). Many within those communities looked to the lawsuit as a chance for change, but its conclusion shattered those dreams. Larry admits surprise at the level of resistance they experienced, stating that he underestimated the political willpower of those who wish to maintain the status quo. None of them expected the lawsuit to last almost 3 decades.

Defeated, Larry noted that he would sunset and retire with his grandchildren to the big cities like Greenville, Charleston, and Columbia, cities that will continue to prosper and grow, unlike his community:

> I'll have to move there, and I'll be happy in my retirement in those nice places where there's roads with no potholes and brand new schools, and everybody's talking about I.B. and the performing arts and all. And I can go watch them perform and my great-grandchildren maybe, in hundred million dollar facilities. So in the big scheme of things, from a personal standpoint, you know, I'm going to eventually live there and not be buried here because I'll probably follow my grandchildren. And so I've acquiesced to them. I've said, "Okay, you've shown me the light. You won, we fought the good fight, you beat the crap out of us. You knocked the slam out. We can't box anymore. I'm acquiescing. I'm at a point in my life where that energy is not there, fighting for the right thing."

In the end, despite their defeat, most of the superintendents did not regret the effort they put into improving the educational conditions for their students. As Frank emphatically summarized, "I'd rather fight for a cause and fail than not fight for a cause at all . . . when you see inequalities in a system; you can't just sit silently and let it go" (Tran et al., 2021, p. 177).

CONCLUSION

After the defeat of the education leaders in court, the plaintiff districts' options for recourse significantly narrowed. From the state perspective, they argued in their defense that they only have a legal requirement to fund the minimally adequate education baseline and not the loftier state standard that they noted were aspirational goals. Furthermore, the state shared that it had increased school funding for all of its districts since the conception of the *Abbeville v. South Carolina* (2014) lawsuit and that most of the plaintiff districts, in particular, received more state funds than other districts in the state.

In response, the plaintiff districts argued that most of the state appropriations that the state pointed to as evidence of progress were allocated to all districts across the state (of which the plaintiffs only received a small share). As mentioned earlier, the superintendents noted that the conditions in their districts were essentially the same as they were when the lawsuit began. Some even claimed that the conditions have worsened. While the leaders noted that the districts were appreciative of any additional funding they received, it was ultimately insufficient to overcome the plaintiff districts' economic and geographical challenges. This assertion was empirically supported by research findings suggesting that while plaintiff districts receive more per-pupil state funds ($\bar{x}$ = \$5,858, *SD* = \$410) when compared to non-plaintiff districts ($\bar{x}$ = \$5,200, *SD* = \$377) from 2000 to 2015 (a year after the Supreme Court of South Carolina initially ruled in favor of the plaintiff districts before the case was ultimately dismissed in 2017), it was insufficient to offset the local advantage as non-plaintiff districts receive more total (local and state) revenue ($\bar{x}$ = \$10,679, *SD* = \$486) than plaintiff districts ($\bar{x}$ = \$9,456, *SD* = \$477) and the gap between the two has been growing (Tran et al., 2021). Federal funds are not considered here as federal dollars are meant to supplement core funds and not supplant them. A more rigorous analysis employing a differences-in-differences estimation methodology found that between 2000 to 2011 (the year the full sets of model variables were available), the plaintiff districts received less revenue than the non-plaintiff districts over time.

The school funding situation was exacerbated by the implementation of Act 388 of 2006, which was approved in South Carolina as a property tax exemption for primary owner-occupied homes, replacing the tax with a 1% increase in sales tax to cover the homeowner school property tax relief and shifting the rest of the tax burden to renters and business owners. Many schools lost funding due to the sales tax increase, failing to generate enough revenue to compensate for the loss of property tax payments, with poor rural schools losing much more due to their lack of revenue base (Tran, 2018). In sum, the evidence from the descriptive and differences-in-differences analysis supports the argument that the revenue gap has grown between the plaintiff and non-plaintiff districts. Please see Tran et al., 2021, for more detail concerning the analysis.

Despite the teetering back and forth with partial victories for both the plaintiff and the defendants along the process, the status quo was reinforced and affirmed by the state Supreme Court. Getting the lawsuit initiated took a lot of willpower, volunteer labor, brave leadership, and political alignment. The superintendents we spoke to were skeptical that this magnitude of change and effort would happen again. So now, they look to the future and hope that progress will come from the very people they fought for. Larry concludes by sharing:

> I can sleep at night with my best and brightest leaving and not staying in my community. Okay? Because I know they're going to go out there and cure cancer and operate on the heart and all that kind of stuff. And that's good. So I'm hoping at some point... before we do ourselves in, that some of them will decide to run for politics in the state for the right reasons. We'll have someone that really cares about moving this state forward and moving it away from this and us still reliving a war that we lost... I see the energy and the excitement and the learning that's going on with my children in this district. Somebody's going to be on Mars. Somebody's going to be that governor. So I have to keep doing that, so that's what keeps me going. It was a lesson learned for me that I better spend my energy on this. I have a better chance of making South Carolina better, focusing on these kids. (Tran et al., 2021, p. 185)

REFERENCES

Abbeville v. South Carolina. Opinion No. 27466. (November 12, 2014). https://cases .justia.com/south-carolina/supreme-court/2014-27466.pdf?ts¼1415808227

Black, D. W. (2017). Kids will suffer because the court refused to do its duty. *The State*. https://www.thestate.com/opinion/op-ed/article186489863.html

Boyd, D., Lankford, H., Loeb, S., & Wyckoff, J. (2005). The draw of home: How teachers' preferences for proximity disadvantage urban schools. *Journal of Policy Analysis and Management, 24*(1), 113–132.

Briggs v. Elliott, 324 SC. 350 (1952). https://supreme.justia.com/cases/federal/us/ 342/350/

Brown v. Board of Education of Topeka, 347 U.S. (1954). https://www.oyez.org/cases/ 1940-1955/347us483

Center for Educator Recruitment, Retention, and Advancement. (2020). *South Carolina annual educator supply and demand report* (2020–21 School Year). https://www .cerra.org/uploads/1/7/6/8/17684955/2020-21_supply___demand_report .pdf

Corbett, M., & White, S. (2014). Introduction: Why put the "rural" in research? In S. White & M. Corbett (Eds.), *Doing educational research in rural settings: Methodological issues, international perspectives and practice solutions* (pp. 1–4). Routledge.

Correll, E. (2021, July 14). *Teacher group finds over 2,000 vacancies in S.C. public schools S.C. for Ed tracks teaching vacancies weekly, and the numbers just keep growing*. News19. https://www.wltx.com/article/news/education/teacher-group-finds -2000-vacancies-south-carolina-schools/101-1efd1df6-5f08-49f7-a23c-d988 03e1ef2f

Cuervo, H. (2016). *Understanding social justice in rural education*. MacMillan.

Edweek. (2021). State grades on school finance: 2021 map and rankings. *Edweek.* https://www.edweek.org/policy-politics/state-grades-on-school-finance-2021 -map-and-rankings/2021/06

Ferillo, B. (2005). *Corridor of shame: The neglect of South Carolina's rural schools* [Film]. Ferillo & Associates.

Kuenzie, J. (2007, August 23). *Obama visits school in S. C. "Corridor of Shame."* WIS News 10. https://www.wistv.com/story/6975244/obama-visits-school-in-sc-corridor-of -shame/

Louis, K. (2016). State constitutional law-minimally adequate education—Qualitative education standards in the South Carolina constitution—Abbeville county school district v. state. *Rutgers University Law Review, 69,* 1457–1474.

National Center for Education Statistics. (2018). *National assessment of educational progress.* https://nces.ed.gov/nationsreportcard/

Richard, A. (2016, August 10). *What's happened in the rural school district Obama fought to save.* The Hechinger Report and PBS. https://www.pbs.org/newshour/ education/rural-school-district-obama-fought-save

Robinson v. Cahill, 62, N.J. 473 (1973). https://law.justia.com/cases/new-jersey/ supreme-court/1973/62-n-j-473-0.html

Rose v. Council for Better Education, 790 S.W.2d 186. (1989). https://law.justia .com/cases/kentucky/supreme-court/1989/88-sc-804-tg-1.html

Scoppe, C. R. (2017). Why the SC Supreme Court washed its hands of poor students. *The State.* https://www.thestate.com/opinion/opn-columns-blogs/cindi-ross -scoppe/article186296138.html

Tran, H. (2018). *Taking the mystery out of South Carolina school finance* (2nd ed.). ICPEL Publications.

Tran, H., & Aziz, M. (2019). South Carolina. In D. C. Thompson, R. C. Wood, S. C. Neuenswander, J. M. Heim, & R. D. Watson (Eds.), *Funding public schools in United States and Indian country* (pp. 613–632). Information Age Publishing.

Tran, H., Aziz, M., & Reinhardt, S. F. (2021). Rage against the machine: The legacy of education leaders' valiant struggle for social justice in Abbeville v. South Carolina. *Journal of School Leadership, 31*(3), 166–188.

Truitt, T. E. (2009). *Going up the river of shame.* AuthorHouse.

Young, I. M. (2006). Education in the context of structural injustice: A symposium response. *Educational Philosophy and Theory, 38*(1), 93–103.

Ziegler, B. (n.d.). Education rankings: Measuring how well states are educating their students. *U.S. News & World Report.* https://www.usnews.com/news/ best-states/rankings/education

PART II

THE DOWNWARD SPIRAL:
ECONOMICS OF SCHOOL FUNDING
AND TEACHER RETENTION

CHAPTER 5

TEACHER SHORTAGES, SCHOOL FUNDING, AND LEGISLATIVE AUSTERITY

The Influence of South Carolina's School Finance Legislation on the Teacher Labor Market

David G. Martínez
University of South Carolina

Henry Tran
University of South Carolina

Concern has grown over the teacher labor market shortage in education across the United States (Carver-Thomas & Darling-Hammond, 2017). Nationally, over a 10-year period (2007–2017), the elementary and secondary teacher labor market decreased by approximately 1% (NCES, 2021). While this decrease seems plausibly negligible, considering that hard-to-staff districts are often forced to hire uncertified and under-qualified individuals to

How Did We Get Here?, pages 79–103
Copyright © 2022 by Information Age Publishing
www.infoagepub.com

have an adult in their classrooms, the shortage understates the challenges across the field (Garcia & Weiss, 2019). The teacher, labor market shortage is not monolithic, exacerbated in specific subjects (e.g., STEM), specific types of schools/ districts (e.g., high poverty), and in specific regional areas (e.g., rural; Cowan et al., 2016; Hutchison, 2012).

The challenge is related to both teacher recruitment and retention, and therefore its remedies must address both, requiring solutions to stimulate growth in the profession and retain those already in the classroom (Kelchtermans, 2017). These challenges quickly become detrimental to the educational success of those communities unable to mediate this complex problem. South Carolina serves as a state-level national case study exhibiting many of the granular details of the teacher labor market shortage. Like many states across the United States, districts in South Carolina face teacher staffing challenges that have continued despite localized efforts to stimulate growth (CERRA, 2019). At all levels, stakeholders are concerned about what efforts could encourage increases in the pipeline and curb attrition.

Addressing teacher staffing issues in South Carolina requires accounting for the states' nuances, which present unique circumstances. South Carolina itself is a predominantly rural state. Hence, efforts must be made to improve teacher pipeline growth in areas of sparsity to meet the needs of all districts. The state has a high degree of localized poverty centralized in rural communities that educate large concentrations of students of color. The poverty limits potential increases in local tax base levies, a prevalent indicator of school funding availability. School funding scarcity limits revenue directed toward salary increases and limits what programs districts can implement to strengthen the pipeline. For decades, the states' political leadership has holistically neglected the education system (Tran et al., 2021), positioning short-term stop-gap remedies instead of sustained improvement efforts over time.

An example is the advent of international teacher hiring. Unable to curb the severe shortages, many districts hire international teachers unfamiliar with the context of the state, the South, and unaccustomed to the needs of South Carolina's students to fill vacancies. However, given that these teachers often are in the country on time-limited VISAs, they do not represent a sustained "solution" to the teacher staffing problem. From the employer's end, the international teachers are often not given appropriate administrative support against xenophobic parents and community or help navigate a foreign land (Tran et al., 2020). It is imperative to unpack all the complications from a nuanced perspective to understand the myriad of complications across the teacher labor market pipeline.

This chapter explores the states' context-specific teacher labor market challenges and its historical policies and legislation that contribute to this shortage. We focus on the salient facts about South Carolina's unique educational context and the function of legislative austerity on the teaching profession within the state. First, we provide a critical review of school finance policies that influence the teacher labor market pipeline. Second, we provide a descriptive analysis that helps us outline how severe the teacher shortage is in South Carolina and whether the media descriptor of "the teacher shortage crisis" (Thomas, 2018) is justified. This analysis helps us measure where teacher shortages are most prevalent and focus on how teacher shortages exist as a function of the region and student demographics makeup. This chapter works to functionally relate educational policy to teacher shortages to systematically address the state's challenges to mediate its labor market.

CRITICAL SOUTH CAROLINA SCHOOL
FINANCE POLICY REVIEW

South Carolina's educational policy landscape has played a role in the continued teacher labor market constriction across the state by implementing school finance policy that directly inhibits fiscal capacity in those districts exhibiting the most need. Acutely, South Carolina's general assembly passed the South Carolina Education Finance Act (EFA) of 1977, Education Improvement Act (EIA) of 1984, and Act 388 for school funding. However, each piece of legislation has functioned to mitigate school district funding availability. This policy contradiction is rooted in ideologies that center property rights and the social benefits amassed by property owners so that school funding is largely predicated on local wealth, often marginalizing minoritized communities, and students, in the pipeline of economic wealth and opportunity (Brewer & Heitzeg, 2008; Brown & De Lissovoy, 2011; Delgado & Sefancic, 2017; Gillborn, 2005; Gillborn & Ladson-Billings, 2010; Ladson-Billings & Tate, 1995). For instance, South Carolina's school finance remedies insufficiently fund its state program of instruction for all students and wholly segregates students, based on geography and race, away from the necessary resources (e.g., labor market, curriculum, pedagogy, and content) foundational for educational attainment, placing minoritized students at an academic disadvantage.

The following section unpacks the policy trajectory leading toward continued deprivation of school funding in South Carolina. Given that the bulk of school district revenue is spent on compensation for personnel (Brimley et al., 2019), we use a state critical policy analysis to examine South Carolina's primary contemporary school funding legislation. A critical policy analysis methodology helps us to comparatively unpack how South Carolina's funding policies have contributed to the underlying historical disparity in the schooling system and reified funding disparity in a manner that further exacerbates needs in minoritized communities (Diem et al., 2014;

Young & Diem, 2018). This policy analysis focuses on EFA, EIA, and Act 388 and the school finance and labor market landscape of South Carolina. Of note is the historical focus on EFA due to its central utility as the funding formula for the state.

Critical Policy Analysis

We employ a critical policy analysis (CPA) to critically interrogate EFA, EIA, and Act 388. CPA is a methodology that grounds a critical investigation of the educational policy process. Young and Diem (2018) and Diem et al. (2014) articulate five policy principles used in CPA:

1. Interrogate the roots and development of educational policy.
2. Probe the difference between policy rhetoric and policy praxis.
3. Examine the distribution of power, resources, and knowledge.
4. Scrutinize the systems and environments in which policy is constructed and implemented.
5. Center the minoritized groups and communities of resistance engaged in activism.

CPA scholars situate their work to explore social stratification and the impact of policy on relationships of privilege and inequality (Diem et al., 2014).

While many CPAs use varied design, methodology, and methods, these five principles differentiate the CPA against a traditional policy analysis. Furthermore, in the tradition of critical race theorists, it is imperative to employ a critical frame to explore a policy and how a particular policy can work to reify the oppression of minoritized communities. The next section uses several of these principles in a critical overview of school finance policy in South Carolina.

Education Finance Act of 1977

The Education Finance Act (EFA) of 1977 is the school finance foundation program South Carolina uses to fund its schools. EFA is primarily funded through property values and tax levies. The history for this local tax structure to fund schools stems back to 1784 when South Carolina's General Assembly created tax levy provisions for properties that relied on valuation and proportionality to assess market value. This funding structure remained in place until adjudication in *Martin v. Tax Collector of St. Luke's Parish* (1 Speers 343, S.C. 1843). Following the *Speers* decision, South Carolina began to tax real property (South Carolina State Constitution, 1865).

Real property remained the central mechanism of property value taxation until *Parker v. Bates* (1949). *Bates* repealed the use of property taxes for an excise tax system to fund in-state infrastructure.

Once again, after adjudication in *Holzwasser v. Brady* (1974), the South Carolina General Assembly changed the property tax mandate to collect levies from private landowners for land used in manufacturing at a rate of 9.5%. Due to *Holzwasser*, Act 208 passed legislation defining four classes of taxable property:

1. Manufacturing property
2. Inventory of business
3. Owner-occupied
4. Agricultural real property (Act 208, 1975)

The South Carolina constitution was once again amended in 1976 to include:

1. Property owned and leased by transportation companies
2. Categorical real property
3. Categorical personal property (S.C. Const. art. V, § 3, 2021).

Following these changes, South Carolina passed the Education Finance Act (EFA) of 1977.

EFA (1977) is the most relevant school funding legislation in South Carolina's history. The bill authorized South Carolina to equalize funding for public schools through a specific funding formula with several components. The formula includes district Base Student Cost (BSC), weighted number of students, and the Index of Taxpaying Ability (ITA):

State Aid = (DWPU × BSC) − (SWPU × BSC × Index × 0.3)
   DWPU = District Weighted Pupil Units
   SWPU = Statewide Weighted Pupil Units
     BSC = Base Student Cost
   Index = School District Index of Taxpaying Ability

The state equalization formula described above also accounts for the additional cost of educating a student by applying multiplier weights in critical areas (S.C. Code § 59-20-40(1)(c)). Table 5.1 shows the weights currently mandated by the South Carolina General Assembly. The General Assembly also considers fiscal capacity in the equalization formula. The index is an inter-district calculation of local district relative fiscal capacity. The calculation is a ratio of the total market value of all taxable property within the district against the total assessed value of property in the state (S.C.

TABLE 5.1 South Carolina Pupil Weights	
Category	**Weight**
K–12	
Base students	1.00
Students in residential treatment facilities	2.10
Weights for Students With Disabilities	
Educable mentally handicapped	1.74
Learning disability	1.74
Trainable mentally handicapped	2.04
Emotionally handicapped	2.04
Orthopedically handicapped	2.04
Visually handicapped	2.57
Hearing handicapped	2.57
Students with autism	2.57
Speech handicapped	1.90
Pre-career technology	1.29
Additional Weights for Personalized Instruction	
Gifted and talented	0.15
Academic assistance	0.15
Limited English proficient	0.20
Pupils in poverty	0.20
Dual credit enrollment	0.15

Source: SC House, Ways, and Means Committee, 2017–18 general appropriations bill (H.3720).

Code of Law § 59-20-20). Districts with high ITA receive less state revenue for schooling than those districts with low ITA.

Education Improvement Act of 1984

The Education Improvement Act (EIA) of 1984 provides funding beyond the BSC through a state sales tax increase from 4% to 5%. The funds support programs targeted at

1. increasing student performance as a function of academic standards;
2. strengthening the teaching and testing of basic skills;
3. elevating the teaching profession;

4. improving leadership, management, and fiscal efficiency;
5. implementing quality controls and reward productivity;
6. creating more effective partnerships among schools, parents, community, and businesses; and
7. providing school buildings that are conducive to improved student learning.

EIA operates by retaining revenue in a trust to appropriate toward districts based on student and teacher eligibility for specific initiatives, including:

1. salary supplement to guarantee teachers are paid the southeastern teacher salary average,
2. advanced placement testing program,
3. services to students identified as gifted and talented, and
4. support for students not meeting state standards.

EIA funds are also appropriated to the South Carolina Department of Education to administer federal programs, assessment, financial auditing, professional licensure, professional development, program leadership, and technical assistance. Finally, school districts are prohibited from supplanting the basic educational program through EIA funding.

Act 388

South Carolina's General Assembly passed Act 388 in 2006. The purpose of Act 388 was to provide property tax relief exempting property owners from paying property levies for school operating costs (Act 388, 2006). Act 388 replaced these tax levies with a 1% state sales tax meant to offset lost revenue from the act. Act 388 eliminated owner-occupied property assessment from its tax base calculation for school districts. Eliminating these tax levies affects local school funding generation by decreasing funding as a proxy of owner-occupied property assessments (Act 388, 2006). Act 388 also limits millage cap increases to a percentage of the local population. While on the surface, South Carolina's school finance policy is positioned as being able to equalize funding disparity based on local property value, and relative community wealth, there are several key critiques of it.

School Funding Policy Critiques

One of the major critiques of the school finance policy environment in South Carolina is that it fundamentally does not provide sufficient revenue for districts to operate. Two major nationally recognized school funding law-suits have taken place in South Carolina, *Briggs v. Elliot* (*Briggs* [1952]) and *Abbeville County School District et al. v. State of South Carolina* (*Abbeville II*), 410 S.C. 619, 767 S.E.2d (2014). In *Briggs v. Elliot* (*Briggs*, 1952), adjudication arose due to frustration over how the state was responding to the educational needs of the Black community in Clarendon County. *Briggs*' (1952) plain-tiffs were denied transportation funding because South Carolina asserted the community had not paid sufficient tax levies to purchase a bus. The state claimed that providing high-poverty Black students of Clarendon County funds for transportation violated the South Carolina statute, favoring Black communities over White communities that could fund transportation. *Briggs* is historically significant to the context of litigation and resources for school-ing and was the first of five National Association for the Advancement of Colored People (NAACP) cases that led to *Brown v. Board of Education* (1952).

Abbeville II (2014) is one among many unresolved school finance cases that question state constitutional requirements to provide equitable fund-ing for all students to fully participate in the state's instruction program (Hinojosa, 2016; Howard et al., 2017). After almost 3 decades, at the cul-mination of the case, the South Carolina Supreme Court ruled against the plaintiffs, asserting judicial overreach and the legislature's good faith effort in their usual business of operations and subsequently vacated all plaintiffs' judgments calling for funding improvement (Tran et al., 2021). Both *Briggs* (1952) and *Abbeville II* (2014) highlight the lack of accountability to mi-noritized districts with little political influence and legislative inaction that sustains school finance inequity, including the equalization formula and subsequent legislation.

For many years, the South Carolina General Assembly adjusted the BSC to account for inflation. However, fiscal austerity measures implemented during the great recession due to fiscal insolvency challenged the state to reconcile a reduced budget. After the great recession, the General Assem-bly began setting arbitrary BSC amounts, and the general assembly has yet to replenish this funding. The last year that the BSC was fully funded was in 1998, and in 2019–2020 the projected state gap in BSC funding was $627; which is the difference between BSC match to inflation of $3,116 and the actual BSC of $2,489 (South Carolina Revenue and Fiscal Affairs Office, 2021a). In 2020–2021 the projected BSC shortfall was $675; the difference between BSC match to inflation of $3,164 and the actual BSC of $2,489 (South Carolina Revenue and Fiscal Affairs Office, 2021b).

Failing to fund the BSC entirely places those districts with low property wealth at a severe disadvantage. It mitigates possible recruitment incentives to attract educators in specific content areas. It limits equity of educational opportunity as a function of revenue availability necessary to operate a func-tional school with up-to-date content, curriculum, and expert pedagogists trained to educate students in today's schooling landscape. Ostensibly, from 2010–2024, the projected capital needs revenue shortfall is $10,197,972,210 (South Carolina Department of Education, 2013; South Carolina Department of Education, 2016; South Carolina Department of Education, 2019). These deficits are detrimental to those districts that require funds and the entire state. Research asserts these deficits are often targeted at low-income and rural districts serving higher proportions of racially and ethnically diverse students who exhibit a higher degree of school funding disparity writ large (Baker et al., 2020; Martínez, 2021; Martínez & Spikes, 2020).

A recent report by EdBuild (2019) calculated a funding gap of $2,200 per pupil and a $23 billion gap nationally. Concurrently, during economic downturns, low-income districts serving higher proportions of minoritized students exhibit decreases in local tax levies that support local education, and state revenue allocation decreases as states work to implement austerity measures (Center on Budget & Policy Priorities, 2019; Lechman & Figueroa, 2019). State-level school revenue constriction creates more significant challenges for districts serving higher proportions of racially and ethnically diverse students because those districts cannot supplement state losses through local tax levies. Act 388 functioned in this manner, decreasing revenue availability locally.

One of the significant critiques of Act 388 is that it disregards property tax levies for educational operations and shifts the funding to burden non-homestead property classifications (e.g., local businesses; Act 388, 2006). This shift creates inequity because communities with lower median income and minimal commerce cannot recapture funding from the 1% adjustment. Districts with high local sales, profitable commerce, and high property value will have a distinct economic advantage. Simultaneously young educators searching for viable areas of residence are likely to choose to reside and work in these areas, thus minimizing teacher workforce availability in areas of high need.

South Carolina's reliance on the 1% to recapture lost funding is presumptive. At the outset of Act 388, South Carolina contended with the Great Recession (2007), and currently, South Carolina faces the second-highest economic downturn exposure due to SARS-CoV-2 (COVID-19), resulting in revenue loss for many high-poverty school districts (IBISWorld, 2021; Saltzman & Ulbrich, 2012). At best, South Carolina's Act 388 exacerbated already dire school funding disparities across the state, decreasing state revenue for education as consumer spending slows during times of personal austerity (Keisler, 2014; Knoeppel et al., 2013; Tran, 2018).

The net influence of these policies invariably negatively influences the teacher labor market, especially given the labor-intensive nature of the education industry. Districts in high-poverty communities rely on state-level revenue to provide their students with a robust program of instruction that includes well-prepared educators. While it is true that each districts' teacher labor market is unique, in South Carolina, districts are forced to contend with fiscal constraints that will influence teacher recruitment and retention. For instance, educators require high-quality facilities and teaching conditions (Sutcher et al., 2019). Nevertheless, according to the December 2013 facilities report, with infrastructure alone, South Carolina calculated a capital needs revenue shortfall of $1,356,035,907 for years 2014–2018 (South Carolina Department of Education, 2013). As of the 2016 report, South Carolina reported a $781,334,902 shortfall in facilities funding from 2016–2021 (South Carolina Department of Education, 2016). As of the 2019 report, South Carolina projected a $3,957,117,535 revenue shortfall for 2019–2024 (South Carolina Department of Education, 2019). Disparate teaching conditions (e.g., unsafe workspaces) often lead to teacher labor market challenges and may lead to class size increases (e.g., due to lack of classrooms), creating unfavorable working conditions that dissuade educators from continuing in the profession (Sutcher et al., 2019).

Additionally, as a state, South Carolina's school system has yet to recover from post-recessionary school funding budget cuts (Center on Budget and Policy Priorities, 2019). This pandemic is creating a scenario where already disparate districts, still feeling the effects of the previous recession, are once again going to exhibit a decrease in state revenue allocations and a decrease in local levies. Thus, the existing inequities may worsen as the pandemic continues and the economic profile of South Carolina continues to develop.

No legislative action has modified the fundamental structure of South Carolina's school funding system. As with *Briggs* (1947) and *Abbeville II* (2017), *when attempts are made*, influential stakeholders stall progress. The most recent attempt to change the school funding formula proposed by the South Carolina Revenue and Fiscal Affairs Office (2019) increased state funds for 55 school districts total, with decreases anticipated for 26. However, pushback from wealthy districts due to their opposition to funding redistribution stalled policy discourse, stalling policy action. The General Assembly has not addressed the revenue loss through Act 388 nor the revenue disparity created by EFA. Education stakeholders recognize that changes must be made but have been unable to overcome policy inertia across the state. In alignment with the purpose of this book, it is crucial to understand South Carolina's teacher labor market as an artifact of South Carolina's continued educational challenges.

EVIDENCE ON SOUTH CAROLINA'S TEACHER LABOR MARKET

To address the central premise of this chapter, we adopt a dual approach to measure South Carolina's teacher labor markets. We use publicly available data aggregated from several sources, including the South Carolina Department of Education and the United States Department of Education National Center for Educational Statistics Common Core of Data. The dataset includes all South Carolina traditional school districts that educate students in grades K–12, reporting finance and other data to the Department of Education National Center for Education Statistics (NCES), from 2007–2008 to 2017–2018.

Independent, private, and charter local educational agencies (LEAs) were excluded in this analysis and are not captured in the primary database for this specific analysis. They are often small sample local educational agencies, structurally incongruous, and would not be comparable with the traditional LEAs. This analysis omits Governor's School for the Arts and Humanities, Governor's School for Science and Mathematics, South Carolina Public Charter School District, Deaf and Blind School, John De La Howe, Department of Juvenile Justice, Department of Correction N04, Charter Institute at Erskine, Felton Lab School of South Carolina H24, South Carolina Department of Disabilities and Special Needs, and Wil Lou Gray Opportunity.

The merged dataset also includes the districts' local poverty index, geography, enrollment, and student demographic information. We use two variables that help to identify majority poverty and majority non-White districts. These variables are calculated for each district and year. The two variables represent districts serving greater than 50% of students in poverty, less than 50% of students in poverty, districts whose enrollment is greater than 50% non-White students, and districts whose enrollment of non-White students is less than 50%. For geography, all rural, city, town, suburb NCES codes were collapsed into their respective categories. The data were merged, compiled, cleaned, coded, and analyzed using Excel v16.51 and Stata v17.0.

The primary variable of interest was teacher turnover; thus, we calculated teacher turnover at the district and year level. We modified a similar methodology used by Chapman et al. (2018), omitting the subject variable as this was not pertinent to the overall analysis. As with Chapman et al. (2018), we calculate turnover at the district level (j) as the number of educators leaving their district for any reason between school year $t-1$ and school year t divided by the number of educators who remained in the district for the corresponding year:

$$Turnover_{jt} = \frac{Teachers\ Leaving_{j(t-1)}}{Teachers_{j(t-1)}}$$

We also estimated, as did Chapman et al. (2018), the 3-year running average of teacher turnover for each district:

$$Average\ Turnover_{jt} = \frac{1}{3} \sum_{k=t-2}^{t} \frac{Teachers\ Leaving_{j(t-1)}}{Teachers_{j(t-1)}}$$

We use a linear estimation strategy to understand how turnover is related to teacher composition, district composition, and student demographics where

$$Y: Turnover\ or\ Average\ Turnover_{jt} = \beta_0 + \beta_1 X_{1jt} + \beta_2 X_{2jt} + \beta_3 X_{3jt} + \gamma_j + \delta_t + \varepsilon_{jt}$$

and (X_{1jt}) is the vector of teacher composition, (X_{2jt}) is the vector of district composition and Caucasian (X_{3jt}) is the vector of student demographics. We specify three subsequent models treating each vector independently. As with Chapman et al. (2018), we also add district (γ_j) and year (δ_t) fixed effects.

FINDINGS

Table 5.2 provides summary statistics for the resulting analytical dataset. The 1-year teacher turnover, and 3-year teacher turnover, are approximately 12%. Of note is the relatively high percentage of teachers with advanced degrees, at 60.19%, compared to teachers with emergent degrees, at 5.56%. South Carolina's students are educated mainly by individuals who show consistent growth in their education. Nevertheless, despite this, across the entire sample, teacher salaries ($46,947) are relatively less competitive than South Carolina's general labor market for individuals with at least a bachelor's degree ($49,440) and lower than the national K–12 teacher salary average ($65,524) and a calculated living wage ($47,000; World Population Review, 2021).

Figure 5.1 shows the comparison of South Carolina's median income for the state, outlined above, graphically. There are gaps in median salary across the state; however, the critical artifact here is that despite having a large proportion of teachers with advanced degrees, teacher wages still lag that of income for graduate and professional degree students in the state ($59,295).

In terms of the district profile, districts exhibit a high degree of poverty, and the mean poverty index across the entire sample is 74.5%. Despite the financial challenges, 78.03% of students in South Carolina are meeting state educational standards. South Carolina has a low student drop-out rate at 2.61%, lower than the national drop-out rate of 5.3% (National Center for Educational Statistics, 2021).

Table 5.3 displays average 1-year and 3-year teacher turnover by geography and districts with greater or less than 50% poverty. Rural regions with greater than 50% poverty have the highest teacher turnover for the 1-year (13.47%) and 3-year sample (13.01%). This high teacher turnover could happen for many reasons, including inadequate resources, lower salaries,

TABLE 5.2 Summary Statistics 2008–2018 Combined Sample

Variable	N	Mean	Std. Dev.	Min	Max
Turnover Measure					
1-Year Turnover	908	11.98	5.08	2.40	340
3-Year Turnover	908	12.08	3.65	5.50	32.30
Teacher Composition					
Percent of Teachers With Adv. Deg.	908	60.19	6.271	36.10	82.90
Percent of Classes w/o Highly Qualified	746	4.20	5.95	0.00	56.40
Percent of Teachers With Emergency Certification	423	5.56	5.29	0.00	30.80
Average Teacher Salary	908	46,947	2,818	38,199	55,023
District Composition					
District Poverty Index	908	74.50	14.50	21.06	98.49
Percent of Students Meeting Standards	827	78.03	14.53	11.76	100.00
Percent of Students Drop Out	908	2.61	1.62	0.00	10.10
Student–Teacher Ratio	894	20.90	3.45	4.35	39.00
Student Demographics (Percentage)					
Black	908	43.96	25.11	0.00	97.34
White	908	47.14	23.21	0.00	86.80
LatinX	908	5.35	5.04	0.00	36.67
Asian	908	0.90	0.90	0.00	5.62
Indigenous	908	0.40	0.73	0.00	5.90
English Learners	908	3.78	4.01	0.00	26.79
IEP	908	14.69	2.99	7.57	27.00
FRLP	908	67.75	19.00	0.00	100.00

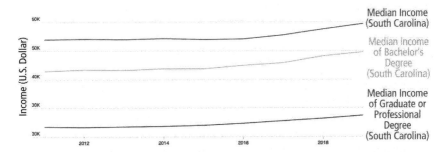

Figure 5.1 Median income of South Carolina. *Source:* https://datacommons.org/place/geoId/45?topic=Economics#Median%20individual%20income

TABLE 5.3	Average Teacher Turnover Rate by Region and Poverty			
	City	Suburb	Rural	Town
1-Year Teacher Turnover				
Greater 50% Poverty	10.71	9.70	13.47	11.63
Less than 50% Poverty	—	8.19	7.75	—
3-Year Teacher Turnover				
Greater 50% Poverty	11.06	10.72	13.01	11.79
Less than 50% Poverty	—	10.09	9.77	—

or more challenging working conditions (Darling-Hammond, 2010; Adamson & Darling-Hammond, 2012; Tran et al., 2021). In South Carolina districts with greater than 50% poverty, towns had a 1-year turnover rate of approximately 11.63%, and cities had a 1-year turnover rate of 10.71. This difference is consistent with 3-year turnover rates of 11.06% for cities and 11.79% for towns. There were no towns or cities designated as having less than 50% poverty in the sample. Community wealth may play a role in teacher turnover, which the subsequent analysis suggests. Suburbs exhibited the lowest 1- and 3-year turnover rate of the entire sample. At its height, suburbs exhibit a 3-year teacher turnover rate of 10.72% for those districts with greater than 50% poverty. The lowest teacher turnover rate is for rural areas with less than 50% poverty at 7.75%.

Table 5.4 and Table 5.5 show the main estimation findings of teacher and district composition and district demographics in correlation with teacher turnover. We use district and year fixed effects to account for any time-invariant characteristics of districts and any time-specific shocks that would affect all districts. The effect of turnover is identified using the within-school variation in the level of teacher turnover from year to year. The first column of both tables displays the coefficients and standard errors of the full estimation strategy using teacher and district composition and district demographics. We exclude the percent of highly qualified teachers and teachers with emergent certification from Model 1. South Carolina did not report highly qualified teachers after 2016 or emergent certification after 2012. Adding them to the full model would have constricted the sample years to 2008–2012. The 2-3-4 columns represent the same estimation strategy; however, we estimate teacher turnover separately based on teacher composition variables, district composition variables, or student demographics.

With the full estimation model, for 1- and 3- year turnover, we detected a statistically significant inverse relationship between teacher turnover and the percentage of teachers with advanced degrees and salary. However, it should be noted that the magnitude of the coefficient is negligible. When examining Model 2 and the four variables of teacher composition, we see that the percentage of teachers with advanced degrees and teacher

TABLE 5.4 Cumulative Effects of Average 1-Year Teacher Turnover by District Characteristics 2008–2018

	Model 1		Model 2		Model 3		Model 4	
Intercept	39.78***	(4.34)	25.14***	(3.09)	14.85***	(1.93)	18.58***	(2.58)
Teacher Composition								
Percent of Teachers With Adv. Deg.	−0.06**	(0.02)	−0.05	(0.03)				
Average Teacher Salary	−0.00***	(0.00)	−0.00***	(0.00)				
Percent of Classes w/o Highly Qualified			0.29***	(0.03)				
Percent of Teachers With Emerg. Cert			0.42***	(0.04)				
District Composition								
District Poverty Index	0.09***	(0.03)			0.13***	(0.01)		
Percent of Students Meeting Standards	−0.08***	(0.01)			−0.13***	(0.01)		
Percent of Students Drop Out	−0.18*	(0.07)			−0.37***	(0.08)		
Student–Teacher Ratio	−0.04	(0.03)			−0.05	(0.04)		

(continued)

TABLE 5.4 Cumulative Effects of Average 1-Year Teacher Turnover by District Characteristics 2008–2018 (cont.)

	Model 1		Model 2		Model 3		Model 4	
Student Demographics (Percentage)								
Black	5.91*	(2.63)					1.65	(2.80)
White	–3.91	(2.62)					–12.44***	(2.64)
LatinX	13.18	(8.31)					–11.37	(8.30)
Asian	11.17	(19.81)					–98.66***	(18.82)
Indigenous	–76.33***	(15.30)					–55.31**	(17.06)
English Learner	–3.18	(9.93)					18.90	(10.37)
IEP	–8.48*	(4.08)					0.45	(4.40)
FRLP	–7.79***	(1.91)					–0.78	(2.58)
N	812		423		812		908	
R^2	0.62		0.60		0.48		0.51	
F	90.41		157.62		180.94		116.47	
Year *FE*	YES		YES		YES		YES	
District *FE*	YES		YES		YES		YES	

Note: Standard errors in parentheses *$p < 0.05$, **$p < 0.01$, ***$p < 0.001$

Note: Model 1 specification excludes the percent of highly qualified teachers and teachers with emergent certification. South Carolina did not report highly qualified teachers after 2016 or emergent certification after 2012; Model 2 specification includes teacher composition measures including highly qualified teachers and teachers with emergent certification from sample years 2008–2012; Model 3 specification includes only district composition measures; Model 4 includes only student composition measures.

TABLE 5.5 Cumulative Effects of Average 3-Year Teacher Turnover by District Characteristics 2008–2018

	Model 1	Model 2	Model 3	Model 4
Intercept	29.57*** (4.36)	25.62*** (3.37)	12.04*** (1.78)	18.50*** (2.23)
Teacher Composition				
Percent of Teachers with Advanced Degree	−0.07** (0.02)	−0.03 (0.03)		
Average Teacher Salary	−0.00*** (0.00)	−0.00*** (0.00)		
Percent of Classes w/o Highly Qualified		0.23*** (0.04)		
Percent of Teachers with Emergency Certification		0.38*** (0.04)		
District Composition				
District Poverty Index	0.08** (0.03)		0.09*** (0.01)	
Percent of Students Meeting Standards	−0.04** (0.01)		−0.07*** (0.01)	
Percent of Students Drop Out	−0.11 (0.07)		−0.22** (0.07)	
Student–Teacher Ratio	−0.04 (0.03)		−0.03 (0.04)	

(continued)

TABLE 5.5 Cumulative Effects of Average 3-Year Teacher Turnover by District Characteristics 2008–2018 (cont.)

	Model 1		Model 2	Model 3	Model 4	
Student Demographics (Percentage)						
Black	0.54	(2.64)			−3.72	(2.43)
White	−4.83	(2.64)			−11.07***	(2.29)
LatinX	23.59**	(8.35)			6.19	(7.19)
Asian	26.36	(19.91)			−46.79**	(16.30)
Indigenous	−53.47***	(15.38)			−37.29*	(14.78)
English Learner	−22.63*	(9.98)			−8.04	(8.98)
IEP	−4.54	(4.10)			0.39	(3.81)
FRLP	−4.22*	(1.92)			1.35	(1.23)
N	812		423	812	908	
R²	0.38		0.50	0.28	0.31	
F	34.12		102.76	78.27	50.97	
Year FE	YES		YES	YES	YES	
District FE	YES		YES	YES	YES	

Note: Standard errors in parentheses *$p < 0.05$, **$p < 0.01$, ***$p < 0.001$. Model 1 specification excludes the percent of highly qualified teachers and teachers with emergent certification. South Carolina did not report highly qualified teachers after 2016 or emergent certification after 2012; Model 2 specification includes teacher composition measures including highly qualified teachers and teachers with emergent certification from sample years 2008–2012; Model 3 specification includes only district composition measures; Model 4 includes only student composition measures.

salaries maintain the same relationship with teacher turnover. However, the percent of classrooms without highly qualified teachers and the percent of teachers with emergent certifications predict teacher turnover. It is plausible that as teachers attain further education, they leave districts for higher salaries or working conditions that align with their preferences (Sutcher et al., 2019; Tran et al., 2021). Indeed, interviews with teachers from hard-to-staff schools in the state seem to suggest that many new teachers treat these contexts as "training grounds" that they leave once they accrue sufficient experience to be attractive elsewhere (Tran et al., 2020). However, further evidence is needed to make these assumptions, and this analysis is incapable of such granularity. In terms of district composition, we see that poverty is predictive of both 1- and 3-year teacher turnover. This relationship held when we examined district composition separately in Model 3.

When examining student demographics, we see from Model 1 that teacher turnover for the 1- and 3-year sample increases as the proportion of Black students increases. This finding holds when examining the isolated 1-year turnover student demographic model; Table 5.4 Model 4. However, when examining 3-year teacher turnover in Table 5.5, the finding is inconsistent. In the full model, the relationship between teacher turnover and the proportion of Black students is not statistically significant, and in Model 4 is inverse. These findings may require greater isolation by year or district to provide further evidence. However, from all of the findings here, we can plausibly assume that teachers are more likely to leave districts at some level of aggregation as the proportion of Black students increases.

Finally, teacher turnover and the proportion of White students have an inverse relationship. For 1-year turnover, the full Model 1 coefficient for White students is not statistically significant, −3.91. In isolation Model 4, 1-year teacher turnover is statistically related to White students, −12.44. These same relationships hold for the 3-year estimation. Thus, we can plausibly assume that as the proportion of White students increases, teacher turnover decreases. That said, prior research suggests that this finding is more systemic than it initially appears. Specifically, Horng's (2009) research showed that it wasn't the students' race that promoted retention and turnover, but rather the school and work conditions correlated with the concentration of student demographics. Unfortunately, concentrations of students of color are primarily educated in high poverty contexts, which, as we mentioned earlier, are often linked with poorer working conditions and less experienced and underqualified teachers (Goldhaber et al., 2015).

DISCUSSION

Currently, South Carolina is fully confronting the impact of the COVID-19 pandemic and the teacher labor market constriction it has created (Garcia & Weiss, 2019). The results show clear indicators of teacher turnover variation by geography, race, and poverty in the short term. Research shows that teacher shortages impact those districts with a higher proportion of students in poverty and minoritized students (Darling-Hammond, 2010). Furthermore, high poverty schools with higher proportions of minoritized students are more likely to be taught by educators with emergent certification or fewer years of training (Darling-Hammond, 2010). These are the same schools that have difficulty hiring and retaining educators upfront, at which point the teacher turnover challenge becomes cyclical. The analysis of South Carolina data supports the national trends.

Schools in high-poverty areas often contend with sparser budgets and, specific to South Carolina, are also congruently rural geographically. In high-poverty rural-exurban areas, budget constraints mediate salaries and working conditions within the district (Brownell et al., 2018). Funding is necessary for salaries, which can offset attrition, and aid in the recruitment of teachers (see Chapter 7). There was an inverse correlation between salaries and teacher turnover in the sample. However, we caution about the assumptions of this specific finding due to the magnitude itself.

It should be noted that this finding is consistent with previous literature. We also show that attrition occurs for educators with advanced degrees, an inverse relationship in the sample, who secure higher salaries due to their education. It is plausible that as educators with advanced degrees leave the district, salaries would correspondingly decrease as new and emergent educators enter the school district to offset the loss. More sensitive data and analyses are necessary to investigate this phenomenon further. It is also well understood that salaries and school facilities are strong predictors of teacher retention in rural areas, with a higher proportion of minoritized students (Williams et al., 2021).

Earlier, we outlined the facility funding gap in South Carolina, and these poor working conditions are a factor in teacher attrition (Bristol, 2020). Educators want to feel as though they are supported through up-to-date facilities, but the reality is that school buildings nationally require a substantial amount of servicing (Filardo et al., 2019). Poorly maintained schools impact how teaching candidates perceive the district and influence their decisions about opportunities that exist in the profession. Local districts are responsible for funding facilities maintenance, and those districts with lower fiscal capacity may not have the necessary funds to do so (Filardo et al., 2019).

Teacher turnover is expensive at the district level, and leaders invest in recruitment and retention initiatives. Teacher staffing problems are also disproportionately concentrated in high-poverty districts that must employ more recruitment and retention efforts to address their staffing challenges, further decreasing their limited operations funds. Furthermore, there are specific subject area constraints (i.e., math, science) that leaders and researchers have yet to historically mitigate, requiring more significant investment (Ingersoll & Perda, 2010; Sutcher et al., 2019). State-level teacher vacancy data does not capture under or unqualified teachers' employment when they are hired to be in the classroom. These types of hires, more likely to occur in marginalized high-poverty districts.

The research field on teacher staffing is rich with information on the factors that impact teacher turnover. As researchers and practitioners, it is crucial to keep sight of critical indicators that lead to more significant attrition. There is no panacea, but as a case study, South Carolina has many variables that together work to disproportionately impact teacher turnover in a specific manner and specific geographic areas. This variation must be continually explored and addressed, yet supplemental teacher policy incentives are insufficient to assist high need districts in overcoming their challenges entirely if they are inadequately funded to begin with. Therefore, one significant change that needs to occur is evaluating South Carolina's school finance policy that adequately considers different teacher employment needs across the state.

CONCLUSION

This chapter serves as a South Carolina case study of the policy-relevant factors that inform teacher turnover. Earlier in the chapter, we outlined the policy context of South Carolina and how it serves to exacerbate educational inequity in high-poverty and rural communities, including the teacher labor market. While this is not an all-encompassing study of teacher turnover in South Carolina, it does help to inform a nuanced perspective on teacher turnover challenges and provides a baseline of evidence to understand the state's teacher labor market. South Carolina will continue to exhibit teacher shortages in specific communities unless the state educational stakeholder leadership addresses the shortages in a systematic manner. If we continue to exhibit the current turnover pattern, we continue to risk the educational health of South Carolina's children. It is imperative to have nuanced research that helps us better understand how the localized context contributes to challenges so that appropriate solutions can be proposed and executed to respond to them to help struggling districts across the nation address their teacher recruitment and retention challenges.

REFERENCES

Abbeville County School District et al. v. State of South Carolina et al., Appellate Case No. 2007-065159. (2014).

Adamson, F., & Darling-Hammond, L. (2012). Funding disparities and the inequitable distribution of teachers: Evaluating sources and solutions. *Education Policy Analysis Archives, 20*(37). https://epaa.asu.edu/index.php/epaa/article/view/1053/1024.

Act 388 of 2006. https://www.scstatehouse.gov/sess116_2005-2006/bills/4449.htm

Baker, B. D., Di Carlo, M., Srikanth, A., Weber, M. A. (2020). *School finance indicators database.* Rutgers Graduate School of Education/Albert Shanker Institute. http://www.schoolfinancedata.org

Brewer, R. M., & Heitzeg, N. A. (2008). The racialization of crime and punishment: Criminal justice, color-blind racism, and the political economy of the prison industrial complex. *American Behavioral Scientist, 51*(5), 625–644.

Briggs v. Elliott. (1952). 342 U.S. 350. https://scholar.google.com/scholar_case?case=16693048563837275531&hl=en&as_sdt=6&as_vis=1&oi=scholarr

Brimley, V., Verstegen, D.A., & Knoeppel, R. (2019). *Financing education in a climate of change* (13th ed). Pearson Education Inc.

Bristol, T. J. (2020). A tale of two types of schools: An exploration of how school working conditions influence Black male teacher turnover. *Teachers College Record, 122*(3), 1–41.

Brown v. Board of Education of Topeka, 347 U.S. 483 (1954). https://supreme.justia.com/cases/federal/us/347/483/

Brown, A. L., & De Lissovoy, N. (2011). Economies of racism: Grounding education policy research in the complex dialectic of race, class, and capital. *Journal of Education Policy, 26*(5), 595–619.

Brownell, M. T., Bishop, A. M., & Sindelar, P. T. (2018). Republication of "NCLB and the demand for highly qualified teachers: Challenges and solutions for rural schools." *Rural Special Education Quarterly, 37*(1), 4–11.

Carver-Thomas, D., & Darling-Hammond, L. (2017). *Teacher turnover: Why it matters and what we can do about it.* Learning Policy Institute.

Center for Educator Recruitment, Retention, & Advancement. (2019). *South Carolina annual educator supply & demand report (2018–19 school year).* Growing Teachers for South Carolina.

Center on Budget and Policy Priorities. (2019). *In more than half of States, combined State-local K–12 funding topped pre-recession levels by 2016.* https://www.cbpp.org/in-more-than-half-of-states-combined-state-local-k-12-funding-topped-pre-recession-levels-by-2016

Chapman, A., Ladd, H. F., & Sorensen, L. C. (2018). *The hidden costs of teacher turnover* (Working Paper No. 203-0918-1). National Center for Analysis of Longitudinal Data in Education Research.

Cowan, J., Goldhaber, D., Hayes, K., & Theobald, R. (2016). Missing elements in the discussion of teacher shortages. *Educational Researcher, 45*(8), 460–462.

Darling-Hammond, L. (2010a). *The flat world and education: How America's commitment to equity will determine our future.* Teachers College Press.

Delgado, R., & Stefancic, J. (2017). *Critical race theory: An introduction.* New York University Press.

Diem, S., Young, M. D., Welton, A. D., Mansfield, K. C., & Lee, P. L. (2014). The intellectual landscape of critical policy analysis. *International Journal of Qualitative Studies in Education, 27*(9), 1068–1090.

EdBuild. (2019). *$23 Billion.* https://edbuild.org/content/23-billion/full-report.pdf

Education Finance Act of 1977. https://www.scstatehouse.gov/code/t59c020.php

Education Improvement Act of 1984. https://www.scencyclopedia.org/sce/entries/education-improvement-act/

Filardo, M., Vincent, J. M., & Sullivan, K. (2019). How crumbling school facilities perpetuate inequality. *Phi Delta Kappan, 100*(8), 27–31.

Garcia, E., & Weiss, W. (2019). *The teacher shortage is real, large and growing, and worse than we thought. The first report in "The Perfect Storm in the Teacher Labor Market"* series. Economic Policy Institute.

Gillborn, D. (2005). Education policy as an act of white supremacy: Whiteness, critical race theory and education reform. *Journal of Education Policy, 20*(4), 485–505.

Gillborn, D., & Ladson-Billings, G. (2010). Education and critical race theory. In M. W. Apple, S. J. Ball, & L. A. Gandin (Eds.), *The Routledge international handbook of the sociology of education* (pp. 37–47). Routledge.

Goldhaber, D., Lavery, L., & Theobald, R. (2015). Uneven playing field? Assessing the teacher quality gap between advantaged and disadvantaged students. *Educational researcher, 44*(5), 293–307.

Hinojosa, D. (2016). Race-conscious school finance litigation: Is a fourth wave emerging. *University of Richmond Law Review, 50*(3), 869–892.

Holzwasser v. Brady, 262 S.C. 481 (1974). https://law.justia.com/cases/south-carolina/supreme-court/1974/19830-1.html

Horng, E. L. (2009). Teacher tradeoffs: Disentangling teachers' preferences for working conditions and student demographics. *American Educational Research Journal, 46*(3), 690–717.

Howard, R. M., Roch, C. H., & Schorpp, S. (2017). Leaders and followers: Examining state court–ordered education finance reform. *Law & Policy, 39*(2), 142–169.

Hutchison, L. F. (2012). Addressing the STEM teacher shortage in American schools: Ways to recruit and retain effective STEM teachers. *Action in Teacher Education, 34*(5–6), 541–550.

IBISWorld. (2021). *South Carolina—State economic profile statistics, economic information and rankings for the Palmetto State.* https://www.ibisworld.com/united-states/economic-profiles/south-carolina/

Ingersoll, R. M., & Perda, D. (2010). Is the supply of mathematics and science teachers sufficient? *American Educational Research Journal, 47*(3), 563–594.

Keisler, J. (2014). *Property tax base erosion: A South Carolina study* [Doctoral dissertation, Clemson University]. https://tigerprints.clemson.edu/all_dissertations/1723

Kelchtermans, G. (2017). 'Should I stay or should I go?': Unpacking teacher attrition/retention as an educational issue. *Teachers and Teaching, 23*(8), 961–977.

Knoeppel, R. C., Pitts, D. A, & Lindle, J. C. (2013). Taxation and education: Using educational research to inform coherent policy for the public good. *Journal of Research in Education, 23*(1). Retrieved from http://www.eeraonline.org/journal/v23n1.cfm

Ladson-Billings, G., & Tate, W. F. (1995). Toward a critical race theory of education. *Teachers College Record, 97*(1), 47–68.

Lechman, F., & Figueroa, E. (2019). *K–12 school funding up in most 2018 teacher-protest states, but still well below decade ago.* Center on Budget and Policy Priorities. https://www.cbpp.org/research/state-budget-and-tax/k-12-school-funding-up-in-most-2018-teacher-protest-states-but-still

Martin v. Tax Collector, 28 S.C.L. 343, 1 Speers 343 (1843). https://cite.case.law/scl/28/343/

Martínez, D. G. (2021). Interrogating social justice paradigms in school finance research and litigation. *Interchange: A Quarterly Review of Education, 52*, 297–317. https://doi.org/10.1007/s10780-021-09418-4

Martínez, D. G., & Spikes, D. D., (2020). Se Acabaron Las Palabras: A post-mortem *Flores v. Arizona* disproportional funding analysis of targeted English Learner (EL) expenditures. *Educational Policy.* https://doi.org/10.1177/0895904820917370

National Center for Educational Statistics. (2021). *Drop out rates.* https://nces.ed.gov/fastfacts/display.asp?id=16

Parker v. Bates, 216 S.C. 52, 56 S.E.2d 723 (1949). https://cite.case.law/sc/216/52/

Saltzman, E., & Ulbrich, H. (2012). *Act 388 Revisited.* The Jim Self Center on the Future, Strom Thurmond Institute of Government and Public Affairs, Clemson University.

South Carolina Constitution Article 1, § 8. (2021). https://www.carolana.com/SC/Documents/South_Carolina_Constitution_1865.pdf

South Carolina Constitution Article X, § 1-16. (2021). https://www.scstatehouse.gov/scconstitution/A10.pdf

South Carolina State Constitution Article I, § 12-37. https://www.scstatehouse.gov/code/t12c037.php

South Carolina Department of Education. (2013). *Statewide school district facilities capital needs analysis.* https://ed.sc.gov/districts-schools/school-planning-building/south-carolina-school-facilities-planning-construction-guides-forms/guides-best-practices-more/forms/2013-capital-needs-report/?showMeta=2&ext=.pdf

South Carolina Department of Education. (2016). *Statewide school district facilities capital needs analysis.* https://ed.sc.gov/districts-schools/school-planning-building/school-facility-building-funds/2016-capital-needs-report/

South Carolina Department of Education. (2019). *Statewide school district facilities capital needs analysis.* https://www.scstatehouse.gov/reports/DeptofEducation/2019%20Capital%20Needs%20Report%20-%20Final.pdf

South Carolina House Bill 4449 (Act 388), 116th Legislature (South Carolina 2006).

South Carolina Revenue and Fiscal Affairs Office. (2019). *Education funding model formula, assumptions, and funding options.* https://governor.sc.gov/sites/default/files/Documents/newsroom/Education%20Funding%20Report%20-Final%202010-03-19.pdf

South Carolina Revenue and Fiscal Affairs Office. (2021a). *EFA factor computation.* https://rfa.sc.gov/sites/default/files/2020-10/EFA22_7-24-20.pdf

South Carolina Revenue and Fiscal Affairs Office. (2021b). *Education finance projections.* https://rfa.sc.gov/data-research/education/education-finance-projections

Sutcher, L., Darling-Hammond, L., & Carver-Thomas, D. (2019). Understanding teacher shortages: An analysis of teacher supply and demand in the United States. *Education Policy Analysis Archives, 27*(35), 1–40.

Thomas, L. (2018, May 8). *There is a teacher shortage crisis': How South Carolina is working to retain teachers.* WLTX 19. https://www.wltx.com/article/news/local/there-is-a-teacher-shortage-crisis-how-south-carolina-is-working-to-retain-teachers/101-550088020

Tran, H. (2018). *Taking the mystery out of South Carolina school finance* (2nd ed.). ICPEL Publications.

Tran, H., Aziz, M., & Reinhardt, S. F. (2021). Rage against the machine: The legacy of education leaders' valiant struggle for social justice in *Abbeville v. South Carolina. Journal of School Leadership, 31*(3), 166–188.

Tran, H., Hardie, S., Gause, S., Moyi, P., & Ylimaki, R. (2020). Leveraging the perspectives of rural educators to develop realistic job previews for rural teacher recruitment and retention. *Rural Educator, 41*(2), 31–46.

U.S. Department of Education, National Center for Education Statistics. (2019). *Digest of education statistics, 2017* (NCES 2018-070). United States Department of Education.

Williams, S. M., Swain, W. A., & Graham, J. A. (2021). Race, climate, and turnover: An examination of the teacher labor market in rural Georgia. *AERA Open, 7.* https://doi.org/10.3886/E131301V1

World Population Review. (2021). *Teacher pay by state 2021.* https://worldpopulation review.com/state-rankings/teacher-pay-by-state

Young, M. D., & Diem, S. (2018). Doing critical policy analysis in education research: An emerging paradigm. In C. R. Lochmiller (Ed.), *Complementary research methods for educational leadership and policy studies* (pp. 79–98). Palgrave MacMillan.

CHAPTER 6

UNDERSTANDING SOUTH CAROLINA'S RURAL RECRUITMENT INITIATIVE

A State Funded Program Developed to Improve Teacher Recruitment and Retention

Henry Tran
University of South Carolina

Douglas A. Smith
Iowa State University

Policymakers have heavily emphasized and promoted financial incentives, such as hiring bonuses, loan forgiveness, and housing assistance, in hopes to "offset" the detracting employment aspects in hard-to-staff schools to recruit and retain teachers to teach in them (Lowe, 2006; Feng & Sass, 2018; Springer et al., 2016; Tran & Smith, 2020). Despite their intuitive appeal, the research on their efficacy is quite mixed. Some research supports

How Did We Get Here?, pages 105–140
Copyright © 2022 by Information Age Publishing
www.infoagepub.com
All rights of reproduction in any form reserved.

the value of financial incentives for teacher staffing. For example, Clotfelter et al. (2008) examined the impact of North Carolina's annual salary
supplement of $1,800 from 2001 to 2004 for teachers certified in math,
science, and special education in high poverty or low performing schools
and discovered that the payment was able to reduce the average teacher
turnover rate by 17%, although survey results suggest there was widespread
misunderstanding of eligibility requirements and criticism concerning the
insufficiency of the bonus size. Likewise, Springer et al. (2016) found that a
$5,000 retention bonus for high-performing teachers in Tennessee's Prior-
ity Schools increased the likelihood of retaining the highest-rated teachers
for tested subjects and grades in high-needs schools by 20%.

There is also research that fails to support the effectiveness of financial
incentive programs. For example, Liu et al. (2004) interviewed 13 of the
original 59 teachers who received financial incentives as part of the Massachusetts Signing Bonus Program (MSBP). The MSBP was instituted in 1998
and received national recognition for its substantial signing bonus amount
of $20,000 to attract high achieving candidates, who would not otherwise
consider teaching, into the profession. Unfortunately, the program did not
achieve its objective. Almost all of the interviewees noted that they had seri-
ously considered teaching before receiving the bonus, and therefore the
money had very little influence on their decision to teach. Additionally,
most were not able to receive all of the bonus as it was paid out over 4 years.
Only five of the interviewees remained in their position by then, suggesting
that the lagged payout was ineffective for teacher retention overall.

Likewise, Prost (2013) examined the impact of a bonus program implemented in 1990 for teachers in disadvantaged schools in France. The bonus
amounted to about a 2.5% wage increase for a novice teacher and a 1% increase for the most experienced teachers. Findings from the study suggest
that "teachers tend to leave schools where there are more students from ethnic minorities, more students from disadvantaged backgrounds and more
students with less educational achievement" while finding no strong evidence
that the bonuses decreased turnover. Turnover increased in 1992 collectively
for the eligible disadvantaged schools. Nearly 2 decades ago in South Carolina, a policy effort aimed at recruiting 500 teacher specialists to work in the
state's weakest schools by providing an $18,000 bonus attracted only 20% of
the target the first year and only 40% after 3 years. Evaluation of the effort revealed several barriers, including a lack of administrative support, poor working conditions, and the need for better preparation for high-need contexts
(Berry et al., 2003). Even an optimistic reading of the body of research would
suggest that there are shortcomings to relying on financial incentives, and
more research is needed to better understand their limitations.

The purpose of this chapter is to report and discuss a comprehensive series
of studies on state-level teacher recruitment and retention policy initiatives

in South Carolina that provides financial support to hard-to-staff school districts. Unlike many prior teacher recruitment and retention policy efforts, the policy approach in South Carolina allowed districts to have discretion in fund utilization for teacher recruitment and retention, as opposed to restricting use to only one strategy (e.g., recruitment bonuses). In the following sections, we introduce the South Carolina context, a rural recruitment policy initiative, and the results of a study that examined the initiative. These findings suggest that funded teacher recruitment and retention efforts should be better aligned with those backed by empirical evidence, and funding should be provided at a level that allows for investment in sustainable and long-term staffing initiatives, not just one-off expenditures.

SOUTH CAROLINA'S TEACHER STAFFING CONTEXT

From 2019–2020 to 2020 to 2021, almost 6,000 South Carolina teachers did not return to their positions in their districts (CERRA, 2020). Early career teachers were overrepresented in departures, with 42% having five or fewer years of teaching in the state and 16% having 1 year or less. From a vacancy perspective, at the beginning of the 2020–2021 school year, 699 vacant teaching positions remained unfilled 55,660 total teaching positions across the 89 public school districts, a 26% increase from the prior year (CERRA, 2020).

In response to the significant and persistent teacher staffing issues that plague many South Carolina school districts, the South Carolina General Assembly General Appropriations Bill for the fiscal year 2015–2016 (H.3701) included $1,500,000 in initial funding for the creation of a Rural Teacher Recruiting Incentive (RRI) distributed by CERRA, with the charge to "recruit and retain classroom educators in rural and underserved districts experiencing excessive turnover of classroom teachers on an annual basis."[1] CERRA was tasked with developing eligibility requirements and an application process for funding. In 2016–2017, H.5001 expanded funding for RRI to $9,748,392 and has continued funding at this level for 2017–2018 (H.3720), 2018–2019 (H.4950), and 2019–2020 (H.4000). However, for 2019–2020, the funds allocated for implementation through CERRA for RRI have been reduced by $2,150,000 to fund educator recruitment/preparation programs at South Carolina State University and the University of South Carolina. Given the upcoming reduction, it is prudent to understand districts' current recruitment and retention incentives utilization.

School district eligibility for RRI is based on their 5-year average teacher turnover. The eligibility cutoff was initially set at 12% in 2015–2016 before being lowered to 11% in 2016–2017.[2] An initial set of 20 eligibility districts in the pilot year (2015–2016) steadily increased to 36 eligible districts by 2018–2019. While the number of eligible districts increased, little was known about the specific recruitment and retention challenges facing these districts and how districts were utilizing RRI funding to complement existing district HR strategies. This chapter reports on a series of studies that sought to better understand district challenges leading to high teacher turnover and subsequent RRI fund utilization and the potential effectiveness of RRI for fund receiving districts thus far.

RRI DISBURSEMENT CATEGORIES

A formula administered by CERRA was utilized to determine how much each eligible district received from the total RRI allocation minus CERRA's administrative costs. This formula considers districts' 5-year average turnover and number of teacher positions in the district to proportion the disbursement by the severity of teacher turnover and district size. Specifically, the formula is:

$$\left(\frac{\text{Total RRI funds available for distribution}}{\text{Total all district's teacher toal with multiplier}} \right)$$

$$\times \text{District teacher total with RRI multiplier}$$

$$= \text{RRI District Distribution}$$

The multiplier is calculated by taking the difference between the 11% eligibility cutoff criteria and the district's 5-year average teacher turnover rate, divided by 100. The total number of teachers does not account for guidance, speech, and media specialists. CERRA notifies eligible districts of their eligibility amount, and districts then submit a request for disbursement to CERRA detailing the specific items they are requesting disbursement for. CERRA maintains a list of pre-approved disbursement categories that function as a suggested, cafeteria-style list of choices for districts to choose from. The disbursement categories and amount disbursed for each category are described in Figures 6.1 and 6.2 for FY17 and FY18.

While most categories are relatively straightforward to interpret, the category "recruitment expenses" requires a bit more explanation. For FY18, this category represented 35% of RRI disbursements ($11.87 million total) from new legislative appropriation and rollover balances. Recruitment expenses for the 30 RRI districts had a median disbursement of $119,250, ranging from $504 to $1,047,916. Given the size and broadness of the recruitment expenses category, a qualitative analysis of these disbursement requests was warranted. Our examination identified five primary areas of recruitment expense disbursements that included (a) international teacher

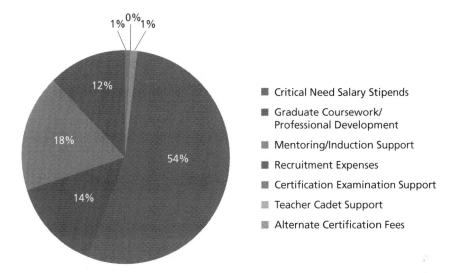

Figure 6.1 RRI Disbursement Categories, FY 2017. *Note:* Because the percentages are rounded, 0% on the graph does not suggest districts failed to receive funding for the categories but rather it suggests only a very small percentage did. RRI funds for each category identified above were allocated to at least one school district.

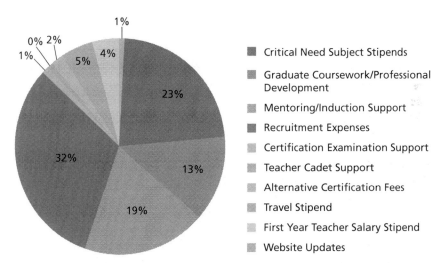

Figure 6.2 RRI disbursement categories, FY 2018.

fees and related expenses, (b) clothing and other district branded items, (c) recruitment fair travel and expenses, (d) recruitment materials, and (e) third party recruiter expenses. International teacher fees and expenses represented the single largest area of **RRI** spending by districts. A total of

17 districts received an average of $189,317 disbursed for this area ($3.2M total), representing 76% of recruitment expenses and 27% of all RRI spending by districts in FY18. The remaining 24% of RRI funds spent on recruitment expenses were spread more widely by districts, including for items such as clothing and district branded items, recruitment fair expenses and travel, physical recruitment materials, and human resource/recruitment vendor expenses.

SURVEY STUDY FOR THE 2018 SCHOOL YEAR: SAMPLE DISTRICTS

To gain further specific insight concerning the teacher staffing challenges RRI funded districts face and how RRI funded strategies complemented current district staffing efforts, we developed an in-depth survey distributed to each of the RRI funded districts. While the survey did ask some historical questions, most of the questions focused on the 2017–2018 school year, the most recently completed school year at the time of the study, to gain depth of information. Of the 30 districts we surveyed, 28 responded with sufficient detail for analysis, representing a 93% response rate.

It is important to note that, despite its name, the Rural Recruitment Initiative is not exclusive to rural school districts, although many eligible districts are rural. Based on the National Center for Educational Statistics (NCES) locale classifications (Table 6.1), eligible districts were 64% rural, 25% town, and 11% town. Regionally, 10 districts were located in the Low-country region, 12 in the Midlands region, 4 in the Pee Dee region, 2 in the Upstate region, and none in the Charlotte region (Table 6.2).

One of the areas affecting teacher staffing that is frequently mentioned in policy and media discussions is teacher salary. Consequently, we reviewed base teacher salary offerings for the sample districts relative to the state average. The average beginning teacher salary in the sample was $32,630, which is 1.3% or $427 lower than the state beginning teacher salary average (Tran & Smith, 2020). Indeed, almost 70% of the RRI funded districts offered lower teacher salaries than the state average.

Personnel wise, the sample employed an average of 4.22 FTE in the HR departments in their districts that averaged 4,171.4 students. However, the FTE count is positively skewed (i.e., the majority of districts have a smaller number) because only three districts reported having more than 10 HR staff members, whereas almost 60% reported having less than three. HR capacity (defined here as HR staff to teacher ratio) was positively related to higher percentages of vacancies ($b = .077$, $p < .001$) and turnovers ($b = .0009$, $p < .0001$), suggesting that districts may have increased their HR bandwidth to respond to their shortages. When accounting for student

TABLE 6.1 NCES's Urban-Centric Locale Categories, Released in 2006	
Locale	**Definition**
City	
Large	Territory inside an urbanized area and inside a principal city with population of 250,000 or more
Midsize	Territory inside an urbanized area and inside a principal city with population less than 250,000 and greater than or equal to 100,000
Small	Territory inside an urbanized area and inside a principal city with population less than 100,000
Suburb	
Large	Territory outside a principal city and inside an urbanized area with population of 250,000 or more
Midsize	Territory outside a principal city and inside an urbanized area with population less than 250,000 and greater than or equal to 100,000
Small	Territory outside a principal city and inside an urbanized area with population less than 100,000
Town	
Fringe	Territory inside an urban cluser that is less than or equal to 10 miles from an urbanized area
Distant	Territory inside an urban cluster that is more than 10 miles and less than or equal to 35 miles from an urbanized area
Remote	Territory inside an urban cluster that is more than 35 miles from an urbanized area
Rural	
Fringe	Census-defined rural territpry that is less than or equal to 5 miles from an urbanized area, as well as rural territory
Distant	Census-defined rural territory that is more than 2.5 miles but less than or equal to 10 miles from an urban cluster
Remote	Census-defined rural territory that is more than 25 miles from an urbanized area and is also more than 10 miles from an urban cluster

Source: Office of Management and Budget (2000).

enrollment, the districts with more HR capacity also utilized more staffing strategies ($b = .805$, $p < .10$). Staffing strategies are discussed in more detail later in this chapter.

RECRUITMENT CHALLENGES

We asked the sample districts to identify the degree of difficulty they experienced recruiting teachers in the last 5 years across 19 challenges identified as significant in the scholarly literature of teacher recruitment. We display the top five most significant challenges with recruiting teachers as

TABLE 6.2   District Locale and Region

District	Locale	Region
Allendale	Rural (Fringe)	Lowcountry Region
Anderson 4	Rural (Fringe)	Upstate Region
Bamberg 2	Town (Distant)	Lowcountry Region
Barnwell 19	Rural (Distant)	Lowcountry Region
Barnwel/Williston 29	Rural (Distant)	Lowcountry Region
Barnwell 45	Town (Distant)	Lowcountry Region
Beaufort	City (Small)	Lowcountry Region
Clarendon 1	Rural (Distant)	Midlands Region
Clarendon 2	Town (Distant)	Midlands Region
Dillon 4	Town (Distant)	Pee Dee Region
Dorchester 4	Rural (Distant)	Lowcountry Region
Edgefield	Rural (Fringe)	Midlands Region
Fairfield	Rural (Fringe)	Midlands Region
Hampton 1	Town (Remote)	Lowcountry Region
Hampton 2	Rural (Distant)	Lowcountry Region
Jasper	Rural (Fringe)	Lowcountry Region
Lee	Rural (Fringe)	Midlands Region
Lexington 4	Rural (Fringe)	Midlands Region
Marion 10	Rural (Fringe)	Pee Dee Region
Marlboro	Town (Distant)	Pee Dee Region
McCormick	Rural (Distant)	Upstate Region
Orangeburg 3	Rural (Distant)	Midlands Region
Orangeburg 4	Rural (Distant)	Midlands Region
Orangeburg 5	Town (Distant)	Midlands Region
Richland 1	City (Midsize)	Midlands Region
Saluda	Rural (Fringe)	Midlands Region
Sumter	City (Small)	Midlands Region
Williansburg	Rural (Distant)	Pee Dee Region

Carlotte Region: Chester, Lancaster, York

Lowcountry Region: Allendale, Bamberg, Barnwell, Baufort, Berkeley, Charleston, Colleton, Dorchester, Hampton, Jasper

Midlands Region: Aiken, Calhoun, Clarendon, Edgefield, Fairfield, Kershaw, Lee, Lexington, Newberry, Orangeburg, Richland, Saluda, Sumter

Pee Dee Region: Chesterfield, Darlington, Dillon, Florence, Horry, Georgetown, Marlboro, Marion, Williamsburg

Upstate Region: Abbeville, Anderson, Cherokee, Greenville, Greenwood, Laurens, McCormick, Oconee, Pickens, Spartanburg, Union

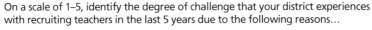

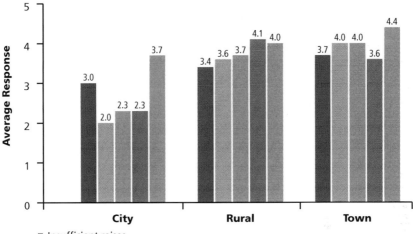

- ■ Insufficient raises
- ▨ Nearby higher paying districts
- ▨ Insufficient teachers w/ appropriate credentials
- ▨ Long distance to closest metro area
- ■ Lacking social opportunities

Figure 6.3   Top 5 challenges for recruiting teachers in the last 5 years by locale.

identified by districts in Figure 6.3 by locale (city, rural, town) and display results for all 19 reasons by locale in Appendix A. Across locales, the insufficient number of teachers with appropriate credentials was ranked as a top challenge for recruiting teachers, followed closely by insufficient raises. Lack of social opportunities, long-distance to the closest metro area, and nearby higher-paying districts were ranked as significant teacher recruitment for rural and town locale districts, but lesser of a challenge for city locale districts. It is important to note that most RRI districts (25 of 28) are classified as rural or town.

We also asked districts to identify their degree of challenge with recruiting specific teaching positions in the last 5 years. The results are presented in Figure 6.4 by district locale type. Overall, significant challenges were reported across locales in recruiting special education, high school English, high school science, high school math, middle-level science, and middle-level math. High school and middle school social studies teachers were reportedly a significant challenge to recruit in town locales, a moderate challenge in rural locales, and a smaller challenge in city locales. Middle school language arts teachers were reportedly a significant challenge to recruit by

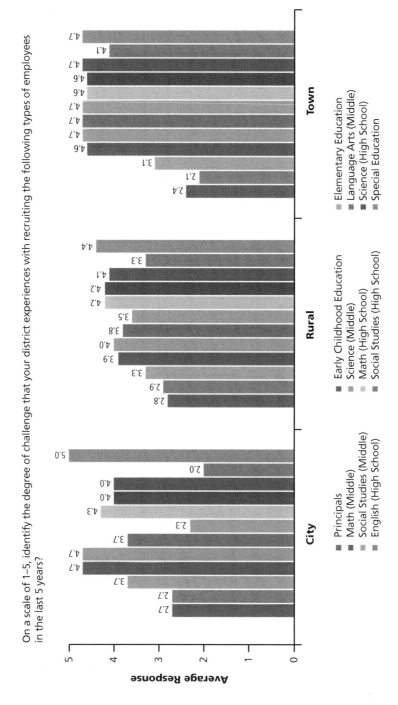

On a scale of 1–5, identify the degree of challenge that your district experiences with recruiting the following types of employees in the last 5 years?

Figure 6.4 Degree of challenge recruiting employees by type.

districts in town locales and a moderate challenge by city and rural locale districts. Principals, early childhood education, and elementary education were reportedly the least challenging to recruit across locales.

VACANCIES

Figure 6.5 depicts the average percentage of vacant teaching positions (at the start of the school year) from 2014–2018 by district. As can be seen, the 5-year average is low (< 2.50%) in most districts, relatively low (2.51%–5.00% in 10 districts, moderate (5.01–7.50%) in 4 districts, and high (> 7.51%) in one district. Figure 6.6 represents the change in the percentage of vacant teaching positions from 2010 to 2018. As can be seen, in 2010, all but one district had low vacancy rates. In contrast, in 2018, 13 districts had relatively low vacancy rates, 3 had moderate rates, and 1 had a high vacancy rate. All vacancy rate maps for 2010–2018 can be found in Appendix B.

Districts were asked to identify how they responded to teacher vacancies in the last 5 years. We provided a list of 12 options identified from the education human resource research literature, that included hiring certified and qualified teachers, substitute teachers, teachers with temporary licenses, teachers with certification in progress, less than the highest quality teacher available in the recruitment pool, teachers from out-of-state, retired teachers, international teachers, increasing class sizes, the number of classes assigned to current teachers, the number of teaching aids, and reducing the number of courses offered.

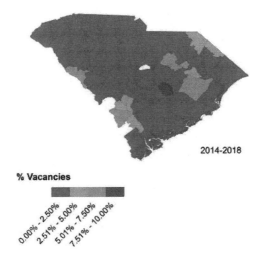

Figure 6.5 Average percentage of vacant teaching positions, 2014–2018.

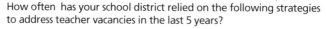

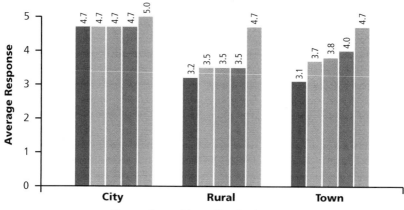

How often has your school district relied on the following strategies to address teacher vacancies in the last 5 years?

■ Hire teachers with certification in progress
▨ Hire retired teachers
▨ Hire certified, qualified teachers
▨ Hire teachers from out-of-state
▨ Hire international teachers

Figure 6.7 Strategies RRI districts rely on to address teacher vacancies.

There was not much difference across locales (city, town, rural) in the most employed responses. Hiring certified and qualified teachers was the most common response, followed by hiring international teachers, retired teachers, teachers from out of state, and teachers with certification in progress. It is important to note that hiring international teachers and retired teachers are more likely to be shorter-term staffing solutions than long-term teacher appointments, given their respective restrictions on employment duration. The distribution of high agreement concerning the use of different staffing responses by districts suggests that they have to actively recruit beyond the traditional in-state pre-retired fully certified teacher candidates. Figure 6.7 shows the top five most common responses by locale.

RETENTION CHALLENGES

Beyond vacancies, we asked districts to identify the degree of difficulty districts experienced with retaining teachers in the last five years across 19 challenges identified as significant in the teacher retention scholarly literature. We display the top five most significant self-reported challenges with retaining teachers by locale (city, rural, town) in Figure 6.8 and display results for all 19 challenges by locale in Appendix C. Mismatch between available personnel

On a scale of 1–5, identify the degree of challenge that your district experiences with retaining teachers in the last 5 years due to the following reasons…

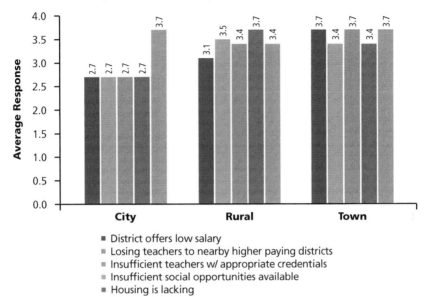

Figure 6.8   Top 5 challenges for retaining teachers during last 5 years by locale.

and required teaching credentials poses a significant challenge for retaining teachers across all locales, as there are insufficient numbers of appropriately certified teachers in the hiring pool. Additional retention issues that were cited as significant for rural and town locales, but were less of a challenge for cities, included a lack of available housing, insufficient social opportunities, high prevalence of districts offering low salaries, and the resulting loss of staff due to the proximity of higher-paying school districts.

TURNOVER

Holme et al. (2018) explain that turnover can be defined and measured in different ways, which results in correspondingly different interpretations of the problem. Consequently, they presented a typology of teacher turnover measures to help understand how teacher instability can differentially affect schools. Among their typology include a measure of short-term teacher turnover and three measures of long-term turnover. The measures include annual turnover, cumulative instability, chronic instability, and instability entry and exit. We will examine the study districts (sample of RRI districts) relative to each of these measures.

Annual Turnover

The measure of short-term teacher turnover used is annual turnover, representing the percent of teachers who did not return from the previous year. This is the most commonly used metric of annual teacher turnover. To provide context, we examined South Carolina's public school district's average teacher turnover between 2010 to 2017. During this period, the average teacher turnover rate increased by 14.57% (see Figure 6.9). In fact, the turnover has been steadily climbing on an annual basis from 2013 to 2017 (a trend that was also captured in Figure 6.9). A recovering economy likely influenced this after the Great Recession, which provided more market opportunities for workers outside of education.

Unfortunately, the story is similar but more severe for the study districts. Between 2010 to 2017, their average teacher turnover rate increased by 18.11%. Similar to the story for all school districts in South Carolina, the turnover rate has been steadily climbing, on an annual basis, since 2013. However, the average turnover rates are much larger for the study districts than the state overall (see Figure 6.10). Teacher turnover also varies significantly by locale. Figure 6.10 stratifies the study districts' percent of teacher turnover in 2017 by different locale types. As can be seen, rural districts, on average, experience a higher percent of teacher turnover than their town and city counterparts.

The 5-year average teacher turnover (2013–2017) for all 81 South Carolina traditional public school districts is 12.01%. Low turnover is prevalent

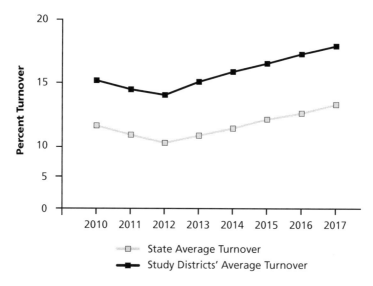

Figure 6.9 South Carolina public school district's teacher turnover, 2010–2017.

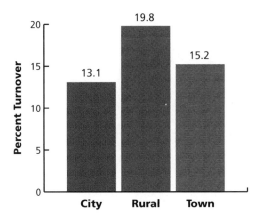

Figure 6.10 Study districts' teacher turnover (2017) by locale.

in the upstate and Charlotte metropolitan area districts. High and moderate turnover districts are mostly located in or near the Lowcountry and Pee Dee regions. Figure 6.11 maps the 5-year average turnover for all South Carolina school districts from 2013–2017. A snapshot of teacher turnover by district in 2010 and 2017 is displayed in Figure 6.12, showing the growing teacher turnover challenges during this period. All teacher turnover by district maps for 2010–2017 can be found in Appendix D.

Longitudinal Measures of Turnover

Cumulative Instability
Cumulative instability represents the proportion of teachers lost over time. This measure emphasizes "depth" of turnover by highlighting how many of

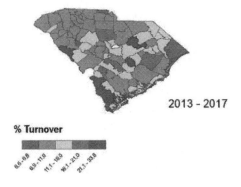

Figure 6.11 5-year average teacher turnover, 2013–2017.

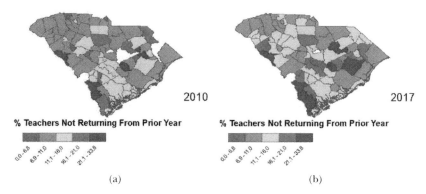

2010   2017

% Teachers Not Returning From Prior Year   % Teachers Not Returning From Prior Year

(a)   (b)

Figure 6.12   Teacher turnover by district, 2010 and 2017.

the original teachers in a given year have left, capturing significant loss over time (even if it may not be reflected on any given year). In this study, cumulative instability was defined as the percentage of teachers in the study districts from 10+ years ago that are no longer employed with the district.

While the average teacher turnover rate for the study's districts was 17.92% in 2017, the cumulative instability rate was 52.47% (see Figure 6.13). This means that, on average, districts lost almost 53% of their original staff from 10+ years ago.

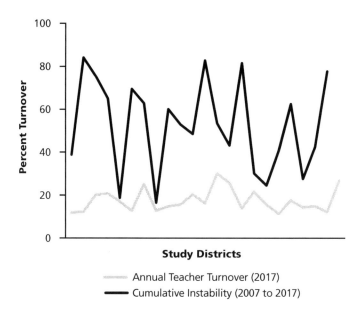

Annual Teacher Turnover (2017)
Cumulative Instability (2007 to 2017)

Figure 6.13   Districts cumulative 10-year instability vs. annual turnover.

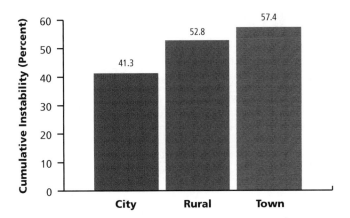

Figure 6.14 Teacher turnover by locale type.

Like annual turnover, cumulative turnover rates appear lower in the city than in rural and town districts (see Figure 6.14). As Holme et al. (2018) suggest, this represents a major human capital loss for these districts. It also represents a major loss in institutional memory and potential long-term continuity.

Table 6.4 ranks each district by various staffing criteria—that is, annual vacancy, annual turnover, 5-year average vacancy, 5-year average turnover, and cumulative instability. Overall, it can be seen that several of the same districts have high single and 5-year average vacancies and turnovers (e.g., Hampton 2, Clarendon 1, Williamsburg, Allendale, Lee), and many of these districts have high cumulative instability as well. Hampton 2, in particular, is amongst the top two districts experiencing the most severe staffing problems across all categories of staffing needs.

Chronic Instability/Instability Entry and Exit

Chronic instability can be defined as "high" annual teacher turnover that persists for a long time. Instability entry and exit refers to the extent districts enter in and out of "high" turnover status. Given that RRI funding is allocated to districts based on a 5-year average teacher turnover of over 11%, we used "over 11%" as the threshold cutoff for our definition of "high turnover." The literature has also relied on a 30% or more turnover cutoff rate given its practical ramifications for school districts (Allensworth et al., 2009; Holme et al., 2018). For the purpose of this study, we designate this cutoff as "severe turnover."

Our review of district data from 2010 to 2017 suggests that the study districts were considered "high turnover" approximately 86% of the time.

TABLE 6.4   District Staffing Criteria Ranking High and Low

Vacancy Ranking (2017)	Turnover Ranking (2017)	5 Year Average Vacancy (2014 to 2018)	5 Year Average Turnover (2013 to 2017)	Cumulative Instability Ranking (10 Years)*
Hapton 2	Hampton 2	Hampton 2	Hampton 2	Bamberg 2
Claredon 1	Williamsburg	Clarendon 1	Lee	Hampton 2
Allendale	Lee	Allendale	Clarendon 1	McCormick
Dillon 4	Clarendon 1	Williamsburg	Allendale	Williamsburg
Lee	Allendale	McCormick	Jasper	Barnwell 19
Williamsburg	Jasper	Lee	McCormick	Clarendon 1
Sumter	McCormick	Dillon 4	Bamberg 2	Barnwell 45
Marlboro	Barnwell/ Williston 29	Barnwell 19	Williamsburg	Dillon 4
Hampton 1	Fairfield	Marlboro	Fairfield	Richland 1
Orangeburg 3	Barnwell 19	Barnwell 45	Barnwell 19	Edgefield
Jasper	Marion 10	Hampton 1	Orangeburg 5	Lee
Barnwell 45	Orangeburg 5	Bamberg 2	Barnwell/ Williston 29	Fairfield
Richland 1	Barnwell 45	Beaufort	Marion 10	Hampton 1
Bamberg 2	Lexington 4	Jasper	Orangeburg 3	Barnwell/ Williston 29
Orangeburg 5	Clarendon 2	Orangeburg 5	Edgefield	Marlboro
Orangeburg 4	Hampton 1	Sumter	Hampton 1	Sumter
Beaufort	Edgefield	Richland 1	Clarendon 2	Orangeberg 5
Clarendon 2	Orangeburg 3	Barnwell/ Williston 29	Lexington 4	Anderson 4
Dorchester 4	Saluda	Orangeburg 4	Saluda	Orangeburg 3
Anderson 4	Dorchester 4	Clarendon 2	Anderson 4	Saluda
Barnwell 19	Richland 1	Orangeburg 3	Richland 1	Orangeburg 4
Barnwell/ Williston 29	Marlboro	Fairfield	Barnwell 45	Beaufort
Edgefield	Beaufort	Marion 10	Dorchester 4	Dorchester 4
Fairfield	Dillon 4	Edgefield	Orangeburg 4	
Lexington 4	Bamberg 2	Anderson 4	Beaufort	
Marion 10	Sumpter	Dorchester 4	Marlboro	
McCormick	Anderson 4	Lexington 4	Dillon 4	
Saluda	Orangeburg 4	Saluda	Sumter	

* Allendale, Clarendon 2, Jasper, Lexington 4, and Marion 10 districts did not provide the requisite data to calculate cumulative instability.

Half of the study districts were "high turnover" districts across the entire time frame, while a few of districts (i.e., Barnwell 19, Barnwell 29, Barnwell 45, Dillon 4, Dorchester 4, Orangeburg 4, Saluda) were able to slip in and out of "high turnover" status. The remaining districts could not exit that designation after meeting the high turnover threshold. Of all the study districts, only one met the criteria for designation as a "severe" turnover district, Hampton 2. Not only has Hampton 2 met the criteria for a "high" teacher turnover district from 2010 to 2017, but the district has consistently exceeded the severe teacher turnover threshold since 2014.

RRI DISTRICT'S PRE-EXISTING STAFFING STRATEGIES

The surveyed districts were each presented with 29 staffing strategies and/or resources identified from the teacher staffing literature and current RRI funding disbursement categories to inquire whether they utilized each one of them. The results of this inquiry were reported in Tran and Smith (2021). Specifically, no districts utilized all 29 strategies or resources. The average number utilized by a district was 14.9 (ranging from 8 to 21). All districts utilized some strategies (participation in job fairs, formal mentoring program for new teachers, teacher professional development). Other strategies were utilized by all but five or fewer districts (post with job banks and database listings, collaborate with colleges or universities to improve recruitment/retention, teacher appreciation programs). On the other end, some strategies were only utilized by five or fewer districts (signing bonus, teacher referral incentive, relocation assistance, performance-based rewards, rental housing assistance, hard-to-staff school incentives, transportation subsidies for commuting teachers). One strategy was not utilized by any districts (homeownership assistance). District level utilization data can be found in Appendix E.

If a district utilized a particular incentive, the HR representatives at the districts were asked to rate how effective that incentive was (for recruitment and retention, respectively, as appropriate). The effectiveness ratings ranged from 1 to 5, with 1 meaning "not effective at all" and 5 "extremely effective." Most incentives were rated with average effectiveness (i.e., 2–3.9). The highest-rated recruitment incentive was transportation subsidies for commuting teachers, at an average of 4 out of 5. Other highly rated recruitment incentives included international teacher repayment and reimbursement fees at 3.76 and the use of applicant tracking and job skills databases at 3.94. For retention, the highest-rated incentive was the use of formal induction programs at 3.74, with the second highest rated being transportation subsidies for commuting teachers at 3.67. It is important to reiterate that not all districts utilized each incentive, and consequently, the number of respondents comprising the average ratings varied significantly between incentives.

Figure 6.15 graphically displays the percent of districts that used each incentive or strategy. As mentioned earlier and seen in the figure, two strategies (i.e., job fair participation and formal mentoring program for new teachers) were used by every sampled district. No districts relied on homeownership assistance, and only one district offered rental housing assistance.

Many districts expressed a desire to offer more incentives but cited cost as a major barrier against them doing so. For instance, several districts expressed a desire to offer housing assistance but indicated "exorbitant local fees and lack of appropriate housing are a challenge." Grow-your-own incentive programs proved difficult for some districts to utilize RRI funding because districts do not have certainty that the legislature continues to fund RRI from year to year if their district remains eligible and what amount they may remain eligible for. The policy aim of RRI is to reduce teacher turnover and the number of districts with an annual turnover greater than 11%. Over time this aim should reduce the number of eligible districts. Given this, investing RRI funds in long-term initiatives proves difficult for some. One district noted the importance of offering travel stipends because "we have many teachers that commute over 100 miles roundtrip. The funds are just not there."

Even those that offered the same incentives provided them at various levels or depths. For instance, the HR officer from one district stated, "Our signing bonuses are so much smaller than other districts." The average signing bonus cost for those districts that shared that information was $2,167.29 per teacher, but that amount ranged from $1,000 per teacher in one district to $5,352.67 in another. Several districts also wanted to offer retention, sign-on, or critical needs bonuses. However, districts cited potential barriers to offering those incentives. One district shared, "Since we are a small district, we feel that it would create a feeling of animosity among others that did not receive the bonus/stipend."

For those incentives that were offered with the assistance of RRI funds, district representatives were asked how challenging would it have been for their district to offer those incentives without RRI funding assistance. Most of the incentives (i.e., relocation assistance, rental housing assistance, international teacher repayment and reimbursement fees, transportation subsidies for commuting teachers, development/purchase of recruitment material, and applicant tracking and job skills databases) were rated 4 (i.e., very challenging) and above, with less than a handful (i.e., participation job fairs, teacher recruitment advertising, collaborate with colleges or universities), rated below 4 and none below 3. One district shared, "Our District is

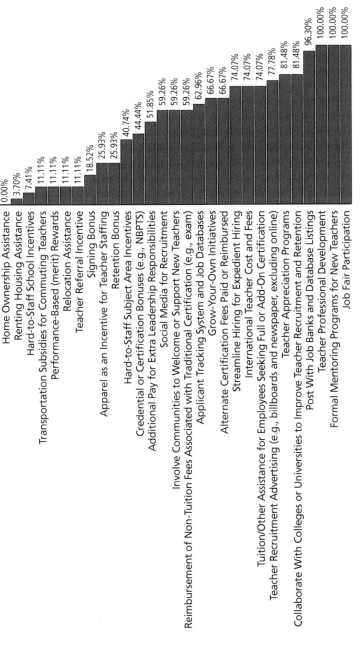

Figure 6.15 Incentives and strategies used by RRI study districts (from Tran & Smith, 2021).

only able to offer what RRI funds us. We have only paid retention bonuses and assistance for foreign teachers in 2018."

DISTRICTS' DEMOGRAPHICS AND STAFFING CHALLENGES BY SOUTH CAROLINA REGIONS

We further examined differences in district demographics and recruitment and retention challenges by geographic regions across the state (the regions were identified in Table 6.2). Table 6.5 displays the averages across various district demographics, staffing, and challenges. Because of a large number of challenges examined, the table only highlights the challenges that identify ratings that are 4 (i.e., *very challenging*) or above (e.g., 5, *extremely challenging*).

As depicted in Table 6.5, districts in the Pee Dee Region offered the lowest starting salary, employed the lowest number of staffing strategies, and had the highest percentage of students in poverty relative to districts in the other region. HR representatives from districts in the region also reported facing more severe challenges with insufficient annual raises for recruitment, low base salaries, and losing teachers to districts that offer better working conditions and pay than other regions. Many of these same factors (i.e., insufficient annual raises, low base salary, and losing teachers to nearby higher-paying districts) were critical challenges for their teacher retention as well. For the Lowcountry region, inadequate housing for teachers represented a major recruitment challenge. They also had the highest percentage of vacancies and turnover. Almost all regions cited an insufficient pool of adequately credentialed teachers as challenging for their recruitment purposes.

THE POTENTIAL EFFECTIVENESS OF RRI

CERRA Report Findings

CERRA's (2020) annual supply and demand report indicates that 29 out of the 35 districts eligible for RRI funds during the 2019–2020 school year "reported some improvement compared to the previous year—fewer teachers leaving, fewer positions still vacant after the school year started, or both... Further data analysis showed that 27 rural districts experienced fewer teacher departures overall" (p. 6). This suggests a surface-level descriptive improvement of the outcomes for RRI funded districts, yet more rigorous analyses are needed to truly determine the program's impact. To look beyond descriptive improvement and each district's ratings of

TABLE 6.5 District Demographics and Challenges by South Carolina Regions

District Demographics	Vacancy	Turnover	Cumulative Instability	Number of Staffing Strategies Employed	Percent of Students in Poverty	Enrollment	Base Pay
Lowcountry Region	0.05	19.03	54.82	15.00	80.42	3,573.70	32,648.70
Midlands Region	0.03	17.23	46.41	17.00	79.91	5,962.67	32,783.78
Pee Dee Region	0.04	17.80	61.27	14.25	86.43	4,242.75	31,817.75
Upstate Region	0.00	16.80	60.19	17.50	70.71	1,829.00	33,234.03

Challenges With Recruitment	Insufficient Annual Raises	Insufficient Pool of Teachers With Appropriate Teaching Credentials	Inadequate Housing for Teachers in Local Community	Low Base Salary	Losing Teacher to Nearby Districts With Better Working Conditions	Losing Teachers to Nearby Districts With Higher Pay
Lowcountry Region	3.80	3.89	4.30	2.90	2.50	3.60
Midlands Region	2.91	4.09	3.36	3.27	3.09	3.64
Pee Dee Region	4.75	4.25	3.75	5.00	4.00	5.00
Upstate Region	2.00	4.50	3.50	1.50	1.50	1.50

Challenges With Retention	Insufficient Annual Raises	Low Base Salary	Losing Teachers to Nearby Districts With Higher Pay
Lowcountry Region	2.90	3.10	3.20
Midlands Region	2.36	2.91	3.27
Pee Dee Region	4.75	5.00	5.00
Upstate Region	2.00	2.00	2.00

Note: None of the sampled/RRI districts were in the Charlotte Region

effectiveness, we conducted a series of studies to examine the effect of RRI on teacher staffing outcomes.

Study 1: How Hard-to-Staff Rural School Districts Use State Funds to Address Teacher Shortages?

Tran and Smith (2021) employed a fixed-effects panel regression on 5 years of data (from 2010 to 2017), with controls for poverty, to gain a preliminary assessment of the potential effects of RRI on teacher turnover. The effect of RRI on recruitment was not determinable as the vacancy data lacked consistency and reliability for rigorous analysis. Furthermore, eligibility to receive RRI funding is based on district turnover. The analysis showed that within the timeframe, teacher turnover had grown annually. While RRI funding could mitigate some of that escalation, it was insufficient to negate the problem completely. In addition, the coefficient for RRI was negative but not statistically significant. Subgroup analysis suggests statistical significance for districts located in NCES classified city regions. One interpretation of this finding could be that RRI allows city districts to leverage their pre-existing resources and strategies better than other locales, especially high poverty rural districts that may not benefit from the added momentum boost from RRI because of their lack of core capacity to do so.

Furthermore, most districts spent their RRI funds on recruitment, which might explain why turnover has not been sufficiently addressed. That said, much of those efforts were spent on "band-aid" temporary solutions, such as paying international teacher fees. Furthermore, research has shown that teacher shortages originate primarily from teacher turnover (Ingersoll, 2001), so addressing recruitment without attuning to retention results in a constant repeat of the teacher replacement cycle because of the "leaky bucket" not being plugged.

Study 2: Do State-Level Teacher Staffing Initiatives Affect Teacher Employment in Hard-to-Staff Schools? Evidence From South Carolina

Tran et al. (2021) conducted a deeper and more rigorous quantitative analysis of the potential impact of RRI on teacher staffing outcomes. Specifically, their work sought to determine the causal effect of RRI on vacancies and retention through an Arellano-Bond maximum likelihood estimation approach. The authors expanded on Tran and Smith's (2021) work by including a decade worth of data (from 2008/2009 to 2018/2019), controlling for a host of control variables (i.e., geographic, economic, districts demographic such as student-teacher ratio and percentage of non-White students) with a methodological approach that addresses the autoregressive nature of the statistical model, given that districts' past teacher turnover rates determine eligibility for RRI fund receipt, which is being used to predict future teacher turnover (the outcome variable of interest). The results suggest that districts that received RRI funding saw a reduction of teacher turnover by 1%.

SUMMARY AND RECOMMENDATIONS

The current South Carolina teacher shortage has been described as a statewide "crisis" (Green, 2021). However, not all districts experience this shortage to the same degree. For instance, across six different measures of staffing difficulties (i.e., vacancy, turnover, 5-year average vacancy, 5-year average turnover, cumulative instability, and chronic instability), Hampton 2 school district is consistently ranked among the top two highest-need districts in each category. In fact, it is the only district that has experienced an annual teacher turnover rate that exceeds 30%, suggesting that the district faces severe teacher turnover.

Indeed, our findings suggest that districts vary in their needs and challenges, with districts in the Lowcountry and Pee Dee facing particularly unique and acute challenges associated with rural employment. For example, for the Lowcountry region, districts cited inadequate housing as a more severe recruitment challenge than other districts. The Pee Dee region offered the lowest starting teacher salaries, employed the least number of staffing strategies, and had the highest percentage of students in poverty relative to districts in the other region. Perhaps it is not a coincidence that this region is the birthplace of the nearly 3-decade-long *Abbeville v. South Carolina* (2014) school funding lawsuit (Tran, 2018).

According to our analysis, the state has been experiencing an annually increasing teacher turnover rate. However, districts that receive RRI funding appear to experience some mitigation (although it does not completely negate the overall escalating trend of teacher turnover). Based on the results summarized in the report, we suggest the following:

While, currently, districts' RRI funding requests can only be spent on a pre-approved list of staffing incentives, these incentives may or may not be evidence-based. Efforts should be made to update the lists to better align the incentives offered with strategies that are backed by empirical evidence, that is, they have been demonstrated to improve teacher staffing outcomes elsewhere, preferably in a similar context to the requesting district (although we acknowledge that the research base often may not be nuanced enough to find such an ideal match). For example, formal induction programs were rated as one of the most effective strategies, and mentoring was one of the most widely used practices. Despite this, districts are largely left to figure out how to execute mentoring strategies with limited funding. Centralizing state financial and knowledge support to highly valued, highly utilized, and empirically based practices are needed. HR capacity is a limiting factor for many districts implementing some talent strategies.

Approximately 60% of the responding districts reported using social media for data collection, whereas districts with more HR capacity were more likely to use social media. Given that social media recruitment is associated with relatively low costs, coupled with reports that 96% of job recruiters use social media for recruitment in the non-education world (Jobvite, 2015), it suggests a lot of untapped potential for proactive recruitment of the districts. The non-use of social media-based recruitment may result from a lack of personnel or technical capacity. Efforts should be made to enhance districts' online recruitment efforts to maximize their potential for success.

While the sample districts reported that RRI funding has been helpful, they also noted that they desired to offer more incentives but could not do so because of cost barriers. One district noted that the lack of assurance and guarantee for annual RRI funding makes it difficult to strategically plan how to use those funds for long-term improvement and initiatives that require more time investment (e.g., grow your own initiatives). Efforts should be made to ensure that RRI funded incentives are sufficient to make an impact and are sustainable/dependable. This means that funding must be substantive, and its receipt must be predictable for planning purposes. Adequacy of funds is particularly critical for high-poverty districts that cannot benefit from current funding supplement allocations because of their lack of core capacity to take advantage of them. More funding and attention are necessary to help these districts develop their core, although this should not come completely from RRI funds but also further state investment from the foundation funding formula.

As a growing number of districts become eligible for RRI funding, care must be taken to ensure that the highest-need districts are not shortchanged in this endeavor to increase the reach of the RRI support. While it is a noble endeavor to maximize the benefit to ensure more districts receive assistance, this is only the case if this does not blunt the potential impact RRI funding could have had for districts that experience the most severe staffing problems. Several districts have expressed concern about this very issue. Helping a larger number of districts in a smaller capacity is likely not as cost-effective as supporting a smaller number of needy districts in a strong and meaningful way. The state has attempted to address this issue by restricting eligibility so that districts within the top fifteen percent of wealth are ineligible for RRI, but this still leaves many districts eligible, which reduces each district's allotment. Ultimately, equity and equality are not synonymous (Tran, 2018), and those that need more support should not be treated the same as those that do not.

Districts should partner with outside agencies and organizations to further support their staffing dilemmas. For example, districts in the

Lowcountry region indicated that inadequate housing for their teachers was a major staffing problem. These districts could partner with the United States Department of Agriculture (USDA). USDA offers a guaranteed housing loan program with low-income limits, zero money down, and no private mortgage insurance. Many teachers in rural areas will likely qualify for the program, and if there are insufficient houses for teachers to live in the community, houses can be built. Because rural districts in particular often do not have the personnel capacity to work on these collaborations, the state could invest funding to support the development of these partnerships, which allows the state to help facilitate the provision of the staffing incentive to the district indirectly. In fact, the Pee Dee region of South Carolina has a consortium, the Pee Dee Education Center. Enhanced state involvement in leveraging and financially supporting similar consortiums could significantly address teacher staffing challenges more collectively as opposed to neighboring districts continuing to compete with each other.

This chapter has demonstrated some initial evidence concerning the potential positive impact of RRI funds for teacher staffing. More sustained funding, coupled with additional accountability to ensure the funds are allocated to evidence-based staffing practices, can improve the likelihood of a more substantive impact. Comprehensive research on the implementation and efficacy of policies meant to address teacher shortages is an important policy topic in the wake of teacher shortages across the country, especially in districts with chronically high turnover.

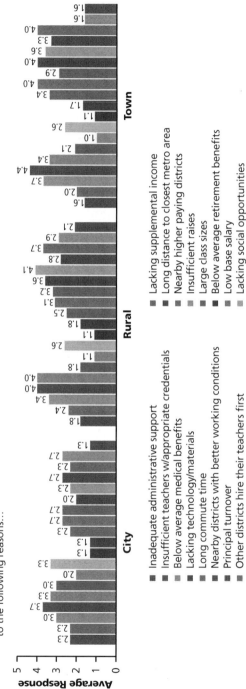

APPENDIX A

Challenges Recruiting Teachers Last 5 Years by Locale

On a scale of 1–5, identify the degree of challenges that your district experiences with recruiting teachers in the last 5 years due to the following reasons...

Legend:

- Inadequate administrative support
- Insufficient teachers w/appropriate credentials
- Below average medical benefits
- Lacking technology/materials
- Long commute time
- Nearby districts with better working conditions
- Principal turnover
- Other districts hire their teachers first
- Housing is lacking or insufficient
- Low academic performance
- Lacking supplemental income
- Long distance to closest metro area
- Nearby higher paying districts
- Insufficient raises
- Large class sizes
- Below average retirement benefits
- Low base salary
- Lacking social opportunities
- Higher paying non-education jobs

APPENDIX B
Percentage of District Teacher Vacancies, 2010–2018

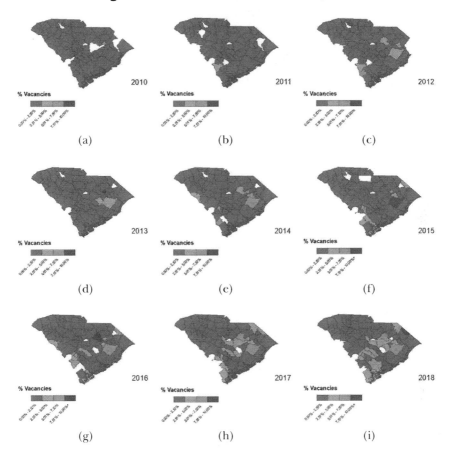

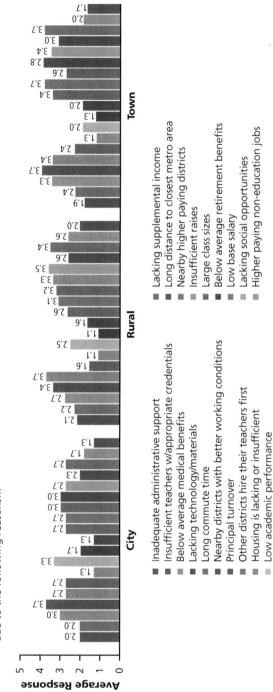

APPENDIX C

Top 5 Challenges Retaining Teachers Last 5 Years by Locale

On a scale of 1–5, identify the degree of challenge that your district experiences with retaining teachers in the last 5 years due to the following reasons....

APPENDIX D
Percentage of Teachers Not Returning From Prior Year by District, 2010–2017

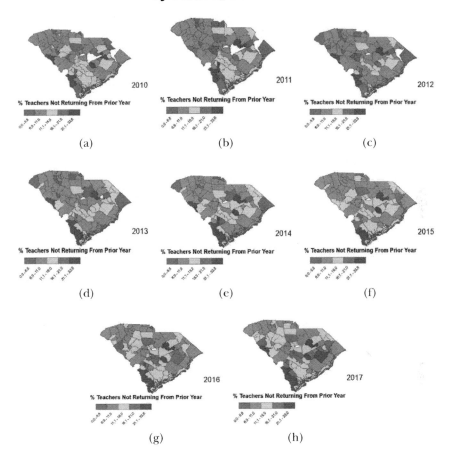

(a) (b) (c)

(d) (e) (f)

(g) (h)

APPENDIX E District Level Strategy Utilization Data

	Allendale	Anderson 4	Bamberg 2	Barnwell 19	Barnwell 45	Beaufort	Clarendon 1	Clarendon 2	Dillon 4	Dorchester 4	Edgefield	Fairfield	Hampton 2	Hampton 1	Jasper	Lee	Marion 10	Marlboro	McCormick	Orangeburg 5	Orangeburg 4	Orangeburg 3	Richland 1	Saluda	Sumter	Williamsburg	Williston/Barnwell 29
Signing Bonus	N	N	N	Y	N	N	N	Y	N	N	N	N	Y	N	N	N	N	N	N	Y	N	N	N	N	N	N	Y
Retention Bonus	N	N	N	Y	N	N	Y	N	N	N	N	Y	Y	N	N	N	N	N	N	Y	N	Y	Y	N	N	N	N
Teacher Referral Incentive	N	N	N	N	Y	N	N	N	N	N	N	N	N	N	N	N	N	N	N	Y	N	N	Y	N	N	N	N
Relocation Assistance	N	N	N	N	N	N	N	N	N	N	N	N	N	N	N	N	N	N	Y	Y	N	N	Y	N	N	N	N
Performance-Based (merit) Rewards	N	N	N	Y	N	N	N	N	N	N	N	N	N	N	Y	N	Y	N	N	N	N	N	N	N	N	N	N
Renting Housing Assistance	N	N	N	N	N	N	N	N	N	N	N	N	N	N	N	N	N	N	Y	N	N	N	N	N	N	N	N
Home Ownership Assistance	N	N	N	N	N	N	N	N	N	N	N	N	N	N	N	N	N	N	N	N	N	N	N	N	N	N	N
Hard-to-Staff Subject Area Incentives	Y	Y	N	N	Y	N	N	Y	N	Y	N	Y	Y	N	N	Y	Y	N	N	N	N	Y	Y	Y	N	Y	N
Hard-to-Staff School Incentives	N	N	N	Y	N	N	Y	N	Y	N	Y	Y	Y	Y	N	Y	N	N	N	N	Y	N	N	N	Y	N	N
Tuition/Assistance for Employees Seeking Full/Add-on Certification	N	Y	Y	Y	Y	N	Y	Y	Y	N	N	Y	Y	N	N	Y	Y	N	Y	Y	N	Y	Y	Y	Y	Y	N
Alternative Certification Fees Paid or Reimbursed	Y	Y	Y	Y	Y	N	Y	N	Y	Y	Y	Y	Y	N	N	Y	Y	N	Y	Y	N	Y	Y	Y	Y	N	Y

(continued)

APPENDIX E District Level Strategy Utilization Data (continued)

Strategy	Allendale	Anderson 4	Bamberg 2	Barnwell 19	Barnwell 45	Beaufort	Clarendon 1	Clarendon 2	Dillon 4	Dorchester 4	Edgefield	Fairfield	Hampton 2	Hampton 1	Jasper	Lee	Marion 10	Marlboro	McCormick	Orangeburg 5	Orangeburg 4	Orangeburg 3	Richland 1	Saluda	Sumter	Williamsburg	Williston/Barnwell 29
Credential or Certification Bonuses	N	Y	N	N	N	Y	N	Y	N	N	N	Y	N	N	N	N	N	Y	Y	Y	Y	N	Y	N	Y	Y	Y
Reimbursement of Non-Tuition Fees for Traditional Certification	Y	Y	Y	Y	Y	N	N	Y	Y	N	Y	Y	Y	N	N	Y	N	N	Y	N	N	Y	Y	Y	Y	Y	N
Apparel as an Incentive for Teacher Staffing	Y	N	N	N	Y	N	N	N	Y	N	N	Y	N	N	Y	Y	N	N	N	N	N	N	N	Y	Y	N	N
International Teacher Cost and Fees	N	N	Y	Y	Y	Y	N	Y	Y	Y	N	Y	Y	N	Y	Y	Y	Y	N	Y	Y	N	N	Y	Y	N	N
Additional Pay for Extra Leadership Responsibilities	Y	Y	N	Y	N	Y	Y	N	N	Y	Y	Y	Y	N	Y	N	Y	N	Y	N	N	Y	Y	Y	Y	Y	N
Transportation Subsidies for Commuting Teachers	N	N	Y	N	N	N	N	N	N	N	N	Y	N	N	N	Y	N	N	N	N	N	N	Y	Y	N	N	N
Streamline Hiring for Expedient Hiring	Y	Y	Y	Y	N	Y	Y	Y	N	Y	Y	Y	Y	Y	N	N	Y	N	Y	Y	Y	N	N	Y	N	N	N
Job Fair Participation	Y	Y	Y	Y	Y	Y	Y	Y	Y	Y	Y	Y	Y	Y	Y	Y	Y	Y	Y	Y	Y	Y	Y	Y	Y	Y	Y

(continued)

APPENDIX E   District Level Strategy Utilization Data (continued)

	Allendale	Anderson 4	Bamberg 2	Barnwell 19	Barnwell 45	Beaufort	Clarendon 1	Clarendon 2	Dillon 4	Dorchester 4	Edgefield	Fairfield	Hampton 2	Hampton 1	Jasper	Lee	Marion 10	Marlboro	McCormick	Orangeburg 5	Orangeburg 4	Orangeburg 3	Richland 1	Saluda	Sumter	Williamsburg	Williston/Barnwell 29
Teacher Recruitment Advertising	Y	N	Y	N	Y	N	N	Y	Y	Y	Y	Y	Y	Y	Y	N	Y	Y	Y	N	Y	Y	Y	Y	Y	Y	Y
Post With Job Banks and Database Listings	Y	Y	Y	Y	Y	Y	Y	N	Y	Y	Y	Y	Y	Y	Y	Y	Y	Y	Y	Y	Y	Y	Y	Y	Y	Y	Y
Collaborate With Colleges or Universities to Improve Recruitment/Retention	N	Y	N	Y	Y	Y	N	Y	Y	N	Y	Y	Y	N	Y	Y	Y	Y	Y	Y	Y	Y	Y	Y	Y	Y	Y
Grown-Your Own Initiatives	N	N	Y	N	Y	N	Y	Y	Y	N	Y	Y	Y	Y	N	Y	Y	N	Y	N	Y	Y	Y	Y	Y	Y	
Involve Communities to Welcome or Support New Teachers	Y	N	N	Y	Y	Y	N	Y	Y	Y	N	N	Y	N	Y	N	Y	N	Y	N	Y	Y	N	Y	Y	N	Y
Applicant Tracking Systems and Job Databases	Y	N	N	N	Y	Y	Y	Y	N	N	Y	Y	N	Y	Y	Y	N	N	Y	Y	Y	Y	Y	Y	Y	N	Y
Formal Mentoring Programs for New Teachers	Y	Y	Y	Y	Y	Y	Y	Y	Y	Y	Y	Y	Y	Y	Y	Y	Y	Y	Y	Y	Y	Y	Y	Y	Y	Y	Y
Teacher Appreciation Programs	Y	Y	Y	Y	Y	Y	N	Y	Y	N	Y	Y	Y	N	Y	Y	Y	N	Y	Y	Y	Y	Y	N	N	N	N
Social Media for Recruitment	Y	Y	Y	N	Y	Y	N	N	Y	N	N	Y	Y	N	Y	Y	Y	N	Y	Y	N	N	Y	Y	Y	Y	N
Teacher Professional Development	Y	Y	Y	Y	Y	Y	Y	Y	Y	Y	Y	Y	Y	Y	Y	Y	Y	Y	Y	Y	Y	Y	Y	Y	Y	Y	Y

NOTES

1   Note that despite the name of RRI, funds are not restricted solely for recruitment but also retention as well.
2   In FY21, eligibility for RRI funds also included the additional criteria that the fund receiving districts are not among the fifteen wealthiest districts per their index of tax paying ability (CERRA, 2020).

REFERENCES

Abbeville v. South Carolina. Opinion No. 27466. (November 12, 2014). https://cases.justia.com/south-carolina/supreme-court/2014-27466.pdf?ts.1415808227

Allensworth, E., Ponisciak, S., & Mazzeo, C. (2009). The schools teachers leave: Teacher mobility in Chicago public schools. *Consortium on Chicago School Research.*

Berry, B., Turchi, L., Johnson, D., Hare, D., Owens, D. D., & Clements, S. (2003). *The impact of high-stakes accountability on teachers' professional development: Evidence from the South.* Southeast Center for Teaching Quality.

Center for Educator Recruitment, Retention, & Advancement. (2020). *South Carolina annual educator supply and demand report (2020–21 school year).* https://www.cerra.org/uploads/1/7/6/8/17684955/2020-21_supply___demand_report.pdf

Clotfelter, C., Glennie, E., Ladd, H., & Vigdor, J. (2008). Would higher salaries keep teachers in high-poverty schools? Evidence from a policy intervention in North Carolina. *Journal of Public Economics, 92*(5–6), 1352–1370.

Feng, L., & Sass, T. R. (2018). The impact of incentives to recruit and retain teachers in "hard-to-staff" subjects. *Journal of Policy Analysis and Management, 37*(1), 112–135.

Green, M. (2021, November 8). SC educator advocacy groups to seek lawmakers' help to remediate teacher shortage "crisis." *WMBF News.* https://www.wmbfnews.com/2021/11/08/sc-educator-advocacy-groups-seek-lawmakers-help-remediate-teacher-shortage-crisis/

Holme, J. J., Jabbar, H., Germain, E., & Dinning, J. (2018). Rethinking teacher turnover: Longitudinal measures of instability in schools. *Educational Researcher, 47*(1), 62–75.

Ingersoll, R. M. (2001). Teacher turnover and teacher shortages: An organizational analysis. *American educational research journal, 38*(3), 499–534.

Jobvite. (2015). *The 2015 Jobvite recruiter nation survey.* https://www.jobvite.com/wp-content/uploads/2015/09/jobvite_recruiter_nation_2015.pdf

Liu, E., Johnson, S. M., & Peske, H. G. (2004). New teachers and the Massachusetts signing bonus: The limits of inducements. *Educational Evaluation and Policy Analysis, 26*(3), 217–236.

Lowe, J. M. (2006). Rural education: Attracting and retaining teachers in small schools. *Rural Educator, 27*(2), 28–32.

Prost, C. (2013). Teacher mobility: Can financial incentives help disadvantaged schools to retain their teachers? *Annals of Economics and Statistics, 111/112,* 171–191.

Springer, M. G., Swain, W. A., & Rodriguez, L. A. (2016). Effective teacher retention bonuses: Evidence from Tennessee. *Educational Evaluation and Policy Analysis, 38*(2), 199–221.

Tran, H. (2018). *Taking the mystery out of South Carolina school finance* (2nd ed.). ICPEL Publications.

Tran, H., Babaei, S., & Smith, D. (2022). *Do state level teacher staffing initiatives affect teacher employment in hard-to-staff schools? Evidence from South Carolina* [Working paper].

Tran, H., & Smith, D. (2020). The strategic support to thrive beyond survival model: An administrative support framework for improving student outcomes and addressing educator staffing in rural and urban high-needs schools. *Research in Educational Administration and Leadership,* 870–919. https://doi.org/10.30828/real/2020.3.8

Tran, H., & Smith, D. A. (2021). How hard-to-staff rural school districts use state funds to address teacher shortages. *Journal of Education Finance, 47*(2), 130–156.

CHAPTER 7

THE RELATIONSHIP BETWEEN TEACHER COMPENSATION AND EMPLOYMENT

Henry Tran
University of South Carolina

Sharda Jackson Smith
University of South Carolina Upstate

Inadequate teacher pay is identified as a major contributor to the discontent in the teaching profession (García & Weiss, 2020; Heubeck, 2021) and is often the focus of policy interventions and discourse aimed at mitigating teacher shortages (Tran & Smith, 2020). It was one of the foundational issues motivating the recent waves of nationwide teacher walkouts (Shapiro et al., 2018) and a major reason why many high potential individuals avoid the teaching profession altogether (Bacolod, 2007; Corcoran et al., 2004; Tran & Smith, 2019). In this chapter, we will analyze academic and public discourse to develop a comprehensive analysis of teacher compensation, emphasizing the state of South Carolina. We begin with the question of whether teachers are underpaid.

How Did We Get Here?, pages 141–178
Copyright © 2022 by Information Age Publishing
www.infoagepub.com

ARE TEACHERS UNDERPAID?

Teaching and low pay have been married in the public consciousness for as long as the profession has existed. Results from a recent poll suggest that the majority (75%) of Americans believe that teachers are underpaid (Goldstein & Casselman, 2018). This belief was validated by results from an analysis by *USA Today* that found beginning teachers "can't afford the median rent almost anywhere in the U.S." (Richards & Wynn, 2019, para. 6), with unaffordability being defined as having to spend more than 30% of one's salary on median rent costs after accounting for federal taxes. This estimate is conservative in that it does not account for other costs like student loan repayment and healthcare. In high-cost cities like San Francisco, new teachers would have to pay close to 90% of their salary for rent (Heubeck, 2021). In fact, in numerous states, teachers qualify for means-tested (i.e., low-income) public welfare services and benefits (Boser & Straus, 2014; Shapiro et al., 2018).

The issue of underpaid teachers exists in absolute terms and comparatively (i.e., to teachers before them and other professionals). For example, the economic returns to becoming a teacher have declined dramatically over time. According to research by the Economic Policy Institute (EPI), compared to other college-educated workers (after adjusting for education, experience, and geographic locale), public school teachers earned six percent less in 1996 than their non-teacher counterparts, with that gap growing to 19.2% in 2019 (Allegretto & Mishel, 2020). Even with similar or even slightly better benefits to their non-teaching counterparts, when considering the lower wages, the overall net teacher compensation penalty was still 10.2% in 2019. To make matters worse, as the purchasing power of teachers fell, so did their professional autonomy and discretion, despite the fact their work responsibilities and duties have increased significantly (Anderson & Cohen, 2015). Some of these duties include the expansion and intensification of duties both inside and outside of the classroom, such as increasing expectations to collaborate, collect, and analyze data, strictly adhering to frequently changing standards, policies and procedures, preparing class content preparation, increased focus on test preparation, engaging in regular communication with parents during online teaching amidst the pandemic and more (Bailey, 2000; Tran et al., 2020; Valli & Buese, 2007). As time goes on, teaching has become an increasingly unattractive career option for many, as reflected by the declining interest in the teaching profession as proxied by dwindling enrollment in teacher education programs and the rising departure of teachers from the profession (Center for Educator Recruitment, Retention, and Advancement, 2020).

With the economic opportunity cost to becoming a teacher rising over time and the growing alternative job opportunities (especially for women), there has been a decline in not only interest in the teaching profession in general, but also a sharp decline in teachers with traditionally identified higher qualifications such as higher standardized test scores and from the more selective undergraduate institutions (Bacolod, 2007; Corcoran et al., 2004). Research suggests that those who enter the teaching profession are more likely to have lower cognitive test scores than those who do not (Hanushek & Pace, 1995). For example, in Corcoran et al.'s (2004) longitudinal research, they found that the percentage of female teachers that ranked in the top 10% in national cognitive assessment scores declined from over 20% in 1964 to 11% in 2000. Because of increased job opportunities for women, many women in the top decile of achievement scores went on to other jobs such as computer specialists, accountants, lawyers, and managers. When both male and female teachers are considered, the decline remains, but is less dramatic given the larger share of women in teaching, at 18.9% for teachers in 1964 to 13.7% in 2000. Bacolod (2007) similarly found a decline across several input "quality" measures, including undergraduate institutions' selectivity and achievement scores for women in the teaching profession from 1960 to 1990. More recent work by Hanushek et al. (2019) suggests that the literacy abilities of American teachers are comparable to those of the average college non-teaching graduate and even those of teachers in the 24 countries they studied, but that their numerical abilities are below average as compared to both comparison groups.

In contrast, in countries where the average student performance on international exams (like the Programme for International Student Assessment) is high, like Singapore or Finland, teachers are recruited from the top third academically performing college students in their respective countries. In sum, numerous studies have linked qualifications such as the teachers' cognitive ability to student achievement test scores (Ehrenberg & Brewer, 1994; Goldhaber, 2007; Rockoff et al., 2011). Given that low pay has deterred teachers with higher cognitive ability from the profession, this illustrates a harmful linkage between low teacher pay for teachers and student outcomes.

It is also worth pointing out the inequity that manifests because of these patterns. Regardless of which of the most commonly defined "quality" metric is used, lower-scoring teachers are more likely to teach in high poverty/low performing schools with large concentrations of students of color (Goldhaber et al., 2015). The inequity is influenced and further compounded by the vicious cycle that often occurs when schools in these communities have lower tax revenue. This lower revenue results in fewer school resources, lower salaries, and more difficult working conditions for their teachers. This ultimately prompts more teacher turnover, forcing districts to spend more on teacher replacement costs, taking away from funds that could support students in the classroom (Tran, 2018; Tran & Smith, 2020).

Conservative estimates suggest that teacher turnover costs the nation 2.2 billion dollars a year. For South Carolina, this equates to about $16,901,022 to $36,787,310 per teacher replacement based on 2008 calculations by Richard Ingersoll (Haynes, 2014). These estimations were calculated over a decade ago, and the replacement costs are undoubtedly higher now. If higher salary offerings can reduce teacher turnover, it makes even less financial sense not to do so as higher retention mitigates turnover and replacement costs.

ARE TEACHERS OVERPAID?

While common knowledge would suggest teachers are underpaid, not everyone believes this is true. Some argue that because teachers have summer off, shorter workdays, strong job security, and generous medical and retirement benefits, they are actually "overpaid" (Greene & Winters, 2007; Richwine & Biggs, 2011). Henderson et al. (2020) implied that the uninformed [were] those who generally support higher wages for teachers. Their study found that "when asked to estimate average teacher salaries in their state, respondents' average guess came in at $41,987 [which was] 30% less than the actual average of $59,581 among [their] sample of educators" (para. 45). Researchers found that when the public is provided with information on average teacher salaries prevailing in their state, about half still believe pay should increase for teachers (Cheng et al., 2019).

Additionally, the U.S. Bureau of Labor Statistics (BLS; n.d.) reported that when compared to other industries, the unemployment rate for the education and health services sector was 4.2 (which is fairly consistent with the total average of 4.6 for all occupations) in October 2021, suggesting that the shortage is exaggerated and not as dramatic as often reported. At this point, you might wonder why there is a discrepancy in opinion between those who argue that teachers are "underpaid" compared to those who determine that they are "overpaid"? Well, to start, the reference points differ. Specifically, EPI compared the pay of teachers to the pay of other college graduates, while the study from the Heritage Foundation and American Enterprise Institute argued that a better comparison is with cognitive assessment scores (e.g., SAT and ACT scores) and that total compensation of teachers is 52% higher than market value based on professionals with comparable assessment scores (Richwine & Biggs, 2011). Delisle and Holt (2017) believed that "in order to justify a federal policy to pay teachers more, policymakers [need] to prove that higher pay would lead to better teachers and outcomes for students" (p. 48).

Let's unpack the "overpaid" argument further. First, while many teachers are technically not contractually obligated to work in the summer, they are also uncompensated if they do not. Furthermore, as Reilly (2018) explains,

"Many regularly work over the summer, planning curricula, taking continuing education and professional development courses, and running summer programs at their schools, making it a year-round job" (para. 23). Secondly, when coupled with research findings concerning the decline in cognitive test scores of incoming teachers into the profession across time, it is interesting that Richwine and Biggs (2011) argue that teachers are overpaid for their cognitive assessment scores. In contrast, many others have suggested that higher-paying alternative occupational opportunities have resulted in the migration of higher-scoring women away from teaching, especially since higher-scoring individuals are more sensitive to wages (Bacolod, 2007; Corcoran et al., 2004; Hanushek & Pace, 1995). The link between higher salary offerings and higher input "quality" for teachers has been supported by research. Leigh (2012), for instance, found that a one percent raise in salary improved the aptitude of the individuals taking teacher education courses by .6 percentile ranks. Research findings such as these suggest that higher salary offerings (and better working conditions) would attract more individuals with higher cognitive assessment scores back into teaching.

Across the world, teachers' cognitive abilities have been linked to their students' performance (Hanushek et al., 2019), and that low pay of the teaching profession deters those with higher cognitive abilities from entering the teaching profession (Hanushek & Pace, 1995). Consequently, the offering of higher teacher wages can improve students' academic performance. Shuffelton (2014) articulated that "traditional teaching pay scales, which reward years of service and credit-hours of professional development, exemplify [the] interpretation of how [skills develop] through time and ought to be recognized" (p. 27). The approximately 20% teacher pay penalty found by EPI (Allegretto & Mishel, 2020) is similar to the one found by Hanushek et al. (2019) when comparing the pay and skills American teachers have to their non-teaching counterparts in the United States. If teacher compensation was held constant (i.e., did not change) but their skills and abilities increased, it would only exacerbate the problem of underpaying teachers in American public schools.

Another issue of criticism from those who argue that teachers are overpaid is the number of hours teachers work. To account for differences in hours worked between teachers and non-teachers, Greene and Winters (2007) from the Manhattan Institute for Policy Research broke salaries down to hourly wages and compared teachers to non-teachers using data from the Bureau of Labor Statistics. They found that the average public school teacher salary (at $34.06/hr in 2005) is 36% higher than white-collar workers (e.g., computer programmers, urban planners) and 11% higher than professional workers (e.g., physical therapists, dental hygienists) based on an average of a 36.5-hour teacher workweek. Podolsky and Kini (2016) found that beginning teachers earn less after adjusting for the shorter work year than individuals with college degrees who enter other fields. If you have spoken to many teachers about the number of hours they put in a week, this number may seem suspiciously "off" to you.

Other more recent work has found this estimate of the average teacher workweek to be grossly underestimated. Research from the National Center for Education Statitstics (2021) "examine[d] whether teachers [were] required to help students with their academic or social and emotional needs outside regular school hours in public and private schools in the United States *before* the coronavirus pandemic" (National Center for Education Statistics, 2021, p. 1), citing that 16% of teachers in traditional public schools and 32% of teachers in charter public schools noted that they helped students with academic needs outside school hours. Additionally, a Bill and Melinda Gates Foundation (2012) report found teachers work closer to 10 hours and 40 minutes a day, with those who advise extracurricular clubs and sports clocking in closer to 11 hours and 20 minutes. A study by EPI noted that "what teachers make in weekly wages compared with similarly educated and experienced workers [moved] from –4.0% to –17.3% [and that] weekly wages have decreased $30 per week (adjusted for inflation), while all college graduates' average weekly wages have increased $124," with stark differences occurring in women and experienced teachers (Mishel et al., 2016).

According to the National Education Association's 2019–2020 Teacher Salary Benchmark Report (NEA, 2020), the starting average teacher salary across the nation is $41,163. In South Carolina, that figure is $37,550, ranking 40th among the 50 states and Washington DC. That said, raw salary numbers are not a great comparison given labor markets. While teachers across the nation earn approximately 20% less in weekly wages than other college graduates, in South Carolina, that amount is slightly less at 13.4% (Allegretto & Mishel, 2020). This smaller gap is likely due to the lower salaries in South Carolina across industries, influenced by the lower cost of living in the state compared to others across the country, such as New York and California. While the nominal average teacher salary has increased

TABLE 7.1 Estimated Average Annual Salary of Teachers in Public Elementary and Secondary Schools, by State: Selected Years, 1970–2020

	1970	1980	1990	2000	2010	2020
United States	**$8,626**	**$15,970**	**$31,367**	**$41,807**	**$55,370**	**$63,645**
Alabama	6,818	13,060	24,828	36,689	47,571	54,095
Alaska	10,560	27,210	43,153	46,462	59,672	70,877
Arizona	8,711	15,054	29,402	36,902	46,952	50,381

(continued)

TABLE 7.1   Estimated Average Annual Salary of Teachers in Public Elementary and Secondary Schools, by State: Selected Years, 1970–2020 (continued)

	1970	1980	1990	2000	2010	2020
Arkansas	6,307	12,299	22,352	33,386	46,700	49,822
California	10,315	18,020	37,998	47,680	68,203	84,659
Colorado	7,761	16,205	30,758	38,163	49,202	57,269
Connecticut	9,262	16,229	40,461	51,780	64,350	78,247
Delaware	9,015	16,148	33,377	44,435	57,080	64,853
Florida	8,412	14,149	28,803	36,722	46,708	48,800
Georgia	7,276	13,853	28,006	41,023	53,112	60,578
Hawaii	9,453	19,920	32,047	40,578	55,063	65,409
Idaho	6,890	13,611	23,861	35,547	46,283	52,875
Illinois	9,569	17,601	32,794	46,486	62,077	68,305
Indiana	8,833	15,599	30,902	41,850	49,986	51,508
Iowa	8,355	15,203	26,747	35,678	49,626	58,917
Kansas	7,612	13,690	28,744	34,981	46,657	52,554
Kentucky	6,953	14,520	26,292	36,380	49,543	53,907
Louisiana	7,028	13,760	24,300	33,109	48,903	50,217
Maine	7,572	13,071	26,881	35,561	46,106	54,967
Maryland	9,383	17,558	36,319	44,048	63,971	73,444
Massachusetts	8,764	17,253	34,712	46,580	69,273	83,622
Michigan	9,826	19,663	37,072	49,044	57,958	62,185
Minnesota	8,658	15,912	32,190	39,802	52,431	58,663
Mississippi	5,798	11,850	24,292	31,857	45,644	45,192
Missouri	7,799	13,682	27,094	35,656	45,317	50,817
Montana	7,606	14,537	25,081	32,121	45,759	52,135
Nebraska	7,375	13,516	25,522	33,237	46,227	55,267
Nevada	9,215	16,295	30,590	39,390	51,524	56,672
New Hampshire	7,771	13,017	28,986	37,734	51,443	60,003
New Jersey	9,130	17,161	35,676	52,015	65,130	76,376
New Mexico	7,796	14,887	24,756	32,554	46,258	54,256
New York	10,336	19,812	38,925	51,020	71,633	87,543
North Carolina	7,494	14,117	27,883	39,404	46,850	54,682
North Dakota	6,696	13,263	23,016	29,863	42,964	52,328
Ohio	8,300	15,269	31,218	41,436	55,958	59,713
Oklahoma	6,882	13,107	23,070	31,298	47,691	54,038
Oregon	8,818	16,266	30,840	42,336	55,224	67,685

(continued)

TABLE 7.1 Estimated Average Annual Salary of Teachers in Public Elementary and Secondary Schools, by State: Selected Years, 1970–2020 (continued)

	1970	1980	1990	2000	2010	2020
Pennsylvania	8,858	16,515	33,338	48,321	59,156	70,258
Rhode Island	8,776	18,002	36,057	47,041	59,686	67,323
South Carolina	6,927	13,063	27,217	36,081	47,508	51,485
South Dakota	6,403	12,348	21,300	29,071	38,837	49,220
Tennessee	7,050	13,972	27,052	36,328	46,290	51,862
Texas	7,255	14,132	27,496	37,567	48,261	57,091
Utah	7,644	14,909	23,686	34,946	45,885	52,819
Vermont	7,968	12,484	29,012	37,758	49,084	61,108
Virginia	8,070	14,060	30,938	38,744	50,015	53,933
Washington	9,225	18,820	30,457	41,043	53,003	72,965
West Virginia	7,650	13,710	22,842	35,009	45,959	50,238
Wisconsin	8,963	16,006	31,921	41,153	51,264	59,176
Wyoming	8,232	16,012	28,141	34,127	55,861	59,014

Note: Table adapted from the National Education Association (n.d.-b)

over time (see Table 7.1), the gap between teachers' average salary and the average income for those with a bachelor's degree has been growing for the last decade in the Palmetto state, as can be seen in Figure 7.1 (Rockefeller Institute of Government, n.d.).

Historically there is an assumption that teachers have spectacular benefits, but those benefits are no longer as attractive as they once were. For instance, most states have underfunded pensions (The Pew Charitable Trusts, 2018). Approximately half of all teachers are estimated to receive no pension at all, given stipulations such as the requirement of pension recipients to stay in the same state to collect the pension (Aldeman & Rotherham, 2014). Various other states (e.g., Iowa and Wisconsin) have passed laws to dramatically reduce collective bargaining rights for teachers and/or reduce their benefits, which has resulted in a decrease in median teacher salaries and benefits and increased teacher turnover (Madland & Rowell, 2017). Yet, signs that conditions may be changing in certain regions of the country surface, such as the case in Connecticut. The NRIG noted that when considering state teacher salary to income metrics, "Connecticut teachers made the largest gains in the last decade with a 16.9% increase. In 2017, they earned 97% of the average bachelor's salary compared to 80% in 2007."

Notwithstanding the reported average pay that prevails across the states that are subject to regional inflation and generally ticks upward over time (see Figure 7.2, Table 7.2, Table 7.3), teachers continue to protest over pay

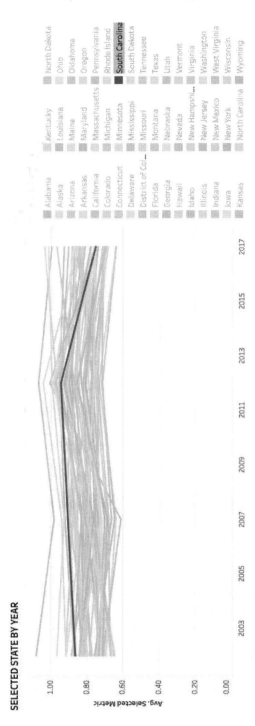

Figure 7.1 Teacher salary trends, 2002–2017. *Data Source:* U.S. Bureau of Labor Statistics, occupational employment statistics, https://www.bls.gov/oes/ & U.S. census bureau, current population survey, https://www.census.gov/programs-survey/cps/data -detail.html

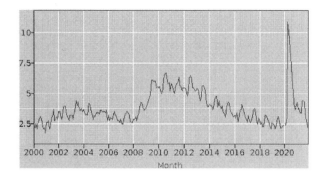

Figure 7.2 Unemployment rate for education and health services (private wage and salary workers), 2000 to 2021. *Note:* Figure adapted from the Bureau of Labor Statistics's Labor Force Statistics Current Population Survey (LNU04032240), https://data.bls.gov/timeseries/LNU04032240?amp%253bdata_tool=XGtable& output_view=data&include_graphs=true

TABLE 7.2 States With the Highest Employment for Elementary School Teachers, Except Special Education

State	Employment	Employment (per thousand jobs)	Annual Mean Wage
California	156,920	9.55	$85,110
Texas	131,370	10.85	$56,760
New York	92,700	10.67	$84,380
Florida	73,840	8.75	$57,520
Illinois	57,880	10.29	$66,140

Note: Table adapted from the U.S. Bureau of Labor Statistics (n.d.)

TABLE 7.3 States With Highest Salary for Elementary School Teachers, Except Special Education

State	Employment	Employment (per thousand jobs)	Annual Mean Wage
California	156,920	9.55	$ 85,110
Massachusetts	29,900	8.93	$84,810
New York	92,700	10.67	$84,380
Connecticut	15,000	0.99	$79,610
District of Columbia	4,150	0.61	$78,840

Note: Table adapted from the U.S. Bureau of Labor Statistics (n.d.)

(Rudick & Dannels, 2020; Wright, 2020) because increases have moved at a negligible pace, with some trends receding from the desired direction. Lytle (2013) noted that a Philadelphia School Reform Commission voted to "negotiate a teacher contract which would dramatically change wages and working conditions for teachers [by imposing] a 15% salary cut, reduce[ing] benefits, eliminat[ing] seniority provisions and transfer rules, and increase[ing] class size" (p. 2).

Regardless of what researchers or their statistics may suggest concerning whether teachers are under or overpaid, the perspective of teachers and potential teachers who might consider the profession matter the most because they are the ones who are ultimately most directly affected by teacher pay. If teachers and potential teachers are telling us the pay is inadequate and low, which prompts them to avoid or leave the profession, we should probably listen. Moreover, from a supply and demand perspective, if the supply is insufficient to meet the demand, higher pay is justified to increase the supply. Consequently, in the next section, we will review the relationship between teacher pay and employment.

WHAT IS THE RELATIONSHIP BETWEEN TEACHER PAY AND EMPLOYMENT?

The compensation challenges endured by teachers have captured the public's attention, and the media has provided a forum for their voices on these issues. Take, for instance, *Time's* spotlight (Reilly, 2018) of the testimonies of several teachers describing their financial struggles. One such teacher was Hope Brown from Kentucky, who, despite being a U.S. history teacher with a master's degree and 16 years of experience, shared that she had to donate plasma twice in a week and sell her clothes, on top of working a secondary evening job manning the metal detectors and security at the local arena, just to barely make enough to pay her bills. Another was Rosa Jimenez, a teacher in California who shares a bed with her young child in a small apartment and spends $1,000 on supplies, but faces constant job and financial uncertainty, having been laid off twice already due to budget cuts. Then there is NaShonda Cooke, a 20-year teacher from North Carolina who cannot afford to fix her car, pay a copay at the doctor's office, or save for her child's college education. In a statement provided to Edweek, Carr, a Black male teacher, succinctly stated, "Almost on a weekly basis I think about doing something else because of the money" (Heubeck, 2021, para. 2).

The fact that teacher pay matters for teacher employment is not only understood from a general perspective through anecdotes, conversations with educators, and communication from the media regularly (Heubeck, 2021; Reilly, 2018), but it has also been validated by studies that have consistently confirmed that relationship (Marvel et al., 2007; Tran & Smith, 2019). Hendricks' (2015) research showed that higher base salaries could attract and retain more experienced teachers, and more teaching experience has been linked to stronger student achievement (Ladd & Sorenson, 2017). The relationship between experience and student achievement is strongest in teachers' initial years (Boyd et al., 2008; Winters et al., 2012) when teachers' employment decisions are most sensitive to salary (Tran & Buckman, 2020).

Beyond attracting individuals to the teaching profession and particular districts, teacher wages also influence retention. In general, higher wages are related to longer retention (Murnane & Olsen, 1990), and those who leave their employer for other school districts often leave for positions that offer higher compensation (Marvel et al., 2007). Case in point, in a March 2021 survey of 1,000 nationally representative educators (approximately 700 teachers and 300 school leaders), the Edweek Research Center found that more than half of the teachers indicated they were "somewhat or very likely" to leave teaching in the next two years. Seven out of ten school leaders indicated pay raises would help reduce teacher turnover, and 57% of teachers suggested it would reduce their likelihood of leaving the profession in the next 2 years (Loewus, 2021). From an empirical perspective, Hanushek et al. (2004) found that a pay increase of 10% reduces the likelihood of teachers leaving a school by one to four percentage points. The link between teacher pay and retention is especially critical because research has suggested that the major source of teacher shortages originate from teacher turnover (Ingersoll, 2001), even though attention is often directed at teacher recruitment.

The suggestion of using salary to improve teacher recruitment and retention may, on the surface, seem misaligned with the research that has found teachers are often primarily motivated to teach because of altruistic reasons, such as making an impact on student lives (Dos Santos, 2019; Morice & Murray, 2003), and not monetary reasons such as compensation. However, from the perspective of Maslow's hierarchy of needs (Maslow & Lewis, 1987), it makes perfect sense. According to Maslow's theory, basic motivational needs such as physiological and safety needs must be met before individuals can be motivated to reach higher-order needs.[1] Like any individual living in modern society, teachers have bills and living expenses to pay for that require appropriate compensation. Many teachers also have their own children that they must provide for and should not be put in a position where they constantly have to prioritize their students' needs relative to their own children's needs. With low relative wages, teachers are 30% more likely to work a second job than their non-teacher college-educated counterparts (Startz, 2018). Secondary teachers are more likely to do so than elementary school teachers. Almost 20% of those second jobs are outside the teachers' school system, such as serving as Uber or Lyft drivers, supermarket cashiers, or working in Amazon Warehouses (Hampson, 2018; Richards & Wynn, 2019).

In addition, most teachers have gone through education, training, and certification that are often associated with a professional career, and there is a societal expectation that such investment in time and financial resources to become a professional yields appropriate economic returns. Perhaps most important of all, like in many other places, in American society, the wages associated with a profession typically signal the amount of respect that profession garners. Consequently, low teacher pay connotes low prestige and respect for teaching, which has implications for interest in the teaching profession.

Tran and Smith's (2019) study on teacher recruitment support that low wages are perceived to represent a lack of respect for the teaching profession and serve as a deterrent for those who may otherwise consider teaching. Specifically, they surveyed over 400 college students at a regional institution in South Carolina and conducted follow-up interviews with 10 of them to determine the influence of financial motivators in their consideration to teach in hard-to-staff schools, and their results yielded several noteworthy findings. First, it further substantiated the importance of base salary and retirement benefits for teaching in the hard-to-staff rural context. While respondents were willing to teach for a lower starting salary than their current chosen non-teaching related occupation, the caveat was that a minimum salary threshold (i.e., $47,606.60) had to be met. That threshold was 36% above the state's average beginning teacher salary at the time of the study. Unfortunately, teacher pay often does not meet the threshold the students have in their mind, and respondents perceived the work input to be incommensurate with the pay. As one business management and marketing major put it:

> Traditionally it is perceived that teachers are not paid enough [...] they feel undervalued and underpaid. I looked into teaching as a career pretty strongly [...] and every person I talked to, be it a grade school teacher or college professor, told me the same thing—that it was a lot of work, it was an unstable work environment, and the pay was very poor for the amount of work that you put in. (Tran & Smith, 2019, p. 161)

Similarly, a female biology major explained, "The thing that is keeping me out of teaching is how little they are paid and how undervalued they are" (Tran & Smith, 2019, p. 161). One respondent even went as far as admitting that she avoids the teaching profession because she did not want to let her parents down, that they would say she could have been "more" with her potential. To these respondents, low pay and a lack of value and respect for teaching are intricately connected.

Respondents noted how the lack of respectability of the profession deterred them from teaching, and their perception that teachers receive low pay contributes to that lack of respectability. Indeed, the issue of the teachers' perception concerning the disrespect they feel originates from multiple levels (e.g., from micro levels like parents and administrators to macro levels like government and policymakers) and often include teachers being told how and what to teach, without their input being valued or considered substantively, and having their creativity and resources stripped away over the years (Tran, 2018). Many of these issues have been publicized by media coverage on the issue of teacher strikes and turnovers (Anderson & Cohen, 2015; Hampson, 2018).

Goldstein (2015) explains that the lack of respect and low pay teachers' experience originates from the historical feminization of the teaching profession. A major downside of this feminization is "because of sexism, the political class would be unlikely to respect and thus fund a profession dominated by women" (p. 41). Teachers were seen as "mother teachers" who performed motherly duties in the classroom. Their profession was not seen as a career, but rather as a "romanticized calling." Consequently, this was used to justify teachers' low pay for their work. Interestingly enough, this has been so ingrained in the consciousness of society that even some teachers see their job as almost missionary-like, with an expectation of self-sacrifice. In their eyes, individuals who do not teach because of the low pay probably are not the type of teachers we want in schools anyway. As discussed earlier, research does not tend to support these theories.

WHAT IS THE PAY STRUCTURE LIKE FOR TEACHERS?

Most public school teachers are paid by the traditional salary schedule that pays teachers based primarily on their years of experience and education level (Springer, 2019). An intricate balance, state teacher salary schedule structures vary extensively with establishing a minimum threshold for local education that is often linked to statute-based funding. Frequently, states mandate the reporting of beginning and average pay to foster a competitive salary distribution, with a high emphasis placed on incentives (Grissom & Strunk, 2012). Recognizing the will to capture the education market that chooses to know the salary bandwidth of their tenure, the minimum and maximum salary amount for teachers hinge on expertise, with the most common indicators being, as mentioned earlier, years of experience and highest degree level (De Brey et al., 2021). Attempting to establish equality in pay for teachers (Horn, 2017; Shuffelton, 2014), a little less than half of the states use a salary schedule to attract teachers (Aragon, 2016). Not to be confused with district-level salary schedules, states choose between whether to establish a state schedule, a minimum salary requirement, pay for performance salaries/bonuses, diversified pay for shortage areas, or a combination of these structures (which excludes Alaska, Arizona, Connecticut,

Kansas, Nebraska, Montana, Pennsylvania, Rhode Island, and Vermont; Aragon, 2016). Other criteria for teachers receiving higher salary range from the number of credit hours taken post-advanced degree to whether a teacher is National Board for Professional Teaching certified.

While the teacher salary schedule structure encourages uniformity of teacher pay within a school district based on common criteria (typically highest degree attained and experience), school district teacher salary offerings can vary depending on their pay structure. To illustrate, districts can lead (pay more than), match (pay the same as), or lag (pay less than) the labor market's average salary offerings. According to Tran's (2017) 3-year study of salary offerings of South Carolina public school districts, districts that matched the labor market for teachers with a bachelor's degree (BA) had more students reach proficiency or above at science than districts that lagged the labor market. Tran and Buckman's (2020) research in the same context found that districts that front-loaded their salary schedules (i.e., pay higher percent raises for beginning teachers) saw an increase in the percent of classes taught by teachers federally identified as "highly qualified teachers" (i.e., they hold a bachelor's degree, have full state certification or licensure and demonstrated competence in the subject they teach). Finally, Figlio (1997) found that districts that offered higher teacher salaries attracted teachers from more selective colleges.

Scores of research have shown that teachers are not interchangeable. Differences in the quality of teachers impact student achievement, although teacher quality is difficult to measure and often not readily observable in traditional input measures of teacher pay such as experience (typically beyond a teacher's initial teaching years) and educational attainment (outside of teachers majoring in the content they teach; Rivkin et al., 2005; Rockoff, 2004). Consequently, a contingent of people argue that teacher pay must be reformed and that teachers should be paid based on performance. They believe only effective teachers should be paid more.

Supporters of performance pay efforts argue that it is not only a way to increase student achievement, but it is also beneficial for the recruitment and retention of high-quality teachers (Glazerman et al., 2011; Shifrer et al., 2017). The argument is the following: When pay is linked to performance, it will increase the motivation of teachers to excel (Springer, 2019). Furthermore, it is also argued that performance pay can have an effect on changing the composition of teachers by attracting high potential professionals into teaching based on their potential higher salary earnings (Bowen & Mills, 2017), given that these individuals resist working at institutions that do not pay employees based on performance-based differences (Erikkson et al., 2009). While there is much enthusiasm for paying teachers based on performance, the vast majority of experimental and non-experimental research on the topic has not found the work to be substantively influential in improving student outcomes (Imberman & Lovenheim, 2015; Marsh et al., 2011; Springer et al., 2012), or increasing the supply of quality teachers (Bowen & Mills, 2017; Goodman & Turner, 2013).

Performance pay programs are not a monolith, and how they are structured and implemented will greatly affect its potential success. Major barriers to the success of performance pay initiatives include the lack of consensus concerning how to define teacher quality (Tran, 2018), the lack of validity of current measures of teacher-value added test scores (Corcoran, 2010), insufficient funds to pay out performance initiatives, or funding incentive pay by lowering base pay of other teachers. The latter negatively affects their take-home income and other areas such as pensions, as well as loan and mortgage applications (Greene, 2019). More to the point, performance pay should not be a substitute for addressing the problem of inadequate teacher base pay (Shapiro et al., 2018). The goal of performance pay systems should not be to save money, and recommendations to use performance pay for budget-cutting purposes are inappropriate.

While reformers look to performance pay as the future of teacher compensation (Springer, 2019), we must know where we came from. Consequently, the next section discusses the historical changes to teacher pay relative to teacher employment.

HOW HAS TEACHER PAY AND EMPLOYMENT CHANGED OVER TIME?

The publication of the controversial Coleman Report (Coleman et al., 1966) and the corresponding rebuke of its sentiment by educational researchers prompted the field to calibrate its stance on equitable funding practices in public education (Atteberry & McEachin, 2020). The report claimed that deep systemic flaws existed in public education, attributed to certain inputs and outputs. Using Coleman Report data, studies attempted to evaluate teacher pay by analyzing salary schedules and income (e.g., Owen, 1971). The teacher salary schedule was developed in 1921 to allocate pay to teachers strictly based on experience and the highest degree held. By doing so, the new system of pay distribution eliminated much of the past pay discrimination that frequently occurred because of nepotism, race, gender, and grade level bias (Goldstein, 2015; Springer, 2019). As a result, teacher pay became highly predictable, uniform, and standardized for teachers receiving the money and distributing districts. In traditional public schools, personnel salaries and benefits comprised approximately 80% of the operating budget, with those expenditures funded by dollars that relied heavily on local property tax revenue (Tran, 2018).

Sensing that funding disparities were prevalent beyond teacher salary, researchers continued to investigate metrics involving students and other related features of the education environment, sometimes in union with teacher salary (Towers, 1992). The National Commission on Excellence in Education published a groundbreaking report in the early 1980s alleging an ever-present deficit in the average teacher salary per year and that many teachers were required to supplement their income (Gardner et al., 1983). Afterward, research on the extent to which teachers were underpaid remained (Abamu, 2018; Jacoby & Nitta, 2012), prompting lingering watchdog reporting of teacher salary and government regulation. Since then, the nation has observed fluctuation in teacher salary advancement. The Nelson A. Rockefeller Institute of Government (NRIG, n.d.) noted:

- The five states with the highest average teacher salary change (2002–2016) in the nation include Alaska, Oregon, Massachusetts, Virginia, and Connecticut.
- The five states with the least average teacher salary change (2002–2016) in the nation include Oklahoma, West Virginia, Alabama, Indiana, and Arizona.
- Alaska's average teacher salary increased by more than $27,000 from 2002 to 2017, while Indiana's increased $6,900.

Understanding that salary is usually unique to the district from which a teacher instructs, educator worth is highly dependent on the balance between state legislation and local ability to fund educators, including a local preference to establish and maintain an aggressive salary scale. To some, the salary schedule is restrictive, generalizes all teaching experience as having the same value, and because other indicators are usually reserved for salary supplements, its definition of expertise is revered as too simplistic (see Table 7.4). It is also important to note that ideas established by state policy about funding mechanisms do not require state funding for local jurisdictions; a state can mandate an increase in teacher pay without providing additional funding. Typically, states at least allow for a redirection of funding or raise taxes to support local school districts when these policies are mandated. Suppose the state does not provide additional funding. In that case, districts view these policies as a loss of fiscal control, arguing that schedules are essentially unfunded mandates for local districts and are slow to be updated (Griffith, 2016).

With this in mind, a distinct atmosphere was created by implementing specific pieces of federal legislation. In 2001, the No Child Left Behind Act (NCLB) was enacted, strengthening teacher accountability and increasing monitoring pressure for educators. Researchers argue that accountability policies prompted a strand of educators to migrate to more affluent

TABLE 7.4 Average Base Salary for Full-Time Teachers in Public Elementary and Secondary Schools, by Highest Degree Earned and Years of Teaching Experience: 1990–91 Through 2017–18

Years of Full- and Part-Time Teaching Experience[a]	Number of Full-Time Teachers	Base Salary[b] (current dollars) Highest Degree Earned				
		All Teachers[c]	Bachelor's Degree	Master's Degree	Education Specialist[d]	Doctor's Degree
1	2	3	4	5	6	7
1990–91 Total	2,336,750 (20,958)	$31,330 (97)	$27,740 (103)	$34,960 (125)	$37,230 (391)	$40,070 (817)
1 year or less	80,770 (2,952)	21,640 (182)	21,170 (172)	25,330 (772)	‡ (†)	‡ n/a
2 years	80,330 (2,981)	21,990 (166)	21,590 (157)	24,650 (527)	‡ (†)	‡ n/a
3 years	77,380 (2,796)	22,770 (189)	22,170 (179)	25,980 (760)	‡ (†)	‡ n/a
4 years	75,400 (3,346)	23,690 (228)	23,090 (232)	25,570 (425)	30,280 (1,601)	‡ n/a
5 years	77,130 (3,280)	24,710 (182)	23,840 (216)	26,530 (394)	29,280 (1,325)	‡ n/a
6–9 years	229,950 (6,518)	26,180 (114)	24,650 (135)	28,570 (215)	29,810 (765)	30,060 (1,551)
10–14 years	406,650 (7,245)	29,120 (120)	26,980 (156)	31,240 (217)	32,940 (601)	35,430 (1,565)
15–19 years	459,540 (7,922)	33,350 (191)	30,580 (234)	35,110 (251)	37,460 (836)	39,890 (1,495)
20–24 years	404,020 (8,354)	36,750 (214)	33,750 (280)	38,330 (243)	39,190 (840)	43,500 (1,387)
25–29 years	233,620 (6,196)	38,070 (279)	34,960 (358)	39,730 (362)	42,320 (1,106)	43,070 (2,031)
30–34 years	106,160 (4,942)	38,430 (379)	34,840 (461)	40,510 (450)	41,460 (1,591)	‡ n/a
35 years or more	35,790 (2,404)	39,180 (744)	34,650 (1,013)	41,430 (983)	48,740 (3,767)	‡ n/a
1999–2000 Total	2,742,210 (20,301)	$39,900 (118)	$35,310 (116)	$44,730 (174)	$48,740 (438)	$48,180 (1,418)
1 year or less	143,610 (4,949)	29,090 (179)	28,110 (160)	33,170 (543)	33,680 (1,012)	‡ n/a
2 years	150,130 (5,012)	29,420 (186)	28,560 (178)	32,990 (423)	‡ (†)	‡ n/a

(continued)

TABLE 7.4 Average Base Salary for Full-Time Teachers in Public Elementary and Secondary Schools, by Highest Degree Earned and Years of Teaching Experience: 1990–91 Through 2017–18 (continued)

Years of Full- and Part-Time Teaching Experience[a]	Number of Full-Time Teachers	All Teachers[c]	Bachelor's Degree	Master's Degree	Education Specialist[d]	Doctor's Degree
1	2	3	4	5	6	7
3 years	144,250 (4,943)	30,270 (150)	29,240 (190)	34,020 (298)	34,050 (1,629)	‡ (n/a)
4 years	127,330 (5,613)	31,810 (249)	30,540 (213)	35,380 (735)	33,960 (1,089)	‡ (n/a)
5 years	121,310 (4,583)	32,220 (272)	30,940 (273)	34,750 (412)	37,240 (2,225)	‡ (n/a)
6–9 years	387,160 (8,145)	34,640 (154)	32,350 (173)	37,480 (227)	39,980 (753)	39,610 (2,802)
10–14 years	375,830 (6,514)	38,710 (254)	35,510 (364)	41,430 (330)	44,560 (1,022)	43,370 (2,096)
15–19 years	325,840 (7,677)	42,940 (222)	39,930 (334)	45,380 (341)	47,150 (942)	46,470 (1,481)
20–24 years	361,420 (7,306)	45,300 (252)	41,160 (290)	48,260 (392)	47,970 (874)	47,150 (1,410)
25–29 years	349,650 (7,057)	48,550 (267)	44,540 (320)	50,400 (390)	53,330 (743)	60,790 (2,519)
30–34 years	199,420 (5,990)	51,910 (375)	47,040 (601)	53,940 (435)	56,590 (1,381)	‡ (n/a)
35 years or more	56,270 (3,030)	50,640 (635)	46,440 (1,234)	52,270 (878)	57,160 (2,395)	‡ (n/a)
2007–08 Total	3,114,690 (41,111)	$49,630 (203)	$43,650 (220)	$54,810 (281)	$58,420 (722)	$59,150 (1,620)
1 year or less	181,340 (10,618)	37,660 (296)	36,210 (301)	42,370 (855)	45,930 (3,571)	‡ (n/a)
2 years	176,370 (10,008)	38,420 (365)	36,860 (372)	42,230 (792)	46,720 (4,534)	‡ (n/a)
3 years	174,150 (8,827)	39,720 (344)	37,570 (366)	44,210 (627)	51,270 (4,903)	‡ (n/a)
4 years	172,750 (7,679)	41,000 (413)	38,440 (416)	45,090 (640)	48,460 (2,574)	‡ (n/a)
5 years	147,760 (7,678)	42,370 (515)	39,200 (449)	46,170 (883)	47,630 (3,308)	‡ (n/a)

Base Salary[b] (current dollars) — Highest Degree Earned

(continued)

TABLE 7.4 Average Base Salary for Full-Time Teachers in Public Elementary and Secondary Schools, by Highest Degree Earned and Years of Teaching Experience: 1990–91 Through 2017–18 (continued)

Years of Full- and Part-Time Teaching Experience[a]	Number of Full-Time Teachers	Base Salary[b] (current dollars)				
		Highest Degree Earned				
		All Teachers[c]	Bachelor's Degree	Master's Degree	Education Specialist[d]	Doctor's Degree
1	2	3	4	5	6	7
6–9 years	546,350 (12,759)	46,020 (265)	41,640 (372)	49,860 (500)	51,030 (1,128)	52,390 (2,491)
10–14 years	515,020 (14,623)	49,920 (369)	44,880 (443)	52,920 (544)	56,120 (1,259)	60,920 (4,249)
15–19 years	351,510 (13,286)	54,550 (465)	48,000 (549)	58,590 (684)	59,930 (1,397)	63,190 (3,501)
20–24 years	297,710 (12,318)	57,570 (591)	52,550 (811)	60,530 (739)	63,620 (1,960)	66,600 (6,196)
25–29 years	236,280 (9,186)	59,890 (676)	54,090 (822)	63,460 (1,025)	64,410 (2,199)	‡ n/a
30–34 years	208,120 (9,566)	60,940 (656)	55,080 (1,007)	63,380 (848)	66,540 (2,552)	71,350 (4,668)
35 years or more	107,310 (6,873)	62,530 (1,002)	55,230 (1,467)	65,570 (1,488)	67,740 (2,872)	‡ n/a
2011–12 Total	3,139,250 (38,342)	$53,070 (213)	$46,340 (225)	$57,830 (352)	$59,680 (642)	$60,230 (1,775)
1 year or less	109,060 (6,116)	38,310 (483)	37,140 (496)	41,650 (1,134)	45,970 (4,231)	‡ n/a
2 years	113,470 (5,654)	39,490 (348)	38,180 (399)	42,690 (695)	41,470 (2,831)	‡ n/a
3 years	127,030 (7,212)	41,170 (451)	38,950 (494)	45,250 (786)	48,160 (2,529)	‡ n/a
4 years	148,720 (8,316)	42,530 (422)	39,900 (423)	45,780 (653)	46,530 (2,181)	‡ n/a
5 years	169,220 (8,284)	43,420 (805)	40,020 (398)	47,220 (1,647)	46,960 (1,639)	‡ n/a
6–9 years	597,980 (16,175)	47,820 (322)	43,020 (334)	50,960 (464)	51,940 (1,177)	51,330 (2,288)
10–14 years	655,560 (17,292)	54,370 (390)	48,360 (542)	57,750 (553)	57,280 (1,075)	60,940 (2,880)

(continued)

TABLE 7.4 Average Base Salary for Full-Time Teachers in Public Elementary and Secondary Schools, by Highest Degree Earned and Years of Teaching Experience: 1990–91 Through 2017–18 (continued)

Years of Full- and Part-Time Teaching Experience[a]	Number of Full-Time Teachers	Base Salary[b] (current dollars)				
		All Teachers[c]	Highest Degree Earned			
			Bachelor's Degree	Master's Degree	Education Specialist[d]	Doctor's Degree
1	2	3	4	5	6	7
15–19 years	435,300 (15,477)	58,800 (600)	51,410 (759)	62,410 (809)	65,390 (1,611)	63,350 (3,950)
20–24 years	312,010 (10,430)	60,880 (599)	54,230 (788)	65,160 (845)	64,460 (1,666)	66,930 (4,546)
25–29 years	230,570 (10,871)	63,300 (778)	56,430 (1,023)	67,330 (1,246)	67,840 (1,906)	‡ (n/a)
30–34 years	153,840 (9,375)	65,770 (796)	58,570 (1,080)	69,180 (1,117)	70,100 (4,586)	‡ (n/a)
35 years or more	86,470 (5,303)	63,570 (953)	59,740 (1,472)	66,250 (1,136)	65,560 (2,379)	‡ (n/a)
2017–18 Total	3,323,200 (22,973)	$57,950 (174)	$49,890 (164)	$63,120 (240)	$66,510 (511)	$69,520 (1,220)
1 year or less	230,500 (6,131)	44,150 (327)	42,130 (317)	49,310 (692)	49,480 (1,197)	50,100 (2,205)
2 years	171,770 (4,940)	46,000 (337)	42,890 (330)	51,180 (669)	52,600 (1,786)	‡ (n/a)
3 years	154,040 (4,999)	47,370 (370)	44,350 (398)	51,440 (598)	52,690 (2,710)	‡ (n/a)
4 years	159,610 (4,784)	47,320 (337)	44,180 (345)	50,950 (513)	55,590 (2,471)	‡ (n/a)
5 years	144,770 (4,745)	48,780 (334)	45,070 (359)	52,180 (588)	51,430 (1,404)	‡ (n/a)
6–9 years	452,970 (8,407)	51,380 (242)	46,410 (277)	54,950 (358)	57,690 (1,035)	60,220 (3,440)
10–14 years	647,230 (8,907)	57,860 (277)	50,630 (358)	61,040 (337)	65,040 (1,087)	66,160 (1,856)
15–19 years	556,500 (9,214)	64,980 (361)	56,600 (509)	68,490 (454)	69,750 (1,013)	79,120 (3,183)
20–24 years	384,560 (7,078)	68,440 (468)	59,690 (702)	72,500 (637)	72,940 (1,331)	73,100 (2,559)

(continued)

TABLE 7.4 Average Base Salary for Full-Time Teachers in Public Elementary and Secondary Schools, by Highest Degree Earned and Years of Teaching Experience: 1990–91 Through 2017–18 (continued)

Years of Full-and Part-Time Teaching Experience[a]	Number of Full-Time Teachers	Base Salary[b] (current dollars) Highest Degree Earned				
		All Teachers[c]	Bachelor's Degree	Master's Degree	Education Specialist[d]	Doctor's Degree
1	2	3	4	5	6	7
25–9 years	237,750 (6,543)	69,170 (616)	59,960 (712)	73,240 (827)	73,240 (1,952)	74,570 (2,633)
30–34 years	119,120 (4,303)	71,000 (729)	64,010 (1,207)	74,680 (991)	74,680 (2,562)	‡ n/a
35 years or more	64,380 (2,845)	69,420 (964)	61,090 (1,256)	72,240 (1,339)	72,240 (2,775)	‡ n/a

Note: Standard errors appear in parenthesis; This table includes regular full-time teachers only: It excludes other staff even when they have full-time teaching duties (regular part-time teachers, itinerant teachers, long-term substitutes, administrators, library media specialists, other professional staff, and support staff). Detail may not sum to totals because of rounding. Figure adapted from the Digest of Education Statistics, 2019 (n.d.-a).

Source: U.S. Department of Education, National Center for Education Statistics, School and Staffing Survey (SASS), "Public School Teacher Data File," 1990–91, 1999–2000, 2007–08, and 2011–12; and "Charter School Teacher Data File," 1999–2000; and National Teacher and Principal Survey (NTPS), "Public School Teacher Data File," 2017–18. (This table was prepared November 2019).

n/a = Not applicable

‡ = Reporting standards not met (too few cases for a reliable estimate).

[a] Teachers were asked how many school years they had worked as a teacher. In 2011–12 and earlier years, teachers were also asked how many of their teaching years were full time and how many were part time. After 2011–12, teachers were no longer asked how many years were full time versus part time. Throughout this table, all school years are counted, regardless of whether teachers taught full time or part time.

[b] Teachers' base salary does not include any supplemental contracts for additional work at a school during the school year (e.g., coaching) or during the summer (e.g., teaching summer sessions). Also does not include any income from non-school sources.

[c] Includes teachers with levels of education below the bachelor's degree (not shown separately).

[d] Education specialist degrees or certificates are generally awarded for 1 year's work beyond the master's level. Includes certificate of advanced graduate studies.

communities with higher achieving students (Malone, 2002). In response, stakeholders had to consider recruiting and retaining educators to areas of high need, which often experienced the most staffing difficulties.

Over time, accountability expanded from academic outcomes to the inclusion of fiscal input in consideration of those outcomes, influencing the collection and publication of school-level financial data. In 2008, America declared an economic recession, signaling sectors of society to evaluate fiscal standing; Education reform was targeted as an area of need. The American Recovery and Reinvestment Act of 2009 (ARRA) elicited states to report teacher salaries (Skinner et al., 2019). This policy capitalized on the idea of attaching dollars to educator effectiveness through grants such as the Race to the Top (RTTT). Aside from the allocation of hundreds of millions of dollars to the Teacher Incentive Fund, Teacher Quality Enhancement, and Statewide Data Systems, the ARRA's RTTT earmarked "$650 million of [its] $5 billion [to] the 'Invest in What Works and Innovation' fund [that was] available through a competition to districts and nonprofit groups with a strong track record of results" (United States Department of Education, 2009). Only accessible for a few years, states and their corresponding districts weighed the intricacy of adjusting its system to federal goals. The magnitude of fiscal devotion prompted a multitude of public opinions. Quinn and Klein (2019) articulated the lack of buy-in for RTTT implementation, stating, "Compliance with state law was the primary motivation behind the local enactment of policies. Most leaders did not believe that the small rewards included in the policies would change teaching practice or student outcomes—they simply felt the need to follow state law and make the changes required" (p. 29). Still, state policy continued to address teacher performance to salary. By 2013, the following national trends in performance-based compensation existed (Behrstock-Sherratt et al., 2013):

- Georgia, Idaho, Nebraska, and South Carolina require[d] that bonuses based on performance be available to all teachers throughout the state.
- In comparison, Florida, Idaho, and Indiana require[d] that summative performance information be used as a factor in determining teacher salaries rather than annual bonuses.
- California, Delaware, Georgia, North Carolina, Texas, and Washington require[d] that school districts provide additional compensation for new teachers who have related experience working in other sectors.
- Sixteen states require[d] districts to pay higher salaries to teachers with advanced degrees.
- Seventeen states provide[d] additional compensation for teachers in hard-to-staff subjects.

- Seventeen states provide[d] additional compensation for teachers who achieve National Board Certification.
- Twenty states provide[d] additional compensation for teachers who work in hard-to-staff schools.
- Twenty-seven states [left] all teacher salary decisions to school districts. (p. 2)

The Every Student Succeeds Act (ESSA) of 2015 continued incentivizing educator pay for performance. ESSA dedicated incentive grant funds for teachers (and school leaders) who "[implemented], as part of a comprehensive performance-based compensation system, a differentiated salary structure, which [could] include bonuses and stipends, to teachers who [taught] in high-need schools; or high-need subjects; who raise[d] student academic achievement; or [took] on additional leadership responsibilities" (§221). This incentive advanced the narrative that teacher pay should be linked to effectiveness, but as mentioned earlier in the chapter, defining effectiveness is not straightforward, and the research has yet to consistently demonstrate robust evidence for the use of educator performance pay.

WHAT ALTERNATIVES TO TRADITIONAL TEACHER PAY ARE OFFERED TO TEACHERS?

After the initial onset of the pandemic, the Center for State and Local Government Excellence (2021) found that education employees were least satisfied with their salary, career advancement, and nontraditional benefits. Although highly dependent on external and subjective means, like the economy or the district leadership's preferences, many practices have been adopted to supplement teacher pay, such as loan forgiveness, signing bonuses, stipends, and retirement incentives.

LOAN FORGIVENESS

As mentioned, a commonly adopted recruitment effort is loan forgiveness. Feng and Sass (2015) stated that some critical teacher shortage programs that exercise loan forgiveness appeal to educators who have taught in high-needs areas, yielding positive retention outcomes. However, they also found that "effects vary across subjects and depend in part on the magnitude of payments" (Feng & Sass, 2015, p. 21). The United States Department of Education currently provides its share of incentives, such as the Stafford Loan to encourage students to enter and remain in the teaching profession via loan forgiveness of up to $17,500 for teachers in certain specialties and up to $5,000 for those who teach for five years in low-income schools and meet other requirements (Stafford Loan Forgiveness Program for Teachers, n.d.). Like any initiative, the concept of loan forgiveness is subject to limitations. For example, the College Cost Reduction and Access Act of 2007 helped establish the Teacher Education Assistance for College and Higher Education (TEACH) Grant Program to make college more affordable and emphasize high-need subject areas. In review, Jacqueline Nowicki (2015) and the United States Government Accountability Office recommended that the field "assess TEACH Grant participants' failure to meet grant requirements, examine why erroneous TEACH grant-to-loan conversions occurred, disseminate information of the TEACH grant-to-loan dispute process, and establish program performance measures" (p. 2). The program's series of drawbacks associated with the grant implementation cast a soured connotation. In 2021, however, the federal government changed the TEACH grant program structure, enhancing the flexibility of the grant to authenticate its necessity and minimize its previous shortcomings (United States Department of Education, 2021). To reach its maximum potential, Podolsky and Kini (2016) deduced that loan forgiveness and service scholarship programs should: (a) cover all or a large percentage of tuition; (b) target high-need fields and/or schools; (c) recruit and select candidates who are academically strong, committed to teaching, and well-prepared; (d) commit recipients to teach with reasonable financial consequences if recipients do not fulfill the commitment (but not so punitive that they avoid the scholarship entirely); and (e) bureaucratically manage participating teachers, districts, and higher education institutions (p. 7). As the nation appeals to new teachers, loan forgiveness will continue to be an important strategy.

SIGNING BONUS

Another financial incentive used to attract teachers is the signing bonus. Signing bonuses are often targeted towards hard-to-staff schools (Clotfelter et al., 2008; Liu et al., 2004) and can be paid out in installments over a time period (e.g., $20,000 over 5 years) to incentive retention. These incentives are often funded by [School Improvement Grants] (SIG), and typically include (a) performance-based pay, (b) compensation for teachers' additional hours worked under SIG, and (c) signing bonuses" (Rosenberg et al., 2014, p. 10). Although attractive in theory, one could suspect that there is a fair level of skepticism in its effectiveness in long-term retention (Blair, 2000; Madison, 2021). Even if the entirety of the bonus is paid out via installments, teachers often do not stay long enough to collect all of it or leave shortly after the bonus period (see Chapter 4).

PERFORMANCE BONUS OR STIPEND

The stipend is geared to retain effective practicing teachers. The Institute of Education Sciences noted that "principals in traditional public schools used teacher performance evaluation results to inform decisions about teachers when granting job protection," with 37% dedicated to determining bonuses or performance-based compensation other than salary increases (Standing & Lewis, 2020, p. 2). Trickling down to higher education recruitment efforts, Sherfinski et al., (2019) discussed how teacher preparation programs used state-mandated teacher performance assessment as a "pathway to increased teacher pay/meritocracy by linking it with the National Boards," which often yields a stipend (p. 2). Some districts have offered a teacher stipend for teaching selected courses, attending required workshops/professional developments, and a student performance incentive (e.g., Houston Independent School District Research and Accountability, 2014). Many stipends are supported by federal initiatives, such as the Teacher Incentive Fund (TIF; authorized by Pub. L. No. 109-149), which offered funding in 2010, 2012, and 2016. TIF promoted "performance-based compensation, and other human capital strategies that enhance[d] and sustain[ed] performance-based compensation [that increased] students' access to effective educators in high-need schools, and to expand the array of promising approaches that can help . . . educators and other personnel succeed" (American Institutes for Research, 2021, para. 1).

RETIREMENT INCENTIVE

Generally, retirement incentives are attractive to educators (Toutkoushian et al., 2011). Incentives, such as pensions, provide a sense of security for teachers who intend to establish and sustain a career in the teaching profession. After settling in a particular location, teachers stand to assume significant gains the longer they invest their time in the profession. Still, Will and Sawchuk (2019) stated, "In 2018, there were a half-dozen statewide protests over educators' salaries and pensions" (para. 1). Teachers protest about pensions largely over the conditions of the formula, such as how much they must contribute to their retirement or the point at which they can retire. Like salary, retirement conditions are contingent on the state and sometimes the district. Critics of teacher pensions often cite unfair incentives, with some researchers pronouncing debatably inaccurate mantras about retirement benefits resonating amongst the profession (Rhee & Fornia, 2016). Costrell and McGee (2016) state, "With benefits delinked from contributions, some individuals receive benefits that cost more than the contributions made on their behalf and some receive less, effectively a system of hidden cross-subsidies" (p. 18). In contrast, however, EPI explained that "school districts contribute an amount based on a fixed percent of pay to prevent costs from increasing as teachers vest or approach retirement, not to give prospective teachers the impression that their benefits will be equal to employer contributions" (Morrissey, 2017, para. 28).

Like other alternatives, retirement incentives are subject to change. An example is South Carolina's discontinued Teacher and Employee Retention Incentive Program (TERI), which permitted teachers to work while drawing retirement benefits (South Carolina Department of Administration, n.d.). By design, the TERI program helped transition career educators from the profession by offering the option of deferred retirement. It allowed qualified teachers to continue to receive a salary, rights, and benefits for years post-retirement. Although a targeted mitigation effort, the program put a band-aid on the degree of shortage in educators. When TERI ended, a relatively low earnings policy cap was applied to retirees, moving many retired professionals to other geographic areas and professions. What lingers of retirement incentives as an alternative to traditional teacher pay lies with the sophistication of the remaining retirement package. Bellwether Education Partners, a nonprofit organization, studied the differences between K–12 and higher education retirement plans, suggesting that pension programs be rated as to whether teachers have a choice over their retirement plan, how long they have to stay in the system to qualify, the value of the benefit, whether the plan builds up unfunded obligations (and how much teachers contribute), and whether teachers are covered by Social Security (Aldeman & Lewis, 2021). Today, South Carolina's Retirement System promotes that it is "based on a formula (1.82% of average final compensation multiplied by years of service), not on [the recipients'] account balance at retirement" ("South Carolina Retirement System," n.d., para. 4), and is generally viewed positively. Still, in the climate of the teacher shortage, with retired teachers leaving the profession and not returning to help mitigate the demand pressure suggests room for improvement.

WHAT DOES THE FUTURE HOLD FOR TEACHER PAY?

Experts cite that the problems concerning the inadequacy of teacher pay, coupled with poor working conditions, funding reductions for benefits and insurance, as well as accumulating work responsibilities have hit a feverish boil, heavily motivating the nationwide teacher walkouts that started to blossom in February and March of 2018, starting in West Virginia (Shapiro et al., 2018). After accomplishing a lawmaker-approved 5% wage increase and agreement to engage in policy discussion to meet the other demands of strikers in 9 school days, the movement spread like wildfire across other states.

States continue to respond to public dissent on teacher pay. For instance, in the state of South Carolina, broad policies like the South Carolina Education Finance Act of 1977, South Carolina Education Improvement Act of 1984, and South Carolina Education Accountability Act of 1998 have attempted to formally address teacher salaries beyond one-time increases (see Table 7.5). Still, unfortunately, the core state funding formula has not been fully funded since the fiscal year 2007–2008 (Tran, 2018). Consequently, teacher annual raise amounts were insufficient to keep teacher salaries up to pace with college graduates in other professions (Allegretto

TABLE 7.5 Examples of South Carolina Code of Laws Excerpts Connected to Teacher Salary

Policy	Excerpt	Teacher Salary Connection
SC Code §59-18-1500	(A)(1)...A school renewal plan must address professional development activities that are directly related to instruction in the core subject areas and may include the use of funds appropriated for technical assistance to provide compensation incentives in the form of salary supplements to classroom teachers who are certified by the State Board of Education. The purpose of the compensation packages is to improve student achievement and to improve the recruitment and retention of teachers with advanced degrees in schools designated as below average or school/district at-risk. If the school renewal plan is approved, the school shall be permitted to use technical assistance funds to provide the salary supplements...	Alongside the established mandate of a formal performance indicator system for school districts (i.e., annual report cards based on statewide standardized achievement assessments), this policy addressed compensation packages as a part of the Education Accountability Act of 1998.
SC Code §59-18-1530	(C) To encourage and recruit teachers for assignment to below average and school/district at-risk schools, those assigned to such schools will receive their salary and a supplement equal to fifty percent of the current southeastern average teacher salary as projected by the Revenue and Fiscal Affairs Office...	This policy was created as a 3-year funding incentive for teacher specialists as a part of the Education Accountability Act of 1998. The language of this policy explicitly identifies a state-level "recruitment" effort. It also identifies the state's intent to address high-needs schools.
SC Code §59-18-1530	(F) The supplements are to be considered part of the regular salary base for which retirement contributions are deductible by the South Carolina Retirement System pursuant to	This policy applies to the recruitment, eligibility, duties, and incentives of teacher specialists as a part of the Education Accountability Act of 1998. The link to the teacher

(continued)

TABLE 7.5 Examples of South Carolina Code of Laws Excerpts Connected to Teacher Salary (continued)

Policy	Excerpt	Teacher Salary Connection
	Section 9-1-1020. Principal and teacher specialists on site who are assigned to below average and school/district at-risk schools shall be allowed to return to employment with their home district at the end of the contract period with the same teaching or administrative contract status as when they left but without assurance as to the school or supplemental position to which they may be assigned.	retirement program is identified as an explicit incentive.
SC Code §59-20-50	(4)(b) . . . The southeastern average teacher salary is the average of the average teachers' salaries of the southeastern states. In projecting the southeastern average, the office shall include in the South Carolina base teacher salary all local teacher supplements and all incentive pay. Under this schedule, school districts are required to maintain local salary supplements per teacher no less than their prior fiscal level. In Fiscal Year 1986 and thereafter teacher pay raises through adjustments in the state's minimum salary schedule may be provided only to teachers who demonstrate minimum knowledge proficiency . . .	This policy outlines the state contribution level requirements and salary schedules established by the Education Finance Act of 1977. It details a minimum value comparative to surrounding states, implying the desire to remain competitive. In lieu of section 4(a), schedules must be defined by "experience" (e.g., years of teaching) and "class" (e.g., degree earned).
SC Code §59-25-57	Notwithstanding another provision of law, school districts uniformly may negotiate salaries below the school district salary schedule for the 2014–2015 school year for retired teachers who are not participants in the Teacher and Employee Retention Incentive [TERI] program. Thereafter, school districts annually may continue to uniformly negotiate salaries below the school district salary schedule for retired teachers who are not participants in the Teacher and Employee Retention Incentive program for each upcoming school year through the 2019–2020 school year. The provisions of this section expire on July 1, 2020.	As a portion of the General Provisions for teachers, this policy addressed the salaries for non-Teacher Employee Retention Incentive (TERI) retired teachers. It articulates a level of flexibility the state intended to provide, signaling a teacher shortage. As articulated in the policy, this provision recently expired.

& Mishel, 2020). In 2017, the South Carolina House of Representatives presented a bill to establish a Teacher Retention Study Committee to review teacher compensation and establish competitive salary distribution. Recent efforts have sought to amend the Code of Laws of South Carolina to set the bar beyond the southeastern average to the national average as a teacher salary requirement, a constantly recurring topic; and after the onset of the COVID-19 global pandemic, South Carolina's General Assembly (124th Session) passed a joint resolution to restore teacher step increases that were suspended, appropriating "fifty million dollars to provide for teacher step increases for the 2020–2021 School Year" (A3, R10, H3609). As can be seen, the topic of teacher salaries continues to be at the forefront of local, state, and federal policy.

Ultimately, improving teacher compensation is necessary but by itself insufficient for improving and maintaining interest in the teaching profession. While not the only or even the most important factor in attracting and retaining teachers to the field of teaching (see Chapter 11; Tran & Smith, 2020 for more details), pay is nonetheless a critical influencer. Research suggests that a pay raise of at least 15 to 20% is necessary to reduce attrition of teachers in high-needs contexts to be comparable to an average district (Imazeki, 2005). Failing to address teacher pay in a *substantive* manner dulls the potential of any other recruitment and retention effort. Any real efforts to improve the appeal of the teaching profession must contend with the issue of teacher compensation.

NOTE

1. The issue of how low pay contributes to job dissatisfaction, whereas work impact on student lives contributes to job satisfaction is discussed in Chapter 12.

REFERENCES

Abamu, J. (2018). *The data tells all: Teacher salaries have been declining for years.* https://www.edsurge.com/news/2018-04-05-the-data-tells-all-teacher-salaries-have-been-declining-for-years

Aldeman, C., Lewis, B., Bellwether Education Partners, & TeacherPensions.org. (2021). Choice and quality among retirement plans for educators. In *Bellwether Education Partners*. Bellwether Education Partners.

Aldeman, C., & Rotherham, A. J. (2014). *Friends without benefits: How states systematically shortchange teachers' retirement and threaten their retirement security.* Bellwether Education Partners.

Allegretto, S., & Mishel, L. (2020). *Teacher pay penalty dips but persists in 2019: Public school teachers earn about 20% less in weekly wages than nonteacher college graduates.* Economic Policy Institute.

American Institutes for Research. (2021). *Educational innovation in teacher incentive fund grants.* https://www.air.org/project/educational-innovation-teacher -incentive-fund-grants

American Recovery and Reinvestment Act of 2009, Pub. L. No. 111-5, Title VIII. https://www.govinfo.gov/content/pkg/PLAW-111publ5/pdf/PLAW- 111publ5.pdf

Anderson, G., & Cohen, M. (2015). Redesigning the identities of teachers and leaders: A framework for studying new professionalism and educator resistance. *Education Policy Analysis Archives, 23*(85), 1–29.

Aragon, S. (2016). *Mitigating teacher shortages: Financial incentives.* https://www.ecs.org/ wp-content/uploads/Mitigating-Teacher-Shortages-Financial-incentives.pdf

Atteberry, A. C., & McEachin, A. J. (2020). Not where you start, but how much you grow: An addendum to the Coleman Report. *Educational Researcher, 49*(9), 678–685.

Bacolod, M. P. (2007). Do alternative opportunities matter? The role of female labor markets in the decline of teacher quality. *The Review of Economics and Statistics, 89*(4), 737–751.

Bailey, B. (2000). The impact of mandated change on teachers. In N. Bascia & A. Hargreaves (Eds.), *The sharp edge of educational change: Teaching, leading, and the realities of reform* (pp. 112–128). RoutledgeFalmer.

Behrstock-Sherratt, E., & Potemski, A. (2013). *Performance-based compensation: Linking performance to teacher salaries. Ask the team.* Center on Great Teachers and Leaders at American Institutes for Research.

Blair, J. (2000). *Districts wooing teachers with bonuses, incentives.* https://www.edweek .org/education/districts-wooing-teachers-with-bonuses-incentives/2000/08 #:~:text=Beginning%20teachers%20earn%20%2433%2C050%20and%20are %20awarded%20%242%2C000,the%20promise%20of%20participation%20 in%20a%20mentoring%20program

Bill and Melinda Gates Foundation. (2012). *Primary sources: America's teachers on the teaching profession.* Scholastic Inc.

Boser, U., & Straus, C. (2014). *Mid-and late career teachers struggle with paltry incomes.* Center for American Progress. https://www.americanprogress.org/issues/ education-k-12/reports/2014/07/23/94168/mid-and-late-career-teachers -struggle-with-paltry-incomes/

Bowen, D., & Mills, J. N. (2017). Changing the education workforce? The relationships between teacher quality, motivation, and performance pay. *Teachers College Record, 119*(4), 1–32.

Boyd, D., Lankford, H., Loeb, S., Rockoff, J., & Wyckoff, J. (2008). *The narrowing gap in New York City teacher qualifications and its implications for student achievement in high-poverty schools* (No. w14021). National Bureau of Economic Research.

Center for State and Local Government Excellence at ICMA-RC. (2021). *K–12 public school employee views on finances, employment outlook, and safety concerns due to COVID-19.* https://slge.org/assets/uploads/2021/02/2021-slge-cv19-k12-report .pdf

Center for Educator Recruitment, Retention, and Advancement (2020). *South Carolina annual educator supply and demand report (2020–21 school year)*. https://www.cerra.org/uploads/1/7/6/8/17684955/2020-21_supply___demand_report.pdf

Cheng, A., Henderson, M., Peterson, P. E., & West, M. R. (2019). Public support climbs for teacher pay, school expenditures, charter schools, and universal vouchers: Results from the 2018 EdNext poll. *Education Next, 19*(1), 8–27.

Clotfelter, C. T., Glennie, E. J., Ladd, H. F., & Vigdor, J. L. (2008). Teacher bonuses and teacher retention in low-performing schools: Evidence from the North Carolina $1,800 teacher bonus program. *Public Finance Review, 36*(1), 63–87.

Coleman, J. S., Campbell, E., Hobson, C., McPartland, F., Mood, A., & Weinfeld, F. (1966). *Equality of educational opportunity study.* United States Department of Health, Education, and Welfare.

College Cost Reduction and Access Act of 2007, Pub. L. No. 110-84. https://www.congress.gov/110/plaws/publ84/PLAW-110publ84.pdf

Corcoran, S. P., Evans, W. N., & Schwab, R. M. (2004). Changing labor-market opportunities for women and the quality of teachers, 1957–2000. *American Economic Review, 94*(2), 230–235.

Corcoran, S. P. (2010). *Can teachers be evaluated by their students' test scores? Should they be? The use of value-added measures of teacher effectiveness in policy and practice. Education policy for action series.* Annenberg Institute for School Reform at Brown University (NJ1).

Costrell, R. M., & McGee, J. B. (2016). *Cross-subsidization of teacher pension normal cost: The case of CalSTRS.* Education Reform Faculty and Graduate Students Publications. https://scholarworks.uark.edu/edrepub/23

De Brey, C., Snyder, T. D., Zhang, A., Dillow, S. A., National Center for Education Statistics, & American Institutes for Research. (2021). *Digest of education statistics 2019, 55th ed.* (NCES 2021-009). National Center for Education Statistics.

Delisle, J., & Holt, A. (2017). The tangled world of teacher debt: Clashing rules and uncertain benefits for federal student-loan subsidies. *Education Next, 17*(4), 43–48.

Digest of Education Statistics. Dos Santos, L. M. (2019). Mid-life career changing to teaching profession: A study of secondary school teachers in a rural community. *Journal of Education for Teaching, 45*(2), 225–227.

Ehrenberg, R. G., & Brewer, D. J. (1994). Do school and teacher characteristics matter? Evidence from high school and beyond. *Economics of Education Review, 13*(1), 1–17.

Erikkson, T., Teyssier, S., & Villeval, M. (2009). Self-selection and the efficiency of tournaments. *Economic Inquiry, 47*(3), 530–548.

Every Student Succeeds Act of 2015, Pub. L. No. 114-95. https://www.congress.gov/114/plaws/publ95/PLAW-114publ95.pdf

Feng, L., & Sass, T. R. (2015). *The impact of incentives to recruit and retain teachers in "hard-to-staff" subjects: An analysis of the Florida Critical Teacher Shortage Program* (Working Paper 141). National Center for Analysis of Longitudinal Data in Education Research.

Figlio, D. N. (1997). Teacher salaries and teacher quality. *Economics Letters, 55*(2), 267–271.

García, E., & Weiss, E. (2020). How teachers view their own professional status: A snapshot. *Phi Delta Kappan, 101*(6), 14–18.

Gardner, D. P., Larsen, Y. W., Baker, W. O., Campbell, A., Crosby, E. A., Foster, Jr., C. A., Francis, N. C., Giamatti, A. B., Gordon, S., Haderlein, R. V., Holton, G., Kirk, A. Y., Marston, M. S., Quie, A. H., Sanchez, Jr., F. D., Seaborg, G. T., Sommer, J., & Wallace, R. (1983). *A nation at risk: The imperative for educational reform. An open letter to the American people. A report to the nation and the Secretary of Education.* National Commission on Excellence in Education.

Glazerman, S., Chiang, H., Wellington, A., Constantine, J., & Player, D. (2011). *Impacts of performance pay under the Teacher Incentive Fund: Study design report.* Mathematica Policy Research, Inc.

Goldstein, D., & Casselman, B. (2018, May 31). Teachers find public support as campaign for higher pay goes to voters. *The New York Times.* https://www.nytimes.com/2018/05/31/us/politics/teachers-campaign.html

Goldstein, D. (2015). *The teacher wars: A history of America's most embattled profession.* Anchor.

Goldhaber, D. (2007). Everyone's doing it, but what does teacher testing tell us about teacher effectiveness? *Journal of human Resources, 42*(4), 765–794.

Goldhaber, D., Lavery, L., & Theobald, R. (2015). Uneven playing field? Assessing the teacher quality gap between advantaged and disadvantaged students. *Educational Researcher, 44*(5), 293–307.

Goodman, S. F., & Turner, L. J. (2013). The design of teacher incentive pay and educational outcomes: Evidence from the New York City bonus program. *Journal of Labor Economics, 31*(2), 409–420.

Greene, J. P., & Winters, M. A. (2007). How much are public school teachers paid. *Manhattan Institute of Policy Research Civic Report, 50*(1), 1–26.

Greene, P. (2019). Teacher merit pay is a bad idea. *Forbes.* https://www.forbes.com/sites/petergreene/2019/02/09/teacher-merit-pay-is-a-bad-idea/?sh=8c596004ffbb

Griffith, M. (2016). *Policy analysis: State teacher salary schedules.* https://www.ecs.org/wp-content/uploads/State-Teacher-Salary-Schedules-1.pdf

Grissom, J. A., & Strunk, K. O. (2012). How should school districts shape teacher salary schedules? Linking school performance to pay structure in traditional compensation schemes. *Educational Policy, 26*(5), 663–695.

Hampson, R. (2018, October 17). We followed 15 of America's teachers on a day of frustrations, pressures and hard-earned victories. *USA Today.* https://www.usatoday.com/in-depth/news/nation/2018/10/17/teachers-appreciation-pay-union-jobs-schools-education/1509500002/

Hanushek, E. A., Kain, J. F., & Rivkin, S. G. (2004). Why public schools lose teachers. *Journal of Human Resources, 39*(2), 326–354.

Hanushek, E. A., & Pace, R. R. (1995). Who chooses to teach (and why)? *Economics of Education Review, 14*(2), 101–117.

Hanushek, E. A., Piopiunik, M., & Wiederhold, S. (2019). The value of smarter teachers international evidence on teacher cognitive skills and student performance. *Journal of Human Resources, 54*(4), 857–899.

Haynes, M. (2014). *On the path to equity: Improving the effectiveness of beginning teachers.* Alliance for Excellent Education. https://all4ed.org/reports-factsheets/path-to-equity/

Henderson, M. B., Houston, D. M., Peterson, P. E., & West, M. R. (2020). Public support grows for higher teacher pay and expanded school choice results from the 2019 Education Next Survey. *Education Next, 20*(1), 8–28.

Hendricks, M. D. (2015). Towards an optimal teacher salary schedule: Designing base salary to attract and retain effective teachers. *Economics of Education Review, 47*, 143–167.

Heubeck, E. (2021). Schools pay a high price for low salaries. *Education Week.* https://www.edweek.org/leadership/schools-pay-a-high-price-for-low-teacher-salaries/2021/07

Horn, B. (2017). Striking out on their own: Lessons learned from student teaching during and after the Chicago teachers union strike. *Critical Questions in Education, 8*(2), 193–205.

Houston Independent School District Research and Accountability. (2014). *2012–2013 SRI payout and student performance report. Research educational program report.* Houston Independent School District.

Imazeki, J. (2005). Teacher salaries and teacher attrition. *Economics of education Review, 24*(4), 431–449.

Imberman, S. A., & Lovenheim, M. F. (2015). Incentive strength and teacher productivity: Evidence from a group-based teacher incentive pay system. *Review of Economics and Statistics, 97*(2), 364–386.

Ingersoll, R. M. (2001). Teacher turnover and teacher shortages: An organizational analysis. *American Educational Research Journal, 38*(3), 499–534.

Jacoby, D. F., & Nitta, K. (2012). The Bellevue teachers strike and its implications for the future of postindustrial reform unionism. *Educational Policy, 26*(4), 533–563.

Ladd, H. F., & Sorensen, L. C. (2017). Returns to teacher experience: Student achievement and motivation in middle school. *Education Finance and Policy, 12*(2), 241–279.

Leigh, A. (2012). Teacher pay and teacher aptitude. *Economics of Education Review, 31*(3), 41–53.

Liu, E., Johnson, S. M., & Peske, H. G. (2004). New teachers and the Massachusetts signing bonus: The limits of inducement. *Educational Evaluation and Policy Analysis, 26*(3), 217–236.

Loewus, L. (2021). Why teachers leave-or don't: A look at the numbers. *Education Week.* https://www.edweek.org/teaching-learning/why-teachers-leave-or-dont-a-look-at-the-numbers/2021/05

Lytle, J. H. (2013). Philadelphia School District deconstruction—A case requiring consideration. *Penn GSE Perspectives on Urban Education, 10*(1), 1–4.

Madison, H. (2021). *America is facing a teacher shortage, and some school districts are giving out signing bonuses to attract staff.* https://www.businessinsider.com/schools-facing-teacher-shortage-as-the-school-year-starts-soon-2021-7

Madland, D., & Rowell, A. (2017, November 15). *Attacks on public-sector unions harm states: How Act 10 has affected education in Wisconsin.* Center for American Progress Action. https://www.americanprogressaction.org/issues/economy/reports/2017/11/15/169146/attacks-public-sector-unions-harm-states-act-10-affected-education-wisconsin/

Malone, D. M. (2002). The No Child Left Behind Act and the teacher shortage. *Policy Briefs: Education Reform, 2*(7). Center for Child and Family Policy, Duke University.

Marsh, J., Springer, M. G., McCaffrey, D. F., Yuan, K., Epstein, S., Koppich, J., Kalra, N., DiMartino, C., & Peng, A. (2011). *A Big Apple for educators: New York City's experiment with schoolwide performance bonuses: Final evaluation report*. RAND Corporation. https://www.rand.org/pubs/monographs/MG1114.html

Marvel, J., Lyter, D. M., Peltola, P., Strizek, G. A., & Morton, B. A. (2007). Teacher attrition and mobility: *Results from the 2004–05 teacher follow-up survey. U.S. Department of Education, National Center for Education Statistics*. U.S. Government Printing Office.

Maslow, A., & Lewis, K. J. (1987). Maslow's hierarchy of needs. *Salenger Incorporated, 14*(17), 987–990.

Mishel, L., Allegretto, S., & Essrow, D. (2016). *Teachers make 17 percent less than similar workers*. Economic Policy Institute. https://www.epi.org/publication/teachers-make-17-percent-less-than-similar-workers/

Morice, L. C., & Murray, J. E. (2003). Compensation and teacher retention: A success story. *Educational Leadership, 60*(8), 40–43.

Morrissey, M. (2017). *Teachers and schools are well served by teacher pensions*. Economic Policy Institute. https://www.epi.org/publication/teachers-and-schools-are-well-served-by-teacher-pensions/

Murnane, R. J., & Olsen, R. (1990). The effects of salaries and opportunity costs on length of stay in teaching: Evidence from North Carolina. *Journal of Human Resources, 25*(1), 106–124.

National Center for Education Statistics. (2021). *Teacher requirements to help students outside regular school hours in 2017–18*. Data point (NCES 2021-054). National Center for Education Statistics.

National Center for Education Statistics. (n.d.-a). Average base salary for full-time teachers in public elementary and secondary schools, by highest degree earned and years of teaching experience: Selected years, 1990–91 through 2017–18 (Table 211.20). https://nces.ed.gov/programs/digest/d19/tables/dt19_211.20.asp

National Center for Education Statistics. (n.d.-b). *Estimated average annual salary of teachers in public elementary and secondary schools, by state: Selected years, 1969–70 through 2018–19* (Table 211.60). https://nces.ed.gov/programs/digest/d19/tables/dt19_211.60.asp

National Education Association. (2020). *NEA 2019–2020 teacher salary benchmark report*. https://www.nea.org/sites/default/files/2021-04/2019-2020%20Teacher%20Salary%20Benchmark%20Report.pdf

National Education Association. (2021). *Rankings of the States 2020 and estimates of school statistics 2021*. https://www.nea.org/research-publications

Nelson A. Rockefeller Institute of Government. (n.d.). *Teacher salary trends, 2002–17*. https://rockinst.org/issue-areas/education/teacher-salary-trends-2002-17/

No Child Left Behind Act of 2001, P.L. 107-110, 20 U.S.C. § 6319 (2002).

Nowicki, J. M. (2015). *Higher education: Better management of federal grant and loan forgiveness programs for teachers needed to improve participant outcomes* (GAO-15-314). U.S. Government Accountability Office.

Owen, J. D. (1971, October). *The determination of teacher salary and quality: An econometric analysis.*

Podolsky, A., & Kini, T. (2016). *How effective are loan forgiveness and service scholarships for recruiting teachers?* [Policy brief]. Learning Policy Institute.

Quinn, D. J., & Klein, C. S. (2019). Pay-for-performance in three Michigan school districts: Lessons for decision makers. *Education Leadership Review of Doctoral Research, 7,* 22–36.

Reilly, K. (2018, September 13). I work 3 jobs and donate blood plasma to pay the bills. This is what it's like to be a teacher in America. *Time.* https://time .com/5395001/teacher-in-america

Rhee, N., & Fornia, W. B. (2016). *Are California teachers better off with a pension or a 401(k)?* University of California, Berkeley Center for Labor Research and Education.

Richards, E., & Wynn, M. (2019). 'Can't pay their bills with love': In many teaching jobs, teachers' salaries can't cover rent. *USA Today.* https://www.usatoday .com/in-depth/news/education/2019/06/05/teachers-pay-cost-of-living -teaching-jobs/3449428002/

Richwine, J., & Biggs, A. G. (2011). *Assessing the compensation of public-school teachers. A report of the Heritage Center for Data Analysis.* Heritage Foundation.

Rivkin, S. G., Hanushek, E. A., & Kain, J. F. (2005). Teachers, schools, and academic achievement. *Econometrica, 73*(2), 417–458.

Rockefeller Institute of Government. (n.d.). *Teacher salary trends, 2007–2017.* https://rockinst.org/issue-areas/education/teacher-salary-trends-2002-17/

Rockoff, J. E. (2004). The impact of individual teachers on student achievement: Evidence from panel data. *American Economic Review, 94*(2), 247–252.

Rockoff, J. E., Jacob, B. A., Kane, T. J., & Staiger, D. O. (2011). Can you recognize an effective teacher when you recruit one? *Education Finance and Policy, 6*(1), 43–74.

Rosenberg, L., Christianson, M. D., Angus, M. H., Rosenthal, E., & National Center for Education Evaluation and Regional Assistance. (2014). *A focused look at rural schools receiving school improvement grants* (NCEE 2014-4013) [NCEE evaluation brief]. National Center for Education Evaluation and Regional Assistance.

Rudick, C. K., & Dannels, D. P. (2020). "Yes, and…": Continuing the scholarly conversation about teacher labor in PK–12 education. Wicked Problems Forum: Teacher labor in PK–12 education. *Communication Education, 69*(1), 130–134.

Shapiro, S., Partelow, L., & Brown, C. (2018). *Fact sheet: Yes, increase the salaries of all teachers.* Center for American Progress. https://www.americanprogress .org/issues/education-k-12/reports/2018/06/14/452130/fact-sheet-yes -increase-salaries-teachers

Sherfinski, M., Hayes, S., Zhang, J., & Jalalifard, M. (2019). "Do it all but don't kill us": (Re)positioning teacher educators and preservice teachers amidst edTPA and the teacher strike in West Virginia. *Education Policy Analysis Archives, 27*(151), 1–45.

Shifrer, D., Turley, R. L., & Heard, H. (2017). Do teacher financial awards improve teacher retention and student achievement in an urban disadvantaged school district? *American Educational Research Journal, 54*(6), 1117–1153.

Shuffelton, A. B. (2014). The Chicago teachers strike and its public. *Education and Culture, 30*(2), 21–33.

Skinner, R. R., Riddle, W., & Library of Congress, C. R. S. (2019). *State and local financing of public schools, version 2* (CRS Report R45827). Congressional Research Service.

South Carolina Department of Administration. (n.d.). *Teacher and Employee Retention Incentive Program.* https://www.admin.sc.gov/dshr/teri

South Carolina Education Accountability Act of 1998. https://www.scstatehouse.gov/code/t59c018.php

South Carolina Education Finance Act of 1977. https://www.scstatehouse.gov/code/t59c020.php

South Carolina Retirement System. (n.d.). PEBA. https://www.peba.sc.gov/plans/scrs

Springer, M. G. (2019). *You get what you pay for: Why we need to invest in strategic compensation reform.* National Institute for Excellence in Teaching.

Springer, M.G., Pane, J. F., Le, V., McCaffrey, D. F., Burns, S. F., Hamilton, L. S., & Stecher, B. M. (2012). *No evidence that incentive pay for teacher teams improve student outcomes. Results from a randomized trial.* Rand Corporation. https://www.rand.org/pubs/research_briefs/RB9649.html

Stafford Loan Forgiveness Program for Teachers. United States Department of Education. (n.d.). https://files.eric.ed.gov/fulltext/ED515844.pdf

Standing, K., & Lewis, L. (2020). *Teacher performance evaluations in U.S. public schools.* Data Point (NCES 2020-133). National Center for Education Statistics.

Startz, D. (2018). Why are teachers more likely than others to work second jobs. *The Brown Center Chalkboard.* https://www.brookings.edu/blog/brown-center-chalkboard/2018/03/23/why-are-teachers-more-likely-than-others-to-work-second-jobs/

The Pew Charitable Trusts. (2018). *The State pension funding gap: 2016, overview.* http://www.pewtrusts.org/en/research-and-analysis/issue-briefs/2018/04/the-state-pension-funding-gap-2016

Toutkoushian, R. K., Bathon, J. M., & McCarthy, M. M. (2011). A national study of the net benefits of state pension plans for educators. *Journal of Education Finance, 37*(1), 24–51.

Towers, J. M. (1992). Twenty-five years after the Coleman report: What should we have learned? *Contemporary Education, 63*(2), 93–95.

Tran, H. (2017). Does the pay stance of South Carolina public school districts influence their math and science achievement scores? *Journal of Education Finance, 43*(2), 105–122.

Tran, H. (2018). *Taking the mystery out of South Carolina school finance* (2nd ed.). ICPEL Publications.

Tran, H., & Buckman, D. G. (2020). The relationship between districts' teacher salary schedule structures and the qualifications of their teacher staffing profile. *Journal of School Administration Research and Development, 5*(1), 6–15.

Tran, H., & Smith, D. (2019). Insufficient money and inadequate respect: What obstructs the recruitment of college students to teach in hard-to-staff schools. *Journal of Educational Administration, 57*(2), 152–166.

Tran, H., & Smith, D . (2020). The strategic support to thrive beyond survival model: An administrative support framework for improving student outcomes and addressing educator staffing in rural and urban high-needs schools. *Research in Educational Administration and Leadership, 5*(3), 870–919. https://doi.org/10.30828/real/2020.3.8

Tran, H., Hardie, S., & Cunningham, K. M. (2020). Leading with empathy and humanity: Why talent-centered education leadership is especially critical amidst the pandemic crisis. *International Studies in Educational Administration (Commonwealth Council for Educational Administration & Management), 48*(1), 39–45.

U.S. Bureau of Labor Statistics. (n.d.). *Occupational employment and wage statistics.* https://www.bls.gov/oes/current/oes252021.htm

United States Department of Education. (2009). *The American Recovery and Reinvestment Act of 2009: Saving and creating jobs and reforming education.* https://www.fr.com/files/Uploads/publications/broadband-stimulus/ARRA-Saving%20and%20Creating%20Jobs%20and%20Reforming%20Education_March72009.pdf#:~:text=The%20American%20Recovery%20and%20Reinvestment%20Act%20of%202009,including%20early%20learning%2C%20K-12%2C%20and%20post-%20secondary%20education

United States Department of Education. (2017). *Teacher shortage areas nationwide listing 1990–1991 through 2017–2018.* https://www2.ed.gov/about/offices/list/ope/pol/ateachershortageareasreport2017-18.pdf

United States Department of Education. (2021). *Department of Education implements TEACH grant program changes to benefit teachers and students.* https://www.ed.gov/news/press-releases/department-education-implements-teach-grant-program-changes-benefit-teachers-and-students#:~:text=TEACH%20Grant%20recipients%20will%20no%20longer%20have%20their,120%20days%20of%20graduating%20or%20separating%20from%20school

Valli, L., & Buese, D. (2007). The changing roles of teachers in an era of high-stakes accountability. *American Educational Research Journal, 44*(3), 519–558.

Winters, M. A., Dixon, B. L., & Greene, J. P. (2012). Observed characteristics and teacher quality: Impacts of sample selection on a value added model. *Economics of Education Review, 31*(1), 19–32.

Will, M., & Sawchuk, S. (2019) *Teacher pay: How salaries, pensions, and benefits work in schools.* https://www.edweek.org/teaching-learning/teacher-pay-how-salaries-pensions-and-benefits-work-in-schools/2018/03

Wright, A. M. (2020). Historical view of accountability and teacher labor. Wicked Problems Forum: Teacher labor in PK–12 education. *Communication Education, 69*(1), 105–118.

PART III

OVERWORKED AND OVERBURDENED:
TEACHER WORKING CONDITIONS

CHAPTER 8

ADVANCING TEACHING AS A PROFESSION

Teacher Working Conditions and the Case of South Carolina

Barnett Berry
University of South Carolina

THE PROFESSIONALIZATION OF TEACHING

The history of the teaching profession in America is complex, often framed by the struggle to determine who teaches what, how, under what conditions—and at what cost. Sociologists have referred to teaching as a semi-profession because its knowledge base has not been well defined and consistently used, and its members have very little control over who enters the field and how they are judged (Etzioni, 1969). Teachers are expected to be authoritarians with their students, but always subservient to political, bureaucratic, and school managerial authorities on policy and practice matters. They are often admired for service by parents but just as often bear the brunt of disdain when public education is being criticized (Berry, 2011). Indeed, efforts to professionalize teaching have been "rife with political dynamics, social

How Did We Get Here?, pages 181–203

drama, and philosophical debate" (Rousmaniere, 2005). Additionally, school workplace structures isolate teachers from each other, preventing them from learning from and leading with their collective expertise, tamping down the prospects for their professionalization (Lortie, 1975).

There has been some progress. For instance, since the late 19th century, teaching has evolved from a short-term occupation for unmarried women who earned little to a stable career with middle-class incomes and pensions that guarantee the ability to retire without falling into poverty. Researchers have also found that "teaching is a complex form of work that requires high levels of formal knowledge for successful performance"—a key element of professionalization (Rowan, 1994, p. 4). However, while social and economic progress for teachers has been made, the legacy of teaching as "social housekeeping" (Apple, 1985) remains in both policy and practice well into the 21st century (Berry, 2011).

As Ingersoll and Collins (2018) noted:

> Professionalization has long been a source of both hope and frustration for teachers. Since early in the 20th century, educators have repeatedly sought to promote the view that elementary and secondary teaching is a highly complex kind of work, requiring specialized knowledge and skill and deserving of the same status and standing as traditional professions, like law and medicine.

The authors examined a series of empirically derived indicators (e.g., credential and licensing levels, induction and mentoring programs for entrants, authority over decision-making, specialization, and compensation levels) and concluded that teaching, based on the characteristics of school workplaces, has fallen short on many of the key features associated with professionalization. For example, their analysis found that teachers have little influence over peer hiring and evaluation. Teachers at the secondary school level are often assigned to teach a substantial portion of their weekly class schedules out of their specialty fields. They also examined indicators of *prestige* and found teaching was rated in the middle of 38 occupations, much less prestigious than law, medicine, and engineering, but more so than most blue-collar work, such as truck driving and pink-collar work, such as secretarial work (Ingersoll & Collins, 2018). In America, professional prestige is often synonymous with how much someone earns. Researchers analyzed salaries for 137 specific college majors, for both bachelor's and graduate degree holders, and those majoring in education ranked in the bottom 25% of median annual salaries (Carnevale et al., 2015). Recent studies have shown that public school teachers earn about 20% less in weekly wages than nonteacher college graduates (Allegretto & Mishel, 2020).

The last several decades of school reform in America had been premised on the assumption that schools did not work well because teachers were either incapable or unwilling to do what needed to be done. As a result, more rigorous academic standards, test-based accountability, and school choice mechanisms were set into motion—in some ways a kind of "heavy policy artillery" to fix education and educators (Calkins, 2015). Teachers were viewed as the problem, not the solution. The headline quote on the cover of the *Time* magazine a few years ago encapsulated the vast disconnect between the teachers' importance and how American society values their work: "I have a master's degree, 16 years of experience, work two extra jobs and donate plasma to pay the bills; I'm a teacher in America" (Reilly 2018).

The COVID-19 forced school closures of 2020 surfaced many daunting stories of disengaged students and stressed parents—not just because of the public health crisis but also because of deepened economic distress, amplified systemic racism, and precarious political tribalism. News reports, Twitter chats, podcasts, and blogs surfaced countless stories of the job of teaching becoming impossible and teachers as "beleaguered" (Noonoo, 2020). Even before the pandemic, stress was the major source of teacher turnover (Diliberti et al., 2021).

At the same time, the pandemic has put a bright light on an emerging truth—education as we have known it may never be the same. Influential think tanks, such as the Learning Policy Institute, have been calling for a re-invention of schooling in the aftermath of COVID-19 that includes strengthening distance and blended learning, more fully assessing what students (and their families) need, providing expanded learning time, and establishing community schools (Darling-Hammond et al., 2020). Suddenly, there is now an opportunity for everyone—policymakers and administrators, parents and their children, and teachers themselves to think of "school" and the teaching profession in deeply different ways (Berry et al., 2021).

Over 30 years ago, Sykes (1990) made the case that teachers will not be professionalized until schools create opportunities to access external knowledge, enhance peer relations, and provide leadership from their classrooms. In other words, the professionalization of teaching does not take root without serious consideration of the conditions under which teachers work. As public schools everywhere face a future of rapid change, intensifying complexity, and growing uncertainty, the teaching profession will need to adapt. Understanding teacher working conditions, past and present, is essential to shaping more effective schooling in the future.

In this chapter, I summarize findings from three distinct studies of teacher working conditions in South Carolina as a way to consider the prospects for the professionalization of an occupation long-considered to be a semi-profession. I begin with a study from 1990, as the state had gained national acclaim for its comprehensive reforms, then to a 2004 survey of teacher working conditions, and finally to a 2020 investigation to understand the lived experiences of those teaching amid the pandemic. But before turning to the descriptive data, I will summarize some more recent evidence on how workplace conditions influence teacher retention, teaching effectiveness, and school performance.

THE IMPORTANCE OF TEACHER WORKING CONDITIONS

Over the last 20 years, the importance of teacher working conditions in school improvement efforts has been well documented. For example, Johnson et al. (2005) found that the "character" of the workplace can influence the overall quality of a school faculty and the likelihood that teachers will persist in the profession. Other studies have pointed to the adverse impact of turnover on student achievement (Ronfeldt et al., 2013) and the high costs for school districts to replace teachers who leave (Barnes et al., 2007). While many teachers leave teaching because of poor salaries, studies often cite opportunities for a better teaching assignment and the lack of administrative support as influential (National Center for Education Statistics, 2004). Working conditions matter for teacher retention, teaching effectiveness, and school performance.

Utilizing 10 years of test scores and survey data from an urban district in North Carolina, researchers found that teachers working in schools with strong professional environments improved their effectiveness, over time, by 38% more than did peers in schools with weak environments (Kraft & Papay, 2016). The workplace conditions that supported teacher improvement included supportive principal leadership, opportunities for peer collaboration, effective professional development, and meaningful feedback, trust, and order (see Figure 8.1).

Ingersoll et al. (2017) used survey data from 900,000 teachers across 16 states, and found a strong relationship between teacher decision-making and school performance. They found that schools with the highest levels of overall instructional leadership from teachers had substantially higher mathematics and English language arts test scores than schools where teachers reported fewer opportunities to lead. The research team also found that in schools that serve high-poverty and minority students, teachers were less likely to report that they can raise concerns, that leaders support them, and that they work in trusting environments.

Berry et al. (2019) pinpointed the strong relationship between teachers' collective efficacy and school-level teacher retention, as well as student performance. Their research, drawing on both surveys and focused group interviews with teachers from high and low poverty schools, also

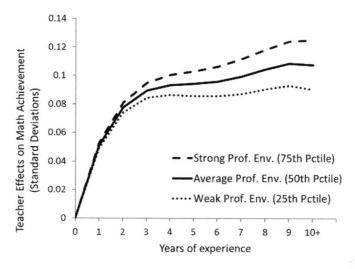

Figure 8.1 Predicted returns to teaching experience across schools with strong, average, and weak professional environments. *Source:* Kraft & Papay, 2016.

highlighted the importance of teacher leadership for developing collective efficacy and that a high concentration of expert teachers in a school (e.g., National Board-certified teachers) is associated with strong student achievement growth.

Simon and Johnson (2015) found that the "working conditions that teachers prize most—and those that best predict their satisfaction and retention—are social in nature" (p. 4). As Huizenga and Sczcesiul have found, teacher leadership is a "socially distributed phenomena" that develops over time as teachers gain efficacy; to do so, they must have "repeated opportunities" to reflect on what they master in the context of structured collaboration (p. 370). Daly et al. (2014) found a strong relationship between teachers reaching out to each other sharing knowledge of teaching strategies and higher student scores on formative assessments. Coburn et al. (2010) found that "social policy can play a role in fostering conditions in schools within which teachers seek out their colleagues, share information, solve problems, and learn from one another in their networks" (p. 331).

The working conditions that allowed teachers to be successful—most notably opportunities for peer collaboration—appear to be the ones that would advance the professionalization of teaching. And while a great deal is known about which factors matter in general, there has been little research and development effort to use local knowledge of these conditions to improve them.

THREE STUDIES OF TEACHER WORKING CONDITIONS
IN SOUTH CAROLINA

Setting the Context

Over the last 30 years, South Carolina has enacted a range of teaching policies supporting the state's education workforce, which comprises approximately 50,000 teachers. During the 1980s, spurred by the landmark report *A Nation at Risk*, nearly every state passed major education legislation focused on school reform. South Carolina was no exception. With the passage of the Education Improvement Act (EIA) of 1984, which was one of the nation's most comprehensive approaches to school improvement with an investment of more than $200 million in new dollars focused on increasing academic standards, improving the teaching of basic skills learning, raising teacher pay, strengthening accountability for schools, and rewarding high performers for higher test scores. The EIA sought to ensure South Carolina teachers were paid at least at the southeastern average.

Timar and Kirp (1989) described the school reform experience in South Carolina as an ideal because it "demonstrate(d) the need for balance between state accountability and local autonomy... [and] it show(ed) that authority and responsibility must be distributed across the entire system of education" (p. 510). In the 1990s, the state was involved in many restructuring efforts, including experiments with National Network for Educational Renewal and a modest effort to launch a lead teacher project (Berry & Ginsberg, 1990). By the mid-2000s, a range of indicators revealed that South Carolina was making progress: More kindergarten students were ready for school; graduation rates began to increase; and national organizations recognized South Carolina for its more rigorous academic standards and service learning opportunities for students (Bartels, 2006; see Figure 8.2).

During the early 2000s, the South Carolina Center for Teacher Recruitment launched and funded by the EIA, changed its name to CERRA (Center for Educator Recruitment, Retention, and Advancement) to reflect a more comprehensive approach to teacher development throughout the state. The programs included recruitment initiatives such as Teacher Cadets and Teaching Fellows and supports for experienced teachers to earn National Board Certification. By then, the state-recognized NBCTs by offering one of the nation's highest salary supplements to those who demonstrated their accomplished teaching skills (Berry et al., 2007). In the mid-2000s, South Carolina recruited teacher specialists to work in the state's lowest-performing schools. However, an $18,000 bonus attracted only 20% of the 500 teachers needed in the program's first year and only 40% after 3 years. Deterrents included location, lack of administrative support, poor working conditions, and a need for better preparation (Berry, 2009).

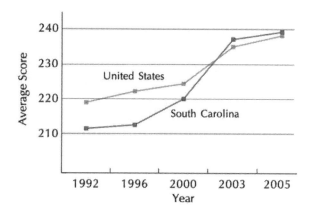

Figure 8.2 Student achievement improved based on the National Assessment of Educational Progress (NAEP).

Since 2001, CERRA has administered the South Carolina Annual Educator Supply and Demand Survey to all public school districts in the state and began publishing data on teacher hires, vacancies, departures, and the supply of new teacher education graduates. Over the last decade, reports have revealed a decline in enrollment in teacher education programs coupled with rising teacher turnover (CERRA, 2020). In 2018–2019, the nation's Red for Ed movement came to South Carolina as teachers walked out of their classrooms because poor salaries and working conditions undermined their capacity to serve students (Will, 2019). In 2021, the state's average teacher salary of $53,316 ranked 40th in the nation (Will, 2021).

The 1990 Study

Even as early as the late 1980s, evidence began to surface that school reform was taking its toll on the teachers of South Carolina. Several studies indicated problems in implementing several programs, including teacher and principal evaluation, that did not consider the complexity of their work and the need for more peer support (Berry & Ginsberg, 1989; Ginsberg & Berry, 1990). A national survey sponsored by the Carnegie Forum found that 43% of South Carolina's teachers reported that morale had worsened since the onset of reform (Ginsberg & Berry, 1990).

In 1989–1990, the South Carolina Educational Policy Center (SCEPC) undertook (what was believed to be) the first study of teacher working conditions in the State. SCEPC surveyed a random sample of 4,000 teachers and conducted focus group interviews with 108 classroom practitioners purposively selected from diverse school districts in the state.[1] The 77-item survey solicited teacher responses to a range of workplace-related factors, including the impact of school reform on teaching, using many of the same items used by a national study, as well as validated instruments to measure role conflict and job-related burnout.[2]

The Impact of Reform

The survey revealed two distinct patterns related to the impact of reform. First, a higher percentage of teachers reported that both in-service education and leadership of the principal had improved more than those who claimed they had gotten worse. Second, for teachers, time away from non-teaching duties, daily preparation time, daily teaching load, time to meet with other teachers, and the burden of paperwork all had gotten worse. Compared to the national sample, South Carolina teachers claimed that school reform worsened these issues. Sixty percent of South Carolina's teachers reported that morale had worsened due to the education reform movement (see Table 8.1).

Role Conflict and Ambiguity

The SCEPC study also drew upon Teacher Responses on the Role Conflict and Ambiguity Questionnaire that links one's behavior and clarity of the behavioral requirements of the job. The results showed little role ambiguity for South Carolina teachers as the prescriptive nature of many of

TABLE 8.1 Teacher Responses to Reform Impact Questions: South Carolina and National Surveys

How has each of the following been affected by the education reform movement?						
Selected Common Survey Items	SCEPC Teacher Study			All Teachers–Carnegie Study		
	Worse	No Change	Better	Worse	No Change	Better
Inservice education	19	27	55	14	22	64
Leadership of principal	24	40	36	9	16	75
Freedom non-teaching duties	51	34	15	43	41	16
Daily preparation time	38	40	22	33	45	21
Daily teaching load	40	40	21	29	43	28
Time to meet w/other teachers	48	37	15	31	39	30
Burden of paperwork	85	10	6	70	23	7
Morale	60	18	21	43	17	40

TABLE 8.2   Teacher Responses on the Role Conflict and Ambiguity Questionnaire (Selected items)

Responses	Percentage Responding		
	True	Neutral	False
I do things which should be done differently.	66	14	20
I have to work on unnecessary things.	68	12	20
I buck rules or policies to carry out an assignment.	24	14	62
I know exactly what is expected of me.	60	16	24
I feel certain about how much authority I have.	55	17	28
I know what my responsibilities are	78	12	10

the reforms led to great job clarity for teachers. Almost 8 in 10 teachers reported they know their responsibilities. Only 1 in 4 teachers believed they had to buck policies. And slightly over 1 in 2 teachers reported knowing how much authority they have. However, 2 in 3 teachers believed they had to do things differently; and 68% reported they had to work on unnecessary things (see Table 8.2).

Teacher Burnout

The study drew upon Maslach Burnout Inventory, a highly respected instrument used with those in the helping professions (Maslach & Jackson, 1981). The MBI has three subscales related to the burnout syndrome—high levels of depersonalization, low levels of personal accomplishment, and high levels of emotional exhaustion. South Carolina teachers reported average feelings of depersonalization and personal accomplishment. This meant that they felt positive about students in the face of the school reform and possessed some sense of work-related efficacy. But teachers reported very high levels of emotional exhaustion. The MBI norms on the EE subscale for teachers was 21.25. In South Carolina, teachers' EE ratings were about 50% higher at 31.13.

The survey revealed that more than 81% of South Carolina teachers reported they felt "used up by the end of the day;" more than 71% often felt

TABLE 8.3   Comparing MBI Mean Scores of South Carolina Teachers With a National Sample of Teachers and Other "Helping Professions"

MBI Subscale	South Carolina Teachers	All Teachers	Other Helping Professions
Depersonalization	8.92	11.00	8.73
Personal Accomplishment	36.63	33.54	34.58
Emotional Exhaustion	31.13	21.25	20.99

emotionally drained by their work, 60% claimed that they worked too hard, and 58% agreed that they felt fatigued in the morning when facing another day of work. These reported feelings of emotional exhaustion spanned every demographic group of teachers of the over 15,000 who responded.

The interviews revealed that most teachers defined burnout in terms of external demands, such as curriculum, testing mandates, teaching evaluation, burdensome paperwork, and their lack of input into policy and practice. Though not as pressing as other areas, parent and community support were cited. The interviews revealed that teachers believe their working conditions were worse than the previous 5 years. In one focus group, a teacher reported:

> I am being made into a machine, and my students are being made into machines. I guess I went to college to be a file clerk. Sometimes I know I am pushing things down their throats, just like pumping gasoline.

The 2004 Study

In 2004, with support from CERRA and the South Carolina Department of Education, the Center for Teaching Quality conducted a study of teacher working conditions for the state, drawing on a similar approach that I had recently used in North Carolina. The survey was anchored in five domains: time, empowerment, professional development, leadership, and facilities and resources, derived from the USDOE School and Staffing Survey, as well as stakeholder input. Every teacher in the state was surveyed, with over 15,000 responding, representing about 33% of the workforce (Center for Teaching Quality, 2004). Some of the descriptive highlights from the survey results for each domain are as follows.

Time

More than one-third of South Carolina teachers reported having *less than* 3 hours of planning time per week (35%), and over three-quarters (76%) reported having 5 hours or less (see Figure 8.3). Teachers also expressed frustration with non-instructional duties (e.g., bus, lunch duty) that often make it more difficult to focus their time on student learning. Only half of the state's teaching corps (52%) *believed* that they are protected from duties that interfere with their role of educating students; one-sixth (15%) *strongly disagreed* that they are protected.

Empowerment

About 75% of teachers *agreed* that they are trusted to make sound professional decisions about instruction and student progress (38% of which *strongly agreed*), and 70% *agreed* that they are recognized as educational

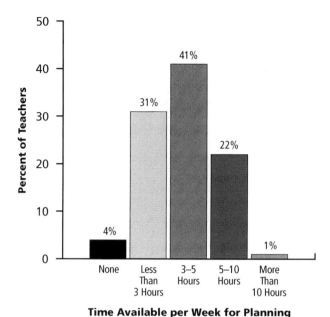

Figure 8.3 Time available per week for planning within the normal instructional day. *Source:* Center for Teaching Quality, 2004.

experts. However, much lower percentages of teachers reported that they had a role in hiring colleagues and determining school budgets. Only 17% *strongly agreed* that they help select what professional development is offered to them. And while two-thirds of the teachers agreed that there is an atmosphere of trust and mutual respect in their school, one-third did not believe this was the case. Over 4 in 10 teachers reported that they did *not* feel comfortable raising issues and concerns that are important to them, and their perception that reasoned educational risk-taking was *not* encouraged and supported in their school.

Professional Development

The majority of teachers gave positive marks to their professional development. More than 2 in 3 teachers believed there are sufficient resources, administrative support (68%), and time (69%) to find and take advantage of professional development opportunities. Additionally, three-quarters of teachers (73%) reported that they are provided opportunities to learn from one another. However, what teachers experienced was not always what was deemed effective. Graduate courses, taken during the last 2 years by 70% of South Carolina teachers responding to the survey, were more likely to be considered beneficial than the more frequently attended workshops and

TABLE 8.4 Method of Professional Development Delivery and Effectiveness

Method	Percentage of Teachers Participating Over Past Two Years	Percentage Participating Who Indicated That it Was the *Most* Beneficial
Workshops, Institutes, or Academies	92%	48%
Attendance at Conferences or Professional Meetings	82%	44%
Informal, Job-Embedded Professional Development Activities	79%	29%
Graduate Courses	70%	55%
Participation in Coaching or Mentoring	38%	17%
National Board Certification	14%	66%

Source: Center for Teaching Quality (2004).

conferences. National Board Certification was most valued but the least accessible. Both job-embedded and coaching were deemed to be the least effective for them (see Table 8.4).

While most teachers' professional development resources appeared sufficient, control over their learning content was not. Slightly over half (53%) of teachers agreed that they assist in determining the content of in-service professional development. The research team found that teachers rated their professional development more highly when they played a role in determining the content.

The 2004 survey posed several questions regarding induction and mentoring in South Carolina. The bottom line was that mentors and mentees shared different perceptions about the frequency of critical components of high-quality induction. In particular, the gap between mentees claiming that they never plan with their mentor, observe their teaching, or are observed is substantially different than what mentors reported (see Table 8.5).

Leadership

South Carolina teachers rated leadership support highly, particularly on communicating policies, expectations, and standards for evaluation and instruction. For example, 2 in 3 teachers reported that school administrators and support personnel are available and prioritize supporting them. The same proportion believed that the school leadership attempted to address their concerns (with 31% who *strongly agreed*). Seventy-seven percent *agreed* that they are recognized for professional accomplishments, and 71% reported that they receive helpful feedback for improving teaching and learning. However, positive ratings of school leadership were not uniform. About

TABLE 8.5   Mentor and Mentee Reporting of the Frequency of Key Characteristics of Induction

Position	Percent Indicating at Least Once a Week	Percent Indicating Several Times a Month to Less Than Once a Month	Percent Indicating Never
Planning During School Day			
Mentees (N = 1,520)	31.4%	31.1%	37.6%
Mentors (N = 2,972)	55.5%	27.9%	16.6%
Observing Mentee's Training			
Mentees	5.5%	76.1%	18.5%
Mentors	13.6%	56.5%	29.9%
Observing Mentor's Training			
Mentees	4.4%	49.8%	45.8%
Mentors	13.4%	59.8%	26.8%

Source: Center for Teaching Quality, 2004.

one-fifth (19%) of teachers indicated that administrators did *not* address leadership concerns. And over one-half (53%) of teachers reported that school leaders did *not* make an effort to minimize required administrative duties or paperwork that interferes with teaching.

Facilities and Resources

Teachers were consistently positive about the facilities and resources available to them. They rated facilities and resources with the highest domain average of any five areas. About two-thirds of South Carolina educators reported they had access to a broad range of educational support personnel, such as tutors, social workers, nurses (66%), and current instructional technology for their classrooms (65%). While this domain had the highest average, it also represents the largest differences in responses among teachers from schools serving low and high-income students. This issue of working conditions for teachers serving low and high-income students became more pronounced in the next study reviewed.

The 2020 Study

In early June 2020, an SC-TEACHER research team studied the state's teachers' teaching experiences amid the COVID-19 pandemic. The study, undertaken in collaboration with two state teacher associations and the South Carolina Department of Education, included the surveying of every South

Carolina teacher (with 1 in 4 responding) and conducting in-depth focus group interviews with 75 of them (who varied in teaching experience, high versus low poverty, and urban and rural contexts). The survey questions focus on various issues, including interactions with students, strategies and tools for remote teaching, access and comfort with online learning, causes of and adjustments to stress, and sources of guidance and support (Berry et al., 2020).

Overall, South Carolina's teachers took on new roles and tasks to reach and teach their students during the pandemic. They faced many barriers. However, on almost every issue raised, teachers who taught in high-poverty and rural schools, and those who worked with elementary students, students with disabilities, and English language learners faced many more challenges than their counterparts. The researchers derived five themes from their analysis (Berry et al., 2020).

Teachers' Commitment to Students and Their Profession

Teachers were *most concerned* about the well-being of their students. At the time of the survey (early June 2020), over 9 in 10 teachers who responded to our survey indicated that they planned to return to teaching in the fall. In each focus group interview, teachers talked about how much they "missed their students" and "struggled in not seeing them." Teachers consistently spoke to their "fear" that their students would be set back emotionally, as well as academically.

Stress Over Their Students and Adjustments to Remote Teaching

Teachers were most stressed about their student's social and emotional health and learning loss, in addition to their safety and what they should be doing now to prepare for next year. Only about one-half of the teachers reported they could interact with their students almost every day—and another 42% were able to do so weekly. Just over 50% of teachers reported they had adjusted to remote teaching.

During the interviews, teachers talked about the stress they experienced because of the lack of time to respond to remote learning in response to the pandemic. Others lamented the lack of clarity from administrators and increased what they thought was needless documentation. However, during the interviews, teachers recognized administrators who "helped them connect with students" and expressed concerns about their stress. They also pointed to and praised counselors who worked with them to address their students with "many mental health needs." On the other hand, not all teachers had the support they needed. One said:

> I was mostly stressed by my school administration as they micro-managed us. We had to redo successful things so that they could check a box. Paperwork seemed more important to them.

Barriers to Reaching and Teaching Students

Teachers went to major lengths to support students during the school closures. However, major barriers stood in their way—especially for those teachers who taught in high-poverty schools and worked with younger (elementary) students, English language learners, as well as those with disabilities. Over 4 in 10 teachers reported that their students did *not* have access to the internet or were not comfortable using digital tools at home. And even if students had access to cell service or broadband at home, it did not translate into access to learning. One teacher said, "This one family had internet access through only mom's cell phone—which had to be shared among six children."

A Whirlwind of New Demands in Teaching and Learning

The survey posed a series of questions regarding how teachers spent time on certain tasks before and after the pandemic. Teachers reported spending *more* (*or much more*) *time* communicating with parents (74%), holding office hours (65%), learning how to use technology (55%), completing paperwork (46%), and preparing lessons (41%). On the other hand, they reported spending *less* (*or much less*) *time* on direct teaching (78%) and attending required professional development (48%).

One teacher talked about how many parents "just did not know how to help their children with the technologies that we did have." Another teacher pointed out, "Our parents just were not familiar with the apps and websites we were using." And for many students, especially those who live in high-poverty communities, parental support for learning at home was difficult at best, "I had many students whose parents had 2–3 jobs to make ends meet." In one focus group, a teacher summarized it this way:

> Many students reported feeling isolated. Teachers made many mental health referrals. Academically, the students completed the assignments but did not engage well during the meetings. Many students just needed and wanted to chat and connect with the teacher and their peers. It was not about the work. They did the best they could.

Teachers had to take on many new and complex tasks as they shifted to remote teaching. Some were successful; others struggled. Most needed a lot more support. Others found new ways to collaborate in serving students and their families.

Important Lessons for the Return to Schooling

The survey also posed a series of questions regarding how teachers spent time on certain pedagogical practices compared to before the pandemic-driven school closures (see Figure 8.4). Teachers reported more time on e-tools and software and locating and using resources outside of their school

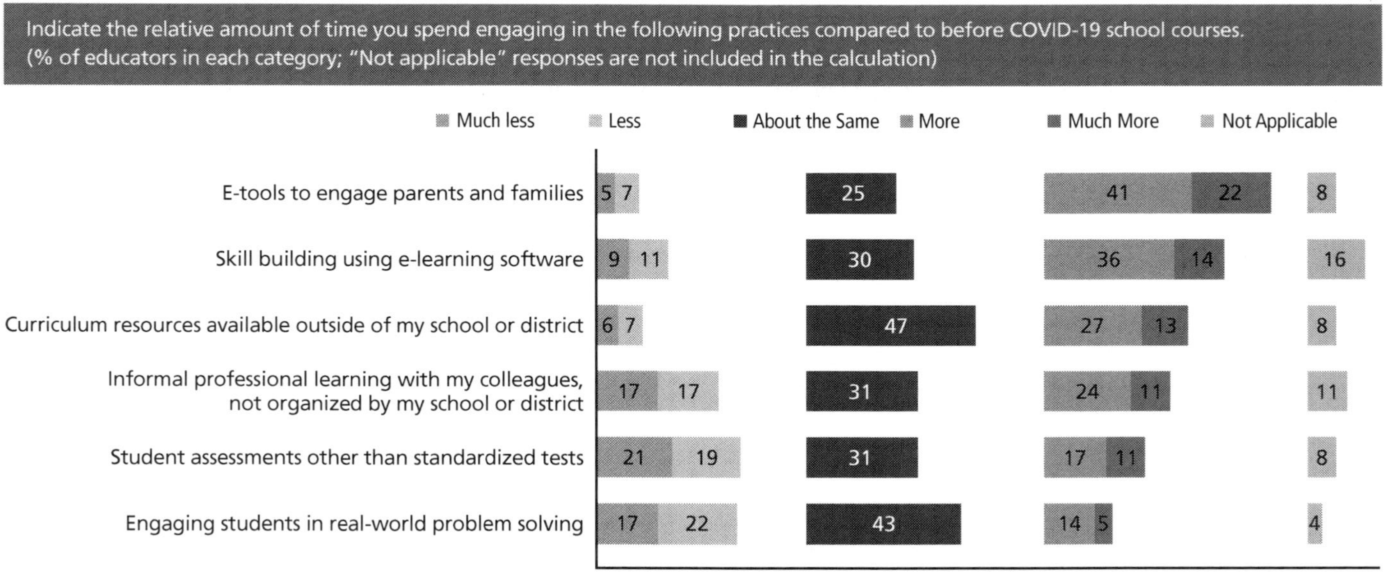

Figure 8.4 Time spent on pedagogical practices (during remote teaching and learning from March to June 2020). *Source:* Berry et al. (2020).

or district. While 1 in 3 teachers reported that they *spent less time* learning with colleagues, 35% indicated that they *had more time* to learn informally with each other. While 28% of teachers *spent more time* using student assessments other than standardized tests, 40% *spent less time.* Almost 1 in 5 teachers spent more time engaging students in real-world problems, but 39% *spent less time.*

The challenges teachers faced and the opportunities that arose during the early days of emergency teaching spurred innovative ideas and important lessons for the return to school and the future of education. While the interviews revealed that not all teachers experienced these opportunities, teachers who did pointed to four major innovations related to parent and family engagement, student-centered learning, curriculum, and teacher leadership.

First, teachers were successful with remote teaching because the school closures led them to find and use new technologies to stay connected to students and their families. In one focus group, a teacher pointed out, "In our school we really used social media effectively to get parents involved and communicate with them about their children's progress."

Second, some teachers could engage students throughout the school closures due to the personalized and project-based learning routines they already had established in their classrooms. In many ways, teachers talked about how the school closures forced a de-emphasis on high-stakes testing and allowed for a focus on real-world learning and anytime-and-anywhere instruction. It was these teachers who found more success in using a variety of e-tools, but only if their students had both the experience in leading their own learning, as well as supports at home. As one teacher said, "Distance Learning has to become second nature to us. Get us a real plan!"

Third, the school closures, and the subsequent need to slow down the pace of curriculum coverage, offered opportunities to think about what was most essential for students to learn. Teachers talked about what South Carolina's schools needed, as one teacher noted, "fewer standards and deeper learning." They also raised the issues of more grade/subject *looping* to allow teachers to work with the same students over several years. As one teacher elaborated, "We must know students better." As they reflected on the impact and opportunities of the pandemic, teachers talked about how their students need to feel more connected to a school curriculum that honors their story and background. One teacher said, "Moving forward, teachers in South Carolina need more support to carry out their students' best interests and motivate them through authentic teaching and learning."

Finally, during the school closures, some teachers found the time to learn from each other. And it was their informal learning and leading that helped them find and use more innovative strategies with students and parents. However, this professional learning and leadership was more likely to result from serendipity than strategy. In general, teachers called for more opportunities to learn from each other. This meant more autonomy in the classroom and more opportunities to lead for many. The survey revealed that most teachers reported their school/district gave them autonomy to make instructional decisions during COVID-19 school closures. However, those who taught in high poverty (74% vs. 82%) and rural schools (78% vs. 81%) were less likely to experience autonomy to make decisions they believed were needed. The kind of professional development teachers sought demanded that they lead their own learning. Teachers were clear that they wanted more voice in how they teach and how their students and themselves are expected to learn. Teachers wanted to lead. One teacher said:

> Teaching this spring really showed the inequity in the education system in both our schools and in our districts. The traditional way of doing things is not sufficient enough for our students. Teachers need to be at the decision-making table as we transform our way of teaching and learning.

Lessons for the Professionalization of Teaching

Decades ago, researchers began to assemble evidence that strongly suggested that education reform cannot fully succeed without support, involvement, and ultimately leadership from teachers—those who work inside schools and most closely with children and families (Ginsberg & Berry, 1998). Since then, many studies have pointed to the influence of more professionalized working conditions (e.g., peer collaboration, decision-making authority, and leadership) on teaching effectiveness, teacher retention, and school performance. Advancing teaching as a profession does not take hold unless teachers teach under more professionalized working conditions.

South Carolina is a state where teacher working conditions have been studied only periodically. And while the findings from these investigations reported herein are not comparable, some general themes have emerged. First, the 1990 study revealed a teaching workforce committed to students and their profession but emotionally exhausted. Teachers reported that they knew what administrators and school reform expected but were burdened by unnecessary tasks and paperwork. Teachers were tired as they sought to cope with state mandates.

Second, the 2004 study found large percentages of the state's teachers giving high marks to school leadership. Teachers also reported that they were trusted to make sound professional decisions about instruction. However, much lower percentages of teachers reported that they had a role in hiring colleagues and determining school budgets. Many teachers reported that they did *not* feel comfortable raising important issues with administrators and that risk-taking on their part was *not* encouraged. Teachers did not have sufficient time to spend on critical matters to their teaching. They again pointed to the burden of unnecessary paperwork. And teachers teaching high-poverty students were less likely to experience more professionalized working conditions.

The 2020 investigation revealed a committed teaching workforce experiencing extraordinary demands and stresses of pandemic-induced emergency teaching. Without sufficient supports, many teachers struggled. Others were able to find innovations with the potential to transform teaching and learning practices. Those who did seemed to do so because of the informal peer collaborations they could create for themselves, a theme anchored in the literature on effective professional learning. Teaching amid the pandemic created space for *some* teachers to find and use innovations in working with parents, the curriculum, and their role as leaders. And again, teachers in high-poverty schools had fewer opportunities to do so.

It is difficult to ascertain with these data as to whether or not the teaching profession has become more professionalized. If anything, one might conclude that for every one step forward in the march to professionalization, teachers have taken three fourths of a step back. After 30 years, several issues are clear: Teachers in South Carolina have had a limited voice in critical pedagogical and policy decision-making. And while some teachers have felt some degree of empowerment from time to time, those who teach the most high-need students reported less authority to exert their professional knowledge.

As pointed out previously, teaching was categorized as a semi-profession partly because its knowledge base has not been well defined and consistently used. These working conditions studies shed little light on these matters. Scant evidence, if any, is available on teachers' preparation into teaching and how schools and their professional education programs support their knowledge and its use. In addition, not much is known about how teachers develop shared conceptions of high-quality instructional practice and how they work collectively toward using evidence to improve their pedagogical skills.

Abbott (1988) makes the case that professional practice involves practitioners assessing a problem and using specialized knowledge and professional judgment in solving it. Future working conditions studies could query teacher reports on these matters. These working conditions studies have pointed to whether or not teachers believe they have sufficient time or whether their professional development is beneficial. However, it is important to know if teachers believe they are empowered and to what end. It is important to know that teachers have more time to learn and lead and how their learning and leadership can lead to better outcomes for children and communities.

South Carolina has placed some value on National Board Certified Teachers and has done so for many years. However, the state has made no systematic use of them in spreading evidence-based teaching and learning practices. Like in other states, South Carolina does not have a career arc for teachers, nor does it have a salary structure to pay different teachers differently based on what they do and accomplish. More needs to be known about how evaluation and compensation attract more capable and well-prepared teachers and encourage the spreading of teaching expertise.

The March 2020 edition of the *Kappan* focused on the status of America's teaching profession, and its editors concluded that teachers still have few occasions to "engage in serious and ongoing conversation about their work and how to improve it" (Heller, 2020). In the face of teacher shortages and the pandemic-fueled disruptions in schooling and colossal inequities made more visible, perhaps now is the time that teachers will lead these conversations with administrators and policymakers as well as with parents and students.

As Lortie (1975) noted almost 50 years ago, the experience of teachers tends to be private rather than shared. The explosion of new technologies has opened up new opportunities for teachers to learn from each other. Perhaps some of these same tools can be used to more systematically understand more nuanced and deeper aspects of teachers' working conditions and communicate the impact of those conditions more broadly to practitioners and policymakers and the public alike. Raising the discourse on teachers' working conditions can provide a window into the professionalization of teaching and the capacity of schools to support deeper and equitable learning of students. As Becker (1962) asserted, professionalization may not always be defined by a "strict application of moral criteria" to existing occupational groups, but by the concerted efforts of its members to "win the honorific label of *profession* for themselves."

In America, the professionalization of teaching has not been an easy task and will continue to require "money, political will, and the audacity" to imagine that teachers could be on "par" with lawyers and doctors (Mehta, 2013). Building on the legacy of a growing body of research, evidence-based conversations on working conditions could provide the basis for making a case for teaching to continue to advance as a profession.

NOTES

1. The 4,054 who responded represented 75% of the random selected sample and 11% of South Carolina total teacher workforce.
2. Maslach Burnout Inventory and the Role Conflict/Role Ambiguity Questionnaire

REFERENCES

Abbott, A. (1988). *A system of professions.* University of Chicago Press.
Allegretto, S., & Mishel, L. (2020). *Teacher pay penalty dips but persists in 2019.* Economic Policy Institute. https://files.epi.org/pdf/207502.pdf

Apple, M. W. (1985). Teaching and "women's work": A comparative historical and ideological analysis. *Teachers College Record, 86*(3), 445–473.

Barnes, G., Crowe, E., & Schaefer, B. (2007). *The cost of teacher turnover in five school districts: A pilot study.* National Commission on Teaching and America's Future.

Bartels, V. (2006) *The history of South Carolina schools.* Commissioned by Center for Educator Recruitment, Retention, and Advancement. https://www.carolana.com/SC/Education/History_of_South_Carolina_Schools_Virginia_B_Bartels.pdf

Becker, H. S. (1962) The nature of a profession. In N. B. Henry (Ed.), *Education for the professions: The 61st yearbook of the National Society for the Study of Education* (pp. 27–46). University of Chicago Press.

Berry, B. (2009). *Children of poverty deserve great teachers.* Paper commissioned by the National Education Association. https://www.teachingquality.org/wp-content/uploads/2018/04/Children_of_poverty_deserve_great_teachers.pdf

Berry, B. (2011). *Teaching 2030: What we must do for our students and our public schools... Now and in the future.* Teachers College Press.

Berry, B., Bastian, K. C., Darling-Hammond, L., & Kini, T. (2019). *How teaching and learning conditions affect teacher retention and school performance in North Carolina.* Learning Policy Institute.

Berry, B., Dickenson, T., Harrist, J., Pomey, K., Zheng, J., Irvin, M., Moon, A., & Hodges. T. (2020). *Teachers and teaching in the midst of a pandemic: Implications for South Carolina's policy leaders.* Research commissioned by The SC Education Association, the Palmetto Teachers Association, and the SC Department of Education. https://sc-teacher.org/wp-content/uploads/2020/08/TG_POLICY_FINAL_AUG5.pdf

Berry, B., & Ginsberg, R. (1988). Legitimizing subjectivity, meritorious performance and the professionalization of teacher and principal evaluation. *Journal of Personnel Evaluation in Education, 2,* 123–140.

Berry, B., & Ginsberg, R. (1990). Creating lead teachers: From policy to implementation. *Phi Delta Kappan, 71*(8), 616–621.

Calkins, A. (2015, December 11). *From 'shock and awe' to systemic enabling.* Next Generation Learning Challenge. https://www.nextgenlearning.org/articles/from-shock-and-awe-to-systemic-enabling

Carnevale, A. P., Cheah, B., & Hanson, A. R. (2015). *The economic value of college majors.* Georgetown University: Center on Education and the Workforce. https://1gyhoq479ufd3yna29x7ubjn-wpengine.netdna-ssl.com/wp-content/uploads/The-Economic-Value-of-College-Majors-Full-Report-web-FINAL.pdf

Center for Teaching Quality. (2004). *Listening to the experts: A report on the 2004 South Carolina teacher working conditions survey.* https://ncpc.info/sites/default/files/EPRU-0504-111-OWI.pdf

Coburn, C. E., Choi, L., & Mata, W. S. (2010). "I would go to her because her mind is math": Network formation in the context of district-based mathematics reform. In A. J. Daly (Ed.), *Social network theory and educational change* (1st ed.; pp. 33–50). Harvard Education Press.

Daly, A. J., Moolenaar, N. M., Der-Martirosian, C., & Liou, Y. (2014). Accessing capital resources: Investigating the effects of teacher human and social capital on student achievement. *Teachers College Record, 116*(7), 1–42. http://www.tcrecord.org/library/abstract.asp?contentid=17486

Darling-Hammond, L., Schachner, A., & Edgerton, A. K. (with Badrinarayan, A., Cardichon, J., Cookson, P. W., Jr., Griffith, M., Klevan, S., Maier, A., Martinez, M., Melnick, H., Truong, N., Wojcikiewicz, S.). (2020). *Restarting and reinventing school: Learning in the time of COVID and beyond*. Learning Policy Institute.

Diliberti, M. K., Schwartz, H. L., & Grant, D. (2021). *Stress topped the reasons why public school teachers quit, even before COVID-19*. RAND Corporation. https://www.rand.org/pubs/research_reports/RRA1121-2.html

Etzioni, A. (1969). *The semi-professions and their organization: Teachers, nurses, social workers*. Free Press.

Ginsberg, R., & Berry, B. (1990). The folklore of principal evaluation. *Journal of Personnel Evaluation in Education in Education, 3*, 205–230.

Ginsberg, R., & Berry, B. (1998). Expanding responsibility to enhance accountability. In R. J. S. MacPherson (Ed.), *The politics of accountability: Educative and international perspectives* (pp. 43–61). Corwin Press.

Heller, R. (2020, February 24). A profession in process. *Kappan*. https://kappanonline.org/teaching-profession-in-process-heller/

Ingersoll, R., Sirinides, P., & Doughtery, R. (2017). *School leadership, teachers' roles in school decision-making, and student achievement* [CPRE Working Paper]. University of Pennsylvania. http://www.cpre.org/sites/default/files/school_leadership_teachers__roles__in_school_decisionmaking_and_1.pdf

Ingersoll, R. M., & Collins, G. J. (2018). The status of teaching as a profession. In J. Ballantine, J. Spade, & J. Stuber (Eds.), *Schools and society: A sociological approach to education* (6th ed.; pp. 199–213). SAGE Publications.

Johnson, S. M., Berg, J. H., & Donaldson, M. L. (2005). *Who stays in teaching and why: A review of the literature on teacher retention*. Harvard Graduate School of Education, The Project on the Next Generation of Teachers.

Kraft, M., & Papay, J. (2016, April). *Developing workplaces where teachers stay, improve, and succeed*. Albert Shanker Institute. http://www.shankerinstitute.org/blog/developing-workplaces-where-teachers-stay-improve-and-succeed

Lortie, D. (1975). *Schoolteacher*. University of Chicago Press.

Maslach, C., & Jackson, S. E. (1981). The measurement of experienced burnout. *Journal of Occupational Behavior, 2*(2), 99–113.

Mehta, J. (2013, April 12). Teachers: Will we ever learn? *The New York Times*. https://www.nytimes.com/2013/04/13/opinion/teachers-will-we-ever-learn.html

National Center for Education Statistics. (2004). *Teacher attrition and mobility: Results for the teacher follow-up survey, 2000-01* (NCES 2004-301). https://nces.ed.gov/pubs2004/2004301.pdf

Noonoo, S. (2020, October 6). 'This job is impossible:' Frustrated teachers share what America's classrooms are really like. EdSurge. https://www.edsurge.com/news/2020-10-06-this-job-is-impossible-frustrated-teachers-share-what-america-s-classrooms-are-really-like

Reilly, K. (2018, September 24). I have a master's degree, 16 years of experience, work two extra jobs and donate plasma to pay the bills. I'm a teacher in America. *Time*. https://time.com/magazine/us/5394910/september-24th-2018-vol-192-no-12-u-s/

Ronfeldt, M., Loeb, S., & Wyncoff, J. (2013). How teacher turnover harms student achievement. *American Educational Research Journal, 50*(1), 4–36.

Rousmaniere, K. (2005). In search of a profession: A history of American teachers. In D. Moss, W. Glenn, & R. Schwab (Eds.), *Portraits of a profession: Teaching and teachers in the 21st century* (pp. 1–26). Praeger.

Rowan, B. (1994). Comparing teacher's work with work in other occupations: Notes on the professional status of teaching. *Educational Researcher, 23*(6), 4–17.

Simon, N. S., & Johnson, S. M. (2015).Teacher turnover in high-poverty schools: What we know and can do. *Teachers College Record, 117*(3), 1–36.

Sykes, G. (1990). Fostering teacher professionalism in schools. In R. Elmore (Ed.), *Restructuring schools: The next generation of education reform.* Jossey-Bass.

Timar, T. B., & Kirp, D. (1989). Education reform in the 1980s: Lessons from the states. *Kappan, 70*(7), 504–511.

Will, M. (2019, May 1) A RedForEd wave: Teachers in North and South Carolina leave classrooms in protest. *Education Week.* https://www.edweek.org/teaching-learning/a-redfored-wave-teachers-in-north-and-south-carolina-leave-classrooms-in-protest/2019/05

Will, M. (2021, April 26). Teacher salaries are increasing. See how your state compares. *Education Week.* https://www.edweek.org/teaching-learning/teacher-salaries-are-increasing-see-how-your-state-compares/2021/04

CHAPTER 9

THE WEIGHT OF ACCOUNTABILITY ON EDUCATORS

Sharda Jackson Smith
University of South Carolina, Upstate

Rinice Sauls
University of South Carolina

Generating a period of public education excitement, 1983's *A Nation at Risk: The Imperative for Educational Reform* prompted the field to take bold steps to appraise K–12 education systems at all levels (American Institutes for Research, 2013; Gardner et al., 1983; Jones, 2009; Kamenetz, 2018). The publication criticized the education system for its inability to provide equitable experiences for all students. One primary area of contention encapsulated the concept of teacher effectiveness and the efficacy of its measurement and evaluation (Kamenetz, 2018). More than ever, public policy began to articulate how teachers' effectiveness, which served as an underlying premise of student success, should be measured. More defined organizational structures were erected across the country, shaping processes to

How Did We Get Here?, pages 205–226
Copyright © 2022 by Information Age Publishing
www.infoagepub.com
All rights of reproduction in any form reserved.

measure teacher value and, ultimately, daily practices accompanying their work environment.

In the season of overwhelming teacher migration and attrition, why teachers leave the profession has often been diluted to reasons such as pay or lack of support, with some of the reasons being present since the indoctrination of public education. So, what connects the many reasons teachers leave? One underlying current that has grown over the last few decades while infiltrating everyday processes in schools is public policy's influence on measuring teacher effectiveness amid varying external and internal conditions. The inquiry that lies therein is the impact that persistent accountability systems have had on teachers' job satisfaction, and subsequently retention. Once again, how do these systems aid in the teacher shortage?

Not to be mistaken, being held accountable for student outcomes is not why teachers leave the profession. Still, it is a fact that in the current age of education, policy-based accountability has had a direct effect on teacher stress and burnout symptoms (Ryan et al., 2017; von der Embse et al., 2016). But, as Wronowski and Urick (2019) state, "Accountability and assessment policies are not congruent with [teachers'] views of their profession ... [and, therefore, teachers do not leave simply] because they are not effective" (p. 22). Rather, the relationship of teacher perception of de-professionalization (loss of influence or control over the technical core of their work, specifically influence over curriculum and instructional decisions) and demoralization (which includes decreased time for instruction due to accountability, administrative tasks, and worry and stress with emotional exhaustion as an endpoint) contributed to teacher turnover (Wronowski & Urick, 2019). These constructs can be defined as *weight.*

This chapter reviews how efforts to improve educational outcomes have negatively affected educator well-being. We rely on von der Embse et al.'s (2016) theoretical framework of the "multifaceted influence of macro-level variables (i.e., accountability policy) on individual variables (e.g., instructional practices and teacher stress)" (p. 309). It argues that good-faith efforts to increase student achievement through teacher effectiveness measurement created a cyclical evaluative system, dependent on measures and practices that can be viewed as impractical and exhaustive. It is designed to walk readers through policies that relate directly to effectiveness measures by beginning with an overview of teacher accountability policy, with the premise that teacher accountability is encapsulated through teacher evaluation that inherently impacts teacher working conditions. Afterward, readers get a similar glimpse of how accountability was exercised at the state level using South Carolina as a case narrative by first identifying the state's relevant policy structure, how effectiveness was measured, and its inherent impact on teacher working conditions. Undoubtedly influenced by policy, procedure, and shared concern for student success, educator effectiveness continues to be a priority of the education field and a factor in overall teacher disposition.

HOW WE GOT HERE: THE EVOLUTION OF THE EDUCATOR EFFECTIVENESS SYSTEMS IN AMERICA

Policy Efforts to Improve Teacher Accountability

For decades, federal education policy has sought to emphasize the importance of accountability in public schools (Murray & Howe, 2017). The No Child Left Behind Act of 2001 (NCLB) included a clause tailored for developing and retaining "excellent" teachers and outlined a series of grant-based initiatives to support the assertion that high-quality teachers were the standard. This sentiment became a sweeping interpretation for teachers and aided the push towards the connection between teacher effectiveness and student outcomes on state-mandated assessments (Domaleski, 2020).

Later, in response to the Great Recession, the federal government enacted the American Recovery and Reinvestment Act of 2009 (ARRA). In union with other areas of priority, ARRA sought to increase the economic wellbeing of education and advance schooling components with a rebuilding undertone, which included holding teachers accountable for their students' success. The act specifically addressed the intent to "[assess] the impact of performance-based teacher and principal compensation" under the title of *Innovation and Improvement.* Like NCLB, performance ratings varied across states, but often highlighted factors associated with standardized testing.

Further, a product of ARRA was the competitive Race to the Top (RTTT) grant. RTTT offered hundreds of millions of dollars to several state departments to reform their education systems by improving data systems to inform instruction and improve teacher "quality" (United States Department of Education, n.d.). Although only some states took advantage of the opportunity provided by the RTTT grants, its message of accountability influenced national discord towards educator effectiveness (Dragoset et al., 2015). Another facet of the ARRA policy addressed the importance of each student, despite their demographic background, to have access to a quality educational environment. To achieve equity in exemplary teacher distribution, the ARRA (2009) declared:

> The State will take actions to improve teacher effectiveness and comply with section 1111(b)(8)(C) of the ESEA [Elementary and Secondary Education

Act] (20 U.S.C. 6311(b)(8)(C)) in order to address inequities in the distribution of highly qualified teachers between high- and low-poverty schools, and to ensure that low-income and minority children are not taught at higher rates than other children by inexperienced, unqualified, or out-of-field teachers. (p. 169)

Afterward, the Every Student Succeeds Act (ESSA) of 2015, the latest incarnation of the Elementary and Secondary Education Act of 1965, continued to elevate the prioritization of holding educators primarily responsible for outcomes. Under Title I, the reauthorization addressed public notification of criteria for measuring teacher effectiveness. Considerable attention was placed on securing tangible data to inform decision-making. An extension of NCLB, ESSA (2015) furthered tenacity promoting an "expectation that there [would] be accountability and action to effect positive change in [the] lowest-performing schools, where groups of students [were] not making progress, and where graduation rates [were] low over extended periods of time."

These policies highlighted the pervasiveness of inequitable experiences in certain areas of the population and pointed at instructors as one of the foundational factors in subsequent associated outcomes resulting from that inequity. At this time, evaluation extended beyond the intention of improving quality instruction—by including the expected outcome of advancing student proficiency in subject areas—through the revamping of state standards and national alignment to make the citizenry competitive on an international stage, for example, through Common Core State Standards (Martinie et al., 2016; McShane, 2014; Rothman, 2014), which encompassed its share of criticism (Tienken, 2013). Essentially, assessments were changing for both teachers and students simultaneously.

Educators grappled with whether they were equipped with enough resources to realize this shared desire for student growth, with attention to outcomes for all students. However, the lack of quantification for particular variables that impact student success created an uneasiness in the use of particular measures, however. Practitioners feared that the climate of the "inclusion of student data at a time when scores on new assessments [were] dropping [alongside] new evaluation systems [would be] magnified by the inclusion of data that [would] get worse before it [got] better" (National Association of Secondary School Principals, 2019, p. 2). Considering this reality, how effectiveness was measured required closer examination. Without clear and precise incorporation, teacher confidence in the evaluation system they were subject to made a necessary process appear less favorable.

Measuring Teacher Effectiveness

Workman and Wixom (2016) pronounced that providing teachers with ongoing feedback and targeted professional development following evaluations is an effective strategy for teacher retention. The practicality in understanding that teacher effectiveness is a product of an adopted appraisal system, variability in how effectiveness was measured was inevitable, and this variability fueled concern about the lack of attention to varying factors that also affect student success. The Education Commission of the States (2018) reflected that consistency in the depth and breadth of the evaluation was an area of concern by stakeholders and advised state policymakers to define perspectives on concepts like the purpose of the evaluation; when, how, and who is responsible for conducting it; which metrics and categories are used to measure and classify teacher performance; whether evaluation procedures should be subject to collective bargaining; and whether districts have the supports they need to ensure proper implementation. Understanding how these measures would be used for teachers, Goe et al. (2008) noted that reliability, validity, credibility, coherence, and the consequences of measures were essential in developing instruments to properly measure and evaluate teaching.

Attempting to move beyond sole dependency on standardized assessment in policy, scholars became explicit about measuring teacher effectiveness. According to Poproski and Green (2018), valid metrics of teaching effectiveness should include student perspectives (student focus groups/discussions, early/mid-course feedback surveys, longitudinal evaluations [alumni exit interviews/surveys]), peer review of teaching (peer observation of teaching, peer review of teaching materials), and instructor reflection/review (teaching portfolios, self-evaluation of teaching effectiveness, self-evaluation using videos of instructor's teaching, scholarship, reflection). In general agreement, Kawasaki et al. (2020) believed that teaching quality should be measured from multiple means such as observation rubrics, teaching artifacts, instructional logs, value-added models, pedagogical content knowledge, surveys of teachers/mentors, and teacher portfolios. These ideas communicated the sophistication of determining effectiveness for teachers.

In the wave of using goals, programs, and outcomes as accountability pieces for teacher effectiveness, attention to the variance of conditions that affect student achievement considered outside teacher control grew. Some metrics attempted to control for these differences but did so in ways that included considerable limitations that affected teachers' effectiveness measures. For example, value-added modeling (VAM) is a popular tool that measures teacher effectiveness. Via large-scale standardized test scores and by statistically controlling for finite confounding variables, VAM purported to predict what students would achieve if the average teacher taught them; after which, VAM calculated the differences between students' actual scores and the relative predictions, averaging the differences together to yield teachers' value-added estimates (Amrein-Beardsley & Holloway, 2019). Related factors could include the number of subject-relevant courses in which a student was enrolled, prior year scores, disability, language, gifted status, attendance, mobility, age in grade, class size, and homogeneity of students' entering test scores in the class (e.g., Florida Admin. Code R. 6A-5.0411). The way VAM measures teachers can be reflected in percentile ranking with an annual predetermined effectiveness level.

Understanding that strong pockets of support serve as the basis for the use of VAM, its statistical and methodological capability to measure teacher effectiveness is contested, especially because stakes are high for teachers. The National Association of Secondary School Principals (2019) noted that VAM scores are used to "make key personnel decisions about retention, dismissal, and compensation of teachers [when] states [are adopting and implementing] challenging academic content and achievement standards" (p. 1), signaling a considerable dependency on its accuracy as a metric.

Yet, considerable reservations in the concept of the value-added model to accurately define teacher effectiveness exist, with a heavy emphasis on external factors that can contribute to teacher effectiveness assessment. Ultimately, the American Statistical Association (2014) found that "teachers account for about 1% to 14% of the variability in test scores, and that the majority of opportunities for quality improvement are found in the system-level conditions [and that] ranking teachers by their VAM scores can have unintended consequences that reduce quality" (p. 2), a valid construct when attempting to understand teacher disdain of particular measures that control their professional fate. Overwhelming assumptions of models like VAM that researchers (and teachers) argued against included (Amrein-Beardsley & Holloway, 2019):

- The influence that students' prior teachers have on student learning (i.e., teacher persistence or residual effects) is negligible, and if not negligible, they can be statistically controlled for under the assumption that these effects decay quickly and, again, at the same rate over time (p. 531).
  Even though multiple teachers teach and interact with students in multiple ways, value-added effects can be attributed solely to single teachers under examination (p. 531).
- Because test-based measurements typically yield a mathematical and assuredly highly scientific value, an appropriate level of certainty or exactness comes along with the numerical scores that result (p. 533).

- A normal distribution, or a bell curve, of teacher effectiveness exists and can and should be used to norm large-scale standardized achievement test scores for VAM analyses (p. 534).
- Large-scale standardized achievement tests are the best and most objective measure we have, and because they are readily available and accessible, but despite the fact that they are designed to measure student achievement and not teacher effects, we should use them to make causal distinctions about teachers regardless (p. 535).

On its surface, teacher evaluations "differentiate performance, inform feedback, improve professional development, provide opportunities for pay increases and advancement, and provide a rationale for teacher dismissals" (Education Commission of the States, 2018, p. 1). Still, upon closer inspection, nuanced measures in teacher effectiveness (and incentives tied to it) prompted a new era in determining the degree to which teachers were subject to equitable circumstances and metrics. Wright et al. (2018) noted that "the use of [student growth models] measures in teacher evaluation, compensation, or both, statistically significantly negatively predicted both teachers' pedagogical and curricular autonomy, as well as job satisfaction" (p. 20). With the previously noted assumptions in mind, although teachers accept and appreciate accountability, the measures used to define their capability have substantial flaws; and thus, the cyclical pieces of assessment used to conclude teacher effectiveness can have full-scale, inequitable effects.

Impact on Teacher Working Conditions

Teachers' lack of trust in effectiveness measures and the resources surrounding them should not be misconstrued as an indicator of a dislike of accountability. On the contrary, inequitable resources, a lack of resources, and unique dispositions of student development and their effects on how outcomes are influenced fuel the discontent. Paufler et al. (2020b) found that "compliance with state accountability demands overshadowed the potential for the evaluator role to focus on support for growth, even in a system that is promoted as growth-based" (p. 45). Acknowledging that the manner in which evaluation systems are currently implemented can negatively impact teacher perceptions of teacher work environments (Wright et al., 2018, p. 21), research persists in defining which pieces breed dissatisfaction.

Teachers report that several factors contribute to student performance. Researchers note that many of these factors are challenges teachers face daily. Challenges include insufficient parent involvement, low student motivation, low/erratic student attendance, low staff morale, poor student discipline, inadequate or substandard facilities, inadequate supports for the lowest-achieving students, too few instructional materials, instructional materials that are not aligned with state standards, a large number of student transfers into schools and classrooms at various points during the year, low teacher expectations for student achievement, large class size or caseloads, lack of safety in or around the school, and insufficient access to technology (Rosenberg et al., 2014). Teachers are subject to regular evaluation with these factors in mind, which often do not articulate the surrounding conditions. When thinking of what teachers actively protest, these constructs loom.

Generally, the profession accepts that evaluations are a means of support for educators, making it an essential component. Nonetheless, the greater question becomes whether the ends justify the means. How the theoretical constructs of evaluation policy matriculate in practice is a complex factor in teacher perception of the weight of accountability. Major components of evaluation systems, such as observations and associated tasks, appear trivial. How this looks across teachers' experiences can vary. For example, one experienced teacher in a study conducted by Derrington and Martinez (2019) noted:

> The problem is that the system does not really do anything to change or improve the practice of successful, tenured teachers, but does require a lot of time that is redundant year in and year out. Spending time on the teacher evaluation rubric is another chore to accomplish, but it is essentially useless to me in my professional practice. I disagree every teacher in the building should go through the same process every year if they have tenure. It's a huge investment of time and paperwork for the teachers and the principals with an unequal benefit. (p. 43)

Administrators recognize the weight of accountability on educators, too. In response to federal legislation, Campbell and Derrington's (2019) study found that evaluators had major concerns regarding teacher evaluation:

> Principal comments included, "One concern I have ... is in the scoring ... having test scores play a major role in a teacher's evaluation score ... we don't always have control over that ... and it's one snapshot of a student"; and "Talk about throwing darts in the dark ... I see a teacher do a really good job ... but on those four days where their students test, they don't do so well." Of value-added measures used for summative effectiveness calculations, one principal said of teachers, "Their value-added score could have a million things that don't have a whole lot to do with how much they [students] learned that year." Some non-tested teachers were required to take school-wide test scores as the quantitative, test-based factor in their final effectiveness rating. This was seen as unreasonable. One principal said, "A lot of teachers might be a 5, but may not be doing level-5 work," indicating that the structurally inflexible rating system misrepresents some teachers' effectiveness. (p. 69–70)

Considering that "teacher perceptions of [performance evaluation systems] characteristics (e.g., fairness of measures, evaluator credibility, and quality of feedback) influence[s] the perceived impact of the evaluation process on teaching and teacher perceptions of its potential benefits" (Finster & Milanowski, 2018, p. 3), the culture of accountability requires a greater degree of support for teachers, as pronounced in protests across the nation. This look at the micro-level becomes important in understanding why this culture has bred an increasingly flimsy pool of educators. To paint a picture of how the evolution of educator effectiveness practices can manifest overtime at the state level, we explore South Carolina's educator evaluation system, illustrating the challenges of converting evaluation policy to everyday processes and the unintended hardship for teachers it can create.

How We Got Here: The Evolution of the Educator Effectiveness System in South Carolina

Policy Efforts to Improve Teacher Accountability

Concurrent to federal efforts, historical precedence at the state level related to teacher accountability was set. South Carolina (a state that did not make use of ARRA funds) passed the South Carolina Education Improvement Act of 1984 decades before the NCLB Act of 2001, advocating the "(a) evaluation for teaching performance as it relates to improved student learning and development; (b) evaluation by a team which includes principals and peers; (c) evidence of self-improvement through advanced training; (d) meaningful participation of teachers in the development of the plan; and (e) working with student teachers whenever possible" (South Carolina General Assembly, 2009, SubPart 2, Section 59-21-810). This legislation set the inflection of liability in the profession and related practices. The South Carolina Education Accountability Act of 1998 outlined teaching incentives, specifically the encouragement and recruitment of teachers for assignments at below average and school/district at-risk schools based on statewide standardized testing; pushing the idea that teachers who were at these schools would be subject to receive salary and a supplement equal to 50% of the current southeastern average teacher salary as projected by the Revenue and Fiscal Affairs Office (S.C. 59-18-1530(b)). The policy (S.C. 59-18-110) emphasized academic subject-specific proficiency, explicitly noting accountability systems, professional development for the state, and linking pay for performance.

Acknowledging the impetus behind evaluation is to support teachers through feedback and professional development, the South Carolina Code of Laws mandated that teacher evaluations be "provided in writing and [that] appropriate assistance [be] provided when weaknesses in performance are identified, noting that goals must be established by the teacher in consultation with a building administrator and must be support-ive of district strategic plans and school renewal plan" (S.C. 59-26-30 (B) (5)), thus ensuring that staff quality and professional development were the central purposes in teacher evaluation systems (e.g., Robertson-Kraft & Zhang, 2018). With this, educators were required to have an annual Profes-sional Growth and Development Plan as a part of their evaluation.

The United States Department of Education (USED; ESEA 2101(c)(4) (B)(ii) and 2103(b)(3)(A)) required student growth measures to be imple-mented by 2015 (South Carolina Department of Education, 2017). South Carolina expanded its evaluation system for educators to require multiple sources of evidence of effectiveness, which included a measure of profes-sional practice, student growth (VAM or another model), and the option for a "district choice" measure (which could include an additional test-score based measure or stakeholder surveys; South Carolina Department of Education, 2017). As it related to VAM, South Carolina preferred to address growth measurement systems in reference to the school and district, offer-ing the option for districts to use VAM to evaluate teachers but defining to whom the measure may be shared and presenting it in the state code of laws as an option that districts may employ (e.g., South Carolina 59-18-1960). In late 2015, the USED reauthorized ESEA legislation, and the South Carolina Department of Education (SCDE) requested that the requirement for VAM be removed as part of an educator's evaluation (South Carolina Depart-ment of Education, 2017).

The ADEPT chronology. The South Carolina Education Accountability Act (1998), the state's system for assisting, developing, and evaluating pro-fessional teaching (ADEPT), was implemented in 1998 to define profes-sional teaching (S.C. Code Ann. 59-26-30 and 59- 26-40). ADEPT "grew out of the knowledge that good teaching is fundamental to student academic growth and achievement" (South Carolina Department of Education, 2017, p. 5). After all, measures of educator effectiveness were designed to provide teachers with actionable, targeted feedback to improve profes-sional practices and positively impact student academic outcomes. In addi-tion to being a vehicle for evaluator feedback and support, completing the year-long summative ADEPT evaluation process was required for teacher eligibility for a professional teaching certificate, making it a high-stakes process for teachers.

Five years after its initial implementation, the ADEPT system was reevalu-ated and revised to directly connect evaluation outcomes to teacher licen-sure and create ADEPT Implementation Guidelines, which would be in use until 2012 (S.C. Code Ann. Regs. 43-20.1; South Carolina Department of Education, 2017). In 2012, upon approval of the waiver from ESEA, the SCDE expanded the evaluation system to include student growth measures and a third component, the "district-choice" measure (South Carolina Department of Education, 2017). By 2014, the South Carolina State Board of Education approved the Expanded ADEPT Support and Evaluation System guidelines for implementation during the 2015–2016 school year.

In December 2015, the ESEA reauthorization granted local education agencies added flexibility in designing educator evaluation systems. The SCDE made requests to the State Board of Education to remove VAM as a part of the educator evaluation system and continue collecting evidence of student growth through student learning objectives (SLOs). The most recent iteration, implemented in 2017, was the *Expanded ADEPT Support and Evaluation System for Classroom-Based Teachers,* which uses the South Carolina Teaching Standards 4.0 Rubric designed by the National Institute for Excellence in Teaching (NIET) to measure professional practice. This rubric is based on performance standards, meets federal requirements, and supports the vision of teaching and learning in South Carolina. The SLO is incorporated as an artifact to support evaluation ratings, not a stand-alone measure (South Carolina Department of Education, 2017).

Measuring Teacher Effectiveness

Teacher effectiveness measurement in South Carolina fostered a climate of added accountability and increased stress on teachers. The Expanded ADEPT system included components not previously used in South Carolina, creating a shift in teacher outcomes. Some of the components of South Carolina's evaluation system and its impact on teacher working conditions include:

Value-added measures.   Although it did not persist as a requirement, the SCDE established a relationship with Statistical Analysis System (SAS) to implement a VAM called the Education Value-Added Assessment System (EVAAS). Like their peers across the nation who implemented VAM years earlier and found VAM potentially punitive (see Ryan et al., 2017), teachers in South Carolina felt like value-added measures were too uncertain and too complex to be attributed to their evaluations (David, 2010). Growing concern about VAM's methodology and its ability to accurately capture a teacher's effectiveness (see Lavigne, 2014) served as an area of stress, which eventually led to VAM not progressing beyond the pilot stage in South Carolina (South Carolina Department of Education, 2017).

Professional practice.   Until 2017, teachers received summative feedback in the previous evaluation system once during the evaluation cycle (South Carolina Department of Education, 2010). In a survey conducted by the American Institutes for Research and the SCDE, South Carolina's teachers suggested that they wanted more opportunities for timely, meaningful, and actionable commentary from their evaluators that provided "[immediate] more direct instructional feedback" (Jaques & Fireside, 2016, p. 34) so that they can adjust their practice (Jaques & Fireside, 2016, p. 35). Considering this criticism, the SCDE sought a professional practice rubric that could be incorporated into the current evaluation structure and provided additional opportunities for teachers to receive feedback and differentiated support. A team of educators, convened by the SCDE, selected the Teaching Standards Rubric from the NIET for use in South Carolina. Later named the South Carolina Teaching Standards 4.0 Rubric, it supported the Profile of the South Carolina Graduate, a framework developed by the South Carolina Council on Competitiveness that identified the knowledge, skills, and dispositions essential for the success of South Carolina's students in college or career. It met federal requirements allowing evaluators to differentiate a teacher's practice for support and created a standard for what effective teaching looks like (South Carolina Department of Education, 2017).

Student learning objectives.   Student learning objectives (SLOs), often described as a vehicle for collecting evidence of student growth in the classroom, allowed teachers to monitor their direct impact on student learning to measure their effectiveness through systematic data analysis, reflection on instruction, and its impact on student learning. The process is benchmarked by three required conferences between the teacher and their evaluator to reflect on student growth and instructional adjustments needed to maximize student growth. Initially developed for teachers in non-tested grades and subject areas, the SLO in South Carolina used student test scores on locally developed assessments to determine the teacher's impact on student growth. This measure was perceived by some as a lesser form of accountability because it was not linked to state standardized tests, like EVAAS VAM.

Impact on Teacher Working Conditions

In the 1980s, South Carolina faced declining enrollment in teacher preparation programs due to diminishing images of the profession, low teacher pay, and challenges in the classroom (CERRA, n.d.-c). Amidst growing concern for the quality of teachers in South Carolina schools, the Commission of Higher Education established a nonprofit organization geared specifically to study the recruitment and retention of South Carolina teachers. The Center for Educator Recruitment, Retention and Advancement (CERRA) administers its Annual Educator Supply and Demand Survey to gather data on teacher hiring, retention, and separation from public school districts in the state. Its most recent survey found that of the approximately 6,000 teachers to leave their positions in 2019–2020, about 6% pursued another profession or career (see Table 9.1 and Figure 9.1; Garett, 2020). Acknowledging that 42% of all teachers who left the profession had 5 or fewer years of teaching experience in the state, why these teachers left the profession early in their careers fueled a discussion. Because educators engage in an arguably rigorous summative evaluation process within the first

TABLE 9.1 Key Teacher Data From CERRA's South Carolina Annual Educator Supply & Demand Reports

School Year	Completers of a SC Bachelor's Level Initial Educator Preparation Program[a]	Completers of a SC Master's Level Initial Educator Preparation Program[b]	Teachers Who Left Their Position[c]	Teachers Who Left With ≤1 Year of Experience in a SC Public School[c]	Teachers Who Left With 2–5 Years of Experience in a SC Public School[c]	Teachers Who Left With >5 Years of Experience in a SC Public School[c]
2016–2017	1,720 (2015–16)	542 (2015–16)	6,482.2	777.8	1,687.6	4,016.8
2017–2018	1,685 (2016–17)	483 (2016–17)	6,705.0	803.0	1,761.3	4,140.7
2018–2019	1,673 (2017–18)	498 (2017–18)	7,339.3	935.7	1,660.4	4,743.2
2019–2020	1,752 (2018–19)	418 (2018–19)	6,649.8[d]	880.4[d]	1,487.0[d]	3,746.5[d]
2020–2021	1,697 (2019–20)	370 (2019–20)	5,995.7	973.6	1,577.4	3,444.7

[a] Data obtained from the SC Commission on Higher Education (CHE). Includes students who graduated from a SC public or private institution with a bachelor's degree eligible for teacher certification.

[b] Data obtained from the SC CHE. Includes students who graduated from a SC public institution with a master's degree eligible for teacher certification. Data for private institutions are not available.

[c] Data obtained directly from SC school district representatives. Includes classroom teachers (and other certified educators who provide instructional and support services) who transferred to another SC public school district.

[d] Representatives from two districts were not able to provide years of teaching experience for their departures reported in 2019–20. Therefore, the total number of teacher departures (column 4) is correct, but it does not equal the sum of the numbers in the 3 "years of experience" columns (columns 5–7).

Note: Adapted from CERRA (n.d.-a). Full reports can be accessed at https://www.cerra.org/supply-and-demand.html

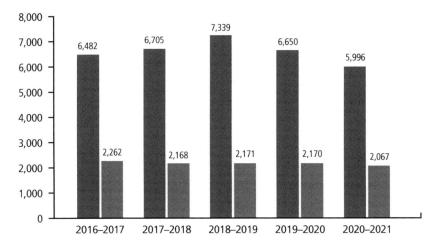

Figure 9.1 Teacher supply and demand (CERRA, 2021). *Note:* Adapted from CERRA (n.d.-b).

3 years of their employment, could the demands of the evaluation process affect teacher attrition and retention?

Teachers' perceptions of SLOs in South Carolina. Despite the messaging around the revised evaluation system's focus on teacher development, educators often conflate administrative supervision with evaluation, creating feelings of chronic tension. In 2016, the American Institutes for Research, in partnership with the Southeast Comprehensive Center (SECC) and the SCDE, conducted surveys and focus groups of more than 11,000 educators in public schools and institutions of higher education (IHEs) across South Carolina about perceptions of the Expanded ADEPT system components. The survey yielded approximately a 20% response rate and explored teacher and administrator perceptions of the evaluation system components (South Carolina Department of Education, 2017). The survey identified that some teachers felt like the SLO process created opportunities to collaborate with other teachers and staff and helped them "identify instructional strengths and challenges, provide useful instructional feedback, improve teaching practice, and learn more about their students' academic strengths and challenges" (Jaques & Fireside, 2016, p. 25).

   In contrast, but consistent with studies that show that test score-based accountability significantly affects teacher stress, burnout, and eventually attrition (Paufler et al., 2020a; Robertson-Kraft & Zhang, 2018; Ryan et al., 2017), some South Carolina teachers explained (Jacques & Fireside, 2016) that they:

- "felt overwhelmed by the SLO process" at first (p. 16);
- "couldn't see the big picture because they [were] up to their eyeballs in everything, even with training," including the "burden of paperwork" (p. 16);
- were "unclear on whether the purpose of the SLO process was to hold teachers accountable for student learning or whether it was to promote professional growth" (p. 30);
- felt like this was "evaluation and not growth" (p. 30);
- perceived the SLO as an accountability measure with no impact on teaching and learning (p. 21); and
- felt this challenge was "depressing" and " I feel like I do a great job, but when they give you back your scores, and only 60% of students met their target . . . I might as well just stay home" (p. 24).

Increased paperwork and evaluation conferences coupled with other added accountability, while not reducing any other responsibilities, contributed to feelings of professional grief so pervasive that the SCDE conducted a Paperwork Reduction Study to streamline and reduce paperwork demands placed on teachers and administrators (South Carolina Department of Education, 2019). Teachers identified the SLO and educator evaluation processes as the third most time-consuming paperwork tasks (p. 15). Consistent with that finding, Jacques and Fireside (2016) reported that some South Carolina teachers felt the SLO created "an undue paperwork burden on teachers that they did not perceive having an impact on their practice" (p. 30).

Ultimately, managing the different evaluations and associated frequencies created an unrelenting undertone. Today, support guidance is offered to streamline and justify supervision techniques as teachers transition through the induction process to a continuing contract (see Table 9.2). While the policy intentions were designed to support teacher professional development and identify ways to capture a teacher's effectiveness, the implementation created additional stress for teachers.

What Does This All Mean?

Conclusively, despite the seemingly straightforward goal of employing quality instructors to promote stronger education systems, dependency on less than perfect evaluation metrics in extremely diverse educational

TABLE 9.2 Classroom-Based Teacher Evaluation Guidance, 2018–2019

Contract Level	Observations of Professional Practice	Forms Used	Collection of Student Growth
First Year Induction	Assessment of Professional Practice using SC Teaching Standards 4.0 > 1—Full Classroom Observation per semester, with conferences* Results are Formative	• Professional Growth and Development Plan (S.C. Code Ann. §59-26-40): SLO Template • Post-Conference Observation Summary, including Teacher Reflection • Professional Review and Self-Review • SLO Scoring Rubric • Final Evaluation Conference Summary	• SLOs are not required at start of year. An SLO with required conferences and a shorter interval (semester or quarter long) is required in second semester. • SLO skills will be supported in induction and work with mentors. • SLOs may serve as one goal on the teacher's Professional Growth and Development Plan; there is space in the SLO form for additional goals if needed.
Annual Diagnostic Assistance	Assessment of Professional Practice using SC Teaching Standards 4.0 > 2—Full Classroom Observations per semester, with conferences* Results are Formative	• Professional Growth and Development Plan, (S.C. Code Ann. §59-26-40): SLO Template • Post-Conference Observation Summary, including Teacher Reflection • Professional Review and Self-Review • SLO Scoring Rubric • Final Evaluation Conference Summary	• Teachers engage in approval, mid-course and summative SLO conferences. • SLO may serve as one goal on the teacher's Professional Growth and Development Plan; there is space in the SLO form for additional goals if needed.
Annual Formal	Assessment of Professional Practice using SC Teaching Standards 4.0 > 2—Full Classroom Observations per semester, with conferences* Results are Formative	• Professional Growth and Development Plan, (S.C. Code Ann. §59-26-40): SLO Template • Post-Conference Observation Summary, including Teacher Reflection • Professional Review and Self-Review • SLO Scoring Rubric • Final Evaluation Conference Summary	• Teachers engage in approval, mid-course and summative SLO conferences. • SLO may serve as one goal on the teacher's Professional Growth and Development Plan; there is space in the SLO form for additional goals if needed.

(continued)

TABLE 9.1 Classroom-Based Teacher Evaluation Guidance, 2018–2019 (continued)

Contract Level	Observations of Professional Practice	Forms Used	Collection of Student Growth
Continuing Contract–Comprehensive Every 5th Year	Assessment of Professional Practice using SC Teaching Standards 4.0 > 1—Full Classroom Observation per semester, with conferences* Results are Formative	• Professional Growth and Development Plan, (S.C. Code Ann. §59-26-40): SLO Template • Post-Conference Observation Summary, including Teacher Reflection • Professional Review and Self-Review • SLO Scoring Rubric • Final Evaluation Conference Summary	• Teachers engage in approval, mid-course and summative SLO conferences. • SLO may serve as one goal on the teacher's Professional Growth and Development Plan; there is space in the SLO form for additional goals if needed.
Continuing Contract and Annual—GBE	Informal observations of and feedback on practice with SC Teaching Standards 4.0 encouraged. Results are Formative	• Expanded ADEPT Process; • Professional Growth and Development Plan, (S.C. Code Ann. §59-26-40): SLO Form • SLO Scoring; SLO Scoring Rubric	• The three required conferences that support a GBE reflect the SLO conferencing process. • SLO may serve as one goal on the teacher's Professional Growth and Development Plan.

Note: Adapted from the South Carolina Department of Education (n.d.).

environments has far-reaching limitations. For example, we know that student performance, like teacher quality and shortages, is subject to several factors: school climate, school leadership, teacher autonomy, teacher respect, student behavior, collaboration, and pension/retirement eligibility (Dillon et al., 2020). Such conditions tighten the conceptual pressure of the profession, catalyzing uneasiness. High levels of stress negatively impact the work environment, morale, and working conditions related to teaching (von der Embse et al., 2016) and lead to teacher burnout, defined as "emotional fatigue, disengagement, irritability, and apathy related to the work environment" (Ryan et al., 2017, p. 3). Research notes a direct connection of "accountability on both teacher migration and teacher attrition [and that accountability] directly affected test stress and burnout, which predicted... teacher turnover" (Ryan et al., 2017, p. 6).

A study conducted by Mintrop et al. (2018) stated that the "interaction of evaluation, bonus pay, artifacts obligated by the system, and teacher learning around instruction shifted over three distinct periods [called] consonance, dissonance, and resonance" (p. 36), a construct articulating the inner turmoil brewing within the profession. The inner systems created to increase student outcomes have, in effect, created a less confident, less stable teacher workforce, largely based on evaluative practices that inconsistently attend to factors that cultivate student growth. Researchers have begun to evaluate the validity and impact of teacher weight on student outcomes a bit further (Cho et al., 2020), with distinct criticism of the "popular thesis that teacher quality is the primary variable limiting student achievement [pointing to] an artificial correlation introduced by omitted variable bias" (Yeh, 2020, p. 1199). We find that the evolution of the art of teacher evaluation, alongside the permissible development of each educator, conflicted with the high-stakes association of relative discourse, policy, and teacher effectiveness (Henderson et al., 2020).

So, what is next for educators? As the teacher shortage lingers, society will have to weigh at which point the balance of accountability from all stakeholders is sufficient in the quest for an education system that supports a quality environment for students, free from the burden of how best to evaluate teachers. So, what can be done to alleviate this pressure? As exercised by the teacher walkout, many believe that advocacy is the beginning of an overhaul of major education reform, which includes educator accountability, amongst others. The unprecedented teacher march on May 1, 2019, drew attention to the challenging working conditions teachers face and their impact on recruitment and retention efforts moving forward. One teacher was quoted as saying, "This goes to really reforming education. I think that this is going to be a great eye-opening experience for not only teachers, but the Legislature and general public" (Schechter, 2019, para. 12). As teachers continue to advocate for education reform that improves working conditions and tangible changes occur as a result, the recruitment and retention of educators will likely improve. Its impact has the potential of evolving the very fabric of what it means to be an educator, adopting teacher activism as a part of curricular and ethical respects (Bradley-Levine, 2018); thus, creating a pool of highly effective, well-rounded educators to serve in public schools.

REFERENCES

American Institutes for Research. (2013). *Three decades of education reform: Are we still "A nation at risk?."* https://www.air.org/resource/three-decades-education-reform -are-we-still-nation-risk

American Recovery and Reinvestment Act of 2009, Pub. L. No. 111-5, 123 Stat. 115 (2009). https://www.congress.gov/111/plaws/publ5/PLAW-111publ5.pdf

American Statistical Association. (2014). *ASA statement on using value-added models for educational assessment.* https://www.amstat.org/asa/files/pdfs/POL-ASAVAM -Statement.pdf

Amrein-Beardsley, A., & Holloway, J. (2019). Value-added models for teacher evaluation and accountability: Commonsense assumptions. *Educational Policy, 33*(3), 516–542.

Bradley-Levine, J. (2018). Advocacy as a practice of critical teacher leadership. *International Journal of Teacher Leadership, 9*(1), 47–62.

Campbell, J. W., & Derrington, M. (2019). Principals' perceptions of teacher evaluation reform from structural and human resource perspectives. *Journal of Educational Supervision, 2*(1), 58–77. https://doi.org/10.31045/jes.2.1.4

Center for Educator Recruitment, Retention, and Advancement. (n.d.-a). *Five-year key teacher supply & demand data.* https://www.cerra.org/uploads/1/7/ 6/8/17684955/2020-21_supply___demand_report.pdf

Center for Educator Recruitment, Retention, and Advancement. (n.d.-b). *Supply and demand.* https://www.cerra.org/supply-and-demand.html

Center for Educator Recruitment, Retention, and Advancement. (n.d.-c). The history of South Carolina schools. https://www.teachercadets.com/uploads/1/7/ 6/8/17684955/history_of_south_carolina_schools.pdf

Cho, J., James, J., & Swarts, G. P. (2020). The impact of U.S. pre-service teachers' high-stakes, accountability era schooling experiences on their future teaching practices. *Journal of Teacher Education and Educators, 9*(2), 143–167.

David, J. L. (2010). What research says about using value-added measures to evaluate teachers. *Association of Supervision and Curriculum Development.* https:// www.ascd.org/el/articles/using-value-added-measures-to-evaluate-teachers

Derrington, M. L., & Martinez, J. A. (2019). Exploring teachers' evaluation perceptions: A snapshot. *NASSP Bulletin, 103*(1), 32–50.

Dillon, E., Malick, S., Regional Educational Laboratory Mid-Atlantic, Mathematica, & National Center for Education Evaluation and Regional Assistance. (2020). Teacher turnover and access to effective teachers in the school district of Philadelphia (REL 2020-037). Regional Educational Laboratory Mid-Atlantic.

Dragoset, L., James-Burdumy, S., Hallgren, K., Perez-Johnson, I., Herrmann, M., Tuttle, C., Angus, M. H., Herman, R., Murray, M., Tanenbaum, C., Graczewski, C., & National Center for Education Evaluation and Regional Assistance. (2015). *Usage of practices promoted by school improvement grants* (NCEE 2015-4019). National Center for Education Evaluation and Regional Assistance.

Domaleski, C. (2020). Breakthrough or breakdown? School accountability in flux. *State Education Standard, 20*(3), 18–23.

Education Commission of the States. (2018). *Policy snapshot: Teacher evaluations.* https://www.ecs.org/wp-content/uploads/Teacher_Evaluations.pdf

Elementary and Secondary Education Act of 1965, Pub. L. No. 89-10, 79 Stat. 27 (1965).

Every Student Succeeds Act of 2015, Pub. L. No. 114-95, 20 USC § 6301 (2015). https://www.ed.gov/essa

Finster, M., & Milanowski, A. (2018, April 2). Teacher perceptions of a new performance evaluation system and their influence on practice: A within- and between-school level analysis. *Education Policy Analysis Archives, 26*(41). http://dx.doi.org/10.14507/epaa.26.3500

Gardner, D. P., Larsen, Y. W., Baker, W. O., Campbell, A., Crosby, E. A., Foster, Jr., C. A., Francis, N. C., Giamatti, A. B., Gordon, S., Haderlein, R. V., Holton, G., Kirk, A. Y., Marston, M. S., Quie, A. H., Sanchez, Jr., F. D., Seaborg, G. T., Sommer, J., & Wallace, R. (1983). *A nation at risk: The imperative for educational reform. An open letter to the American people. A report to the nation and the Secretary of Education.* National Commission on Excellence in Education.

Goe, L., Bell, C., & Little, O. (2008). *Approaches to evaluating teacher effectiveness.* National Comprehensive Center for Teacher Quality. https://gtlcenter.org/sites/default/files/docs/EvaluatingTeachEffectiveness.pdf

Henderson, M. B., Houston, D. M., Peterson, P. E., & West, M. R. (2020). Public support grows for higher teacher pay and expanded school choice: Results from the 2019 "Education Next" poll. *Education Next, 20*(1), 8–27.

Jacques, C., & Fireside, D. (2016). *Educator perceptions of educator evaluation in South Carolina.* American Institutes for Research. https://ed.sc.gov/newsroom/educator-perceptions-of-educator-evaluation-in-south-carolina-report/

Jones, L. (2009). The implications of NCLB and a nation at risk for K–12 schools and higher education. *International Journal of Educational Leadership Preparation, 4*(1), 1–4.

Kamenetz, A. (2018). *What 'A Nation At Risk' got wrong, and right, about U.S. schools.* NPR. https://www.npr.org/sections/ed/2018/04/29/604986823/what-a-nation-at-risk-got-wrong-and-right-about-u-s-schools

Kawasaki, J., Quartz, K. H., & Martínez, J. F. (2020). Using multiple measures of teaching quality to strengthen teacher preparation. *Education Policy Analysis Archives, 28*(128), 1–19.

Lavigne, A. L. (2014). Exploring the intended and unintended consequences of high-stakes teacher evaluation on schools, teachers, and students. *Teachers College Record, 116*(1), 1–29.

Martinie, S. L., Kim, J. H., & Abernathy, D. (2016). "Better to be a pessimist": A narrative inquiry into mathematics teachers' experience of the transition to the Common Core. *Journal of Educational Research, 109*(6), 658–665.

McShane, M. Q. (2014). Navigating the Common Core. *Education Next, 14*(3), 24–29.

Mintrop, R., Ordenes, M., Coghlan, E., Pryor, L., & Madero, C. (2018). Teacher evaluation, pay for performance, and learning around instruction: Between dissonant incentives and resonant procedures. *Educational Administration Quarterly, 54*(1), 3–46.

Murray, K., & Howe, K. R. (2017). Neglecting democracy in education policy: A-F school report card accountability systems. *Education Policy Analysis Archives, 25*(109), 1–34.

National Association of Secondary School Principals. (2019). *Position statement: Value added measure in teacher evaluation.* https://www.nassp.org/top-issues-in -education/position-statements/value-added-measures-in-teacher-evaluation/

No Child Left Behind Act of 2001, P.L. 107-110, 20 U.S.C. § 6319 (2002). https:// files.eric.ed.gov/fulltext/ED556108.pdf

Paufler, N. A., King, K. M., & Zhu, P. (2020a). Promoting professional growth in new teacher evaluation systems: Practitioners' lived experiences in changing policy contexts. *Studies in Educational Evaluation, 65*, 1–9. https://doi .org/10.1016/j.stueduc.2020.100873

Paufler, N. A., King, K. M., & Zhu, P. (2020b). Delivering on the promise of support for growth? Evaluator perceptions of a new state teacher evaluation system. *Journal of Educational Supervision, 3*(2), 32–50. https://doi.org/10.31045/ jes.3.2.3

Poproski, R., & Greene, R. (2018). *Metrics and measures of teaching effectiveness.* https:// ctl.gatech.edu/sites/default/files/documents/poproski_greene_2018_ metrics_and_measures_of_teaching_effectiveness.pdf

Robertson-Kraft, C., & Zhang, R. S. (2018). Keeping great teachers: A case study on the impact and implementation of a pilot teacher evaluation system. *Educational Policy, 32*(3), 363–394. https://doi.org/10.1177/0895904816637685

Rosenberg, L., Christianson, M. D., Angus, M. H., Rosenthal, E., & National Center for Education Evaluation and Regional Assistance. (2014). *A focused look at rural schools receiving school improvement grants. NCEE evaluation brief* (NCEE 2014-4013). National Center for Education Evaluation and Regional Assistance.

Rothman, R. (2014). The Common Core takes hold. *Education Next, 14*(3), 16–22.

Ryan, S. V., von der Embse, N. P., Pendergast, L., Saeki, E., Segool, N. S., & Schwing, S. (2017). Leaving the teaching profession: The role of teacher stress and educational accountability policies on turnover intent. *Teaching and Teacher Education, 66*, 1–17. https://doi.org/10.1016/j.tate.2017.03.016

Schechter, M. (2019). 10,000 people marched. Where does the SC teacher movement go from here? *The State.* https://www.thestate.com/news/politics -government/article229939669.html

South Carolina Department of Education. (2010). *Summative ADEPT formal evaluation of classroom-based teachers: A guide for teachers and evaluators.* https://ed.sc .gov/sites/scdoe/assets/file/programs-services/50/documents/SAFET GuideTeachersEvaluators.pdf

South Carolina Department of Education. (2017). *Expanded ADEPT support and evaluation system guidelines for classroom-based teachers.* https://ed.sc.gov/sites/scdoe/ assets/File/educators/teacher-evaluations/20170313_ADEPT_Guidelines _FINAL_Edited.pdf

South Carolina Department of Education. (2019). *Paperwork reduction and streamlining report.* https://www.scstatehouse.gov/reports/DeptofEducation/Paper%20 Reduction%20Final%20Report%207.31.19.pdf

South Carolina Education Accountability Act of 1998, Section 59-18-500 (1998).

South Carolina Education Improvement Act of 1984, S.C. Code Ann. § 59-29-55 (1984).

South Carolina General Assembly. (2009). *1983–1984 Bill 3267 Part II Section 8 Education Improvement Act.* https://www.scstatehouse.gov/sess105_1983-1984/bills/ eia.htm

Tienken, C. H. (2013). Neoliberalism, Social Darwinism, and consumerism masquerading as school reform. *Interchange: A Quarterly Review of Education, 43*(4), 295–316.

United States Department of Education. (n.d.). *Race to the top fund.* https://www2 .ed.gov/programs/racetothetop-district/index.html

von der Embse, N. P., Pendergast, L. L., Segool, N. K., Saeki, E., & Ryan, S. (2016). The influence of test-based accountability policies on school climate and teacher stress across four states. *Teaching and Teacher Education, 59,* 492–502. http://dx.doi.org/10.1016/j.tate.2016.07.013

Workman, E., & Wixom, M. (2016). *Mitigating teacher shortages: Evaluation and feedback.* https://www.ecs.org/wp-content/uploads/Mitigating-Teacher-Shortages -Evaluation-and-Feedback.pdf

Wright, K. B., Shields, S. M., Black, K., Banerjee, M., & Waxman, H. C. (2018, May 14). Teacher perceptions of influence, autonomy, and satisfaction in the early Race to the Top era. *Education Policy Analysis Archives, 26*(62). http://dx.doi .org/10.14507/epaa.26.3449

Wronowski, M. L., & Urick, A. (2019). Examining the relationship of teacher perception of accountability and assessment policies on teacher turnover during NCLB. *Education Policy Analysis Archives, 27,* 86.

Yeh, S. S. (2020). Educational accountability, value-added modeling, and the origin of the achievement gap. *Education and Urban Society, 52*(8), 1181–1203.

CHAPTER 10

THE ROLE OF PRINCIPALS
IN SOUTH CAROLINA'S
TEACHER SHORTAGE

David Buckman
Kennesaw State University

SOUTH CAROLINA DATA OVERVIEW

Considering school leadership turnover is often ignored in the media, this chapter fills this void by addressing how school leadership may influence teacher turnover and shortages. Evidence of teacher shortage and school leader and teacher turnover found in the literature will be further discussed. As all states have their specific issues caused by state-specific dynamics, this chapter begins with an overview of district, school, and personnel data to better understand the nuances of the focal state, South Carolina.

Data from a sample of public schools throughout South Carolina was collected to analyze the relationship between school principals and the teacher shortage crisis. The South Carolina Department of Education and National Center of Education Statistics served as data sources. The researcher acquired the school, teacher, principal, and student data from 2016 to 2020 for analysis and discussion purposes. Only schools with complete data

How Did We Get Here?, pages 227–255
Copyright © 2022 by Information Age Publishing
www.infoagepub.com
227

TABLE 10.1   Descriptive Statistics (Central Tendency): South Carolina Teacher, Principal, and Student Data AY 2016–2020

	Range	Minimum	Maximum	Mean	Std. Deviation	Percent Over Time
Teacher Count	247	8	255	43.91	22.86	1.03
Poverty %	90.3	8.37	99.30	66.31	19.00	−4.23
Average Teacher Salary[a]	$25,221	$37,759	$62,980	$49,903	$3,602.86	−7.44
Returning Teacher[b]	76.5	23.5	100	83.88	8.76	2.03
Principal Years at Current School	36	0.0	36	5.55	4.97	104.23
School Enrollment[c]	4,016	53.0	4,069	674.72	408.46	1.83
White Enrollment[c]	3,338	0.0	3,338	352.70	297.50	8.17
Non-White Enrollment[c]	1,471	5.0	1,476	321.95	210.25	−3.19

Note: Number of observations = 2,795. Number of schools = 559.

[a] U.S. dollars, [b] percentage, [c] students

(i.e., had available data across all variables) remained in the analysis. Table 10.1 describes the continuous variables used in the chapter.

The total number of schools in the sample is 559. As noted above, the reported *N* is the total number of schools combined over the 5 years. When analyzing teacher and principal-related components of the sample, the average number of teachers employed at the schools was roughly 44, ranging from 8 to 255, while the average teacher salary was $49,903 ranging from $37,759 to $62,980. To demonstrate the comparative difference between teacher salaries and principal salaries, the Bureau of Labor Statistics' Occupational Employment and Wage Statistics (OEWS) 2020 data indicated the average principal salary in South Carolina was $91,490 (https://www.bls.gov/oes/). The average percentage of teachers returning to their school from the previous year was 83.88% ranging from 23.5% to 100%. Finally, the average number of years school principals remained at their same school was 5.55 years, ranging from 0 to 36 years, but you will learn later in the chapter that that principal retention varies by school level (i.e., elementary, middle, and high) and often falls below 5 years.

School variables in reference to student characteristics were also used in the chapter. For example, student poverty, which will be discussed later in the chapter, influences the teacher and principal labor markets. The sample indicates that the average poverty percentage of students, as defined by the percentage of students on free and/or reduced lunch, is 33.31% ranging from 8.37% to 99.30%. School enrollment (i.e., the total number of students in a school) ranged from 52 students to 4,069 students, with an average of approximately 674 students.

The average number of White student enrollment across the sample was approximately 352 students ranging from 0 to 3,338 students and represents 50.6% of the state's total enrollment. In comparison, the average number of non-White students was approximately 322 students ranging from 5 to 1,476 students and represented 49.3% of the state's total enrollment.

Table 10.2 describes the sample regarding frequencies and percentages of the schools that fall into specific categories. Schools were classified by their level, location, region, Title I status, and principal turnover. School levels were classified as elementary, high, middle, and primary schools. Between

TABLE 10.2 Descriptive Statistics (Frequency & Percentages): South Carolina School Level Data (AY 2016–2020)

	Frequency[a]	Percent of Schools per Category	Percent Over Time
School Level			
Elementary	304	54.0	–0.32
High	114	20.2	–2.56
Middle	119	21.1	5.30
Primary	22	5.0	–21.40
School Location			
City	76	13.6	10.14
Suburb	171	30.4	–5.00
Town	79	14.0	2.59
Rural	233	41.4	–1.68
Title I Status			
Non-Title I	277	49.2	2.59
Title I	277	49.2	–5.40
Targeted Title I	5	0.9	500
Principal Turnover			
No Turnover	476	84.5	0.63
Turnover	83	14.7	–7.77
Region			
Savannah River	75	13.3	0
Low Country	126	22.4	–1.56
Pee Dee	95	16.9	–1.05
Midlands	87	15.5	–1.13
Upstate	176	31.3	0

[a] Number of schools in the category. Observed over a 5-year period.

AY 2016–2020, approximately 54% of the sample schools were elementary schools, and approximately 20%, 21%, and 5% were high school, middle school, and primary schools, respectively. The sample schools were disaggregated by location (i.e., city, suburb, town, rural) and provided the following approximations: 13% city, 30% suburban, 14% town, and 41% rural.

Title I, also known as Title I, Part A of the Elementary and Secondary Education Act, is a school assistance program funded by the federal government that provides funds to schools to ensure that all children receive a free, equitable, and high-quality education. Schools in the sample were categorized as non-Title I, Title I, or Targeted Title I (i.e., services provided to select students in the school). The sample consisted of approximately 49% non-Title I schools, 49% Title I schools, and less than 1% Targeted Title I schools.

Principal turnover is analyzed in this chapter and is assessed as a predictor of teacher turnover. For the observation period (2016–2020), schools that had a principal leave during a given year were flagged. In the sample, roughly 84% of the schools experienced no principal turnover, while 14.7% had a principal turnover during the observation period.

South Carolina is divided into five major regions (i.e., Savannah River, Lowcountry, Pee Dee, Midlands, and Upstate. The Savannah River portion of the state is located on the western border connected to Georgia and accounted for roughly 13% of the sample schools. South Carolina's Lowcountry is the southernmost and coastal portion of the state and accounted for roughly 22% of the sample. Pee Dee, which accounted for approximately 17% of the sample schools, is also located on the state's coastal region and the eastern border. South Carolina's midland area is found in the central northeast portion of the state and accounted for approximately 15% of the sample. Finally, the Upstate region of the state is found in the northwestern region and accounted for approximately 31% of the sample. Figure 10.1 depicts South Carolina and highlights all five regions and the respective school districts in each region.

Qualitative data was also used to capture participant voices to supplement the quantitative data. A purposive sample of five school personnel who had experienced principal turnover during the focal years of the study were interviewed. The participants served as either assistant principals or teachers. Table 10.3 provides details of the participants who were interviewed.

NATIONAL TEACHER SHORTAGE

According to the National Education Association, since 2001, all U.S. states have been affected by teacher supply shortages. When analyzing shortages at micro levels such as state to state, across districts, and even across subject

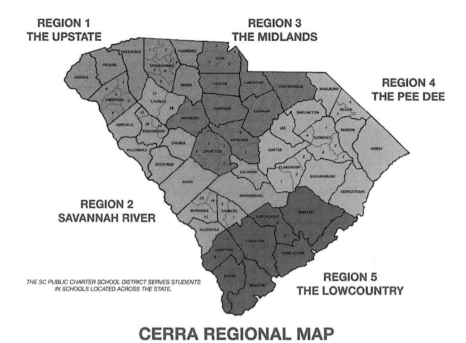

Figure 10.1   Regional map of South Carolina with school districts. *Source:* Center of Educator Recruitment, Retention, & Advancement (n.d.).

TABLE 10.3 Qualitative Data: Participant Information			
Role	Years of Experience	Region	School Level
Assistant Principal	10	Midlands	High School
Teacher	7	Upstate	Elementary School
Assistant Principal	4	Midlands	Middle
Assistant Principal	9	Low Country	High School
Teacher	12	Pee Dee	Middle School

areas, the issue is more nuanced, and researchers indicate the problem is more localized than national (Sutcher et al., 2019). Regardless of the debate, many studies have been published supporting the presence of a national teacher shortage crisis (e.g., Lewis-Spector, 2016; Garcia & Weiss, 2019). In their 2016 study, Sutcher et al. analyzed the national teacher labor market and uncovered an annual dearth of roughly 250,000 teaching vacancies. In addition to teaching vacancies, they also found that teacher education enrollments at colleges and universities decreased by 35% between 2009 and 2014.

In their more recent study, Sutcher et al. (2019) reported an estimated national shortage of 112,000 teachers in 2017–2018. They indicated further that even if the supply of teachers were to increase to pre-recession levels (i.e., 260,000 teachers a year), the demand for teachers would still surpass the supply by approximately 40,000 teachers. Additionally, they indicate that the persistent areas of critical shortages (i.e., special education, mathematics, and science) have shown few signs of response to labor market demands, and states continue to report shortages in these areas.

Because the sources of and solutions to teacher shortages are localized, examining the topic at a lower level is important. Take, for instance, the state of South Carolina. According to Garrett (2019), roughly 7,300 teachers left their teaching position in AY 2018–2019, and the majority of these teachers (72%) are no longer working in public schools in the state. The report further identified that the number of teacher vacancies at the beginning of AY 2018–2019 was a 13% increase compared to vacancies reported at the beginning of the previous year.

To corroborate the CERRA finding highlighted above, Figure 10.2 suggests that between 2016 and 2020, the schools of South Carolina had a

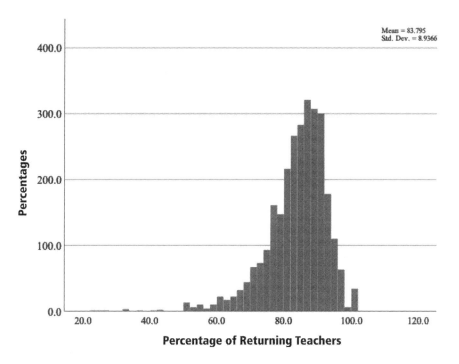

Figure 10.2 Percentage of South Carolina returning teachers 2016–2020.

teacher return rate of 83.7%, which means that the schools turned over approximately 17% of their teachers. The data supplied does not distinguish if the teachers in the sample left the teaching field completely or just changed schools; nonetheless, the figure displays the percentage of teacher turnover across all school levels (i.e., primary, elementary, middle, and high).

The turnover trends highlighted in Figure 10.2 are critical because of the harmful effects repeated turnover has on organizational outcomes, most notably student achievement. For example, Ronfeldt et al. (2013) found that when studying the impact of teacher turnover in New York from 2002–2010, the students did worse in years where teacher turnover rates were high compared to years when fewer teachers turned over. They indicated that student math scores were 8.2% to 10.2% lower in years when there was complete (i.e., 100%) turnover than in years when there was no turnover. Ultimately their study provides empirical evidence suggesting that teacher turnover has a significant negative effect on student achievement.

Henry and Redding (2020) utilized 2009–2014 administrative data from North Carolina to evaluate the impact of teacher turnover on fourth through eighth-grade students. Their analysis, similar to Ronfeldt et al. (2013), concluded that teacher turnover had a negative effect on student achievement. Some of their findings indicated consistent adverse effects when teachers turned over during the academic year (i.e., ELA = –0.045; Math = –0.1.), and teacher turnover was more detrimental at the elementary school level than middle school. Hanushek et al. (2016) allude that the effect of teacher turnover on student achievement may be because (a) turnover reduces the amount of general or specific human capital at the school, (b) many new teachers who replace movers tend to have no prior teaching experience, and (c) new teachers who replace movers are often less efficient.

TEACHER AND LEADER TURNOVER LOCATION CHARACTERISTICS

To better understand the impact of principal turnover on teacher attrition, we must first understand the factors that influence both independently. In the literature, teacher and leader turnover trends recognize that specific types of schools have significantly more turnover than others (Reininger, 2012).

Teacher Turnover

This section will provide background research and data on teacher retention/turnover based on (a) school level (i.e., primary, elementary, middle, high), (b) community location (i.e., urban, rural, suburban), (c) school demographics, and (d) region.

School Level

Some research has identified school level as a predictor of teacher turnover. For example, Redding and Henry's (2018) research determined that teachers were more likely to turnover at the middle and high school levels than elementary and middle school levels. They further indicated that the relationships were more robust for within-year turnover for middle school (114%) and high school (312%) compared to elementary school. The researchers did not indicate why the difference occurred at different levels or provided a theoretical underpinning that alludes to a cause within their discussion. Instead, their primary focus was on the impact of turnover for the students at each level.

Figure 10.3 provides a sample of South Carolina's teacher retention data from 2016–2020. Unlike the findings highlighted by Redding and Henry (2018), the South Carolina data indicates elementary (84.3% retention) and high school (84% retention) had the lowest teacher turnover percentages (i.e., 15.7% and 16%, respectively). Middle school (82.5% retention, 17.5% turnover) and primary school (82.7% retention, 17.3% turnover) reported higher teacher turnover percentages than elementary and high school. One can suspect that teacher turnover by school level is nuanced and determined by other factors such as poverty or geographic location.

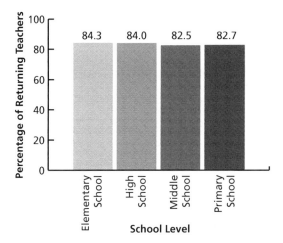

Figure 10.3 Percentage of South Carolina returning teachers by school level 2016–2020.

Community Location

When studying teacher turnover by community type in the United States, Carver-Thomas and Darling Hammond (2017) highlight that urban schools in the southern region of the United States produced the highest teacher turnover (i.e., 17.3%) when compared to suburban, town, and rural schools. Their research also indicated that southern regional suburban, town, and rural schools reported the following teacher turnover percentages: 15.8%, 14.3%, and 14.7%, respectively. As noted in the statistics above, both urban and suburban schools reported the highest percentage of teacher turnover, followed by rural and town schools.

Compared to Carver-Thomas and Darling-Hammond's (2017) report, this chapter utilized poverty to further examine the differences between school locations and teacher turnover. The National Center for Education Statistics's (NCES) 2021 classification for high poverty schools (i.e., schools with 50% or more free and reduced priced lunch) and low poverty (i.e., schools with less than 50% free or reduced priced lunch) were used to further disaggregate the schools. South Carolina's 2016–2020 data highlights that the highest teacher turnover occurred in high-poverty city schools (80.9% returning teachers; see Figure 10.4). It is important to note that the most considerable portion of South Carolina schools are in rural areas (i.e., 41.9%), and Figure 10.4 indicated that high poverty town and rural schools reported the second and third highest teacher turnover percentages. There was very little variation in teacher retention in low poverty areas; however, a school located in a town setting displayed lower teacher retention than city, suburban, and rural schools.

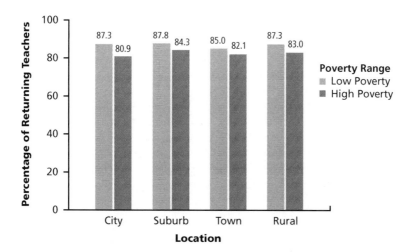

Figure 10.4   Percentage of South Carolina returning teachers by location and poverty 2016–2020.

Hammer et al. (2005) identified that the main challenges within rural schools are related to both recruitment and retention. More pointedly, they associate rural school recruitment and retention issues with lower teacher salaries, teacher isolation (i.e., geographic and social), and poor working conditions. Research suggests that strategically recruiting teachers with rural backgrounds and teachers with general knowledge of the region and school can alleviate the annual shortages in rural schools (Beesley et al., 2008; Hammer et al., 2005; Maranto, 2013; Monk, 2007; Ulferts, 2016). This suggestion is corroborated by Tran et al. (2020), who found that many of the participants in their South Carolina study did not have prior experience working in rural settings, which caused added stress on teachers.

School Demographics (Poverty and Diversity)

Research has heavily identified poverty and students' composition as significant determinants of teacher turnover. More specifically, higher levels of turnover have been in schools with high percentages of low-performing and minority students (Boyd et al., 2005; Hanushek et al., 2004). Poverty and diversity are closely related to factors that heavily influence teacher turnover. For instance, as previously stated, studies have repeatedly purported that teachers who work in schools with high concentrations of low-income, low-achieving students of color were more likely to turnover as compared to teachers of other schools (Boyd et al., 2005; Clotfelter et al., 2011; Hanushek et al., 2004; Scafidi et al., 2007).

Figure 10.5 displays the relationship between the percentage of returning teachers and poverty percentages in South Carolina. Poverty was operationalized by the percentage of students identified as receiving free and/or reduced lunch in schools. The scatter plot provides a best fit line that identifies the slope of the relationship. There is a negative relationship between student poverty and teacher retention ($r = -.329$, $p < .001$). In Figure 10.5, the percentage of students identified as free and/or reduced lunch recipients increases as the percentage of the returning teachers in the school's decreases. This finding is not uncharacteristic of the literature and indicates further, South Carolina teachers, like teachers of other states, are more likely to leave less affluent schools.

Also aligned with the literature, Figures 10.6 and 10.7 display the relationship between percentages of returning teachers and White students and the percentage of returning teachers and non-White students, respectively. The best fit line of Figure 10.6 indicates a positive relationship between the percentage of returning teachers and White students ($r = .285$,

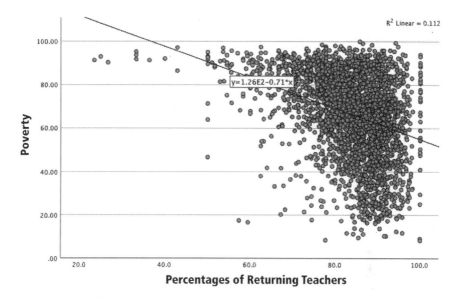

Figure 10.5   Scatterplot of percentage of South Carolina returning teachers and poverty 2016–2020.

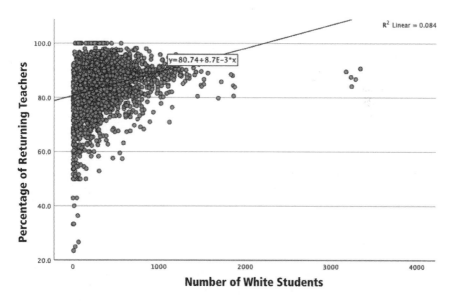

Figure 10.6   Scatterplot of percentage of South Carolina returning teachers and White students 2016–2020.

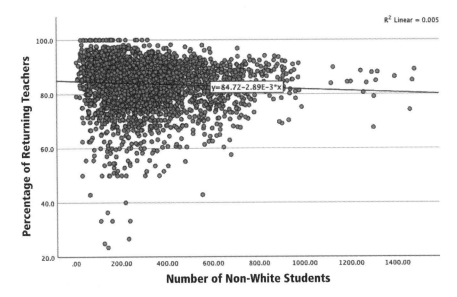

Figure 10.7 Scatterplot of percentage of South Carolina returning teachers and non-White students 2016–2020.

$p < .001$). In short, as the percentage of White students at school increased, the percentage of returning teachers also increased.

Contrarily, Figure 10.7 represents the relationship between the percentage of returning teachers and non-White students. Data highlights a negative slope indicating that as the percentage of non-White students increased, teacher retention decreased ($r = -.079$, $p < .001$). This finding is alarming, but unfortunately, predictable based on the abundance of literature with similar findings.

Regional Characteristics

This section disaggregates the state regionally and identifies teacher turnover/retention trends to provide further context on teacher retention in the focal state. Throughout the book, readers will discover that South Carolina has had a history of inequity (e.g., *Abbeville v. South Carolina* [2018]), a large rural population, and has one of the highest poverty indexes in the country per the U.S. Census. These factors impact education as South Carolina ranks 44th in the *U.S. News & World Report's* national education rankings (Ziegler, n.d.).

Figure 10.8 provides the percentages of South Carolina returning teachers by region. Although vastly different in culture and geography, the percentage of returning teachers are very similar. The geographic regions, historically known to have higher levels of student achievement (i.e., Upstate

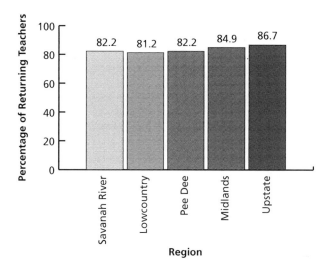

Figure 10.8 Percentage of South Carolina returning teachers by region 2016–2020.

and Midlands), also have the highest teacher retention ratings (i.e., 86.7% and 84.9%, respectively). The Savannah River and Pee Dee areas reported 82% teacher retention, and the Lowcountry reported 81.2%, the lowest teacher retention regionally.

Principal Turnover

Because teacher turnover captures most of the public's attention, principal turnovers are often neglected. This chapter focuses on the relationship between principal turnover and teacher turnover; therefore, this section will highlight South Carolina principal turnover data to provide further context. Specifically, this section will provide background data on principal retention/turnover based on school level (i.e., primary, elementary, middle, high), community location (i.e., urban, rural, suburban), school demographics, and region.

School Level

As noted in the research (Barnes et al., 2007; Carroll, 2007; Grissom et al., 2015; Guarino et al., 2006), principal turnover, albeit costly (i.e., average SC principal replacement cost $23,974; Tran et al., 2018), is a growing problem and it has been reported their turnover rate is even higher than that of teachers. Goldring and Taie (2018) report in their NCES study, a national principal turnover rate of approximately 18% as compared to the national teacher turnover rate of 16% (NCES, 2015). Principal turnover exceeding teacher turnover is confirmed in the data reported in this chapter, whereby South Carolina's 5-year teacher turnover rate is approximately 16% (see Table 10.1, "Returning Teacher").

Research has reported a host of consequences for principal turnover, including but not limited to decreased student achievement (Branch et al., 2009; Burkhauser et al., 2012; Kearney et al., 2012; Mascall & Leithwood, 2010), lower graduation rates (Weinstein et al., 2009), poor school climate and culture (Hanselman et al., 2016; Noonan & Goldman, 1995), and increased teacher turnover (Beteille et al., 2012; Miller, 2013; Ronfeldt et al., 2013). Likewise, principal retention research has directly linked principal stability to student achievement (see Akiba & Reichardt, 2004; Branch et al., 2009; Fuller & Young, 2009; Miller, 2009; Vanderhaar et al., 2006). Principal retention is essential for school stability. Research has suggested that it takes time for school reform initiatives to come to fruition; therefore, principal stability remains vital because it can take a principal, on average, 5 years to positively change the culture of the school (Ringel et al., 2004; Weinstein et al., 2009).

To further illustrate the principal retention concerns across the United States, Fuller and Young's (2009) Texas study indicated that the average elementary school's principal tenure at a school was 4.96 years, while high school principals reported 3.38 years. Seashore Louis et al. (2010) reported similar findings in their analysis which determined that the average school in the United States reported a principal retention rate of 3 to 4 years per school. They also indicated that principals who served low-income and high minority communities experienced decreased levels of principal retention. Finally, Taie and Goldring's (2017) U.S. study further confirms that principals, on average, remain in a school for 4 years. Figure 10.9 indicates South Carolina's data is very similar, demonstrating that elementary principals during the observation period remained at their school longer than all other school levels (i.e., 6.18 years). The figure also identifies that primary and middle schools displayed the lowest principal retention metrics (i.e., 4.43 years and 4.70 years, respectively). It is important to note that high school, middle, and primary school all fell below the 5-year metric, the benchmark for a principal to see leadership impact (Ringel et al., 2004; Weinstein et al., 2009).

Community Location

Figure 10.10 provides a breakdown of the retention of South Carolina principals by location from 2016 to 2020. The figure indicates schools located in town areas experienced lower retention than all other locations (i.e., 4.93 years). The average principal years at a school for rural principals were 5.44 years, suburban principals were 5.75 years, and city schools were 5.99 years.

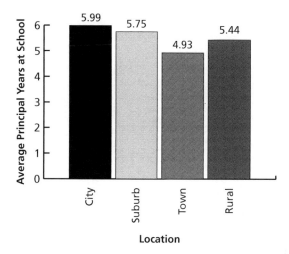

Figure 10.9   Average South Carolina principal years by school level 2016–2020.

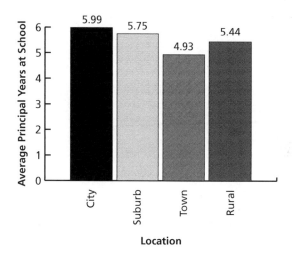

Figure 10.10   Average South Carolina principal years at school by location 2016–2020.

School Demographics (Poverty and Diversity)

Figure 10.11 displays the relationship between principal retention (i.e., the average years a principal stays at their school before turning over) and poverty percentages in South Carolina. The scatter plot's best fit line suggests a negative relationship between student poverty and principal retention ($r = -.080$, $p < .001$). The findings mean that as the percentage of students identified as free and/or reduced lunch recipients increase, principal retention decreases.

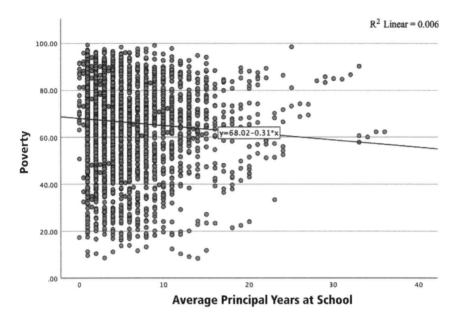

Figure 10.11 Scatter plot of poverty percentage and average South Carolina principal years at school 2016–2020.

To demonstrate this relationship further, Figure 10.12 provides a bar graph that captures actual principal turnover based on student poverty percentages. As in Figure 10.11, Figure 10.12 shows that as poverty percentages increase, the number of principal turnovers increases. The bar graph shows that the largest principal turnover occurred in schools with over 70% poverty, while schools with no turnover remained below 66% poverty. This data highlights the need for support and sustainability in high-poverty schools.

Similar to the data found in Figures 10.6 and 10.7 regarding teacher turnover and diversity, Figures 10.13 and 10.14 display the relationship between principal retention (i.e., the average number of years a principal stays at a school before turning over) and the percentage of White students at school, as well as principal retention and non-White students, respectively. The best fit line of Figure 10.13 shows a positive relationship between the years a principal stays at a school and the percentage of White students ($r = .024$, $p > .05$). To interpret, as the percentage of White students at school increases, the number of years a principal stays also increases. This relationship lacks statistical significance, so the findings may be due to chance.

As expected, when observing the relationship between principal retention and percentage of non-White students in Figure 10.14, the data displays a negative relationship indicating that as the percentage of non-White students increases, principal retention decreases ($r = -.103$, $p < .001$).

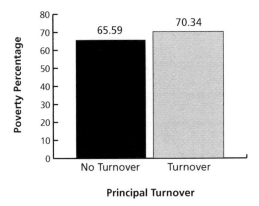

Figure 10.12 Poverty percentage and teacher turnover in South Carolina 2016–2020.

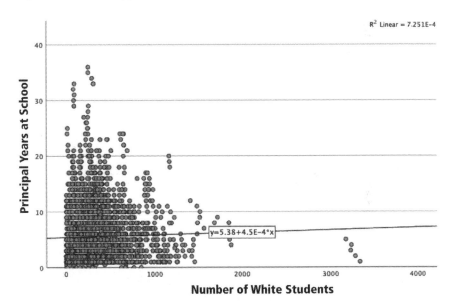

Figure 10.13 Scatterplot of principal years at school and White students 2016–2020.

Considering principals can impact student achievement, graduation rates, school climate, culture, and teacher turnover, this finding is concerning. Schools with high percentages of students of color, particularly those in urban, high needs areas, are often associated with a host of environmental concerns that disrupt the education setting; principal stability should not have to be one of them. As such, all human resources offices, particularly those serving large populations of students of color, should make efforts to

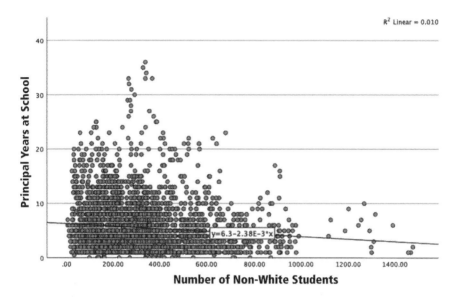

Figure 10.14 Scatterplot of principal years at school and non-White students 2016–2020.

identify incentivizing mechanisms, administrative supports, and leadership development to foster principal retention.

Regional Characteristics

Figure 10.15 provides the principal retention by region. Principal retention by region almost identically models the regional teacher retention trends in Figure 10.8. The Upstate and Midlands areas report the highest

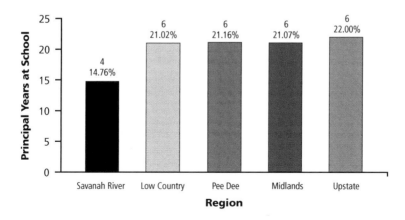

Figure 10.15 Principal years at a school by region 2016–2020.

principal retention. The difference between Figure 10.14 and Figure 10.8 can be found with the Savannah River area, which reported the lowest principal retention (i.e., 4 years). The Lowcountry and Pee Dee areas reported similar principal retention (i.e., approximately 6 years) as the Midland and Upstate areas. Factors such as principal wages and student achievement by region could further explain the difference in principal retention by region (see Tran & Buckman, 2017).

PRINCIPAL ATTRITION AND TEACHER TURNOVER

Considering that a school's culture, climate, and procedural organization are developed and maintained by principals (Edwards et al., 2018), it is not uncommon that these elements are disrupted when principals leave. Upon a principal's departure, schools can suffer from a lack of shared purpose, question leadership commitment, and demonstrate an inability to maintain school improvement (Fink & Brayman, 2006). Additionally, schools with principal turnover often struggle to maintain teacher retention efforts (Grissom & Bartanen, 2019). In short, beyond principal quality and support, principal turnover can ultimately influence a teacher's propensity to stay or leave.

Research has provided evidence to support a link between principal turnover and teacher turnover. For example, Beteille et al.'s (2012) study found that teachers were 17% more likely to leave the year after a principal turned over. Similarly, Jacob et al. (2015) found evidence that teachers were less likely to leave if their principals stayed. Henry and Harbatkin (2019) purport that voluntary principal turnover was associated with a 1.7 percentage point increase in teacher turnover. Finally, Miller (2013) analyzed teacher turnover related to principal turnover and student achievement and found a 1.3% ($b = -1.221$) increase in teacher turnover in the year before a principal left a school. Her finding also indicated an additional 1.6% ($b = -1.407$) in teacher turnover in the year after the principal's departure. These findings suggest that principal and teacher turnover are not isolated events but often occur in patterns.

As previously noted, principals play a crucial role in either helping to mitigate or exacerbate the existing teacher shortage. From the 2013 School and Staffing Survey (SASS), 21% of teachers who voluntarily left their positions over-highlighted that administration dissatisfaction was important or very important in their decision to leave (Learning Policy Institute, 2017). Their dissatisfaction stemmed from the principal's inability to support teachers and promotion of authoritative leadership styles (i.e., top–down leadership). Additionally, dissatisfaction with leadership is more potent in high poverty and high needs schools (i.e., schools with historically high levels of teacher turnover; Grissom, 2011). To mitigate teacher turnover

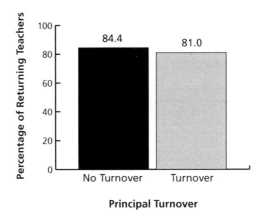

Figure 10.16 Percentage of returning teacher and principal turnover in South Carolina 2016–2020.

in high-needs schools, Simon and Johnson (2015) recommend selecting high-quality principals. They define principal quality as principals who employ (a) effective school management, (b) effective instructional leadership, and (c) inclusive decision-making practices. These attributes can also assist in creating a positive school climate and culture and ultimately influence teacher turnover determinants such as satisfaction and self-efficacy (Aldridge & Fraser, 2016).

As noted in the previous sections and throughout the literature, principals influence the complete operational function of a school, and the role of the principal impacts not only student achievement but also the culture and climate of a school and personnel dispositions. Figures 10.16 and 10.17 provide some insight into the potential influence of principal departures, particularly in terms of teacher turnover. Figure 10.16 provides data on the percentage of returning teachers and principal turnover. The data indicates that, on average, schools that did not have any leadership turnover had higher percentages of returning teachers than schools that had a principal turnover.

To further illustrate the link between principal turnover on teacher turnover, Figure 10.17 plots the relationship between the percentage of returning teachers and principal retention. The data indicates a positive relationship between the percentages of returning teachers and teacher retention ($r = .185$, $p < .001$). Based on this finding, the prevention of principal turnover appears to be one viable mechanism to reduce teacher turnovers.

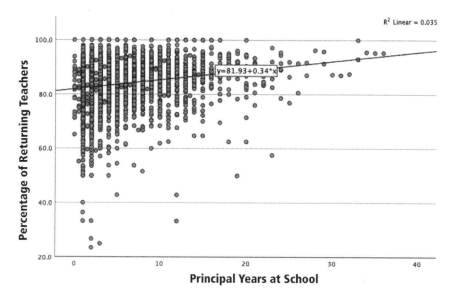

Figure 10.17   Scatter plot of percentage of returning teachers and average South Carolina principal years at school 2016–2020.

COMMENTARY FROM THE FIELD

To deeper the understanding of the findings, the voices of teachers and school leaders employed in public schools in South Carolina were obtained via semi-structured interviews. A qualitative phenomenological approach to the interviews was taken with a purposive sample of five school personnel who were either assistant principals or teachers (i.e., three assistant principals and two teachers) who had experienced principal turnover during the years of focus.

These individuals shared their narratives on issues on the importance of the school principal in retaining teachers, how principals can improve teacher retention, the climate and culture of the school pre and post principal turnover, how principal turnover impacted faculty and staff, and the extent the principal turnover influenced their decisions to stay or leave was discovered. From the conversations, four themes were rendered: (a) the importance of principal retention, (b) principal strategies to improve principal retention, (c) the effects of faculty after principal turnover, and (d) principal behaviors that influence teacher turnover.

Theme 1: The Importance of Principal Retention

According to a Midlands assistant principal with 10 years of experience:

> Principal retention creates stability within the school and provides an atmosphere to develop a consistent, positive school culture. Unfortunately, principal turnover often results in lack of standard operating procedures supporting the growth of students and faculty.

Similarly, an Upstate teacher with 7 years of experience explained:

> I think principal retention is crucial to the livelihood of the school. The principal is the key factor when building and maintaining the culture of the school. If the principalship is consistently changing, then the school culture is never consistent either. The teachers within the school rely on the principal for leadership and continuity. Having that leader there each year allows the teachers to foster a relationship of trust with the principal. This will help the teachers in that school tremendously as well because they will be more confident in their teaching. They know they have that principal there whom they have established trust with over the previous year.

A Midlands assistant principal with 4 years of experience shared:

> Principalship retention is extremely important to establish stability inside of a building. Stability strengthens the educational foundation to fertilize other key aspects. All stakeholders have a clear expectation and trust the decisions made by the principal.

Theme 2: Principal Strategies to Improve Teacher Retention

In discussing the types of strategies principals use to improve teacher retention, a Lowcountry assistant principal with 9 years of experience explained:

> Internal communication is critical for the retention of teachers. Teachers want to be informed and contribute to the decision-making process within the school building. While some decisions are executive in nature, many decisions can be handled through a shared decision-making process. Principals improve teacher retention by communicating clear expectations and building positive relationships.

Related to communications, one Pee Dee teacher with 12 years of experience suggested that principals:

> Provide the opportunity to have a genuine conversation with their staff members. Show appreciation often, expressing how valuable each person is in a thoughtful way, always show support in successes and failures.

An Upstate teacher with 7 years of experience recommended that

> principals can seek to improve teacher retention by building a community within their school. They must work alongside other key stakeholders within the school to build a strong school culture where it is a place everyone wants to be. While this may be challenging if done successfully, teachers will want to come back year after year. Principals can also help to improve teacher retention by supporting the staff throughout the school year and giving feedback to help them.

Theme 3: The Effects on Faculty After Principal Turnover

To help us interpret the findings between principal and teacher turnover, a Midlands assistant principal with 10 years of experience shared:

> While every situation is different, the continuity of leadership is vitally important to maintaining a strong school culture. In my experience, the transition of educational leadership creates anxiety among the faculty, and teachers wait to see which instructional philosophies and programs will be retained.

Meanwhile, the Midlands assistant principal with 4 years of experience indicated:

> [We had feelings of] anxiousness, uncertainty, and self-preservation. From my experience, I can sense/feel the atmosphere shifting in either direction. Shifting towards stability or petal to the medal towards uncertainty.

The Upstate teacher with 7 years of experience elaborated:

> School culture takes time to build. Therefore, when a principal leaves the school, culture doesn't immediately disappear. I think among the staff, there may be questions and a sense of nervousness. However, if a new principal comes in and doesn't try to maintain or add to the school culture, the staff morale and students will suffer.

Theme 4: Principal Behaviors that Influence Teacher Turnover

In addressing principal behaviors that are related to turnover, the Lowcountry assistant principal with 9 years of experience shared,

Poor instructional leadership directly influenced my decision to pursue a degree in educational leadership. After a dynamic principal retired, I was deeply disappointed in the successor. The inability of the young principal to clearly communicate expectations and manage the day-to-day tasks influenced my decision to leave the classroom.

The Midlands assistant principal with 4 years of experience elaborated,

[The principal was] confined in their office 95% of the time, no positive interactions with teachers or students, drastic changes without teacher/student input, stern disciplinarian versus compassion and empathy, and displays lack of wisdom. For these reasons I chose to leave.

SUMMARY

From the review of research and data, this chapter provided evidence supporting a relationship between teacher turnover and principal turnover, which likely contributes to the teacher shortage crisis. The analysis results identified high poverty and high minority schools as having high attrition for teachers and leaders. Considering these schools are generally the most at risk for poor academic achievement (Childs & Russell, 2017), the turnover statistics are somewhat expected. Nonetheless, teacher and leader stability remains a necessity to increase the stability and performance of these types of schools. Other school characteristics such as school level, community, and geographic region were inconclusive. There were few similarities in teacher attrition and principal attrition across those areas.

The analysis indicated a clear relationship between teacher retention and principal retention. The scatter plot and the bar graph indicated that the percentage of returning teachers increased as the same principals remained in the school, and there were higher percentages of returning teachers each year when there was no principal turnover. In their principal movement study, Tran and Buckman (2017) and Tran (2017) highlight that principals often leave when they are less satisfied with their pay and seek higher salaries; however, school districts in high poverty areas often cannot pay principals the same as more affluent districts. Therefore, we see the revolving door of the principalship begin the turnover sequence that trickles down to teachers. While not the only factor that matters for principal retention, money likely plays an influential role that precipitates the teacher turnover cycle, contributing to the teacher shortage crisis.

Principal attributes, experience, and disposition can play a role in retaining teachers. Walker and Slear (2011) indicated that principals should (a) provide clear instructional expectations, (b) be an effective communicator, and (c) be able to motivate. Similar to the quotes from the practitioner commentary in this chapter regarding poor instructional leadership and communication, the literature indicates that the aforementioned principal qualities are needed to maintain a positive school culture and ultimately retain teachers. However, all principal turnover may not be bad if the principals who leave are ineffective (Bartanen et al., 2019).

As evident from the other chapters in this book, addressing teaching shortages is not a quick fix. The teacher shortage phenomenon has many layers, and the root cause can be found within a host of areas (i.e., federal and state policy, financial and job markets, local communities, districts, and schools). This chapter, instead, informs school and district leaders of an area they may be able to better control, retention of *school leadership*. The South Carolina statistics suggest that if principals stay, teachers are more likely to stay as well.

When interpreting the findings and recommendations found in this chapter, it is important to note that no causal relationships should be made when interpreting the data. The scatter plots and bar graphs do not account for concomitant variables. Instead, the data found in the figures should be viewed as trends. Future researchers are encouraged to analyze the "principal retention influence on teacher retention" phenomenon using more rigorous research methods to determine if the relationship between teacher turnover and principal turnover is causal and whether the relationship has a sizeable impact.

REFERENCES

Abbeville v. South Carolina. Opinion No. 27466. (November 12, 2018). https://cases .justia.com/south-carolina/supreme-court/2014-27466.pdf?ts¼1415808227

Akiba, M., & Reichardt, R. (2004). What predicts the mobility of elementary school leaders? An analysis of longitudinal data in Colorado. *Education Policy Analysis Archives, 12*(8), 1–21.

Aldridge, J. M., & Fraser, B. J. (2016). Teachers' views of their school climate and its relationship with teacher self-efficacy and job satisfaction. *Learning Environments Research, 19*(2), 291–307.

Barnes, G., Crowe, E., & Schaefer, B. (2007). *The cost of teacher turnover in five states: A pilot study.* National Commission on Teaching and America's Future.

Bartanen, B., Grissom, J. A., & Rogers, L. K. (2019). The impacts of principal turnover. *Educational Evaluation and Policy Analysis, 41*(3), 350–374.

Beesley, A., Atwill, K., Blair, P., & Barley, Z. (2008). *Strategies for recruitment and retention of secondary teachers in central region rural schools.* Mid-continent Research for Education and Learning.

Béteille T., Kalogrides, D., & Loeb, S. (2012). Stepping stones: Principal career paths and school outcomes. *Social Science Research, 41*(4), 904–919.

Boyd, D., Lankford, H., Loeb, S., & Wyckoff, J. (2005). Explaining the short careers of high-achieving teachers in schools with low-performing students. *American Economic Review, 95*(2), 166–171.

Branch, G. F., Hanushek, E. A., & Rivkin, S. G. (2009, January). *Principal turnover and effectiveness* [Paper presentation]. American Economics Association, San Francisco, CA.

Burkhauser, S., Gates, S. M., Hamilton, L. S., & Ikemoto, G. S. (2012). *First-year principals in urban school districts: How actions and working conditions relate to outcomes* (Technical Report). RAND Corporation.

Carroll, T. G. (2007). *Policy brief: The high cost of teacher turnover* (Technical report). National Commission on Teaching and America's Future.

Carver-Thomas, D., & Darling-Hammond, L. (2017). *Teacher turnover: Why it matters and what we can do about it.* Learning Policy Institute.

Center of Educator Recruitment, Retention, and Advancement. (n.d.). *Regional map.* https://www.cerra.org/program-facilitators1.html

Childs, J., & Russell, J. L. (2017). Improving low-achieving schools: Building state capacity to support school improvement through race to the top. *Urban Education, 52*(2), 236–266.

Clotfelter, C. T., Ladd, H. F., & Vigdor, J. L. (2011). Teacher mobility, school segregation, and pay-based policies to level the playing field. *Education Finance and Policy, 6*(3), 399–438.

Edwards, W. L., Quinn, D. J., Fuller, E. J., & Pendola, A. (2018). *Impact of principal turnover.* University (Policy Brief 2018-4). Council for Educational Administration.

Fink, D., & Brayman, C. (2006). School leadership succession and the challenges of change. *Educational Administration Quarterly, 42*(1), 62–89.

Fuller, E. J., & Young, M. D. (2009). *Tenure and retention of newly hired principals in Texas.* University Council for Educational Administration, Department of Educational Administration, University of Texas at Austin.

Garcia, E., & Weiss, E. (2019). *The teacher shortage is real, large, and growing, and worse than we thought.* Economic Policy Institute.

Garrett, J. (2019). *South Carolina annual educator supply and demand report: 2018–2019 school year.* Center for Educator Recruitment, Retention, and Advancement.

Goldring, R., & Taie, S. (2018). *Principal attrition and mobility: Results from the 2016–17 principal follow-up survey* (NCES 2018-066; Technical report). National Center for Education Statistics.

Grissom, J. A. (2011). Can good principals keep teachers in disadvantaged schools? Linking principal effectiveness to teacher satisfaction and turnover in hard-to-staff environments. *Teachers College Record, 113*(11), 2552–2585.

Grissom, J. A., & Bartanen, B. (2019). Strategic retention: Principal effectiveness and teacher turnover in multiple-measure teacher evaluation systems. *American Educational Research Journal, 56*(2), 514–555.

Grissom, J. A., Kalogrides, D., & Loeb, S. (2015). Using student test scores to measure principal performance. *Educational Evaluation and Policy Analysis, 37*(1), 3–28.

Guarino, C. M., Santibañez, L., & Daley, G. A. (2006). Teacher recruitment and retention: A review of the recent empirical literature. *Review of Educational Research, 76*(2), 173–208.

Guin, K. (2004). Chronic teacher turnover in urban elementary schools. *Educational Evaluation and Policy Analysis, 12*(42), 1–25.

Hammer, P. C., Hughes, G., McClure, C., Reeves, C., & Salgado, D. (2005). *Rural teacher recruitment and retention practices: A review of the research literature, National Survey of Rural Superintendents, and case studies of programs in Virginia.* Appalachia Educational Laboratory at Edvantia. https://files.eric.ed.gov/fulltext/ED489143.pdf

Hanselman, P., Grigg, J. K., Bruch, S., & Gamoran, A. (2016). The consequences of principal and teacher turnover for school social resources. In G. Kao & H. Park (Eds.), *Family environments, school resources, and educational outcomes* (pp. 49–89). Emerald Group.

Hanushek, E. A., Kain, J. F., & Rivkin, S. G. (2004). Why public schools lose teachers. *Journal of Human Resources, 39*(2), 326–354.

Hanushek, E. A., Rivkin, S. G., & Schiman, J. C. (2016). Dynamic effects of teacher turnover on the quality of instruction. *Economics of Education Review, 55,* 132–148.

Henry, G. T., & Harbatkin, E. (2019). *Turnover at the top: Estimating the effects of principal turnover on student, teacher, and school outcomes* (EdWorkingPaper: 19-95). Annenberg Institute at Brown University. http://www.edworkingpapers.com/ai19-95

Henry, G. T., & Redding, C. (2020). The consequences of leaving school early: The effects of within-year and end-of-year teacher turnover. *Education Finance and Policy, 15*(2), 332–356.

Jacob, R., Goddard, R., Kim, M., Miller, R., & Goddard, Y. (2015). Exploring the causal impact of the McREL balanced leadership program on leadership, principal efficacy, instructional climate, educator turnover, and student achievement. *Educational Evaluation and Policy Analysis, 37*(3), 314–332.

Kearney, W. S., Valdez, A., & Garcia, L. (2012). Leadership for the long-haul: The impact of leadership longevity on student achievement. *School Leadership Review, 7*(2), 24–33.

Learning Policy Institute. (2017). *The role of principals in addressing teacher shortages* (Research brief). Learning Policy Institute.

Lewis-Spector, J. (2016). State-level regulations for alternative routes to teacher certification in the U.S.: Are candidates being prepared to develop their students' literacy? *Literacy Practice & Research, 42*(1), 5–15.

Maranto, R. (2013). How do we get them on the farm? Efforts to improve rural teacher recruitment and retention in Arkansas. *The Rural Educator, 34*(1), 1–9. https://doi.org/10.35608/ruraled.v34i1.406

Mascall, B., & Leithwood, K. (2010). Investing in leadership: The district's role in managing principal turnover. *Leadership and Policy in Schools, 9*(4), 367–383.

Miller, A. (2009). *Principal turnover, student achievement and teacher retention.* Princeton University.

Miller, A. (2013). Principal turnover and student achievement. *Economics of Education Review, 36,* 60–72.

Monk, D. H. (2007). Recruiting and retaining high-quality teachers in rural areas. *Future of Children, 17*(1), 155–174. https://doi.org/10.1353/foc.2007.0009

National Center for Education Statistics. (2015). Teacher turnover: Stayers, movers, and learners. *The Condition of Education*.https://nces.ed.gov/programs/coe/pdf/coe_slc.pdf

National Center for Education Statistics. (2021). *The condition of Education 2021* (NCES 2021-144). U.S. Department of Education.

Noonan, W., & Goldman, P. (1995). *Principal succession and elementary school climate: One year's experience in an urban school division* (ED396426). http://files.eric.ed.gov/fulltext/ED396426.pdf

Redding, C., & Henry, G. T. (2018). New evidence on the frequency of teacher turnover: Accounting for within-year turnover. *Educational Researcher, 47*(9), 577–593.

Reininger, M. (2012). Hometown disadvantage? It depends on where you're from: Teachers' location preferences and the implications for staffing schools. *Educational Evaluation and Policy Analysis, 34*(2), 127–145.

Ringel, J., Gates, S., Chung, C., Brown, A., & Ghosh-Dastidar, B. (2004). *Career paths of school administrators in Illinois: Insights from an analysis of state data.* Rand Education.

Ronfeldt, M., Loeb, S., & Wyckoff, J. (2013). How teacher turnover harms student achievement. *American Educational Research Journal, 50*(1), 4–36.

Scafidi, B., Sjoquist, D. L., & Stinebrickner, T. R. (2007). Race, poverty, and teacher mobility. *Economics of Education Review, 26*(2), 145–159.

Seashore Louis, K., Leithwood, K., Wahlstrom, K., & Anderson, S. (2010). *Learning from leadership project: Investigating the links to improved student learning* (Final report of research findings). The Wallace Foundation. https://conservancy.umn.edu/bitstream/handle/11299/140885/Learning-from-Leadership_Final-Research-Report_July-2010.pdf?sequence=1&isAllowed=y

Simon, N. S., & Johnson, S. M. (2015). Teacher turnover in high-poverty schools: What we know and can do. *Teachers College Record, 117*(3), 1–36.

Sutcher, L., Darling-Hammond, L., & Carver-Thomas, D. (2016). *A coming crisis in teaching? Teacher supply, demand, and shortages in the U.S.* Learning Policy Institute.

Sutcher, L., Darling-Hammond, L., & Carver-Thomas, D. (2019). Understanding teacher shortages: An analysis of teacher supply and demand in the United States. *Education Policy Analysis Archives, 27*(35), 1–40.

Taie, S., & Goldring, R. (2017). *Characteristics of public elementary and secondary school teachers in the United States: Results from the 2015–16 National Teacher and Principal Survey. First Look.* NCES 2017-072. National Center for Education Statistics.

Tran, H. (2017). The impact of pay satisfaction and school achievement on high school principals' turnover intentions. *Educational Management Administration & Leadership, 45*(4), 621–638.

Tran, H., & Buckman, D. G. (2017). The impact of principal movement and school achievement on principal salaries. *Leadership and Policy in Schools, 16*(1), 106–129.

Tran, H., Hardie, S., Gause, S., Moyi, P., & Ylimaki, R. (2020). Leveraging the perspectives of rural educators to develop realistic job previews for rural teacher recruitment and retention. *Rural Educator, 41*(2), 31–46.

Tran, H., McCormick, J., & Nguyen, T. T. (2018). The cost of replacing South Carolina high school principals. *Management in Education, 32*(3), 109–118.

Ulferts, J. D. (2016). A brief summary of teacher recruitment and retention in the smallest Illinois rural schools. *The Rural Educator, 37*(1), 14–24.

Vanderhaar, J., Munoz, M. A., & Rodosky, R. J. (2006). Leadership as accountability for learning: The effects of school poverty, teacher experience, previous achievement, and principal preparation programs on student achievement. *Journal of Personnel Evaluation in Education, 19,* 17–33.

Walker, J., & Slear, S. (2011). The impact of principal leadership behaviors on the efficacy of new and experienced middle school teachers. *NASSP Bulletin, 95*(1), 46–64.

Weinstein, M., Schwartz, A. E., Jacobowitz, R., Ely, T., & Landon, K. (2009). *New schools, new leaders: A study of principal turnover and academic achievement at new high schools in New York City* (New York University Wagner Research Paper No. 2011-09). Institute for Education and Social Policy.

Ziegler, B. (n.d.). Education rankings: Measuring how well states are educating their students. *U.S. News & World Report.*

PART IV

MOVING FORWARD:
HOW THE TEACHING PROFESSION CAN ASCEND
AND FLOURISH

CHAPTER 11

RURAL TALENT MANAGEMENT

Recruiting and Retaining Teachers in Rural Hard-to-Staff Schools

Douglas A. Smith
Iowa State University

Henry Tran
University of South Carolina

Christine M. Cain
Iowa State University

We have seen an unprecedented amount of education policy reform, research, and attention focused on urban schools across the United States in the past few decades. Yet despite the fact that half of all U.S. school districts and one third of all schools are located in rural areas (Johnson et al., 2014), rural education has not received near comparable attention to their urban counterparts, relegating it to the periphery of educational improvement

How Did We Get Here?, pages 259–286
Copyright © 2022 by Information Age Publishing
www.infoagepub.com

efforts (Corbett & White, 2014). Given that underrepresented students of color from low-income backgrounds are already neglected in the education system, the urban bias doubly marginalizes those from rural communities (Cuervo, 2016). From a teacher staffing perspective, rural neglect is extremely problematic given that rural schools experience higher educator turnover than schools in any other geographic space (Goldring et al., 2014; Ingersoll, 2019). While data from the National Center for Education Statistics (NCES) 2012–2013 Schools and Staffing Survey (SASS) shows that annual teacher turnover in low-poverty suburban schools averaged 11%, high-poverty urban schools averaged 19%, and high-poverty rural schools faced even higher overall teacher turnover at an average of 25% per year (Ingersoll, 2019). Repeated turnovers are costly both from an academic (i.e., more turnover is related to lower student achievement scores; Ronfeldt et al., 2013) and financial perspective (i.e., teacher replacements in high-turnover, resource-constrained districts can cost schools upwards of $20,000 per teacher; Carver-Thomas & Darling-Hammond, 2017).

While some general teacher staffing policies have applicability across contexts, rural schools experience many unique challenges and benefits that differ from their non-rural counterparts (Smith & Tran, 2019). Tran et al. (2020) reviewed the research on rural teacher recruitment and retention and summarized numerous commonly identified challenges. These challenges include lower pay (due to lower property tax wealth of the regions), limited resources, professional isolation (away from universities and other sources of professional development), less desirable locations with fewer amenities (e.g., lack of Broadway plays or large shopping malls), highly visible teachers in small communities (e.g., the community is more concerned with and knowledgeable about teachers' personal lives), among others. Berry et al. (2020) also pointed to the lack of broadband internet access, fewer colleagues in the same grade level or topic for collaboration, and a lack of autonomy in decision-making during difficult times. Unique benefits to rural communities include smaller class sizes, lower cost of living, access to nature, school camaraderie, and greater community engagement (Tran et al., 2020).

It is important to note that rurality is not a monolith, and different rural communities have different opportunities and challenges. For example, individuals living in rural communities on the edge of a large metropolitan area can more easily access urban amenities than their remote rural counterparts. Some rural communities have a high concentration of people of color, while others do not. Some rural communities have thriving rich local resources (e.g., agriculture or oil), while others live in perpetual poverty. Common to many rural communities is that schools often represent the hub of their community (Eppley, 2015), and educators are the most important school input for student learning (Goldhaber, 2015; Stronge et al., 2007). Consequently, the University Council for Education Administration

(UCEA) noted the critical importance of "stabilizing the rural educator workforce" (UCEA, 2018, p. 1) as a key element in responding to the challenges of rural education.

The purpose of this chapter is to highlight a series of studies that the authors conducted to better understand the influence of personal characteristics, educational preparation, employment experiences, and external influences on teacher recruitment and retention in rural hard-to-staff schools. The highlighted studies, focusing on the South Carolina context, include a span of perspectives from potential teachers (e.g., college students and pre-service teachers) to current and former teachers (e.g., administrators). The chapter reviews findings from studies that explore the influence of various factors motivating college students and preservice teachers to consider teaching in hard-to-staff rural schools. The chapter then shifts to the perspectives of current teachers by exploring retention insights (including identifying advantages and challenges associated with rural teaching) of present rural educators from hard-to-staff schools in South Carolina's Lowcountry. Given the consistent findings concerning the importance of administrative support for teacher employment, teachers' perceptions of the most important types of administrative support from across the state are then reviewed, followed by an analysis of what motivates teachers from non-rural backgrounds to stay in rural schools. The chapter concludes with a discussion about making sense of these findings from a theoretical perspective and their implications for policy and practice. Collectively, these studies provide a more holistic understanding of the conditions necessary to recruit and retain teachers in some of the most challenged districts in the Palmetto State. Because the shortages are influenced by both a declining supply of teachers (i.e., declining interest in the teaching profession exemplified by falling teacher education program enrollment over time) and a rising frequency of teacher turnover that exceeds the number of teachers that enter the profession annually (Center for Educator Recruitment, Retention, and Advancement [CERRA], 2020), we focus our attention on both ends of the spectrum, beginning with potential and pre-service teachers.

POTENTIAL AND PRE-SERVICE TEACHERS

For the 2020–2021 school year, 44% of all new public school district hires in South Carolina were new to the profession, of which 24% were recent graduates from teacher education programs in the state (CERRA, 2020). These figures remind us of the prominent role new teachers play in the teacher staffing environment. While researchers, practitioners, and policymakers have identified numerous factors and staffing incentives that are important for prospective teachers, it is largely unknown which staffing incentives should hold priority when budgetary constraints necessitate a prioritization of incentives, especially for rural school districts with severely constrained resources. To address this question, Tran and Smith (2020a) conducted a mixed-method (i.e., quantitative and qualitative) study to examine the relative importance of various working characteristics for regional college students in their consideration of teaching in a rural high-need (i.e., high poverty and staffing demand) school district. A comprehensive review of the teacher recruitment research results in a robust array of evidence to support the importance of 25 particular working conditions for teacher employment (Table 11.1). As can be seen, many of these conditions affect both teacher recruitment and retention. For example, attractive working conditions and compensation can both draw and keep employees.

The 25 working conditions identified from the body of research were categorized along three dimensions: financial incentives, personal factors, and school environment. Financial incentives represented the largest

TABLE 11.1   Working Conditions Related to Acquiring and Sustaining Teachers

Working Conditions Related to Acquiring and Sustaining Teachers		Working Conditions Related to Development of Teachers	Working Conditions of Rural Schools (as compared to other locales)
Base Salary	College Tuition Pre-Paid	Input on School Decisions	Longer Commute Time
Medical Benefits			
Retirement Benefits	Forgivable Home Mortgage Loans/ Housing Assistance	School Administrative Support	Lengthier Distance to Metropolitan Area
Annual Raises			
Work Schedule That Provide Summers Off	Signing Bonus	Provision of Ongoing Teacher Coaching	Smaller Class Size
	Teacher Licensure Requirements		Lower Academic Performance of Students
Sufficient Textbooks and Class Materials	Responsiveness During Hiring Process		
Up-to-Date School Technology	Parental Involvement at School		
Clean and Safe School Facilities			
Forgiveness of College Student Loans	Amicable Colleagues		
	Connection to Students		
	Self Confidence in Being an Effective Teacher		

dimension that included longitudinal commitments such as base salary (Milanowski, 2003; Ulferts, 2016), annual raises (Allegretto & Mishel, 2016; Lankford et al., 2002), and employee benefits such as medical and retirement (Handal et al., 2013; Ulferts, 2016). Other financial incentives were limited-duration monetary incentives that included signing bonuses (Clotfelter et al., 2005; Rosenberg et al., 2014), the forgiveness of college student loans (Collins, 1999; Ulferts, 2016), and prepaid college tuition (Tran et al., 2015). Forgivable home mortgage loans and housing assistance incentives have also been useful in employment decision-making, particularly in rural areas with limited quality housing availability (Berry et al., 2019, Shuls & Maranto, 2014; Ulferts, 2016).

Important personal recruitment factors that were identified in the literature included commute time (Rosenberg et al., 2014), distance to a metropolitan area (Boyd et al., 2005), individual's self-confidence in being an effective teacher in specific contexts (Milanowski, 2003; Tran et al., 2015). Likewise, teacher licensure processes have proven to be a point of intimidation that deters individuals from pursuing teaching careers (Milanowski, 2003), but work schedules that provide for summers off have been an attractive factor (Ulferts, 2016). In terms of factors related to the school environment in teacher employment decision-making, prior research has established the importance of the availability and quality of sufficient textbooks and class materials (Handal et al., 2013), up-to-date school technology (Milanowski, 2003), clean and safe school facilities (Hirsh & Emerick, 2006), and parental involvement in the school (Liu & Johnson, 2006). Relationally, a school environment that has amicable colleagues promotes a sense of connection to students (Goodpaster et al., 2012) and allows for teachers to have the ability to provide input on school decisions (Berry et al., 2019; Ingersoll, 2002) has been established as attractive employment decision-making factors. From an academic perspective, the performance of students (Goodpaster et al., 2012), class sizes (Allen, 2005), school administrative support (Rosenberg et al., 2014), and provision of ongoing teacher coaching (Handal et al., 2013) are important school environment factors. Lastly, from a human resources management perspective, responsiveness in the hiring process (Liu & Johnson, 2006) is also important for employment consideration (Plaskoff, 2017). Given the long list of important work attributes, Tran and Smith (2020a) sought to understand potential teachers' perception of the relative importance of these attributes for their employment consideration in rural hard-to-staff contexts.

The survey issued in Tran and Smith's (2020a) study captured respondents' preferred rankings for 25 working conditions (Table 11.1) when presented with a sample profile of a rural district with extremely high-teacher turnover in the state of South Carolina. Based on the results of a utility ranking methodology with 403 regional college students, participants identified the following five working conditions as most influential for their employment decision process: (a) school administrative support, (b) self-confidence in being an effective teacher in the profile district, (c) strong sense of connection to students, (d) clean and safe school facilities, and (e) responsiveness during the hiring process. An especially noteworthy item is that the base salary for the teaching position was ranked as 18th most influential, medical benefits were 10th, and annual raises were 6th. These findings reveal that salary and monetary benefits are necessary to improve interest in the teaching profession, but they alone are insufficient without consideration for non-monetary working conditions and altruistic considerations (e.g., connection to students, amicable colleagues). Keep in mind that past research and policy have identified all working conditions as important for teacher considerations. This means that the results do not suggest that those ranked lower on the list are unimportant to potential teachers, just less than those ranked higher.

The qualitative aspect of Tran and Smith's (2020a) study sought to better understand the utility rankings and participants' perceptions of teaching in rural high-need schools. Interviews with ten randomly selected survey respondents reinforced that respondents prioritized working for an employer that would provide support and resources to successfully fulfill their job responsibilities. However, there was skepticism from many participants that a rural high-need district could meet this need due to scarcity of resources and small district size. In many small resource-limited schools, teachers often have to wear "multiple hats," as a result, administrative support was perceived to be particularly important in these schools to help reduce the non-instructional duties and tasks of overworked teachers. Furthermore, administrative support was seen to be particularly critical for rural schools, given that many of their teachers are isolated from professional support opportunities. In short, strong administrative support is seen as a buffer to mitigate some of the more challenging aspects of rural teaching. Alternatively, weak support could serve as a deterrent. As one 20-year-old political science major shared, "If the school's administration has a reputation of habitually invading the teacher's classroom and enforcing counterproductive, or ineffective teaching strategies, that would hinder me from applying" (Tran & Smith, 2020a, p. 468).

The participants interviewed in the study also expressed concerns and pause in potentially seeking teaching employment because of the perceived safety concerns associated with the school and community, especially if they were to reside and work in the same rural high-needs district presented in the profile. One 20-year-old criminal justice major noted that the following questions he would wonder before deciding whether to work in the environment "The area around the school district. If it is safe? Welcoming?

If I would be able to start a family in the future here, etc." (Tran & Smith, 2020b, p. 468).

The study respondents further raised concerns about their ability to relate to students in the district if there was a mismatch between teacher and students in three areas: racial, socioeconomic, and cultural background. In part, there was a fear of cultural clash with many participants. They worried that the profile district would be different from their own prior experiences and thus would limit their ability to connect with students and community members. This finding aligns with those from Tran et al.'s (2015) survey with 64 early childhood (P–2nd grade) teacher preparation students at the University of South Carolina, where they found that students with high confidence in their self-efficacy reported more willingness to teach in rural high-need schools for at least 5 years. Lastly, interview participants that expressed the greatest levels of openness to pursuing a teaching career in rural high-need schools often included those with altruistic motivations to help students. Considering both the qualitative and quantitative findings, policymakers and district leaders must look comprehensively (i.e., from teacher training/pre-service and onwards) at working conditions to improve teacher recruitment.

UNDERSTANDING FINANCIAL FACTORS

State and district teacher staffing policies most frequently identify financial incentives as a vehicle to improve teacher recruitment and retention (Strunk & Zeehandelaar, 2011). Yet, financial incentives come in many forms (e.g., higher base pay, higher bonuses, retention bonuses, housing allowances, etc.) and can serve many purposes. For rural hard-to-staff schools, stronger financial incentives are often justified based on the theory of compensating differentials (Horng, 2009; Milanowski et al., 2009; Steele et al., 2010). The theory suggests that more compensation (e.g., signing bonuses and salary enhancements) can be used to offset and overcome the deterrent factors (e.g., lack of local amenities) associated with rural hard-to-staff schools in the employment decision-making process (Strunk & Zeehandelaar, 2011). However, many of these additional compensation benefits are temporary, and although they may support improvement recruitment initially, they often add significantly less benefit for long-term retention (Clotfelter et al., 2008). Additionally, potential and current teachers operate within the larger labor market where education occupations vie against non-education occupations that are often able to offer higher salaries, which often results in school employers trying to narrow the gap between their non-education competition as opposed to beating their wage offerings. While non-salary benefits have traditionally offset the lower wages associated with teaching, the weakening of employee retirement, insurance benefits, and contributions have eroded some of their offsetting influence for public educators (Bureau of Labor Statistics, 2020).

Rural school leaders often have smaller applicant pools for vacant teaching positions (Jimerson, 2003) and struggle to offer financial packages to attract quality teachers to accept teaching positions (Kolbe & Strunk, 2012). Even when they can offer recruitment incentives, their wealthier counterparts can often outmatch them with a counter offer (see Chapter 4). Rural districts often operate under finite resources and have to prioritize one method over another in terms of retention and recruitment strategies. However, not much is known about the financial factors used to attract teachers (Kolbe & Strunk, 2012), especially in impoverished rural settings.

Working with the same sample as the Tran and Smith's (2020a) study, Tran and Smith (2019) sought to more deeply understand the specific influence of financial factors as motivators for college students to consider the teaching profession and teaching in rural hard-to-staff schools. Respondents were asked various questions about this focus, and several illuminating findings were discovered. Case in point, the average beginning teacher salary offered in South Carolina at the time of the survey was $33,057. Respondents' average reported starting salary needed to seriously consider teaching in the profile hard-to-staff rural school was $47,607. This represents a sizeable gap but demonstrates the need for a continued policy focus on improving starting salary conditions, among other incentives. In Tran et al.'s (2015) survey findings, their sample of early childhood education student survey respondents underestimated the average beginning salary for teachers with a bachelor's degree in South Carolina by about $3,000, showing a need for more public awareness about teacher pay, especially when underestimations may harm the consideration of employment in rural high-need schools.

Returning to Tran and Smith's (2020a) work, the higher the salary the college students' expected for their current chosen field, the less likely they would have interest in considering rural teaching (or teaching altogether for many). Students majoring in fields that have some of the highest average starting salaries (e.g., physical sciences, engineering) were the least interested in considering teaching in the rural profile district and those majoring in fields that have some of the lowest average starting salaries (e.g., social sciences, communication, interdisciplinary) were some of the most interested. Results from an ordinal logistic regression found that the proper financial incentives can influence decisions to pursue a rural teaching profession.

Qualitative interview findings help further explain that beginning teacher salary and other working conditions (e.g., community amenities, administrative support) combine to influence teaching career decision-making. It was also revealed that most participants associated lower starting salaries as a strong signal towards perceived lower respectability of the teaching profession. Perceptions of low respectability of the teaching profession were quantitatively and qualitatively associated with respondents' lower likelihood of teaching consideration. While non-salary benefits in public sector employment have historically offset lower base salaries, students expressed little understanding of public sector retirement (e.g., pension) and medical benefits and how these may vary from private-sector employer benefits. This is important because potential teachers may overlook important benefits to public teaching employment that they are unaware of and may not be widely promoted.

Teachers' motivation to teach is often not money (Dos Santos, 2019; Morice & Murray, 2003). But as explained in Chapter 8, teachers, like all other adult citizens in our modern society, require sufficient compensation to live and make ends meet. Furthermore, low pay is connotated with low respectability of the profession, which deters individuals from teaching to preserve their self-esteem, pride, and sense of self-image. We saw this highlighted in Tran and Smith's (2019) findings when one participant noted,

> Traditionally it is perceived that teachers are not paid enough [...] they feel undervalued and underpaid. I looked into teaching as a career pretty strongly [...] and every person I talked to, be it a grade school teacher or college professor, told me the same thing—that it was a lot of work, it was an unstable work environment, and the pay was very poor for the amount of work that you put in. (p. 161)

Consequently, while low pay is not the sole barrier for teaching consideration, it remains a significant barrier to entry into teaching for many, especially in rural schools.

CURRENT TEACHERS

Don't neglect to highlight the positives of rural teaching.

While rural schools are frequently associated with unappealing characteristics for potential employees, they also have many opportunities and advantages seldom mentioned. Furthermore, some individuals prefer the country to the hustle and bustle of the big cities or the commuter traffic in suburban communities. When attempting to build a sustainable rural teacher workforce, school employers can support their recruitment and retention efforts by identifying individuals with a predisposition or compatibility with the rural environment (Tran, Smith, & Fox, 2018). This requires that schools highlight rural advantages to interest candidates while simultaneously engaging with them honestly about the challenges, balancing the pros and cons of rural teaching. Centering a place-based education approach has become a relevant topic for researchers and the greater educational community for its positive impact on developing students' sense of place, promoting community and environmental engagement, and improving student learning and teacher/student motivation. From a human resources perspective, it is useful to learn how place-based advantages could also be emphasized to help respond to rural teacher staffing issues.

Traditional recruiting methods focus primarily on standardized financial incentives (Shuls & Maranto, 2014). However, evidence supports idealistic appeals to teaching (e.g., student-centered classrooms or public service) as effective recruitment messages for difficult-to-staff jobs such as rural teaching in high-poverty communities. Partly because altruism (as opposed to material incentives such as salaries) is often the motivating factor for individuals to enter the teaching profession in the first place (Hess, 2010; Shuls & Maranto, 2014).

Tran et al.'s (2020) study leverages the voices of rural teachers from South Carolina's Lowcountry to better understand how to utilize realistic job previews (RJPs) as a recruitment strategy for rural school districts. Accuracy, transparency, honesty, and credibility in recruitment are at the center of RJPs. RJP's purpose is to provide honest information to applicants to make better employment decisions. It includes emphasizing strategies such as: using current employee perspectives, highlighting positive and negative aspects of the position and organization, describing what a typical workday looks like, describing the positive and negative aspects of the organizational culture, and being transparent in presenting all relevant data about compensation, benefits, and turnover.

In the study, Tran et al. (2020) conducted interviews with 11 teachers and one principal from five rural, high-need school districts in South Carolina. The work centers on spotlighting the advantages and challenges identified by rural educators to better understand the rural teaching environment. Advantages identified included a stronger emphasis on administrative support, family-oriented culture, strong community relations and tight networks, smaller class sizes, and teacher autonomy (see Figure 11.1). For example, interviewees in the study talked about the importance of belonging or inclusion in the community's social fabric as an advantage of teaching in the rural community. Likewise, many teachers discussed the family-like environment their small schools foster. As one rural teacher explained, "Coming from a school with a thousand students to a school with 400–500 students, there is a big difference…With the teachers, I felt welcomed at that [small, rural] school. They are willing to help me with anything that I need help with…I felt that they were there for me" (p. 37).

On the other hand, when challenges exist, a district should be transparent in identifying these to potential employees to avoid a new employee feeling bait-and-switched or hiring someone who will unlikely stay with the school given the discrepancy between their expectations and the reality of

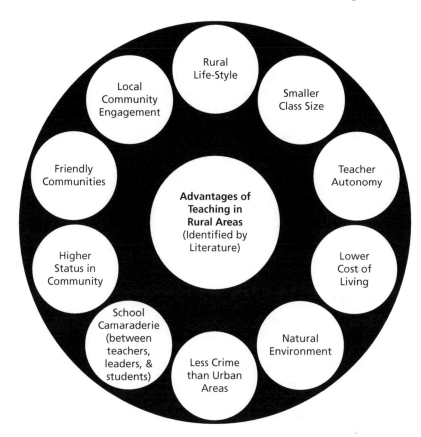

Figure 11.1 Advantages of teaching in rural areas (identified by participants).
Source: Tran et al., 2020.

the work setting. In other words, the relationship won't last if it is built on a lie. Challenges identified by participants as important include a lack of economic opportunities, cultural isolation, and small-town politics, among others (see Figure 11.2).

The lack of economic and professional opportunities often results in a brain drain of talent in rural communities, who, without other avenues for progress, often leave the community, which reinforces and sustains the lack of human capacity in the region. This can be very demoralizing to the educators that develop and cultivate that talent. One rural teacher reflects,

> I hate the fact that we do have families that are in poverty, that the children that I am teaching have nowhere to go once they graduate. There are no businesses here for them, that they'll probably leave and not come back. (Tran et al., 2020, p. 39)

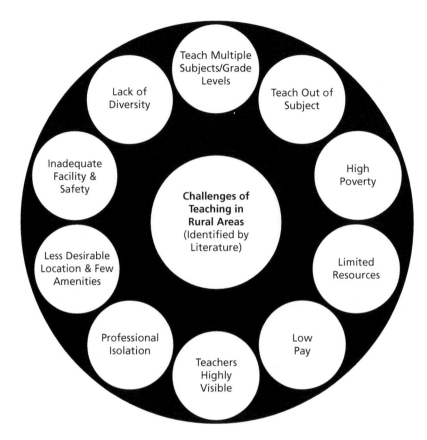

Figure 11.2 Challenges of teaching in rural areas (identified by participants). *Source:* Tran et al., 2020.

Another rural teacher shared how conflicted she felt about it all. On the one hand, she was happy for her students who could gain more opportunities in life, but it saddened her that they had to leave to do so. "You want them to stay, but again you want them to live the life the fullest they can live. That's what I told my children. I don't want you to leave me, but you have to, you know. I want to give those wings you find your way and being success. No matter what."

While amenities like zoos and theaters may be commonplace in urban locales, many rural teachers indicated that their students have to be driven an hour or more to get to these locations. Furthermore, many students' first experiences with these places are with their teachers who bring them on field trips. Had it not been for their teachers, many students may never have received such an experience in their childhood.

Finally, numerous participants in this study did not have prior experience in rural settings before teaching in their schools, which resulted in added stress (on top of teaching in general) for them as they had to adjust to their lack of familiarity with the geographical contexts and working with students from a different background than they are used to. The lack of rural-specific preparation is a constant theme that has emerged in several of the studies mentioned.

ADMINISTRATIVE SUPPORTS THAT MATTER MOST

While money and resources are significant influences, administrative support has been frequently identified as the most important factor influencing teachers' retention decisions (Burkhauser, 2017; Ladd, 2011). There is a common saying, "People don't leave bad jobs, they leave bad bosses." Tran and Dou (2019) studied teacher perspectives on different types of administrative supports that mattered to their retention in a rural school and whether those preferred supports differed for beginning teachers (in their initial 3 years of teaching) or more seasoned teachers. Data consisted of survey results from 28 rural South Carolina teachers and interviews conducted with the 12 educators from the Tran et al. (2020) study. The findings were consistent with past research in that the most important factor for teacher employment (e.g., Boyd et al., 2011, Burkhauser, 2017; Glazer, 2018), despite the specific focus on rural teacher retention. Family-oriented culture and community willingness to offer support came in second and third place. Given the importance of administrative support, the qualitative follow-up interviews focused on understanding the rural administrative support necessary for teacher retention. Administrative support for new teachers often centered on mentorship and direct support, while veteran teachers expressed a greater need for having their voices heard by the administration. One theme across all participants emphasized the need for improved teacher preparation specific to the rural contexts. As one rural teacher succinctly stated, "The actual teacher preparation itself, I don't think prepared me for a rural, small school district" (p. 140). This rural-specific preparation is necessary for teacher and principal preparation to support rural teachers' needs. Overall, Tran and Dou's (2019) findings suggest that rural leaders should

- provide rural specific administrative support given the general lack of rural context-specific teacher preparation;
- provide mentorship and offer financial incentives;
- advertise the community;
- maintain administrative consistency and stability (e.g., constant principal turnover affects teacher turnover);
- provide a positive, collaborative, and open work culture; and
- build relational trust from open communication.

In Tran (2020) and Tran et al.'s (2020) study of the relative importance of different types of administrative support, they found that the issue of respect was foundational to all the attributes based on their survey of 178 teachers across 13 schools throughout South Carolina, and interviews with a subsample of that group. Specifically, in that study, the authors utilized an experimental design to randomly assign 13 different attributes of administrative support (that are important in prior research, see Figure 11.3) to the teachers to estimate their perceptions of the relative importance of these attributes for teacher retention. The results of their analysis can be seen in Figure 11.4.

The number on the right of each attribute indicates how important the teachers perceived that attribute relative to the least important attribute. For example, according to the teacher respondents, the demonstration of "respect" was ranked a little over 27 times more important than community leadership for their retention. The salience of respect was found across the sub-analyses for low retention, high retention, middle, high, urban, and particularly relevant to this chapter, rural schools. As a beginning rural middle school teacher shared in her interview,

> I think it boils down to . . . that human need that we want to feel accepted and like we're doing something, and that someone appreciates us, and to me, that's really what respect is. That [principals] understand, okay, you might not get it right 100% of the time, but I know you're trying. Thank you for what you do. I mean, that goes a huge way.

As you might have noticed, the importance of respect was echoed earlier with the pre-service and potential teachers and had once again emerged as an important theme for current teachers. We will revisit this point in our culminating analysis of the joint findings of these studies.

RETAINING NON-RURAL TEACHERS IN RURAL SCHOOLS

Because teachers are more likely to teach where they grew up (Boyd et al., 2005), and those from rural environments are more likely to consider rural teaching (Tran et al., 2020), significant attention has been placed on initiatives such as "grow-your-own" programs (e.g., Cary, 2015; Dwyer, 2007; Lavalley, 2018; Lowe, 2006) that seek to train, develop, and hire home-grown talent into the teaching positions. Despite these efforts, many rural schools remain understaffed in key areas and must rely on recruiting and retaining non-rural talent. Turnover is frequent in hard-to-staff rural districts that are viewed as a starting point, or transitional employer, to new teachers who, upon and gaining some experience, move to a non-rural district that is perceived to be better resourced and located in a more desirable location (Barnes et al., 2008; Keiser, 2011). This sentiment was captured by a

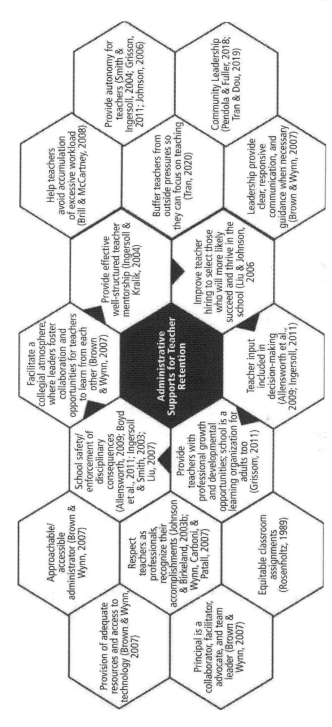

Figure 11.3 Administrative supports for teacher retention. *Source:* Tran, 2021.

Figure 11.4 Best–Worst estimate rankings for different types of administrative support. Relative importance of administrative support characteristics. Full sample ($N = 178$ teachers from at least 13 schools).

rural teacher from the Lowcountry of South Carolina, who shared, "We're a training ground. They recruit the teachers from Ohio, Pennsylvania, New Jersey, those areas. Bring them down here, they work for three to five years, and then go back because they realize, at least [this] county, is challenging" (Tran & Dou, 2019, p. 143). Literature seeking to better understand the retention of rural teachers fails to recognize and differentiate between teachers that have a rural background and those that do not.

Smith et al. (2021) studied the factors and conditions necessary to retain teachers identifying as not from a rural background in rural high-turnover schools. Their phenomenological study focused on understanding the experiences of 11 teachers across six rural districts identified by the state as experiencing high turnover. They each had at least 5 years of teaching experience and self-identified as not having a rural background before employment. Guided by Chapman's (1983) model of the influences on teacher recruitment, which argues that retention is an overall result of career satisfaction, this study focused on understanding teacher attrition through the influence of personal characteristics, educational preparation, quality of first employment experience, and external influences that lead to career satisfaction or dissatisfaction.

The findings of the phenomenological interviews identified several core themes (Table 11.2). First, the teacher sample revealed unique rural perks that include various benefits or opportunities teachers receive employed in their specific district. These perks include financial benefits (e.g., signing and retention bonuses, loan repayment assistance, licensure, and other fee payment) and housing benefits (e.g., ample availability and low cost). While no participants received direct housing subsidies from a district, housing regularly emerged as a positive factor in employment for availability and low housing costs in rural communities compared to suburban and urban contexts. Several participants noted that they were also extremely motivated by signing bonuses offered by school districts (ranging from $4–$5k). Others described the importance of their dependent children's opportunities in the school district for involvement in programs and activities that may not be available or accessible to the extent that they are in their rural district. Many of these benefits would be lost if teachers moved to a different district.

Second, culture and climate were emphasized, including how teachers feel about each other in the district. It includes a family-like feeling amongst colleagues that the administrators lead. Other positive behaviors of administrators, including support and providing a feeling of professional autonomy, are included in this theme. Third, many participants described a sense of complacency and comfort in their job positions, therefore negating teachers seeking opportunities outside of their current school due partly to a fear of rejection or teachers being comfortable and satisfied with

TABLE 11.2 Core Themes and Subsidiary Themes	
Themes	**Subsidiary Themes**
Unique Perks	• Financial Benefits (e.g., bonuses, loan repayment, licensure fee payment) • Housing Benefits (e.g., availability of housing, low housing costs) • Opportunities for Teachers' Dependent Children (e.g., activities, programs, and connections)
Culture and Climate	• Family-Like Feeling in District • Commitment to Highly Respected Leaders • Administrator Support • Professional Autonomy
Complacency and Comfort	• Rejection or Fear of Rejection • Personal Choice to Avoid Change
Commitment to the Community	• Relationship With Students and Families • Holding Leadership Roles in Extra-curricular Activities • Altruistic Motivations

their current situation. Lastly, the findings revealed a strong sense of commitment to the community, which includes a strong feeling of commitment to students, working with the community, or roles in extra-curricular activities in which teachers have a strong commitment.

Collectively, these themes describe the interconnectedness of factors influencing non-rural originating teachers in rural high-turnover schools. Alone, a single factor described in the themes may not be enough to retain a teacher. However, retention decisions are multifaceted and complicated, often influenced by multiple factors simultaneously that must be considered when developing a culture of support or allocating funding to support retention initiatives.

THEORETICAL INTERPRETATION OF THE RESEARCH FINDINGS AND IMPLICATIONS FOR POLICY AND PRACTICE

To help make sense of the findings in the aforementioned studies, Tran and Smith (2020b) introduce the *sustaining teacher employment* model (see Figure 11.5). The model draws on Herzberg et al.'s (1959) motivation-hygiene theory that theorizes that the factors that create job dissatisfaction differ from those that create job satisfaction. An important implication stemming from motivation theory work is that it suggests what may attract teachers to rural areas (recruitment efforts) may not be the same factors that keep them in those communities (retention efforts). For example, earlier

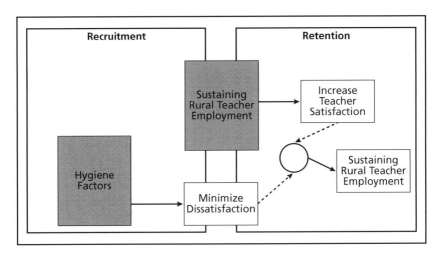

Figure 11.5 Sustaining teacher employment model. *Source:* Tran & Smith, 2020b.

research has explained that teachers often choose the teaching profession because of altruistic reasons, such as wanting to make a difference in the lives of students (Dos Santos, 2019; Morice & Murray, 2003) and would consider seeking or staying in the profession only with sufficient administrative support (Tran & Smith, 2020a; Tran & Dou, 2019; Tran, 2020). While pay does not motivate people to teach, inadequate pay certainly deters college students away from the profession (Tran & Smith, 2019) or prompts those within the field to leave (see Chapter 8). So what does this all mean?

Using Herzberg et al.'s (1959) motivation theory language, salary is an example of a hygiene factor. For example, salary can affect job dissatisfaction, but it does not have equal ability to generate job satisfaction. Therefore, while having more money can mitigate job dissatisfaction, it does not generate job satisfaction in the same way that factors such as a strong connection to students, having a positive influence on student lives, maintaining a strong sense of professional self-efficacy, and receiving consistent and robust administrative support to excel in their work does.

When it comes to self-efficacy, many college students had expressed their trepidation with teaching in rural schools because of their lack of familiarity with the rural context and concern that they could do more harm than good if working in that environment with their lack of preparation to succeed there (Tran et al., 2015). Relatedly, many rural teachers also shared the lack of rural-specific preparation they received, which made their work particularly challenging (Tran et al., 2020). In the pre-service space, rural-specific development can help improve pre-service teachers' confidence to teach in rural spaces (Tran, 2020). In the field, the lack of rural preparation requires administrative support from administrators and school leaders to help teachers succeed in the foreign environment.

Respect is key to sustaining rural teacher employment, both at the macro-level regarding respect for the profession (Tran & Smith, 2019) and at the micro-level in terms of respect to teachers as shown by their administrators and employers (Tran & Smith, 2020a). For school administrators, Tran and Smith (2020c) introduced a conceptual model known as the *thrive beyond survival* model that positions the principal as the lead talent developer in schools. This model theorizes that administrative support is essential for principals and teachers in high-need contexts to not only "survive" but to "thrive" in their positions.

Teachers commonly cite a lack of administrative support as a significant reason for departing teaching positions in hard-to-staff rural schools (Robinson, 2012; Tran & Dou, 2019), yet principals often report not having the knowledge to develop teachers (Barber et al., 2010), and indicate not receiving sufficient development themselves (Grissom & Harrington, 2010; Tran & Bon, 2015), which can lead to principal turnover (Tran, McCormick, &

Nguyen, 2018). Principal turnover often leads to reduced administrative support for teachers and further increases teacher turnover. To make matters worse, both teacher and principal turnover result in a lack of curricular coherence, trust, and consistency. Consequently, this turnover is negatively associated with school student achievement and learning outcomes (Jacob et al., 2015; Miller, 2012).

An underlying argument of the thrive beyond survival model is that school districts and university-based principal preparation programs can and should be providing the support needed to emerging leaders that enables school administrations to support teachers' needs. Tran and Smith's (2020c) thrive beyond survival model (Figure 11.6) centers on the role of the principal as the chief talent developer in schools. In doing so, principal preparation programs should provide context-specific principal preparation focused on developing and supporting teachers in rural and urban hard-to-staff schools. It is critically important that principal preparation programs provide aspiring principals with experience and training beyond preparation for leadership in "idealistic" high-functioning, well-funded, suburban school contexts.

Principal development with a rural focus should prepare administrators to wear many hats and sometimes serve as both principal and superintendent (Canales et al., 2008). Rural principals should also be prepared for additional duties and responsibilities not typically designated to an urban or suburban principal because of a lack of supporting administrators to delegate work to (Stewart & Matthews, 2015). In a rural school, the principal is often involved in all aspects of decision-making and regularly is the lead intermediary connecting teachers to the community and the community to the school. The rural principal is looked at as a school leader and a community leader (Pendola & Fuller, 2018). Principal development programs should focus on preparing principals for the collaboration and partnership skills essential for a rural principal in navigating the rural-specific context. This focus should lead to a heightened awareness of the six rural-specific community attributes Bauch (2001) describe as attributes school leaders can lean on for support in rural communities: social capital, sense of place, parent involvement, strong church ties, school-community-business partnership, and community as curriculum.

Contextualized rural administrative support provided to teachers is necessary across a number of areas that include providing detailed feedback to teachers (Seashore Louis et al., 2010), building teacher capacity (Wallin & Newton, 2013), empowering teachers (Bartling, 2013), developing strong individual, interpersonal relationships with faculty (Preston & Barnes, 2017), providing flexible schedule and personal days (Ulferts, 2016), and developing external partnerships to connect teachers with the community (Pendola & Fuller, 2018).

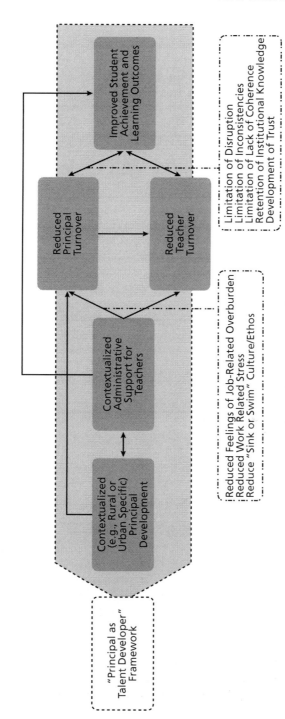

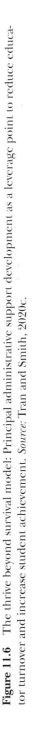

Figure 11.6 The thrive beyond survival model: Principal administrative support development as a leverage point to reduce educator turnover and increase student achievement. *Source:* Tran and Smith, 2020c.

CONCLUSION

Research has consistently demonstrated that teachers are the most vital resource for improving student outcomes (Goldhaber, 2015; Stronge et al., 2007), yet national data reports that an average of a quarter of teachers in high poverty schools leave annually (Ingersoll, 2019). Discontent in the teaching profession has been exacerbated by the "wage penalty" experienced by teachers (Allegretto & Mishel, 2016), the rising workload (e.g., additional time commitments, increasing responsibilities of teachers beyond the contractually compensated duties), decline in discretion, and autonomy in the classroom, which has jointly served as a foundation for the rise of teacher strikes and walkouts across the United States (Tran & Smith, 2021). Recruiting and retaining teaching staff is vital, especially for rural hard-to-staff districts. We focus our attention on the state of South Carolina, given that it is a largely rural state that is experiencing severe "teacher shortages" (Correll, 2021).

Over the course of this chapter, we have highlighted a series of studies to better understand the complex nature of teacher recruitment and retention in rural hard-to-staff schools. By incorporating a variety of perspectives (college students and pre-service teachers, current teachers, and administrators), we address the teaching and employment needs that span the education career lifecycle.

Tran and Smith's (2020b) sustaining teacher employment model encourages school leaders and policymakers to consider the career life cycle of a teacher and specifically the intrinsic factors that can lead to increased job satisfaction and external factors that can minimize job dissatisfaction. This consideration begins with developing a holistic view of the teacher's career and understanding that teacher needs over time. Tran and Smith's (2020c) thrive beyond survival model centers the principal as the chief talent developer in schools to drive much of this work. For the principal to fill this role, they need to receive context-specific principal preparation. This requires a change in the mindset of principal preparation and principal professional development partners to move away from training for idealistic, well-resourced suburban schools, but rather to provide experiences and expertise specific to high-need rural and urban contexts, the realities, and the challenges of leading these schools.

In conclusion, there is a need for rural context-specific training for teachers and principals (pre-service and current) to better prepare practitioners for the unique needs of rural schools. These efforts should consider where staff are in their career lifecycle to effectively strategize retention efforts. Leaders and policymakers are often reactive and do not consider teachers' holistic and stage-specific needs when addressing teacher shortages. Too often, the focus is on getting teachers in the door initially and not on keeping quality teachers in rural classrooms. Financial incentives are important and should be implemented to reduce job dissatisfaction and barriers that deter individuals from rural teaching. However, they are necessary but insufficient to improve teacher working conditions to increase the attractiveness of the job. The inclusion of non-monetary leverage points in teacher recruitment and retention requires a shift away from deficit thinking and moving towards a greater understanding of how rural school leaders can meet the needs of teachers through existing resources, community relationships, and administrative support. Mentoring, recognition programs, improved transparency and communication, and responsiveness in the hiring process are all relatively low-cost and high-impact efforts for rural school leaders to undertake.

Rural context is important and should be incorporated into both policy and school-level decisions related to teacher recruitment and retention. Whether that means prioritizing and highlighting the unique needs of rural areas in policy decision making, providing context-specific teacher and leader preparation, or accurately framing the school and community for employee fit, rurality must be intentionally attuned to improve the teacher staffing conditions in rural spaces.

REFERENCES

Allegretto, S. A., & Mishel, L. (2016). *The teacher pay gap is wider than ever: Teachers' pay continues to fall further behind pay of comparable workers.* Economic Policy Institute.

Allen, M. B. (2005). *Eight questions on teacher recruitment and retention: What does the research say?* Education Commission of the States.

Barber, M., Whelan, F., & Clark, M. (2010). *Capturing the leadership premium. How the world's top school systems are building leadership capacity for the future.* McKinsey and Company.

Barnes, G., Crowe, E., & Schaeffer, E. (2008). *What keeps good teachers in the classroom? Understanding and reducing teacher turnover.* Alliance for Excellent Education.

Berry, B., Bastian, K. C., Darling-Hammond, L., & Kini, T. (2019). *How teaching and learning conditions affect teacher retention and school performance in North Carolina.* Learning Policy Institute. https://learningpolicyinstitute.org/sites/default/files/product-files/Leandro_Working_Conditions_REPORT.pdf

Berry, B., Dickenson, T., Harrist, J., Pomey, K., Zheng, J., Irvin, M., Moon, A., & Hodges, T. (2020). *Teachers and teaching in the midst of a pandemic: Implications for South Carolina's policy leaders.* The South Carolina Teacher Advancement Consortium. https://sc-teacher.org/wp-content/uploads/2020/08/TG_POLICY_FINAL_AUG5.pdf

Bartling, E. M. (2013). *Female high school principals in rural Midwestern school districts: Their lived experiences in leadership* [Unpublished doctoral dissertation]. University of Wisconsin–Milwaukee.

Bauch, P. A. (2001). School–community partnerships in rural schools: Leadership, renewal, and a sense of place. *Peabody Journal of Education, 76*(2), 204–221.

Boyd, D., Lankford, H., Loeb, S., & Wyckoff, J. (2005). The draw of home: How teachers' preferences for proximity disadvantage urban schools. *Journal of Policy Analysis and Management: The Journal of the Association for Public Policy Analysis and Management, 24*(1), 113–132.

Boyd, D., Grossman, P., Ing, M., Langford, H., Loeb, S., & Wyckoff, J. (2011). The influence of school administrators on teacher retention decisions. *American Education Research Journal, 48*(2), 303–333.

Burkhauser, S. (2017). How much do school principals matter when it comes to teacher working conditions? *Educational Evaluation and Policy Analysis, 39*(1), 126–145.

Bureau of Labor Statistics. (2020, September). *Employee benefits in the United States— March 2021.* https://www.bls.gov/news.release/pdf/ebs2.pdf

Canales, M., Tejeda-Delgado, C., & Slate, J. R. (2008). Leadership behaviors of superintendent/principals in small, rural school districts in Texas. *The Rural Educator, 29*(3), 1–7.

Cary, N. (2015, January 14). *Haley Budget: teacher incentives, more reading coaches.* http://www.greenvilleonline.com/story/news/education/2015/01/12/haley-budget-teacherincentives-reading-coaches/21662411/

Carver-Thomas, D., & Darling-Hammond, L. (2017). Teacher turnover: Why it matters and what we can do about it. *Learning Policy Institute.* https://learningpolicyinstitute.org/sites/default/files/product-files/Teacher_Turnover_REPORT.pdf

Center for Educator Recruitment, Retention, and Advancement. (2020). *South Carolina Annual Educator Supply and Demand Report* (2020–21 School Year). https://www.cerra.org/uploads/1/7/6/8/17684955/2020-21_supply___demand_report.pdf

Chapman, D. W. (1983). A model of the influences on teacher retention. *Journal of Teacher Education, 34*(5), 43–49.

Clotfelter, C., Glennie, E., Ladd, H., & Vigdor, J. (2008). Would higher salaries keep teachers in high-poverty schools? Evidence from a policy intervention in North Carolina. *Journal of Public Economics, 92*(5–6), 1352–1370.

Clotfelter, C. T., Ladd, H. F., & Vigdor, J. (2005). Who teaches whom? Race and the distribution of novice teachers. *Economics of Education Review, 24*(4), 377–392.

Collins, T. (1999). *Attracting and retaining teachers in rural areas.* ERIC Digest.

Corbett, W., & White, S. (2014). Introduction: Why put the 'rural' in research? In M. Corbett & S. White (Eds.), *Doing educational research in rural settings: Methodological issues, international perspectives and practice solutions* (pp. 1–4). Routledge.

Correll, E. (2021, July 14). *Teacher group finds over 2,000 vacancies in SC public schools: SC for Ed tracks teaching vacancies weekly, and the numbers just keep growing.* News19. https://www.wltx.com/article/news/education/teacher-group-finds-2000-vacancies-south-carolina-schools/101-1efd1df6-5f08-49f7-a23c-d98803e1ef2f

Cuervo, H. (2016). *Understanding social justice in rural education.* Macmillan.

Dos Santos, L. M. (2019). Mid-life career changing to teaching profession: A study of secondary school teachers in a rural community. *Journal of Education for Teaching, 45*(2), 225–227.

Dwyer, C. A. (2007). America's challenge: Effective teachers for at-risk schools and students. *National Comprehensive Center for Teacher Quality.* https://files.eric.ed.gov/fulltext/ED543777.pdf

Glazer, J. (2018). Leaving lessons: Learning from the exit decisions of experienced teachers. *Teachers and Teaching, 24*(1), 50–62.

Goldhaber, D. (2015). Teachers clearly matter, but finding effective teacher policies has proven challenging. In H. F. Ladd & M. E. Goertz (Eds.), *Handbook of research in education finance and policy* (pp. 157–173). Routledge.

Goldring, R., Taie, S., & Riddles, M. (2014). *Teacher attrition and mobility: Results from the 2012–13 teacher follow-up survey. First look* (NCES 2014-077). National Center for Education Statistics.

Goodpaster, K. P., Adedokun, O. A., & Weaver, G. C. (2012). Teachers' perceptions of rural STEM teaching: Implications for rural teacher retention. *The Rural Educator, 33*(3), 9–22. https://doi.org/10.35608/ruraled.v33i3.408

Grissom, J. A., & Harrington, J. R. (2010). Investing in administrator efficiency: An examination of professional development as a tool for enhancing principal effectiveness. *American Journal of Education, 116*(4), 583–613.

Eppley, K. (2015). "Hey, I saw your grandparents at Walmart": Teacher education for rural schools and communities. *The Teacher Educator, 50*(1), 67–86.

Handal, B., Watson, K., Petocz, P., & Maher, M. (2013). Retaining mathematics and science teachers in rural and remote schools. *Australian and International Journal of Rural Education, 23*(3), 13–27.

Herzberg, F., Mausner, B., & Snyderman, B. (1959). *The motivation to work* (2nd ed.). Wiley.

Hess, F. M. (2010). *Education unbound: The promise and practice of Greenfield schooling.* ASCD. https://doi.org/10.1080/15582159.2011.577677

Hirsh, E., Emerick, S., Church, K., & Fuller, E. (2006). *Teacher working conditions are student learning conditions: A report on the North Carolina teacher working conditions survey.* CTQ.

Ingersoll, R. M. (2002). The teacher shortage: A case of wrong diagnosis and wrong prescription. *NASSP Bulletin, 86*(631), 16–31.

Ingersoll, R. M. (2019, October 24). *"Why schools have difficulty staffing their classrooms with qualified teachers?"* [Presentation]. Talent Centered Education Leadership Initiative: Rural Educator Talent Management Seminar, University of South Carolina, Columbia.

Jacob, R., Goddard, R., Kim, M., Miller, R., & Goddard, Y. (2015). Exploring the causal impact of the McREL balanced leadership program on leadership, principal efficacy, instructional climate, educator turnover, and student achievement. *Educational Evaluation and Policy Analysis, 37*(3), 314–332.

Jimerson, L. (2003). *The competitive disadvantage: Teacher compensation in rural America* [Policy brief]. Rural School and Community Trust.

Johnson, J., Showalter, D., Klein, R., & Lester, C. (2014). *Why rural matters 2013–2014: The condition of rural education in the 50 States.* Rural School and Community Trust.

Keiser, D. R. (2011). *Teacher retention in a rural school district* [Unpublished doctoral dissertation]. University of Virginia.

Kolbe, T., & Strunk, K. O. (2012). Economic incentives as a strategy for responding to teacher staffing problems: A typology of policies and practices. *Educational Administration Quarterly, 48*(5), 779–813.

Ladd, H. F. (2011). Teachers' perceptions of their working conditions: How predictive of planned and actual teacher movement? *Educational Evaluation and Policy Analysis, 33*(2), 235–261.

Lankford, H., Loeb, S., & Wyckoff, J. (2002). Teacher sorting and the plight of urban schools: A descriptive analysis. *Educational Evaluation and Policy Analysis, 24*(1), 37–62.

Lavalley, M. (2018). *Out of the loop: Rural schools are largely left out of research and policy discussions, exacerbating poverty, inequity, and isolation.* National School Boards Association, Center for Public Education.

Liu, E., & Johnson, S. M. (2006). New teachers' experiences of hiring: Late, rushed, and information-poor. *Educational Administration Quarterly, 42*(3), 324–360.

Lowe, J. M. (2006). Rural education: Attracting and retaining teachers in small schools. *Rural Educator, 27*(2), 28–32.

Milanowski, A. (2003). An exploration of the pay levels needed to attract students with mathematics, science and technology skills to a career in K–12 teaching. *Education Policy Analysis Archives, 11*(50).

Milanowski, A. T., Longwell-Grice, H., Saffold, F., Jones, J., Schomisch, K., & Odden, A. (2009). Recruiting new teachers to urban school Districts: What incentives will work? *International Journal of Education Policy and Leadership, 4*(8), 1–13.

Miller, L. C. (2012). Situating the rural teacher labor market in the broader context: A descriptive analysis of the market dynamics in New York State. *Journal of Research in Rural Education, 27*(13), 1–30.

Morice, L. C., & Murray, J. E. (2003). Compensation and teacher retention: A success story. *Educational Leadership, 60*(8), 40–49.

Pendola, A., & Fuller, E. J. (2018). Principal stability and the rural divide. In E. McHenry-Sorber & D. Hall (Eds.), The diversity of rural educational leadership [Special issue]. *Journal of Research in Rural Education, 34*(1), 1–20.

Plaskoff, J. (2017). Employee experience: The new human resource management approach. *Strategic HR Review, 16*(3), 136–141.

Preston, J., & Barnes, K. (2017). Successful leadership in rural schools: Cultivating collaboration. *The Rural Educator, 38*(1), 6–15.

Robinson, N. (2012). Pre-service music teachers' employment preferences: Consideration factors. *Journal of Research in Music Education, 60*(3), 294–309.

Ronfeldt, M., Loeb, S., & Wyckoff, J. (2013). How teacher turnover harms student achievement. *American Educational Research Journal, 50*(1), 4–36.

Rosenberg, L., Christianson, M. D., Angus, M. H., & Rosenthal, E. (2014). *A focused look at rural schools receiving school improvement grants* (NCEE 2014–4013) [NCEE evaluation brief]. National Center for Education Evaluation and Regional Assistance.

Smith, D. A., & Tran, H. (2019). Teaching in rural America: Talent management, challenges, and potential solutions. In M. D'Amico & C. Lewis (Eds.),

Community college teacher preparation for diverse geographies: Implications for access and equity for preparing a diverse teacher workforce. Information Age Publishing.

Smith, D. A., Tran. H., & Prowell, H. (2021). *Retaining non-rural teachers in high-turnover rural schools* [Unpublished manuscript].

Shuls, J., & Maranto, R. (2014). Show them the mission: A comparison of teacher recruitment incentives in high need communities. *Social Science Quarterly, 95*(1), 239–252. https://doi.org/10.1111/ssqu.12011

Seashore Louis, K., Dretzke, B., & Wahlstrom, K. (2010). How does leadership affect student achievement? Results from a national US survey. *School Effectiveness and School Improvement, 21*(3), 315–336.

Stewart, C., & Matthews, J. (2015). The lone ranger in rural education: The small rural school principal and professional development. *The Rural Educator, 36*(3), 49–60.

Stronge, J. H., Ward, T. J., Tucker, P. D., & Hindman, J. L. (2007). What is the relationship between teacher quality and student achievement? An exploratory study. *Journal of Personnel Evaluation in Education, 20*(3–4), 165–184.

Strunk, K. O., & Zeehandelaar, D. (2011). Differentiated compensation: How California school districts use economic incentives to target teachers. *Journal of Education Finance,* 268–293.

Tran, H. (2020). *Retaining teachers with talent centered education leadership.* SC-Teacher Report. https://sc-teacher.org/retaining-teachers-through-talent-centered -education-leadership/

Tran, H., & Bon, S. C. (2015). Assessing multiple stakeholders' perceptions of an effective principal evaluation system. *Education Leadership Review, 16*(2), 1–18.

Tran, H., Cunningham, K., Hardie, S., & Yelverton, V. (2020). What types of administrative support matter for teacher retention in hard-to-staff schools? *NASSP Bulletin, 104*(2), 85–109.

Tran, H., & Dou, J. (2019). An exploratory examination of what types of administrative support matter for rural teacher talent management: The rural educator perspective. *Education Leadership Review, 20*(1), 133–149.

Tran, H., Hogue, A. M., & Moon, A. M. (2015). Attracting early childhood teachers to South Carolina's high needs rural districts: Loan repayment vs. tuition subsidy. *Teacher Education Journal of South Carolina, 8,* 98–107. https://www.researchgate .net/profile/Henry-Tran-12/publication/325177186_Attracting_Early_ Childhood_Teachers_to_South_Carolina's_High_Needs_Rural_Districts_ Loan_Repayment_vs_Tuition_Subsidy/links/5afc4546a6fdccacab1a0fbd/ Attracting-Early-Childhood-Teachers-to-South-Carolinas-High-Needs-Rural -Districts-Loan-Repayment-vs-Tuition-Subsidy.pdf

Tran, H., McCormick, J., & Nguyen, T. T. (2018). The cost of replacing South Carolina high school principals. *Management in Education, 32*(3), 109–118.

Tran, H. E., Smith, D. A., & Fox, E. C. (2018, September). *The perspectives of potential and current rural teachers for rural teacher recruitment and retention in South Carolina.* Center for Innovation in Higher Education. https://www.usccihe. org/s/SC-Rural-Teacher-Staffing-Report.pdf

Tran, H., & Smith, D. A. (2019). Insufficient money and inadequate respect: What obstructs the recruitment of college students to teach in hard-to-staff schools. *Journal of Educational Administration, 57*(2), 152–166.

Tran, H., & Smith, D. A. (2020a). What matters most for recruiting teachers to rural hard to staff districts: A mixed-methods analysis of employment related conditions. *American Journal of Education, 126*(3), 447–481.

Tran, H., & Smith, D. A. (2020b). Designing an employee experience approach to teacher retention in hard-to-staff schools. *NASSP Bulletin, 104*(2), 85–109.

Tran, H., & Smith, D.A. (2020c). The strategic support to survive then thrive cycle: An administrative support model for improving student outcomes and addressing educator staffing in rural and urban high-needs schools. *Research in Educational Administration & Leadership, 5*(3), 870–919.

Tran, H., & Smith, D. A. (2021). Talent center education leadership: Using the employee experience to improve teacher-school relations. *Journal of Cases in Educational Leadership, 24*(1), 42–54.

University Council for Education Administration. (2018). *UCEA's comments and recommendations about U.S. Department of Education report on rural education, section 5005 of P.L. 114-95. ED-2017-OCO-0139.* http://3fl7112qoj4l3y6ep2tqpwra .wpengine.netdna-cdn.com/wp-content/uploads/2018/03/UCEAcomments -Sect5005Report-on-Rural-Education.pdf

Ulferts, J. D. (2016). A brief summary of teacher recruitment and retention in the smallest Illinois rural schools. *The Rural Educator, 37*(1), 14–24.

Wallin, D., & Newton, P. (2013). Instructional leadership of the rural teaching principal: Double the trouble or twice the fun? *International Studies in Educational Administration, 41*(2), 19–31.

CHAPTER 12

NEGATIVE DISCOURSE AND FALSE CLAIMS

Confronting the Myths and Lies That Devalue Teachers and the Teaching Profession

Davíd G. Martínez
University of South Carolina

Henry Tran
University of South Carolina

South Carolina is frequently described as being amidst a teacher labor market crisis (Mintzer, 2021; Thomas, 2018), influenced by teacher recruitment, attrition, and vacancy challenges across the state. According to the Center for Educator Recruitment, Retention, and Advancement (CERRA, 2021), estimates from the 2021 school year suggest that within a 3-month timeframe (December 2020 to February 2021), an average of approximately 170 teachers left their positions each month, with 500 vacancies still unfilled at

How Did We Get Here?, pages 287–309

the end of that period. In years prior, the state has seen a trend of declining enrollment in in-state teacher preparation programs (an average of 1705.4 from 2016–2017 to 2020–2021) and an increase in teachers who leave their positions (an average of 6,634.4 from 2016–2017 to 2020–2021).

Teacher attrition is endemic in education, creating national teacher quantity and quality gaps, often stratified by region and racialized nuance (Cowan et al., 2016; Scafidi et al., 2007). This reality is reflected in South Carolina. Some of the hardest to staff districts in South Carolina are often located in communities with the highest concentrations of student diversity and poverty. To prosper and progress, the South Carolina education community, reformers, and public stakeholders must have a vested interest in maintaining full classrooms and strengthening the teaching workforce.

Challenges to teacher staffing, both from a recruitment and a retention perspective, catalyze negative outcomes through the educational pipeline (e.g., larger class sizes, workload increases, underqualified personnel teaching, erosion of stability and trust) that impairs student learning (Ronfeldt et al., 2013). There are efforts to mitigate these challenges, especially in hard to staff areas, including legislative appropriations through the South Carolina General Assembly (i.e., HB 3720; Proviso 1A.59.; Rural Recruitment Initiative (RRI) appropriation of $9,748,392), 2018 (i.e., HB 4950; Proviso 1A.55.; RRI appropriation of $9,748,392), 2019 (HB 4000; Proviso 1A.54.; RRI appropriation of 9,748,392), and 2020 (HB 5201; Proviso; RRI appropriation of 9,748,392). These efforts have made some improvement, but many consider South Carolina's teacher labor market crisis to be a function of disparity gaps between districts within the state (Mintzer, 2021; Thomas, 2018). Many scholars, and policymakers, have confronted the crisis through efforts aimed at triaging gaps, but rarely do teacher stakeholders confront the constant attacks on the professionalization of the field that render the profession undesirable.

For example, in a mix-methods analysis of responses from college students at a regional South Carolina university, Tran and Smith (2019) found that their respondents often avoided considering teaching as a career due to lack of respect associated with the teaching profession. Indeed, potential teachers are threatened with potentially becoming victims of the pervasive barrage of attacks on education and the consistently perpetuated misconceptions of the teaching profession that continue to disrespect, degrade, and devalue teachers. The lack of prestige and constant disrespect to the profession potentially damages the self worth and pride of those who choose to enter the teaching profession based on the public perception of their career choice. The causes, symptoms, and treatment of teacher career avoidance and attrition are frequently explored in research, but few have considered how specific attacks on teaching, created by rhetorical positions, can influence policy in a manner that creates symptomatic attrition.

Thus, our chapter attempts to focus on this nuance by using empirical evidence to dispel the myths about the teaching profession in South Carolina.

This chapter, written in the tradition of Berliner et al.'s (2014) *50 Myths and Lies That Threaten America's Public Schools*, explores a series of myths and lies related to the teaching profession that harm the reputation of teachers and contributes to teacher attrition, especially in South Carolina. Specifically, this chapter outlines eight myths that directly impact the discourse about teachers and their lives. These include:

1. Myths about teacher's relaxing work schedules that provide them
   a. Only partial workdays (e.g., 8:00 a.m.–3:00 p.m.)
   b. Summer and many holidays off
2. Myths about teacher compensation
   a. Teachers are adequately compensated.
   b. Pay has no relationship with educational quality.
3. Myths about the professional resources
   a. Teachers are well resourced; working in comfortable environments with little to no challenges.
   b. Attending to teacher needs take away from student needs because it caters to "adult interest."
4. Myths about the professionalization of teaching; the unskilled worker
   a. Teaching is easy. Those who can, DO, and those who can't, TEACH;
   b. Employment is perpetual and plentiful; teachers are easily replaceable.

SIGNIFICANCE AND BACKGROUND

South Carolina is currently facing a teacher supply emergency that requires intervention (Thomas, 2018). Specific shortages in the pipeline, coupled with attrition, have left many wondering what combination of resources is necessary to help schools reach full teaching capacity once again. However, part of the challenge is grounded directly in beliefs about teachers and how these beliefs are positioned to create direct challenges to the teaching battery. For instance, outdated beliefs about teachers' abundance of personal time considering their leisurely schedules no longer hold and likely never have. Teachers often find themselves working long hours through the summer months and winter holidays on personal development, classroom improvement, and educational enrichment that are often required but uncompensated (Krantz-Kent, 2008; Stoddard & Kuhn, 2008).

When accounting for education and experience, teachers are often amongst the leanest salary consumers. For instance, in South Carolina, first year teachers earn approximately $37,916. The work intensity and load have only escalated in recent years (Tran, 2020), as teachers often find themselves in stressful and under-resourced environments, with working conditions that cry for severe improvements (Ornstein, 1994; Wakefield, 2002). For example, while not as influential as the social conditions of the workplace, numerous studies have nonetheless linked school facilities with teacher satisfaction and retention (Buckley et al., 2005; Moore et al., 2012). Moreover, poor building conditions have been linked with lower student achievement (Earthman, 2017). While school buildings across the country need extensive repairs, these repair needs are significantly worse in rural buildings in high-poverty areas (DeWees & Hammer, 2000). As a rural state, South Carolina must combat these challenges to help teachers in their environment.

Teachers often have little say over the policies in their classrooms, let alone schools. For example, teachers are often confronted with a lack of freedom over curriculum and pedagogy (Hursh, 2005; Wills & Sandholtz, 2009). This lack of agency is sustained and rooted in the continuous disrespect towards teachers undergirded by mistrust and assumptions concerning their lack of skills and competence. This discourse has pervaded how the teaching profession operates and led to accountability measures that scrutinize and control every major teaching function. Furthermore, across the United States, calls for educational opportunity for all pivoted toward stringent accountability, standards-based reform, and high-stakes testing as the increasingly conservative political context of the United States shaped the educational landscape away from civil rights arguments imploring greater resources and care for students of color (Baker et al., 2014).

Ultimately, educational reform, including accountability, increased calls for funding efficiency, focus on specific content/curricular areas, has further damaged the career and moved teaching away from democratic educational environments, critically undermining one of the key stakeholders of schooling, the teachers (Evans, 2014). South Carolina must ask why these myths pervade the profession and how we can fundamentally address the realities of teaching. We conclude this chapter by exploring what critical actions South Carolina can take to curb the declining interest in the teaching profession and dissolve those myths and lies that threaten our educational paradigm.

EVIDENCE ON SOUTH CAROLINA'S TEACHING PROFESSION MYTHS

To address the main purpose of this chapter, we use descriptive and correlation analysis. We use publicly available data aggregated from several sources for our analysis, including the South Carolina Department of Education and the United States Department of Education National Center for Educational Statistics Common Core of Data. Our dataset includes all South Carolina's traditional school districts that educate students in any Grade K–12, reporting finance and other data to the Department of Education National Center for Education Statistics (NCES), from 2007–2008 to 2017–2018.

Independent, private, and charter LEAs were excluded from this analysis. These districts are often small sample districts, structurally incongruous to traditional districts, and as a result, would not be comparable with South Carolina's traditional LEAs. This analysis omits Governor's School for the Arts and Humanities, Governor's School for Science and Mathematics, South Carolina Public Charter School District, Deaf and Blind School, John De La Howe, Department of Juvenile Justice, Department of Correction N04, Charter Institute at Erskine, Felton Lab School of South Carolina H24, South Carolina Department of Disabilities and Special Needs, Wil Lou Gray Opportunity.

Our merged dataset includes the districts' local poverty index, geography, enrollment, and student demographics. We use two variables that help to identify majority poverty and geography. These variables are calculated for each district and year. Poverty is represented by those districts serving greater than 50% of students in poverty, while for our geography variable, we collapsed all rural, city, town (exurban), and suburban districts into their respective NCES categories. The data were merged, compiled, cleaned, coded, and analyzed using Excel v16.51 and Stata v17.0.

MYTH 1: TEACHERS WORK SHORT DAYS AND HAVE SUMMERS OFF

Currently, it is difficult to ascertain how many hours a day teachers work in South Carolina or how much time off they have. However, nationally, the common notion that teachers work 8 hours per day for approximately 190 days per year, while the average worker is responsible for 8 hours per day for 260 days a year, is categorically false. For instance, according to Scholastic Inc. and The Bill & Melinda Gates Foundation (2021) report, nationally, teachers spend on average an additional 90 minutes per day mentoring students, providing supplemental or after school instruction in staff meetings, and another 95 minutes per day at home on their grading, classroom preparation, and in some job-related task completion. For those teachers with extracurricular, coaching, or teacher leader duties, the workday quickly expands to 11 hours and 20 minutes (Scholastic Inc., & The Bill & Melinda Gates Foundation, 2021). Relatedly, Drago et al. (1999) found that teachers work approximately 9.7 hours per day regularly. In an updated analysis, West (2014) found teachers work at least 38 hours per week during the school year, but could work as much as 45 hours per week using the American Time Use Survey. Furthermore, the authors found teachers work at least 21.5 hours per week in the months of June–August, the supposed summertime off, and as much as 43.6 hours per week according to the American Time Use Survey. West (2014) reports that teachers work 41.7 hours per week during the school year, and as much as 33.3 hours per week June–August, as reported on the Current Population Survey.

Compared with other developed countries, teachers in the United States tend to spend many more hours working than their international counterparts. For example, an Organization for Economic Cooperation and Development (OECD) report states that U.S. teachers work approximately 1,004 hours per year in the primary grades and 966 hours in secondary grades (OECD, 2021). The teacher work hours for the United States is the highest of any developed country in the world. The evidence also shows that many teachers are not completely duty-free in the summer months. Teachers make decisions, like most professions, based on a complex web of variables. One of those variables is the workday and the work schedule, but in a competitive labor market, it appears teachers are subject to normative labor market work-hour conditions.

Many rhetorical arguments for teacher pay structure include the work schedule as reasons why teachers are underpaid. These arguments, however, have little supportive evidence, and in fact, evidence supporting the normative 40-hour workweek schedule for teachers is stronger than the evidence supporting a workweek schedule that is less than 40 hours. In this first myth, we move beyond the rhetorical into an evidence-based framework. We maintain this evidence-based framework using primary empirical data and analyses to address the subsequent myths.

MYTH 2: TEACHERS ARE WELL PAID

As a career, teaching is known as a low-wage profession. This is common knowledge among the public at large (which has deterred interest away from the field; Tran & Smith, 2019) and has been demonstrated empirically (see Chapter 7). Historically teachers are often asked to bear the responsibility for the education of millions of children. The pay structure of the teaching profession is a function of gendered beliefs about the teaching profession and how women in the workplace should be compensated (García & Weiss, 2019). Women in the workplace are often less compensated than men and segregated into lower-wage employment. The average starting salary expectations for women in the United States is also lower than men (Gradín, 2019; Statista, 2019). This gendered persecution leads to more damaging discourse asserting that teaching and teachers are glorified babysitters and should be paid accordingly (Nelson & Lewis, 2016). Relevant to these deficit ideologies, it is important to acknowledge that teachers are skilled individuals with advanced education, discussed further below, and experts in content, curriculum pedagogy, and management. This type of discourse also falls apart when recognizing current wages in 2021 and if we are to follow the "babysitter" comparison, the current cost of private childcare nationally.

Full-time workers across the United States earn on average $51,480 (Federal Reserve Bank of St. Louis, 2021). These wages decrease for women to $47,299 and increase substantially for men to $57,456 (Federal Reserve Bank of St. Louis, 2021). Furthermore, in 2019, before the SARS-CoV-2 (COVID-19) pandemic, families spent between $9,200 and $9,600 per child on childcare (Childcare Aware, 2020). We computed[1] a student–teacher ratio of approximately 21 students from our data, and when coupled with Childcare Aware data, we can calculate a classroom rate of between $193,200–$201,600. The Childcare Aware estimation includes the cost of infrastructure, but as we will discuss below, the $9,200–$9,600 estimate is well above the per-pupil state revenue allocation of $5,837.45 for areas with less than 50% poverty and $5,794.00 for areas with greater than 50% poverty that also includes infrastructure funds. Critics could also plausibly argue that a better comparison when discussing childcare is the comparison of childcare worker salaries versus teacher salaries. However, we caution against this argument as this is in line with our overall logic that those skilled professionals entrusted with our students' educational care are grossly under-compensated. With these first assertions settled, we can turn to address the salient facts about the compensation of South Carolina teachers.

South Carolina publishes their yearly teacher minimum salary schedules. This minimum is the least amount public school districts must pay to still receive state foundation funding. While wealthier districts can pay more than the minimum salary schedules, many districts pay at or near the minimum. In the 2020–2021 release, South Carolina's minimum base rate salary for teachers was $28,190.00, with a minimum salary of $35,000 for a beginning teacher with no experience (South Carolina Department of Education, 2021). According to the salary schedule, the highest salary for a teacher in South Carolina would be $67,320, including the base rate of $59,997 and the EIA adjustment. This salary is for an individual with a doctorate and 23 years of experience. Comparatively, the Bureau of Labor Statistics (BLS) data shows that nationally individuals with a doctorate make approximately $97,916 (BLS, 2021). BLS also shows that individuals with a baccalaureate degree earn on average $64,896. However, in South Carolina, our data shows the average teacher salary is much lower.

Figure 12.1 shows mean teacher salary and year-to-year inflation-adjusted mean teacher salary. Our figure shows that teacher salaries in South Carolina are not competitive nationally, even for someone with a baccalaureate degree,

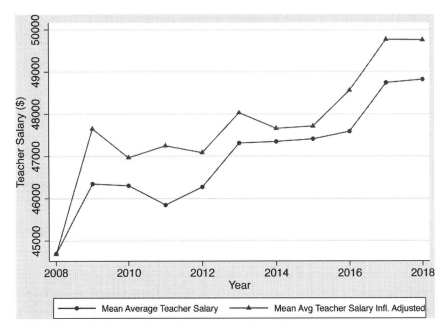

Figure 12.1   Mean teacher salary vs. year-to-year inflation adjusted teacher salary 2008–2018.

at the mean salary of $46,946.63 in 2018. Our figure shows that even considering inflation, as computed using the Federal Reserve Bank of St. Louis Inflation estimates, teacher salaries are not competitive against inflation.

Critics would likely argue that a federal vs. state-level comparison is inappropriate given the differences in cost of living and labor market costs in South Carolina. However, even if we compare wages across South Carolina for all workers, as demonstrated in Figure 12.2 that reflects the last 4 years of data available, we see that teacher salaries are minimally competitive with other 4-year degree earners. For instance, in 2018, the average 4-year degree earners surpassed teachers' earnings. If we look at graduate and professional degree salaries, in general, we see the base rate of a 23-year veteran teacher with a doctorate, $59,997, is minimally competitive with a sample of all graduate and professional degree salaries in the state. The fact is, in this case, South Carolina teachers are underpaid compared to their national peers and their South Carolina intra-educational attainment peers.

Given the low relative salaries, perhaps it is unsurprising that South Carolina is exhibiting high teacher turnover and attrition. The teacher staffing problem requires many different nuanced components, requiring nuanced and balanced solutions. Any solution, however, must address the compensation structure of teachers, and specifically salaries. Districts and students

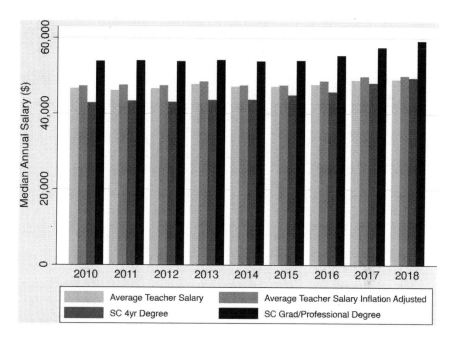

Figure 12.2 Median salaries teacher, inflation adjusted teacher, 4-year degree, graduate or professional degree 2008–2018.

need capable teachers and a stable teacher workforce, but in South Carolina, many districts do not have the teacher labor market to support all their classroom staffing needs. Teacher shortages are also worse in specific geographic regions, rural and exurban, and specific types of districts, such as those serving high percentages of students of color from high poverty backgrounds (Jimerson, 2003; Tran & Dou, 2019).

The publicly reported teacher vacancy rates only represent part of the teacher labor market constriction. These numbers do not reflect that many districts are often forced to hire under-prepared, out-of-subject matter, emergency credentialed, or international teachers just to ensure there is an adult in front of the classroom. The consequences also include inflation of class sizes, lack of diversity of course offerings, and lack of curriculum for students. In sum, these events put the education of students at risk. A stable teacher workforce means that a state can educate all children (Demi et al., 2010; Tran & Smith, 2020; Ulferts, 2016).

At this point, it is worth recognizing that despite rhetorical critiques that teacher salaries are not correlated with student achievement, the research asserts they are (Akiba et al., 2012; Goldhaber & Walch, 2012; Grissom & Strunk, 2012; Woessmann, 2011). In South Carolina, this is true as well. Table 12.1 shows correlation coefficients for several variables in our dataset

TABLE 12.1 Correlation Coefficients 2008–2018						
Variables	% Standards Met	Average Teacher Salary	% Poverty	% FRLP	% Black	% White
% Standards Met	1.000					
Avg. Tch. Sal.	0.36***	1.000				
% Poverty	–0.54***	–0.62***	1.000			
% FRLP	–0.64***	–0.37***	0.77***	1.000		
% Black	–0.58*** *	–0.46***	0.75***	0.68***	1.000	
% White	0.60***	0.40***	–0.72***	–0.65***	–0.96***	1.000

*** $p < 0.01$, ** $p < 0.05$, * $p < 0.1$

related to the percent of students in a district who met standards. Our table shows that teacher salaries are positively correlated to the percent of students meeting achievement metric standards in a district. We can interpret this to mean that as teacher salaries increase, achievement seems to increase. Of course, a correlation between the two variables does not imply a causal relationship and should not be interpreted as such. However, it does provide evidence to support the extant literature that these variables are related in some capacity.

Researchers understand that money matters in the landscape of educational policy and that teacher pay matters in the context of student achievement (Martínez, 2021; Springer et al., 2010). The relationship between teacher salaries and student achievement is further supported by research that teacher pay scale increases, through incentives, are linked to improvements in student achievement (Goldhaber & Walch, 2012; Woessman, 2011). Our descriptive/correlational analysis here also supports what research in South Carolina has asserted, that there is a relationship between better compensation of teachers and greater student achievement (Tran, 2017). Finally, achievement requires many different inputs, but one must certainly include fiscal inputs that are at least competitive with the regional labor market. Next, we discuss those myths about the professional environment that impacts educators writ large.

MYTH 3: TEACHERS ARE WELL RESOURCED

One of the rhetorical arguments against teachers, and the teaching profession, centers on the comfort of the work environment. There are some prominent truths about schools and infrastructure in the United States. For example, many school buildings are often left unrepaired and under-resourced and have been for some time.

Alexander and Lewis (2014) reported that, on average, school construction has remained stagnant for approximately 44 years, and most buildings have lacked major renovations for 12 years or more. Since that time, things have not improved. Across the United States, approximately 54% of all public school districts require updates or replacement of infrastructure, including heating, ventilation, and air conditioning systems (Government Office of Accountability, 2020). On average, districts serving a higher proportion of students in poverty spend $300 less per pupil on facilities and capital maintenance. The American Society of Civil Engineers (2021), in their report, also found that public school facilities require an annual $145 billion of funding to maintain and operate schools and replace those structures that require full updating.

In South Carolina, the picture of schools and infrastructure funding is similar. It's important to understand that part of the revenue allocations to districts includes funding for maintenance, operations, and construction. Table 12.2 shows the mean of construction capital outlay expenditures, including expenditures on property and construction of facilities. It also shows the mean expenditures for maintenance and operations (MO), both related to the tending of school facilities and operation sites. The table shows that South Carolina spends approximately $9,178,095 per year on construction expenditures and approximately $8,242,142 on maintenance and operations. While this certainly seems like a substantial amount, a much clearer picture emerges when we account for per-pupil differentiation. Table 12.2 shows that South Carolina is spending approximately $823 per year on construction and $967 on maintenance on operations. At the 25th percentile of the distribution, some districts are spending $72.67 per pupil on construction. Stakeholders should question upgrades districts could make for $73 per pupil, especially given the costs related to other

TABLE 12.2 Descriptive Statistics of Construction and Maintenance and Operations Expenditures 2008–2018

	Construction Expense	Construction Expense per Pupil	MO Expense	MO Expense per Pupil
N	904.00	904.00	905.00	908.00
Mean	9,718,095.13	823.56	8,242,142.54	967.65
SD	20,786,353.48	1,428.62	10,670,803.47	254.15
Min	0.00	0.00	0.00	0.00
p25	201,000.00	72.67	1,992,000.00	801.55
p50	1,303,500.00	305.46	4,350,000.00	928.85
p75	8,684,500.00	897.40	9,154,000.00	1,113.63
Max	198,204,000.00	14,988.50	67,921,000.00	2,188.90

TABLE 12.3 Descriptive Statistics of Construction and Maintenance and Operations Expenditures by Geographic Region 2008–2018

Geographic Region	Construction Exp. per Pupil	MO Exp. per Pupil
City	1,368.49	1,071.20
Rural	680.27	1,028.55
Suburb	1,184.75	867.31
Town	524.60	854.29

areas of the school. It is also worth noting that there are differences in amount by geographic area and poverty.

Table 12.3 shows that districts in major cities and suburbs spend much more than those located in rural areas. There is a difference of $843.89 between the city and exurban districts in per-pupil construction expenditures, approximately as much as the mean across the entire sample for 2008–2018; $823.56. Those concerned stakeholders should then question if these disparities are also concentrated by other demographics.

Examining Table 12.4, we see that the disparities in facilities-associated expenditures in South Carolina are concentrated in districts with higher poverty. Those districts with greater than 50% of poverty spend approximately $758.90 per pupil on construction expenditures and $966.67 on maintenance and operations, while those with less than 50% poverty spend $2,087.23, approximately $1,328.33 more per pupil on construction expenditures. Concurrently, wealthy districts also spend approximately $20 more per pupil on maintenance and operations expenditures, and while this seems negligible, this should be taken into context of overall funding availability in high poverty districts serving a majority of minoritized students. This funding is then compounded when considering that wealthy districts are typically larger. This disparity has implications that extend beyond the aggregate funding as wealthier districts end up with more pupils, more per-pupil funding, and thus a larger operating budget supporting more teacher hires. We must also consider the importance of fiscal capacity in this relationship which gives a discrete advantage to wealthy districts; if poorer districts hire similar numbers of teachers, then they are subject to decreased fiscal capacity due to the necessary teacher expenditures consuming a larger share of revenue than what is available to wealthier districts for the same category.

TABLE 12.4 Descriptive Statistics of Construction and Maintenance and Operations Expenditures by Poverty 2008–2018

Concentration of Poverty	Construction Exp. per Pupil	MO Exp. per Pupil
Less than 50% Poverty	2,087.23	986.76
Greater 50% Poverty	758.90	966.67

In the 2021–2022 legislative session, South Carolina passed their omnibus appropriations bill, House Bill (HB) 4100. Among this piece of legislation were the education appropriation for the year and the allocations to school districts. HB 4100 ultimately decreased funding in specific areas, including state aid to classrooms. The state aid to classrooms budget is an allocation that is a function of the Education Finance Act of 1977. For 2020–2021, the state aid to classroom allocation decreased from 65.59% to 65.11%, with projected per-pupil state aid to classroom allocation decreasing from $3,889 to $3,773. Furthermore, there are substantial increases to local revenue per pupil, from $6,406 to $7,423, while state allocations increase minimally from $6,556 to $6,773. As can be seen, South Carolina's school finance policy is deliberately one-sided, forcing communities to produce more and more revenue while decreasing the state's responsibility substantially.

In terms of facilities, this has led to a projected capital needs shortfall of $10,197,972,210 from 2010–2024 (South Carolina Department of Education, 2013; South Carolina Department of Education, 2016; South Carolina Department of Education, 2019). Figure 12.3 shows the shortfall has increased year over year. This revenue shortfall impacts how facilities are maintained and sustains substandard work conditions for teachers and the learning environment for their students.

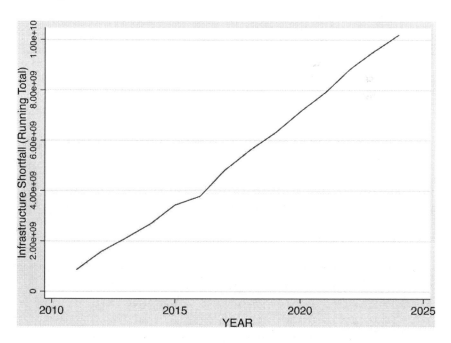

Figure 12.3 South Carolina school infrastructure funding shortfall 2010–2024.

School stakeholders require facilities and resources that provide healthy and safe environments with clean water, HVAC/climate-controlled systems, and modern technology (American Society of Civil Engineers, 2021; Filardo et al., 2019). In South Carolina, however, schooling apathy has proliferated funding inequity, and now many teachers readily do not have a quality environment to address their student's learning needs. On the whole, South Carolina as a state has not prioritized district spending on facilities, nor has it prioritized spending overall on education, leaving historically marginalized districts in a status quo of funding insufficiency.

Table 12.5 shows the per-pupil revenue and expenditure differences between districts with greater than 50% poverty and those with less than 50% poverty. From Table 12.5, we see that in districts with greater than 50% poverty total revenue, local, state, and instructional revenue per pupil is less than in those districts with less than 50% poverty. This distinction is important because we see that in all categories, including instructional expenditures (expenditures on classroom and instructional areas), teachers working in areas with higher poverty contend with the intersection of the effects of poverty and funding insufficiency.

Educators focus on the holistic needs of their students, which includes the quality of the environment. Anecdotally, it is not uncommon for teachers to lament the decreases in funding availability for classroom supplies. From a research standpoint, we also understand that teachers are spending their funding to maintain a healthy, positive classroom, and in communities whose schools are at 75% percentile or more of students eligible for free or reduced-price school lunch, a higher percentage of teachers spend more than $1,000 (NCES, 2021c).

Improving student achievement is crucial for South Carolina's national competitiveness, but teachers require resources that support student learning, including well-kept facilities. Research shows the physical environment influences student achievement. However, many South Carolina schools have inadequate structural facilities and facilities funding. Teachers

TABLE 12.5 Descriptive Statistics of Per-Pupil Revenue and Expenditure by Poverty 2008–2018

	Tot. Rev. per Pupil	Tot. Loc. Rev. per Pupil	Tot. State Rev. per Pupil	Tot. Fed. Rev. per Pupil	Tot. State+Loc. Rev. per Pupil	Tot. Instructional Exp. per Pupil
Less than 50% Poverty	12,456.55	6,012.41	5,837.45	606.45	11,849.86	5,773.45
Greater 50% Poverty	11,610.48	4,284.51	5,794.00	1,531.98	10,078.51	5,406.31

educating students in poverty and minoritized students are more likely to work in schools with inadequately funded districts and ineffective structural facilities (Alexander & Lewis, 2014).

Finally, the South Carolina community cannot stifle funding for improved schooling environments without consequences. The classroom environment must, at a minimum, have enough funding to maintain its structural quality, but in South Carolina, it appears these minimums are not met. Overall, the aforementioned findings suggest that resource supports to teachers are not only meant to serve the "interest of adults," but rather attending to teachers' needs benefits students. Research has consistently shown that better working conditions (e.g., stronger administrative support, respectful and collaborative work environments) for teachers have been linked to positive student learning outcomes (Bear et al., 2014; Kraft et al., 2016). It is a simple concept. If teachers are well supported, they are better positioned to support their students. Consequently, the myth that teachers' needs take away from students represents a false dichotomy (Tran, 2020). Our final section addresses the myth that anyone can teach, and those who cannot do, teach.

MYTH 4: ANYONE CAN TEACH

The final myth we will address in this chapter is that anyone can teach or teachers are unskilled workers. Earlier, we partially addressed why this myth occurs. Namely, it is used to reinforce low wages for teachers, especially given their work schedules, resulting in a deprivation of adequate resources and respect. These myths help legislators underpay teachers, devalue the teaching profession, and overlook necessary change. In the previous three myths, we have shown evidence that most rhetorical critiques on teaching are not true, and in fact, evidence completely contradicts these myths. The adage, "those who can't do, teach," helps to publicize and reinforce the idea anyone from other industries can step foot into teaching and easily address issues of content, curriculum, pedagogy, classroom management, and the daily politics of schools immediately without any substantive training. This stance is nothing short of disrespectful yet is consistently repeated by critics of the teaching profession.

At the surface, it neglects that teacher candidates enrolling in traditional teacher certification/training programs complete a 4- or 5- year baccalaureate degree and that within that training, there are typically at least 2 years of courses related to pedagogy and education content (Boyd et al., 2007; McCarty & Dietz, 2011). Additionally, most teachers are required to spend time in an apprenticeship with teacher educators and mentors (Qu & Becker, 2003). Moreover, it is common for teachers to return to school to obtain post-baccalaureate education. Table 12.6 shows that approximately 60% of

TABLE 12.6   Percentage of Teachers With Advanced Degrees by Poverty 2008–2018

Year	Less than 50% Poverty	Greater 50% Poverty	Average
2008	60.65	55.24	55.49
2009	62.65	57.15	57.41
2010	63.57	58.63	58.86
2011	65.55	60.87	61.09
2012	66.35	62.04	62.25
2013	66.38	61.46	61.71
2014	66.65	61.40	61.66
2015	67.40	60.79	61.12
2016	67.35	61.32	61.62
2017	66.83	60.78	61.07
2018	66.25	59.84	60.16
Total	**65.42**	**59.92**	**60.19**

teachers have an advanced degree in South Carolina for all years and all poverty levels. Furthermore, if we look at those teachers in districts with less than 50% of students in poverty, for 2016, approximately 67% of all teachers had advanced degrees.

Additionally, in Table 12.7, we see the pattern of teachers having an advanced degree holds despite geographic area. In fact, in city districts, approximately 63% of all teachers have an advanced degree.

By and large, South Carolina teachers are well trained, not complacent with their initial training, and seek to enhance the student experience in the classroom with greater training. In South Carolina, not everyone can do, and those that do, work extremely hard to make sure their pedagogy is up to date. Teachers in South Carolina are not easily replaceable, and it takes well-educated and trained individuals to fill classrooms.

Table 12.8 shows that the percentage of classrooms without a highly qualified teacher[2] is 1.72% in those districts with less than 50% poverty and 4.32% in classrooms with greater than 50% poverty. Individuals teach our classrooms with a highly qualified skill set in both environments. The number of teachers with emergency certification is also quite low at 2.02% in districts with less than 50% poverty. This number increases for districts with greater than 50% of students in poverty to 5.73%. However, it is important to contextualize this as part of a national discussion where 4% of teachers hold a provisional or temporary certificate, 3% a probationary certificate, 2% no certification, and 1% a waiver or emergency certificate for all schools regardless of poverty (NCES, 2021d). South Carolina teachers are not only highly educated but also highly certified.

TABLE 12.7   Percentage of Teachers With Advanced Degrees by Geographic Area 2008–2018

Year	Geographic Area				
	City	Rural	Suburb	Town	Average
2008	58.86	54.22	58.87	53.68	55.49
2009	60.29	56.26	60.48	55.82	57.41
2010	61.14	57.40	61.74	58.73	58.86
2011	62.86	59.98	63.69	60.45	61.09
2012	64.20	61.42	64.30	61.24	62.25
2013	63.89	60.57	63.95	61.09	61.71
2014	63.13	60.82	63.71	60.82	61.66
2015	63.31	60.33	63.41	59.38	61.12
2016	63.54	60.86	63.69	60.22	61.62
2017	63.10	60.27	62.94	60.04	61.07
2018	63.20	58.89	62.32	59.69	60.16
Total	**62.50**	**59.14**	**62.65**	**59.12**	**60.19**

South Carolina teachers face some labor market constraints in job availability overall, including the contract conditions in the state. Table 12.8 shows that the number of teachers per district is approximately 1,050 for those districts with less than 50% of poverty and approximately 571 for those with greater than 50% of poverty. We can also see that not all teachers work with annual contracts. In fact, 83.53% of teachers work with an annual contract, and in those districts with more than 50% of poverty, only 77.53% of teachers work with a viable contract. Ultimately teaching jobs are not infinitely plentiful.

By region, these patterns exhibit some similar characteristics. We see the percentage of classrooms without highly qualified teachers is low, peaking in rural districts at 5.19%. We also see the percentage of teachers with an

TABLE 12.8   Descriptive Statistics Teacher Labor Market Conditions by Poverty 2008–2018

	Number of Teachers	Teacher Retention	Teacher Turnover	3-Year Teacher Turnover	% of Teachers on Annual Contract	% Classrooms Without Highly Qualified Teachers	% Emergency Certification Teacher
Less than 50% Poverty	1,046.55	91.92	8.08	10.01	83.53	1.79	2.02
Greater 50% Poverty	571.02	87.82	12.18	12.18	77.53	4.32	5.73

TABLE 12.9   Descriptive Statistics Teacher Labor Market Conditions by Geographic Region 2008–2018

	Number of Teachers	Teacher Retention	Teacher Turnover	3-Year Teacher Turnover	Percent of Teachers on Annual Contract	% Classrooms Without Highly Qualified Teachers	% Emergency Certification Teacher
City	1,509.60	89.29	10.71	11.06	74.86	4.83	4.49
Rural	237.25	86.66	13.34	12.93	77.18	5.19	6.56
Suburb	1,297.18	90.55	9.45	10.62	80.54	1.98	2.70
Town	342.79	88.37	11.63	11.79	77.79	3.63	6.49

emergent certification is low and peaking at 6.56% again in rural districts. Attending to the idea that teaching jobs are plentiful, Table 12.9 shows labor market constraints in job availability in rural and exurban areas.

Rural districts, on average, have approximately 237 total teaching positions available, while exurban areas have approximately 343. This scale of potential job availability increases for city and suburban schools; however, it should be noted that in 2018, the latest year of data available in this analysis, there were only seven city districts and 18 suburban districts. More than double the number of rural and exurban districts (56) as city districts (25); 43 rural and 13 exurban. Thus, the ideology that jobs are plentiful is not holistically accurate. Furthermore, it is important to recognize that across South Carolina, there are teacher shortages, but the relationship between shortages and vacancies is complicated, often a function of geographic or curricular supply and demand.

The purpose of this section was to dispel the myth that anyone can teach and that jobs are plentiful and perpetual. From our findings, we can assert that not everyone can teach, and in fact, South Carolina teachers' preparation should give the state some hope. The teaching battery is strong regarding who they are and what type of individuals enter the profession. South Carolina's teachers are well prepared, pedagogically sound, and highly certified. This standing benefits students, as these educators think about teaching the whole child instead of vacuously focusing on one aspect of the teaching, such as the curriculum.

Finally, South Carolina teachers care enough about their profession to continually train and update their skills to create novel learning environments. Having these expert teachers available allows incoming teacher trainees to observe good teaching practices modeled for them (Darling-Hammond, 2010). These expert teachers then help support a positive learning environment that benefits the school holistically (Boyd et al., 2007; Moffett & Davis, 2014).

CONCLUSION

The education of South Carolina's children is at stake, and the General Assembly must recognize how bias embedded within the current system can influence how teachers are treated. South Carolina can no longer enable substantive lies about the teaching profession to pervade the common discourse. In this chapter, we problematize the negative discourse about teachers through empirically driven knowledge to bring truth to power to rectify false narratives about South Carolina's teachers. Education is one of the greatest resources in the United States, and this, like many of our great resources, suffers from resource insufficiency.

Our chapter shows that outright lies are told about educational talent as part of that insufficiency. Educating children is one of our state's highest priorities, and South Carolina's teachers know this, working against countless efforts to demean them and their working environment. Despite this, South Carolina's teacher labor force has made strides in their training, contending with a hostile environment that underpays them, forcing them to work long hours in buildings that are practically falling apart.

South Carolina's school stakeholders must now acknowledge that their teachers have made a concerted effort to hold up their "part of the bargain" in that promise to educate all children. The Palmetto State must now be willing to uphold its responsibility and ensure that all children and teachers have the necessary resources and respect to move forward. If not, then we may see South Carolina continue to trudge through year after year of academic mismanagement.

For now, we hope this chapter demystifies and clarifies many common misconceptions about public school teachers. In no uncertain terms, we have shown that those myths about teachers, and the teaching profession, in South Carolina are often lies. Teachers have known the deficit ideologies and conjecture about their field filled with half-truths and negative propaganda. This chapter adds to what they've known and hopefully works to dispel those inaccuracies.

NOTES

1. Student–teacher ratio is calculated as the quotient of the total numbers of students in each district by the total number of teachers in each district, for each year of data; District Student–Teacher$_t$ = District Total Student Enrollment$_t$/ District Total Number of Teachers$_t$.
2. A highly qualified teacher is someone who (a) has earned at least a bachelor's degree, (b) demonstrates content knowledge in each core content area he or she teaches, and (c) has full state certification appropriate for the teaching assignment.

REFERENCES

Akiba, M., Chiu, Y. L., Shimizu, K., & Liang, G. (2012). Teacher salary and national achievement: A cross-national analysis of 30 countries. *International Journal of Educational Research, 53*, 171–181.

Alexander, D., & Lewis, L. (2014). *Condition of America's public school facilities: 2012–13. National Center for Education Statistics.* https://nces.ed.gov/pubs2014/2014022.pdf

American Society of Civil Engineers. (2021). *2021 Infrastructure report card.* https://infrastructurereportcard.org/wp-content/uploads/2020/12/Schools-2021.pdf

Baker, S., Myers, A., & Vasquez, B. (2014). Desegregation, accountability, and equality: North Carolina and the nation, 1971–2002. *Education Policy Analysis Archives, 22*(117), 1–30. https://doi.org/10.14507/epaa.v22.1671

Bear, G. G., Yang, C., Pell, M., & Gaskins, C. (2014). Validation of a brief measure of teachers' perceptions of school climate: Relations to student achievement and suspensions. *Learning Environments Research, 17*(3), 339–354. https://doi.org/10.1007/s10984-014-9162-1

Berliner, D. C., & Glass, G. V. (Eds.). (2014). *50 myths and lies that threaten America's public schools: The real crisis in education.* Teachers College Press.

Boyd, D., Goldhaber, D., Lankford, H., & Wyckoff, J. (2007). The effect of certification and preparation on teacher quality. *The Future of Children, 17*(1), 45–68.

Buckley, J., Schneider, M., & Shang, Y. (2005). Fix it and they might stay: School facility quality and teacher retention in Washington, DC. *Teachers College Record, 107*(5), 1107–1123.

Bureau of Labor Statistics. (2021). *Median weekly earnings and unemployment by education attainment, 2019.* https://www.bls.gov/careeroutlook/2020/data-on-display/education-pays.htm

Center for Educator Recruitment, Retention, & Advancement. (2021). *South Carolina annual educator supply & demand report update (2020–2021 school year).* https://www.cerra.org/uploads/1/7/6/8/17684955/2021-22_supply_demand_report__1_.pdf

Childcare Aware. (2020). *Picking up the pieces: Building a better child care system post COVID-19.* https://info.childcareaware.org/hubfs/Picking%20Up%20The%20Pieces%20—%20Building%20A%20Better%20Child%20Care%20System%20Post%20COVID%2019.pdf?utm_campaign=Picking%20Up%20The%20Pieces&utm_source=Full%20Report%20PDF

Cowan, J., Goldhaber, D., Hayes, K., & Theobald, R. (2016). Missing elements in the discussion of teacher shortages. *Educational Researcher, 45*(8), 460–462.

Darling-Hammond, L. (2010). Teacher education and the American future. *Journal of Teacher Education, 61*(1–2), 35–47.

Demi, M. A., Coleman-Jensen, A., & Snyder, A. R. (2010). The rural context and post-secondary school enrollment: An ecological systems approach. *Journal of Research in Rural Education, 25*(7), 1–26.

Dewees, S., & Hammer, P. C. (2000). *Improving rural school facilities: Design, construction, finance, and public support.* AEL Inc.

Drago, R., Caplan, R., Constanza, D., & Brubaker, T. (1999). New estimates of working time for elementary school teachers. *Monthly Labor Review, 122*(4), 31–40.

Earthman, G. I. (2017). The relationship between school building condition and student achievement: A critical examination of the literature. *Journal of Ethical Educational Leadership, 4*(3), 1–16.

Evans, R. W. (2014). *Schooling corporate citizens: How accountability reform has damaged civic education and undermined democracy.* Routledge.

Federal Reserve Bank of St. Louis. (2021). *Real median personal income in the United States.* https://fred.stlouisfed.org/series/MEPAINUSA672N

Filardo, M., Vincent, J. M., & Sullivan, K. (2019). How crumbling school facilities perpetuate inequality. *Phi Delta Kappan, 100*(8), 27–31.

García, E., & Weiss, E. (2019). *Low relative pay and high incidence of moonlighting play a role in the teacher shortage, particularly in high-poverty schools. The third report in "the perfect storm in the teacher labor market" series.* Economic Policy Institute.

Goldhaber, D., & Walch, J. (2012). Strategic pay reform: A student outcomes-based evaluation of Denver's ProComp teacher pay initiative. *Economics of Education Review, 31*(6), 1067–1083.

Government Office of Accountability. (2020). *School districts frequently identified multiple building systems needing updates or replacement.* https://www.gao.gov/assets/gao-20-494.pdf

Gradín, C. (2020). Segregation of women into low-paying occupations in the United States. *Applied Economics, 52*(17), 1905–1920.

Grissom, J. A., & Strunk, K. O. (2012). How should school districts shape teacher salary schedules? Linking school performance to pay structure in traditional compensation schemes. *Educational Policy, 26*(5), 663–695.

Hursh, D. (2005). Neo-liberalism, markets and accountability: Transforming education and undermining democracy in the United States and England. *Policy Futures in Education, 3*(1), 3–15.

Jimerson, L. (2003). *The competitive disadvantage: Teacher compensation in rural America. Policy brief.* Rural School and Community Trust.

Kraft, M. A., Marinell, W. H., & Shen-Wei Yee, D. (2016). School organizational contexts, teacher turnover, and student achievement: Evidence from panel data. *American Educational Research Journal, 53*(5), 1411–1449. https://doi.org/10.3102/0002831216667478

Krantz-Kent, R. (2008). *Teachers' work patterns: When, where, and how much do US teachers work.* Bureau of Labor Statistics.

Martínez, D. G. (2021). Interrogating social justice paradigms in school finance research and litigation. *Interchange: A Quarterly Review of Education, 52*(1), 297–317. https://doi.org/10.1007/s10780-021-09418-4

McCarty, W. L., & Dietz, D. (2011). Alternative teacher certification: The case for transition to teaching. *Journal of Applied Learning in Higher Education, 3*, 45–57.

Mintzer, A. (2021, July 9). Teachers concerned about worsening teacher shortage ahead of upcoming school year. *WISC News 10.* https://www.wistv.com/2021/07/09/teachers-concerned-about-worsening-teacher-shortage-ahead-upcoming-school-year/

Moffett, E. T., & Davis, B. L. (2014). The road to teacher certification: Does it matter how you get there? *National Teacher Education Journal, 7*(4), 17–26.

Moore Johnson, S., Kraft, M., & Papay, J. (2012). How context matters in high-need schools: The effects of teachers' working conditions on their professional satisfaction and their students' achievement. *Teachers College Record, 114*(10), 1–39.

National Center for Educational Statistics. (2021c). *Public school teacher spending on classroom supplies.* https://nces.ed.gov/pubs2018/2018097/index.asp

National Center for Educational Statistics. (2021d). *Teacher qualifications.* https://nces.ed.gov/fastfacts/display.asp?id=58

Nelson, J. L., & Lewis, A. E. (2016). "I'ma teacher, not a babysitter": Workers' strategies for managing identity-related denials of dignity in the early childhood workplace. In *Research in the sociology of work* (pp. 37–71). Emerald Group Publishing Limited.

OECD. (2021). *Teaching hours.* https://doi.org/10.1787/af23ce9b-en

Ornstein, A. C. (1994). School finance and the condition of schools. *Theory Into Practice, 33*(2), 118–125.

Qu, Y., & Becker, B. J. (2003, April 21–25). *Does traditional teacher certification imply quality? A meta-analysis* [Paper presentation]. Annual meeting of the American Educational Research Association, Chicago.

Ronfeldt, M., Loeb, S., & Wyckoff, J. (2013). How teacher turnover harms student achievement. *American Educational Research Journal, 50*(1), 4–36.

Scholastic Inc., & The Bill & Melinda Gates Foundation. (2021). *Primary sources America's teachers on teaching in an era of change.*

South Carolina Department of Education. (2013). *Statewide school district facilities capital needs analysis.*

South Carolina Department of Education. (2016). *Statewide school district facilities capital needs analysis.*

South Carolina Department of Education. (2019). *Statewide school district facilities capital needs analysis.*

South Carolina Department of Education. (2021). *2020–2021 state minimum salary schedule.* https://ed.sc.gov/finance/financial-data/historical-data/teacher-salary-schedules/fiscal-year-2020-2021-state-minimum-teacher-salary-schedule/

Springer, M. G., Ballou, D., Hamilton, L., Le, V. N., Lockwood, J. R., McCaffrey, D. F., Pepper, M., & Stecher, B. M. (2010). *Teacher pay for performance: Experimental evidence from the Project on Incentives in Teaching.* National Center on Performance Incentives.

Statista. (2019). *Average starting salary expectations of recent university graduates in the United States in 2019, by gender.* https://www.statista.com/statistics/1052637/average-starting-salary-expectations-recent-university-graduates-gender-us/#statisticContainer

Stoddard, C., & Kuhn, P. (2008). Incentives and effort in the public sector: Have US education reforms increased teachers' work hours? *Economics of Education Review, 27*(1), 1–13.

Thomas, L. (2018, May 8). *There is a teacher shortage crisis': How South Carolina is working to retain teachers.* WLTX 19. https://www.wltx.com/article/news/local/there-is-a-teacher-shortage-crisis-how-south-carolina-is-working-to-retain-teachers/101-550088020

Tran, H. (2017). The impact of pay satisfaction and school achievement on high school principals' turnover intentions. *Educational Management Administration & Leadership, 45*(4), 621–638.

Tran, H. (2020). Revolutionizing school HR strategies and practices to reflect talent centered education leadership. *Leadership and Policy in Schools,* 1–15. https://doi.org/10.1080/15700763.2020.1757725

Tran, H., & Dou, J. (2019). An exploratory examination of what types of administrative support matter for rural teacher talent management: The rural educator perspective. *Education Leadership Review, 20*(1), 133–149.

Tran, H., & Smith, D. (2019). Insufficient money and inadequate respect: What obstructs the recruitment of college students to teach in hard-to-staff schools. *Journal of Educational Administration, 57*(2), 152–166.

Tran, H., & Smith, D. A. (2020). What matters most for recruiting teachers to rural hard-to-staff districts: A mixed methods analysis of employment-related conditions. *American Journal of Education, 126*(3), 447–481.

Ulferts, J. D. (2016). A brief summary of teacher recruitment and retention in the smallest Illinois rural schools. *The Rural Educator, 37*(1), 14–24.

Wakefield, J. (2002). Learning the hard way: The poor environment of America's schools. *Environmental Health Perspectives, 110*(6), A298–A305.

West, K. L. (2014). New measures of teachers' work hours and implications for wage comparisons. *Education Finance and Policy, 9*(3), 231–263.

Wills, J. S., & Sandholtz, J. H. (2009). Constrained professionalism: Dilemmas of teaching in the face of test-based accountability. *Teachers College Record, 111*(4), 1065–1114.

Woessmann, L. (2011). Cross-country evidence on teacher performance pay. *Economics of Education Review, 30*(3), 404–418.

CHAPTER 13

WHY ARE TEACHERS MARCHING IN SOUTH CAROLINA?

Tim Monreal
University at Buffalo

Will McCorkle
College of Charleston

On May 1, 2019, over 10,000 people, many of them public school teachers, attended a "walkout" event at the state capitol in downtown Columbia, South Carolina. The event, organized by the teacher advocacy group SC for ED, is believed to be the largest teacher protest in South Carolina history, a state defined by its lack of worker protections and unions and its status as a right-to-work state (Schechter, 2019). So many teachers requested a day off that it forced the closure of several districts across the state (Cueto & Barton, 2019). While the reasons why individual teachers attended the rally are myriad, Figure 13.1 alludes to how a major contributing factor is likely how the profession in South Carolina is routinely undervalued and ultimately disrespected. In the image, a large sign reads #FullyFundED, a direct

How Did We Get Here?, pages 311–330
Copyright © 2022 by Information Age Publishing
www.infoagepub.com
All rights of reproduction in any form reserved.

Figure 13.1 Tim's photo from South Carolina Teacher Walkout, May 1, 2019.

reference to the South Carolina legislature refusing to meet the minimum per-pupil base cost mandated by state law (Street, 2018). A smaller sign held up by a march participant states, "My 2nd and 3rd jobs paid for this sign," tying such underfunding to teacher experiences of low salaries, unpaid workplace demands, insufficient benefits, and the need to find other sources of income. Before, during, and after the march, teachers expressed that inadequate education funding and salaries caused a variety of other woes such as large class sizes, minimal resources, overworked and tired employees, poor facilities, and severe staffing shortages. Paired with such overt financial concerns, teachers expressed disdain for ever increasing amounts of paperwork, standardized testing, and restrictive curriculum (see also Bartell et al., 2019). Perhaps, one May 1st teacher attendee summed it up best, saying, "There's just no break, day after day" (Cueto & Barton, 2019, n.p.). Setting a typically muggy Columbian, South Carolina May 1st day as the backdrop and outcome of extreme yet daily teacher frustration, we forward South Carolina as one point to help us understand larger regional and national trends of both educator alienation and a resultant resistance.

Specifically, in this chapter, we examine the South Carolina context in two ways. First, we outline how the teaching profession intersects with a larger state history of anti-unionism, minimal employee protections, and increasing neo-liberalism. Such a history necessarily highlights decades of teacher resistance and advocacy that seeks to change this norm and its impact on schools. Second, we examine data from a pilot study where teachers reflected on and explained their (seemingly) sudden shift to public teacher advocacy during 2018–2019. Thus, this chapter explores how and why particular South Carolina teachers insert themselves into the fight for their profession, taking on new (political) subjectivities within a restrictive context that opposes such action through policy, rhetoric, and history. This chapter is significant in beginning a scholarly conversation about recent teacher advocacy in South Carolina, in addition to better understanding how teachers (re)conceptualize their political commitments at this moment when teachers are continually under attack. We also think through how teacher education programs can use these findings to take up the responsibility to prepare future educators for political agency within restrictive contexts.

HISTORICAL CONTEXT: SOUTH CAROLINA LABOR AND EDUCATION ADVOCACY

South Carolina Labor History

South Carolina has historically been antagonistic towards teacher advocacy or worker activism of any type. The roots of a contemporary Southern economic strategy, anti-union, low taxes, minimal regulation, and pro-industry and business, emerged in the last quarter of the 19th century to stymie the short-lived push for inclusive democracy during Reconstruction (Du Bois, 1935; Flanagan, 2003; Woodward, 1971). In his overview of the historical narratives on the lack of unions in the South, Simon (1997) points out that scholars have often focused on racism, xenophobia, individualism, and paternalism as the cultural reasons for the lack of union activity in the South. Although Simon (1997) argues that widespread White Southern poverty plays an under-examined role in larger organizing, it is important to understand how white supremacy would rather see racial privilege than class solidarity. The White South fought bitterly and worked tirelessly to link power relations to White material and political privilege spaces. Du Bois (1935) speaks clearly to this point that racial privilege is often maintained under the veil of unregulated, capitalist growth. In other words, controlling labor is part and parcel of the economic injustices resulting from racial injustice.

As such, (racialized) capital consistently wins vis-a-vis labor in South Carolina; the discourse and veneer of free labor and industrial growth is used to recreate a system of labor disempowerment. The rise of the New Right in the 1980s in South Carolina is one way to understand how such logic plays out and continues to impede labor (unions) and the investment in government programs for the public good (like schooling). The New Right sought to reverse the large-scale redistribution of political and economic power that resulted from the social programs and movements of the 1960s by using racially coded language to (re)stoke White resentment (Omi & Winant, 2015). In particular, the New Right used discourses of private property, individual rights, tradition, and government overreach as a way to reify White beliefs that expanded government programs benefited the "underserving (and implicitly Black) poor, who had the nerve to demand 'handouts'" (Omi & Winant, 2015, p. 195). Thus, any expansion and intervention of the state into social life were fervently fought in lieu of an "efficient," "color-blind," and inherently "fair" free market. This resistance laid the foundation for a current neoliberal agenda in South Carolina that focuses on economic well-being and competitiveness over state programs (fully funded schools) and labor protections/organizing (unions). In sum, low taxes, low wages, low regulations, and low worker protections emphasize the needs of business profit making above those of employees and the public good.

Still, there have been numerous attempts from labor groups in South Carolina to disrupt this anti-union, neoliberal thinking. For example, at the turn of the 20th century, there was an attempt among unions such as the Knights of Labor to organize mill workers in the state. Though the efforts were not successful, they did show that Southerners were open to the idea of unionization, but also that it was in the best interest of management to be hostile towards any union activity (McLaurin, 1971). In 1969, African American nurses organized a union and strike to protest racialized wages and working conditions at Charleston's Medical College. Although state officials did not recognize the union, the strike made national news, created an employee grievance process, increased wages, and inspired a complementary strike by the city's Black sanitation workers (Hale, 2019b). More recently, in 2017, Boeing workers in North Charleston organized a union campaign and secured a vote. Showing how deeply entrenched such anti-union thinking is, however, 74% of Boeing workers rejected the attempt to unionize (Scheiber, 2017).

Anti-unionism is also ingrained into, and supported by, South Carolina law. South Carolina is a right to work state; its legal code bars workplaces from requiring employees to pay union fees, allows union members to cancel their deductions a year after any agreement is made, and makes it illegal "to compel or attempt to compel any person to join, or support, or refrain from joining or supporting any labor organization" (South Carolina Code of Laws, 2012, para. 7). Even though state law does not prohibit strikes, South Carolina is one of only six states that do not allow collective bargaining by public employees (Garcia & Han, 2021). Given this context, it is not surprising that South Carolina ranks 50th in the nation for union membership, with just 3.6% of its employed residents represented by a union (Bowers, 2019b). In sum, the above restrictions have furthered a common feeling that any labor activism or union-type activity is illegal, creating a chilling effect on any teacher/public employee strikes in the state (Bowers, 2019a). To add anecdotal evidence about this context, both of us were recently public-school teachers in South Carolina and heard from our colleagues how participation in any type of organizing would get us fired. Hannah Timmons, a teacher who led organizing efforts in the 1970s and 1980s, recently explained this ingrained resistance (even by teachers) to unions and/or employee advocacy saying, "They have an anti-labor attitude which is what you find in a feudalistic society, which is what we still have" (Bowers, 2019b, para. 18). Such state anti-unionism, in general, intersects with recent national discourse to paint teacher unions in particular as an "enemy" of public-school reforms and efficiency (Goldstein, 2011, p. 557). As Goldstein (2014) shows, media often focuses on how unions (supposedly) protect incompetent teachers and impede new learning directives, rather than union efforts to improve work conditions, raise public school funding, and achieve educational justice. Thus, as we see next, teacher/education advocacy in South Carolina tends to be grassroots and mercurial.

South Carolina Teacher/Education Advocacy

Though widespread teacher political action in South Carolina is rare, there have been notable exceptions, particularly as Black teachers fought for equal education rights throughout and beyond the civil rights era. For example, one of the most famous teacher activists in the history of South Carolina is Septima Clark, who worked for equal rights for Black teachers and later helped lead citizenship schools during the Civil Rights Movement (Hall et al., 2010). She set a model for South Carolina educators to show that their role was not merely to remain passive and follow the instructions of their superiors and state officials but to push for structural change. Similarly, Hale (2019a) highlights how Black teachers resisted the gutting of public education that occurred in the 1960s, standing against the myriad school "integration" education ploys and actions that reinscribed white supremacy. For example, Black teachers organized for their right to continue teaching and leading newly desegregated schools even as White educators were given priority in the new educational arrangements (Hale, 2018, 2019a). This happened even as new teacher organizations like the Palmetto State Teacher Association (PSTA), a non-union professional association without national affiliation, were formed to reject the radical racial ideas of traditional (and Northern) teacher unions.[1]

As the overt racial tension of, and intersections with, the civil rights era drew to a close, Bowers (2019b) highlights increased teacher advocacy and the union movement in the late 1970s and early 1980s. Teachers joined school board meetings to protest for better conditions, and there were prominent examples of teacher demonstrations in Oconee County, which may have factored into the school board acquiescing to some teacher demands. Likewise, in 1985, the Richland County Education Association sued for equal pay for female teachers and greater transparency. Though there was this growing teacher advocacy in the state at the time, as is an important theme, this movement was both anti-union and "color-blind." To elaborate, Hale (2019a) writes how nascent teacher associations like the PTSA grew in large part because they were *not* unions; they tied teacher professionalism and respect to measures of individual freedom that included support of right-to-work legislation and critique of government overreach (i.e., busing).

Even as teacher advocacy ebbs and flows during the 1990s and 2000s, several education groups like the South Carolina Educational Association (SCEA) and the Palmetto State Teachers Association (PSTA) continue to lobby on behalf of teachers. PSTA goes to great lengths to separate itself from union activity stating, "All educators have the right to choose their professional association,"[2] but does offer legal protection, lobbying campaigns, and professional development. With considerably less power than its chapters in more unionized states, SCEA has still influenced public education in the state. The most recent example of this was in 2020 when the SCEA and several other organizations filed a suit against the governor of South Carolina, Henry McMaster, who was planning on using the federal education funds for COVID-19 to bolster private schools. As a result of this legal support, the case went to the South Carolina Supreme Court who ruled against McMaster and in favor of the SCEA and public education (Mallory, 2020).

Still, lobbying efforts from these "legacy" teacher groups and associations did little to stymie the devastating effects of the Great Recession of 2008 on an already underfunded public school system in South Carolina. As education budgets lagged behind pre-recession levels, the state of South Carolina continued a long history of failing to meet its state constitution-mandated "minimally adequate" education funding (Walker, 2019). Ten years after the Great Recession, teacher pay was stagnant, teachers were leaving the profession in droves, and many schools struggled to maintain basic resources (Bowers, 2018). In sum, teachers (including the two of us) felt overworked and undervalued. Feeling the sting of accountability and facing ever-increasing demands on their practice, many described doing more for, and with, less (Cueto & Barton, 2019).

Mirroring the frustration of many, one individual teacher launched a Facebook page in the Spring of 2018 to counter the "lack of respect for teachers" in South Carolina (Schechter, 2019). Created for about 20 of her friends, she originally posted, "Hey, is anybody else discouraged and frustrated and tired?" (Schechter, 2019). Within a week, there were 1,000 members, a year later, more than 25,000. Expanding from this Facebook page, a new grassroots group, SC for Ed quickly embraced a larger organizing and advocacy mission. A core group of individuals and board members soon traveled the state, created educator forums, and attempted to summarize a large set of teacher grievances. Rooted in a grassroots ethos of "for us, by us" the group focused on three topics: (a) increasing salary and improving benefits, (b) improving working conditions, and (c) improving the funding of public schools (SC for ED, n.d). While the group first sought more conservative means of influence (e.g., letter writing, legislative listening sessions, state lobby days), it also connected to the larger "Red for Ed" teacher activism gripping the nation. Foregrounding how local disinvestment in public schools led South Carolina to a number 50 ranking in education (Pan, 2017) with national momentum, SC for ED pushed for big changes in the state through engagement, community, and advocacy. However, sensing little improvement or attention from state lawmakers, SC for Ed organized a "walkout" event on May 1, 2019, that brought over 10,000 people to the state capital. This more direct action was one of the largest grassroots demonstrations in South Carolina since the civil rights movement. Perhaps most remarkable is how all of this is advanced in a South Carolina context defined by its lack of worker protections and status as a right-to-work state. Given how rapidly SC for ED grew, we now explain and examine data from a pilot study where two teachers reflected on their (seemingly) sudden shift to public advocacy within such a restrictive state/local context during 2018–2019.

BECOMING PUBLIC EDUCATION ADVOCATES

Pilot Study Rationale and Methodology

Similar to other contemporary state teacher movements (e.g., Kentucky, North Carolina, Virginia, and Arizona), a major component and driver of this new wave of teacher advocacy in South Carolina came through public dialogue via social media (Krutka et al., 2018). In particular, SC for ED used Facebook as a primary means of communication, growth, messaging, and eventually, a major tool to mobilize large numbers of classroom teachers for direct action. Although Krutka et al. (2018) speak to the local context of Oklahoma and the #OklaEdWalkout movement, we agree that teacher advocacy in South Carolina through social media "signaled their [teacher] power to alter narratives, cause disruption, and effect some desired legislative change" (p. 389). Classroom teachers felt like they finally had a collective space to share, connect, complain, and hope. Given the ambiguity and impact of social media on SC for ED, we were interested in the intersections of emerging (public) advocacy, a more political teacher identity, and online activity. We wanted to create a method of collecting data that allowed for teachers to communicate and make sense of their entrance and continuation of public advocacy via their social media presence.

As such, Author 1 (Tim) developed a modified photovoice method where participants found "photos" from their own social media accounts that spoke to their emerging public advocacy. The "photos" consisted of actual photography posted on social media and more traditional social media posts (text-based) the participants wanted to share. Mitchell et al. (2017) note that finding photographs (or in this case, past social media posts) is sometimes regarded as a type of photovoice and can be "representative of what they saw as change, rather than taking photographs with a camera themselves" (p. 27). Similar to more traditional photovoice (Annang et al., 2016; Wang & Burriss, 1997), the photos became the focus of an open-ended interview where participants answered questions about (a) how they came to understand themselves as public education advocates; and (b) why, and for what reasons, did they start to publicly advocate for education/teachers. Subsequently, the data sources for this examination lie in the teachers' reflections and explanations about their social media posts and event pictures.

The data shared in this chapter come from a pilot study of two public school teachers, Ashley and Garrett (both pseudonyms), in South Carolina. Each teacher individually selected 10 "photos" and individually participated in an accompanying interview with Tim in Summer 2019. The interviews lasted about one hour long, were recorded, and transcribed for accuracy. Data analysis was an emergent process of reading the transcripts and outlining key themes. After Tim outlined his initial themes with supporting quotes, Author 2 (Will) reread the data to confirm and/or modify the themes.

Given the small sample size, the focus is not on generalizability but rather on seeking to understand and describe the experience of individuals. We also counter that the two teachers, one White male, and one White female, are worthy of detailed analysis and study for at least four reasons. First, before SC for Ed, the two teachers had little experience, or even desire to be involved, in "politics." Second, the two teachers are both 10+ year veterans but still relatively young (approximately 35 years old). This matters because they have chosen to stay and make their career in the teaching profession, even as they actively push back against its construction in the state. Third, although the pair do not hold "official" positions in the SC for Ed leadership, they are among a small group who have used sick/personal days to lobby at the statehouse, in addition to attending numerous local events. This is important because it speaks to a group of teachers who may eschew official titles or positions but are crucial to a prolonged movement. Fourth, the teachers have since become involved in other political issues and are increasingly vocal at their school sites. This points to a shift in how they perceive themselves and is crucial to understanding how others may transform. Before sharing the themes, we offer a brief moment for theory.

THEORY

While we find it important to center the two teachers' reflections in the remainder of this chapter, we also find it essential to highlight how discourses about teaching in South Carolina created the normalized teacher subject, and correspondingly how teacher advocacy might create opportunities for resistance and counter-conduct (see Monreal, 2021; Zembylas, 2021). In particular, we center post-structural notions of subjectivity (Foucault, 1982, 1990, 2017) to understand how teachers are subject to a myriad of discourses and knowledge about teaching, for example, what it means to be a "professional," or what it means to be a "good" teacher. In other words, the teacher subject is the embodied site of different power relations—university preparation, macro, and micro educational policy, state politics, neoliberal and instrumental discourse, pedagogical norms, and community expectations—that struggle for the teacher's soul (Popkewitz, 1998). As many scholars (Apple, 2013; Daniels & Varghese, 2019; Hara & Sherbine, 2018; Popkewitz, 1991, 1998; Webb, 2009) note, the teaching subject is increasingly tied to amorphous performances of "professionalism" that reproduce neoliberal logic about color-blindness, apolitical practice, accountability, instrumentalism, surveillance, efficiency, and perpetual self-improvement (Au, 2016; Ball, 2003; Melamed, 2006; Sleeter & Bernal, 2004). Specific to South Carolina, we see how the history and context of anti-unionism and low worker protections factor into these subject locations and appropriate behavior for teachers. Poststructuralists, then, shift away from theories of *a* subject and toward an understanding of the ongoing processes of subjectification and subjection. As we see in our articulation of the participant reflections, emergent teacher advocacy created new and explicitly political ways of seeing oneself as a teacher.

FINDINGS

"I Think We Have Been Conditioned by the System...": Starting Small and Testing the Waters

> *I think we have been conditioned by the system and by all those that came before us ... you don't rock the boat. Nobody wants to be that teacher that, that stirs the*

pot . . . so I was real afraid to, you know, step outside that because I didn't want to be seen as a troublemaker or disgruntled at all.

—Ashley

Ashley felt she needed to add context before she shared her first "photo," a screenshot of a Facebook post where she reposted an article about teaching conditions in South Carolina. She explained how she came from a family of educators and grew up idolizing her mother, a teacher, who showed her that good teachers were "caring," "hard-working," and "respectful," but also accepting of the "challenges and problems" that came with the job. Thus, as she stated in the opening quote, teachers don't "rock the boat" lest they be labeled "troublemakers" and/or "disgruntled." This certainly fits within a normed teacher subjectivity of being a "good employee" and a "professional" who eschews labor politics (and their close association to unions) and accepts workplace difficulties as part of the job. Yet joining the SC for ED Facebook group provided some safety for Ashley because she found a place where others were dialoguing about common concerns. Seeing other teachers speak publicly gave her a model to do the same, and she communicated that it was a "big deal" for her to (re)post that first article. After posting the first article, she posted a second, adding a hashtag, #SCforED (see Figure 13.2). Soon, she was sharing articles with her commentary and experiences. Ashley showed "photos" of longer posts and a profile picture where she was clad in red complete with a Red for Ed filter. The red dress was an

Figure 13.2 Ashley's first use of #SCforED on Facebook.

explicit wedding of South Carolina with the larger "Red for Ed" teacher activism gripping the nation. Thus, for Ashley, she started small and tested the waters but came to realize that she had "a voice" and that she could no longer "keep quiet."

Similarly, Garrett shared how teacher behavior has historically and contemporary been controlled and gendered (Apple, 2013; Quantz, 1985). He mentioned his grandmother, who, as a teacher in the 1950s, was made to quit when she got pregnant. While he said those situations were "just accepted back then," he said similar actions continued today. He mentioned that many teachers are forced out of the profession because of the lack of affordable daycare and/or inflexibility regarding parenting from their administration. He also cited "traditional" beliefs about teachers for comments made from one of his administrators that he shouldn't have a beer in public or go to bars. However, what made him most frustrated was the announcement of Betsy Devos as the nominee for secretary of education. He said he was sick of "leaders who don't have credibility, who have never been in public schools, and then want to tear down public schools." He began to notice teacher movements from other states organizing against such moves and ideas. Joining SC for ED gave him ideas to start advocating on his own. In particular, the Wear Red on Wednesday initiative was a crucial starting point for him. Seeing other teachers post selfies wearing red each Wednesday motivated him to do the same. It also allowed him to give teachers at his school a tangible starting point for advocacy, wearing red each Wednesday. Thus, some of the "photos" he shared were pictures of dozens of teachers at his middle school posing together after wearing red on different Wednesdays. This community building started from simply reading about and posting his red shirt Wednesday. As Garrett got more involved and vocal in his advocacy, this reference to increased social connections would come back as vital.

"Some of the Best Teachers I've Worked With Are Involved in This...": Building Connections and Working to Redefine Good Teachers

I think some of the best teachers I've worked with are involved in this ... and real leadership is standing up for what is right.

—Garrett

Garret consistently stated how social media and his emerging advocacy helped build connections with other teachers across the state. His public stance increased in response to teachers who supported teacher advocacy and those that ignored it. It was not only that the "best teachers"—one's he identified as pedagogically progressive, hard-working, and child-centered—he worked with were involved in SC for ED, but also the reverse. Garrett stated, "And I know that some of the teachers that aren't the best are against it." Thus, for Garrett, being involved with teacher advocacy meant he was part of a group fighting for his profession, and ultimately the betterment of children and the state. In his mind, this was "real leadership"; this was what educators were expected to do. In his own words, being publicly involved showed a commitment to "stick my neck out for the benefit of all of us." While he understood that teachers had been trained to remain "neutral," he started to see that the only way public education would improve in South Carolina was for teachers to come together, build relationships, and demand something different. He saw actions, typically those connected to union activity, such as "walkouts" and "strikes," had worked elsewhere and shared social media posts where he stated the same needed to happen in South Carolina.

Similarly, Ashley stated that the connections she started to make through her online engagement with SC for ED made her feel like "she wasn't alone." Yet, even more than remedying alienation, Ashley started to feel pride in the relationships she was forming. She shared a Tweet where she reached out to a local state representative that was also a family friend. The state representative acknowledged her, wrote back, and started a dialogue that other teachers joined. She stated, "I saw this momentum...and there were all these people doing it with me...and I'm like I'm proud to be a teacher. I'm proud of my colleagues for advocating for our profession." In her mind, creating relationships fueled participation, strengthened motivation, and built solidarity. Buoyed by colleagues at her school and online excitement, Ashley felt safe and confident publicly urging other teachers to walkout on May 1st. She even changed her profile picture (Figure 13.3) to an image that read #alloutMay1. It is no surprise then that Ashley explained watching so many teachers come together on May 1st as "a spiritual experience...that brought me to tears many times over the day." The

Figure 13.3 Ashley's Facebook profile picture.

event rejuvenated her desire to be a teacher and reframed her purpose in education. She posted on Facebook, "I've rediscovered the spark inside of me that led to this career in the first place." Importantly, Ashley and Garrett show a redefinition of the subject position "good teacher." They both explain how in the past they saw (themselves as) good teachers in terms of their practice of, and compliance to, certain norms grounded in pedagogical and professional knowledge. Now they see "good teachers" as those who "fight for public education . . . and get involved in politics" (Ashley), especially since it remains relatively unpopular to do so in their state context that is anti-labor (and anti-union).

"This Is Something That Benefits All of Us As Teachers, But Also the Future of Our Community": Choosing Certain Political Engagements

> *Whether you have kids or if you are just neighbors, our future is worth advocating for. This is something that benefits all of us as teachers, but also the future of our community.*
>
> —Garrett

Both Garrett and Ashley (re)conceptualized their political commitments through a pragmatic economic frame. They saw their advocacy both as a personal financial necessity and a way to fight for greater public investment in education. Garrett consistently noted his young child as a reason he took on public advocacy. He shared a picture of his son in a Red for Ed t-shirt by saying, "Teacher pay directly impacts my family and his future." However, beyond the simple fact that he wanted more financial security, he reasoned that low salaries and poor benefits impacted "all kids because the attrition rates continue to grow." In his mind, this affected the quality of teachers and limited a career in education to those who were "well off" or "with rich spouses." One of the things that appealed to Garrett was that SC for ED was not content on pushing for one or two percent raises but rather fundamentally changing how education was imagined and funded in the state. Ultimately, funding education and paying teachers was a pragmatic economic move to help his family, recruit more teachers, and provide future prosperity for the state. Ashley shared a similar tact stressing the economics of teacher recruitment (see her picture at the May 1st Walkout, Figure 13.4) as a way to move the state and profession "forward and not backward."

However, given the context of South Carolina (labor) history as previously outlined, it appeared that an emphasis on economics was also a way to deemphasize more controversial (potentially union-aligned) issues like political parties and race. Ashley was clear that she was still wary of "politics"

Figure 13.4 Ashley's photo and sign from the May 1st Walkout.

and thus couched her political action as "non-partisan." In her words, "Education is a non-partisan issue. It's an everyone issue. It's everybody's responsibility to educate ourselves and to vote for people who will support public education, regardless of party lines . . . it's about having kids' best interests at heart." Yet, it was clear that education funding and policy in South Carolina was very much a partisan issue in which Republican lawmakers consistently worked to restrict unions, open up school choice, limit curriculum, and privatize any remaining remnant of benefits like retirement and health care.

Moreover, economics was a way to evade conversation about race and racialized inequality in the state. Garrett discussed being part of a continuing education PD called the poverty cohort. He consistently talked about how these classes evidenced the deep and unjust disparities in funding resulting from the policy of "minimally funding" schools. However, he did not mention race once in these discussions, even as he alluded to the "Corridor of Shame," a portion of rural South Carolina with notoriously under-resourced schools that serve many majority Black communities (see Ferillo, 2013; Moore, 2018; Ohue, 2017; Wellington, 2004; Chapter 4, this volume). Similarly, as Ashley described the need to "stay woke" going forward, she did not mention how this applied to racialized outcomes, funding, and resources in schools. More research is needed to determine whether such color-evasiveness was a covert strategy to make advocacy more palatable and/or an overt response to the racist history of teacher advocacy in the state.

"I Have Been Told That I Need to be Quiet to Get Promoted": Professional Risk

So, I have a master's degree plus 30 [units], was top of my class in elementary education and also in my educational admin program. I'm about to start my 15th year. But I have been passed up for every administration job I applied to. I have been told that I need to be quiet to get promoted.

—Garrett

While both participants expressed a great deal of self-pride in their identification as a teacher advocate and larger feelings of efficacy, support, and motivation from most colleagues, there was also risk. In particular, Garrett expressed how his vocal support of teachers and SC for ED limited career advancement. He was told directly by a district administrator that his advocacy was "too political," and as such, he would need to "be quiet to get promoted [to a vice principal job]." More than the increase in pay that such a job entailed, he was frustrated that administrator's writ large had an "unspoken code of neutrality." Ashley, too, wondered why administrators weren't more vocal in their support of SC for ED as she believed this advocacy would ultimately benefit their ability to recruit and retain teachers. In her mind, administrators should be instructing us on policy just "as they do for classroom management and content." She wanted administrators to be part of the solution but found many instances when her school leadership tried to dissuade participation. Ashley shared that one international teacher from a Latin American country was told that participating in the walkout would jeopardize her ability to stay in the United States. Thus, it appears that there are still limits to tying political and teacher advocacy to the subject of (good) teachers in the South. However, both participants shared how much they would appreciate working for a school leader that supported them in this way, leading credence to research that emphasizes the teacher-administrator relationship (Scallon et al., 2021).

CONCLUSION

In this chapter, we shared the context of teacher advocacy in one restrictive labor state, South Carolina, and pilot research where two teachers reflected on their (seemingly) sudden shift to public advocacy during 2018–2019. The two participants redefined their subjective understanding of a good teacher to include pedagogical and curriculum knowledge and political advocacy. This is significant because even in a state context hostile to labor organizing and teacher unions, these two teachers acknowledged the importance of and participated in direct political advocacy. As the four themes demonstrate, the two teachers used social media to start small, build connections, and link their advocacy to a broader improvement of their community. In this way, their emergent self-knowledge of teaching (and the teacher self) transformed to include work that was "outside the classroom." This points to a series of entry points to building teacher solidarity in restrictive settings while disrupting neoliberal (and anti-union) logics, discourses, and definitions of teaching. Such work is crucial to shifting perceptions of teaching toward the inherent political work it is. Additionally, it is vital to note that Ashely and Garrett's advocacy was personally risky and couched in neoliberal understandings of efficacy, economic pragmatism, and nonpartisan politics. More research is needed to determine whether this was a covert strategy to make advocacy more palatable and/or an overt response to the racist history (of teacher advocacy) in the state.

Such research is important because a more explicit embrace of so-called partisan politics may be necessary, as there continues to be a disconnect between politicians from the two major parties in South Carolina regarding education. Educational advocates in the state have noted that this continues to be a large issue in 2020 as many teachers continue to vote for conservative Republican candidates who would weaken public education and stand against teachers' rights. In fact, in the 2020 election, the GOP gained a supermajority in the South Carolina legislature, allowing them to push through almost any legislation, including bills detrimental to public education.

These political and partisan realities were also at play in the Spring of 2021 when Governor McMaster signed an executive order to prevent school districts from enforcing mask mandates if parents opted out (Koeske, 2021). There were individuals on the SC for Ed Facebook page supportive of McMaster and pushed back against the leadership of SC for Ed for being too political about these types of issues. Hence, we see that there are limits to the economic pragmatism of teacher advocacy when their support of smaller class sizes, better teacher pay, and more benefits are secondary to larger political ideologies such as partisan politics or matters of racial justice. It also gives little incentive for GOP legislators in the state of South Carolina to listen to the voices of teachers when they realize they have many of their votes regardless of what they do.

Thus, and in sum, we believe this research mirrors Bartell et al.'s (2019) call for higher education and teacher preparation to nurture and support teachers to work as change agents. Such education would equip new teachers with "the ability to access or create a network of support, and strategies for connecting [advocacy] to the everyday practices of teaching" (Bartell et al. 2019, p. 302). Teacher education would then take on the responsibility of preparing practitioner advocates with an understanding of local context, in the case of South Carolina that of neoliberal anti-unionism, while providing ideas and tactics for navigating and disrupting these realities. Listening to, learning from, and building upon the voices and actions of teachers themselves, as we emphasize here, should be a central part of this program as stakeholders learn how to unravel this complicated puzzle of teacher advocacy in South Carolina and across the United States.

NOTES

1. For a detailed examination of how White teacher associations responded to desegregated schools see Hale (2019a).
2. On the "History and Vision" page of its website, PSTA also states, "You do not have to join a national association in order to be a member of PSTA. All dues collected remain in South Carolina to support our educators through benefits such as advocacy, liability insurance coverage, and professional development... PSTA does not endorse candidates" (para. 3; https://palmetto teachers.org/about-us/history-vision/)

REFERENCES

Annang, L., Wilson, S., Tinago, C., Wright Sanders, L., Bevington, T., Carlos, B., Cornelius, E., & Svendsen, E. (2016). Photovoice: Assessing the long-term impact of a disaster on a community's quality of life. *Qualitative Health Research, 26*(2), 241–251.

Apple, M. W. (2013). Controlling the work of teachers. In D. J. Flinders & S. J. Thornton (Eds.), *The curriculum studies reader* (4th ed.; pp. 167–182). Routledge.

Au, W. (2016). Meritocracy 2.0: High-stakes, standardized testing as a racial project of neoliberal multiculturalism. *Educational Policy, 30*(1), 39–62. https://doi .org/10.1177/0895904815614916

Ball, S. J. (2003). The teacher's soul and the terrors of performativity. *Journal of Education Policy, 18*(2), 215–228. https://doi.org/10.1080/0268093022000043065

Bartell, T., Cho, C., Drake, C., Petchauer, E., & Richmond, G. (2019). Teacher agency and resilience in the age of neoliberalism. *Journal of Teacher Education, 70*(4), 302–305. https://doi.org/10.1177/0022487119865216

Bowers, P. (2018, October 30). South Carolina teachers are poorer today than in 2008, according to salary study. *Post and Courier.* https://www.postandcourier .com/news/south-carolina-teachers-are-poorer-today-than-in-2008-according -to-salary-study/article_56c297d8-dc50-11e8-b47c-8715f4b62dda.html

Bowers, P. (2019a, April 29). In anti-union South Carolina, May 1 teacher protest could make history. *Post and Courier.* https://www.postandcourier.com/news/ in-anti-union-south-carolina-may-1-teacher-protest-could-make-history/ article_76411ace-6a82-11e9-a6a8-bf94ad68223c.html

Bowers, P. (2019b, April 28). South Carolina teachers flex their activist muscles after decades of labor losses. *Post and Courier.* https://www.postandcourier .com/news/south-carolina-teachers-flex-their-activist-muscles-after-decades-of -labor-losses/article_e25dd566-6605-11e9-b779-63a44d23af8b.html

Cueto, I., & Barton, T. (2019, May 2). Why they marched: At historic rally, SC teachers declare 'state of emergency.' *The State.* https://www.thestate.com/news/politics-government/article229869584.html

Daniels, J. R., & Varghese, M. (2019). Troubling practice: Exploring the relationship between Whiteness and practice-based teacher education in considering a raciolinguicized teacher subjectivity. *Educational Researcher, 49*(1), 1–8. https://doi.org/10.3102/0013189X19879450

Du Bois, W. E. B. (1935). *Black reconstruction.* Harcourt, Brace and Company. http://ouleft.org/wp-content/uploads/2012/blackreconstruction.pdf

Ferillo, B. (2013). *Corridor of shame: The neglect of South Carolina's rural schools.* University of South Carolina Press.

Flanagan, B. E. (2003). *Race, employment and poverty in two New South cities: The case of Greenville-Spartanburg.* University of North Carolina.

Foucault, M. (1982). The subject and power. *Critical Inquiry, 8*(4), 777–795.

Foucault, M. (1990). *The history of sexuality: An introduction, volume 1.* Vintage Books.

Foucault, M. (2017). *Subjectivity and truth: Lectures at the Collège de France, 1980–1981.* Palgrave Macmillan.

Garcia, E., & Han, E. (2021, April 29). *The impact of changes in public-sector bargaining laws on districts' spending on teacher compensation.* Economic Policy Institute. https://www.epi.org/publication/the-impact-of-changes-in-public-sector-bargaining-laws-on-districts-spending-on-teacher-compensation/

Goldstein, R. A. (2011). Imaging the frame: Media representations of teachers, their unions, NCLB, and education reform. *Educational Policy, 25*(4), 543–576. https://doi.org/10.1177/0895904810361720

Hale, J. N. (2018). On race, teacher activism, and the right to work: Historicizing the Red for Ed movement in the American South. *West Virginia Law Review, 121*(3), 851–881.

Hale, J. N. (2019a). 'We are not merging on an equal basis': The desegregation of southern teacher associations and the right to work, 1945–1977. *Labor History, 60*(5), 1–19. https://doi.org/10.1080/0023656X.2018.1561103

Hale, J. (2019b, April 29). Honor the past by respecting teachers today. *Post and Courier.* https://www.postandcourier.com/opinion/commentary/honor-the-past-by-respecting-teachers-today/article_9a7cf250-6a8c-11e9-af8d-f3aea4ba44a2.html

Hall, J. D., Walker, E. P., Charron, K. M., Cline, D. P., & Clark, S. P. (2010). Voices from the Southern oral history program: "I train the people to do their own talking": Septima Clark and women in the civil rights movement. *Southern Cultures, 16*(2), 31–52.

Hara, M., & Sherbine, K. (2018). Be[com]ing a teacher in neoliberal times: The possibilities of visioning for resistance in teacher education. *Policy Futures in Education, 16*(6), 669–690. https://doi.org/10.1177/1478210318758814

Koeske, Z. (2021, May 12). SC schools, local governments may no longer impose mask mandates, governor orders. *The State.* https://www.thestate.com/news/local/education/article251317653.html

Krutka, D. G., Asino, T. I., & Haselwood, S. (2018). Eight lessons on networked teacher activism from #OklaEd and the #OklaEdWalkout. *Contemporary Issues in Technology and Teacher Education, 18*(2), 379–391.

Mallory, L. (2020, October 7). *SC Supreme Court rules against McMaster's grants for private schools.* WIS News. https://www.wistv.com/2020/10/07/sc-supreme-court-rules-against-mcmasters-grants-private-schools/

McLaurin, M. A. (1971). Early labor union organizational efforts in South Carolina cotton mills, 1880–1905. *The South Carolina Historical Magazine, 72*(1), 44–59.

Melamed, J. (2006). The spirit of neoliberalism: From racial liberalism to neoliberal multiculturalism. *Social Text, 24*(4), 1–24. https://doi.org/10.1215/0164 2472-2006-009

Mitchell, C., De Lange, N., & Molestane, R. (2017). *Participatory visual methodologies: Social change, community, and policy.* SAGE Publications.

Monreal, T. (2021). Stitching together more expansive latinx teacher self/ves: Movidas of Rasquache and spaces of counter-conduct in El Sur Latinx. *Theory, Research, and Action in Urban Education, 7*(1), 17–31.

Moore, E. (2018). Shamed—Court rules S.C. must help poor rural schools. *Free Times.* https://www.free-times.com/cover_story/shamed—court-rules-s-c-must-help-poor/article_b39afdd3-3635-5692-927b-3a690daaa578.html

Ohue, E. (2017, July 6). At Duke, I realized how badly many South Carolina schools are failing students like me. *The State.* http://www.thestate.com/opinion/op-ed/article160018914.html

Omi, M., & Winant, H. (2015). *Racial formation in the United States* (3 ed.). Routledge.

Pan, D. (2017, March 1). South Carolina ranks last in education in U.S. News & World Report study. *Post and Courier.* https://www.postandcourier.com/news/south-carolina-ranks-last-in-education-in-u-s-news-world-report-study/article_5a7d26c8-fe9d-11e6-9644-2bab813ed6f7.html

Popkewitz, T. S. (1991). *A political sociology of educational reform: Power/knowledge in teaching, teacher education and research.* Teachers College Press.

Popkewitz, T. S. (1998). *Struggling for the soul: The politics of schooling and the construction of the teacher.* Teachers College Press.

Quantz, R. A. (1985). The complex visions of female teachers and the failure of unionization in the 1930s: An oral history. *History of Education Quarterly, 25*(4), 439–458. https://doi.org/10.2307/368834

Scallon, A. M., Bristol, T. J., & Esboldt, J. (2021). Teachers' perceptions of principal leadership practices that influence teacher turnover. *Journal of Research on Leadership Education,* 19427751211034216. https://doi.org/10.1177/1942 7751211034214

SCforED. (n.d.). *Our focus.* https://www.scfored.org/our-focus

Scheiber, N. (2017, February 15). Boeing workers reject a union in South Carolina. *The New York Times.* https://www.nytimes.com/2017/02/15/business/boeing-union-south-carolina.html

Schechter, M. (2019, February 10). This SC teachers' group caught fire overnight. Meet the educator who lit the match. *The State.* https://www.thestate.com/news/politics-government/article225915545.html

Sleeter, C. E., & Bernal, D. D. (2004). Critical pedagogy, critical race theory, and antiracist education: Implications for multicultural education. In J. A. Banks & C. A. M. Banks (Eds.), *Handbook of research on multicultural education* (pp. 240–258). Jossey-Bass.

Simon, B. (1997). Rethinking why there are so few unions in the south. *The Georgia Historical Quarterly, 81*(2), 465–484.

South Carolina Code of Laws. (2012). *Title 41-Labor and employment.* South Carolina Legislature. https://www.scstatehouse.gov/code/t41c007.php

Street, L. (2018, March 30). *New budget keeps underfunding education by hundreds of millions.* Statehouse Report. https://www.statehousereport.com/2018/03/30/news-new-budget-keeps-underfunding-education-by-hundreds-of-millions/

Walker, T. (2019, May 2). *#RedforEd wave gets bigger in North and South Carolina.* Education Votes. https://educationvotes.nea.org/2019/05/01/redfored-wave-gets-bigger-in-north-and-south-carolina/

Wang, C., & Burris, M. A. (1997). Photovoice: Concept, methodology, and use for participatory needs assessment. *Health Education and Behavior, 24*(3), 369–387. https://doi.org/10.1177/109019819702400309

Webb, T. (2009). *Teacher assemblage.* Sense Publishers.

Wellington, D. L. (2004). Ambiguous legacy: Summerton, South Carolina, and *Briggs v. Elliott. Dissent, 51*(3), 45–51.

Woodward, C. V. (1971). *Origins of the New South: 1877–1913* (2nd ed.). Louisiana State University Press.

Zembylas, M. (2021). The affective dimension of everyday resistance: Implications for critical pedagogy in engaging with neoliberalism's educational impact. *Critical Studies in Education, 62*(2), 211–226. https://doi.org/10.1080/17508487.2019.1617180

CHAPTER 14

LOOKING AHEAD

The Future of the Teaching Profession

Henry Tran
University of South Carolina

Douglas A. Smith
Iowa State University

In recent years, news headlines and scholarship about the teacher shortage crisis have become increasingly commonplace (Edelman, 2021; Garcia & Weiss, 2019). These shortages have been fueled by dramatic enrollment declines in teacher preparation programs across the nation (Partelow, 2019) and large concentrations of teacher attrition (Carver-Thomas & Darling-Hammond, 2017). While some critics argue against the existence of a nationwide teacher shortage (Cowan et al., 2016), less controversial is the robust body of evidence that suggests, for teachers of certain subject matters/specialty areas (e.g., science, technology, engineering, math, special education) or contexts (e.g., high poverty and low performing districts; Partelow, 2019; Tran & Smith, 2020), the presence of the shortage problem is less disputable.

How Did We Get Here?, pages 331–352
Copyright © 2022 by Information Age Publishing
www.infoagepub.com

Despite the common lip service by many who claim to acknowledge the importance of teachers, according to results from Phi Delta Kappa (PDK) International's parent survey in 2018, for the first time, the majority of parents across the nation stated that they did not want their children to grow up to be teachers (Starr, 2021). In response, JoAnn Bartoletti, executive director of the National Association of Secondary School Principals, commented that "we cannot be comfortable with the stunning contradiction that a majority of Americans both recognize the importance of the teaching profession and want their own kids nowhere near it. The recent series of teacher strikes and the public support for more should wake us up to the need to invest more purposefully and creatively in the professionals who do nothing less than build our collective future" (Stringer, 2018, para. 8). Unfortunately, the low status of teaching has resulted in most college students concurring with the sentiments of their disapproving parents regarding the lack of attractiveness of the teaching profession (Tran & Smith, 2019).

The negative reputation and poor working conditions associated with the teaching profession were exacerbated by the emergence of the COVID-19 pandemic and the associated organizational and governmental responses to the catastrophic event. Many teachers were forced to decide between facing punitive disciplinary actions from their employers or putting themselves and their families at risk by complying with regulations and policies (Tran et al., 2020). Many of these policies required mandatory physical teacher attendance in classrooms packed with students where the recommended 6-feet social distancing guidelines were impractical to enforce. Workplace inflexibility further promoted turnover when requests for virtual teaching were rejected after in-person mandates were implemented (Flannery, 2020). Parents hailed teachers as "heroes" at the onset of the pandemic when they received a small taste of what the teacher's job entailed, as parents were forced to supervise home school for their children during the societal shutdown. However, the status of teachers quickly reverted to "zeros" when teachers were treated as expendable once teachers were forced to return to their densely packed classroom (often without the protection of a mask mandate for the people in the school due to contentious resistance from disapproving parents on the polarizing issue of mandatory mask enforcements in the classroom) despite the widespread rising COVID-19 infection rates (Tran & Jenkins, 2022).

To make matters worse, COVID-19 related support staff shortages have resulted in many teachers adding uncompensated staff duties to their already full workload, "sacrificing their lunch periods to cover unsupervised classrooms, monitor lunch lines, and get behind the wheel of school buses" (Lieberman, 2021, para. 1). Many teachers lost their planning periods and served as substitute teachers, janitors, and whatever other role was needed. The National Education Association's nationwide poll of teachers indicated that 28%

expressed a higher likelihood of leaving the profession due to the pandemic (Flannery, 2020). The unattractiveness of teaching has been further amplified by teachers being caught in the crossfire of intense political wars (e.g., calls for book bans, attacks against critical race studies) and concerns of potential verbal and/or physical abuse from parents and even students.

It is worth pointing out that while teacher shortages appear across the country, they are often highly localized phenomena. For example, the reasons a large urban metropolitan school district might struggle with attracting and retaining teachers likely differs from the reasons a small remote rural school district would experience the same struggles. Small remote rural districts, for example, often suffer from challenges attracting candidates because of potential candidates' perception of the lack of professional growth opportunities, as well as a lack of amenities or "things to do" in their community relative to larger cities (Tran & Smith, 2019). Furthermore, state policy differences can result in differential laws and regulations that impact teacher working conditions, such as workplace employment protection, the presence of teacher unionization, accountability, and salaries.

Given the localized issue of teacher shortages, this book has focused on examining the topic through a case study of a specific state described as being in a teacher shortage "crisis" due to its rising teacher vacancies and turnover (Chuck, 2019). Throughout this book, we have heard from the voices of hundreds of educators (including both teachers and administrators, as well as those engaging in teacher activism and those involved in the legacy lawsuit to fight for equitable school funding for South Carolina's most disenfranchised students), traced the history of teacher working conditions across decades, reviewed policy efforts aimed at mitigating teacher shortages and reviewed nationwide, and explored localized empirical research related to the topic.

Collectively, the chapters paint a picture of a decaying teaching profession that has suffered from racist and sexist origins, which fuels the disrespect of professionals in the industry both in the local school setting and its broader reputation at the state national level. For example, Goldstein (2015) documents how pay declined when the profession became feminized (i.e., majority women; Chapter 1, this volume). Relatedly, a dearth of people of color in the teaching profession (7%) relative to the broader labor market (13%; U.S. Bureau of Labor Statistics, 2017) was heavily influenced by the lack of recovery from school employers' response to the desegregation ruling in *Brown v. Board of Education* (1954). Specifically, post ruling, school employers purged tens of thousands of Black educators from their positions (Chapter 3, this volume; Grooms et al., 2021; Tillman, 2004) because Black students were integrated and now can be taught in White schools, which in the eyes of many employers, rendered Black teachers and principals obsolete.

Racism and sexism are only examples of the dehumanization that is endemic to the decay of the teaching profession, especially in South Carolina. They go hand in hand with the lack of respect for the profession overall at the societal level, which often trickles down to how teachers are perceived and treated at the school level. In the next section, we will provide a synthesis of the major elements of this book, with an emphasis on implications for the future of not only the teaching profession, but education as a whole and how the information shared throughout the book should be of concern to the general public.

WHAT HAVE WE LEARNED?

This book was organized into four parts. In Part I: "How Did We Get Here: The Historical and Racial Context of the Teacher Profession's Decay," Tran and Smith (Chapter 1) situated the current teacher labor issues in a historical context. This context originates from a history of lower wages being associated with the increase of female representation in the public education workforce (Goldstein, 2015), and whose workers are uncoincidentally compensated at a much lower rate than those in male-dominated labor and mechanical industries, tracing back to the 1800s. In introducing the illustrative case state of South Carolina, this chapter focused on painting a vivid picture of teacher attrition and working condition issues that have festered for decades in the state. At present, South Carolina has more departures from public school teaching positions than it prepares each year through in-state teacher preparation programs (Center for Educator Recruitment, Retention, & Advancement [CERRA], 2020). At the same time, the state legislature has consistently underfunded public school districts from the legislatively mandated minimum base student cost. Since 1989, the appropriated base student cost has only met or exceeded the minimum 11 times, the last time being 2008–2009, with a current shortfall of $606 per pupil (Tran, 2018). The consistent underfunding of education, coupled with the wide gap in compensation between those in the education profession relative to other professional fields (Allegretto & Mishel, 2020), reflects a lack of respect for the profession—a theme that re-emerges several times in this book.

In Chapter 2, Hale and Getowicz discussed Black teacher progress in southern states and their historical influence on teacher reform movements dating back to the reconstruction era. Although progress has undoubtedly been made, there remains a significant lack of diversity in the teacher workforce (U.S. Department of Education, 2016). Moreover, while many school employers publicly state that they seek to diversify their workforce, the underrepresentation of teachers of color, particularly Black teachers, culminated from decades of rejection of that diversity. Focused specifically on the underrepresentation of Black teachers in the South Carolina teacher labor market, in Chapter 3, Holden and Tran discussed historical discriminatory influences in school district human resource decision making and policies stemming from school employers' response to desegregation. During school segregation, segregated Black schools were often described as having excellent, supportive teachers and leaders, despite receiving unequal fiscal support (Siddle-Walker, 2009; Tillman, 2004). Research has long-established that Black students have improved academic outcomes when paired with black teachers (Egalite et al., 2015; Gershenson, Hart, et al., 2018; Gershenson, Holt, et al., 2016). Post-school desegregation, many Black educators were displaced from or denied entry into the educator labor force as they were no longer seen as needed now that White teachers were also educating Black students (Fultz, 2004; Oakley et al., 2009). Black student enrollment in teacher preparation declined for decades, and the profession's diversity remains hindered by the legacy of Black educator treatment during desegregation (Horsford, 2011). Lastly, in Chapter 4, Tran, Aziz, and Frakes Reinhardt highlighted a court battle lasting nearly 30 years. In this case, the most rural and impoverished districts along the state's I-95 corridor sued the state over inequitable, inadequate school funding claims. While the state supreme court initially ruled in favor of the plaintiff districts, the ruling was dismissed entirely upon a change in justices, leaving the majority of districts with limited, if any, substantive change in their conditions. Transportation costs, poverty, and teacher quality were issues identified by the court as reasons inequity had been and would continue to be sustained in the plaintiff rural districts, even if equal financial resources per pupil to more affluent districts were available. The court's reference to teacher quality is directly a function of and compounded by teacher recruitment and retention challenges, especially in the state's most rural and economically impoverished communities. In the chapter, we heard from superintendents of the plaintiff district about their persistent and longstanding staffing woes.

In Part II: "The Downward Spiral: Economics of School Funding and Teacher Retention," Martínez and Tran examined the historical labor market and school finance state policies and their influence on the teacher shortage in Chapter 5. This work draws attention to the disparate impact of teacher shortages in school districts with higher proportions of students in poverty and from racially minoritized backgrounds. Likewise, this examination showed an inverse correlation between salaries and teacher turnover. These results further detail the facility funding gap for schools in South Carolina that is especially hard-felt in rural, high-poverty districts. This funding gap undoubtedly contributes to poor physical working conditions experienced by many teachers in those locales. In Chapter 6, Tran and Smith examined a state policy initiative to provide financial support directly to high-turnover school districts to aid in their teacher recruitment and retention efforts. While the findings of this examination determined that the state funding appeared to have some mitigating effects on teacher turnover, both quantitative and qualitative data suggest that the efforts are insufficient for the policy initiative to reach its full potential at current funding levels. More work is needed to ensure that sufficient funding is available to high-need districts to make investments sustainable and dependable and better align districts' selected incentives with empirically supported evidence. Lastly, in Chapter 7, Tran and Jackson analyzed teacher shortage mitigation discourse, focusing on the relationship between teacher pay and teacher employment trends and policy efforts. The general sentiment held by the majority of Americans is that teachers are underpaid (Goldstein & Casselman, 2018). Even in comparative terms, teachers earn nearly 20% less than equivalently credentialed peers in non-teaching occupations, and this differential remains over 10% even when considering the retirement and medical benefits typically offered to public school teachers (Allegretto & Mishel, 2020). Higher base salaries are linked to improved job attraction, teacher retention, and, subsequently, teacher experience, all of which contribute to student achievement (Ladd & Sorenson, 2017). While many factors undoubtedly influence initial and continued employment decision-making, compensation remains a foundational barrier for many in their consideration for seeking teacher employment. However, confronting issues of inadequate compensation is necessary, but alone insufficient, in improving teacher employment attractability, job satisfaction, and retention. School employers must also address the broad array of working conditions that influence future and current employee decision-making.

Berry begins Part III: "Overworked and Overburdened: Teacher Working Conditions," with Chapter 8, where he reviews the current knowledge base of teacher working conditions related to teacher recruitment, effectiveness, and school performance. He then summarizes three separate research projects related to the topic that spans three decades, starting from 1990 to 2020. The occupation of teaching has long been considered a semi-profession in the eyes of many (Berry, 2011; Etzioni, 1969; Lortie, 1975; Rousmaniere, 2005). To improve the professionalization of teaching, policymakers and leaders should focus on key working conditions that are linked with positive employee sentiments, such as improving opportunities for peer collaboration (Szczesiul & Huizenga, 2015), providing more time for planning (Center for Teaching Quality, 2004), giving autonomy back to teachers that were taken away reform movements (Berry et al., 2020), empower and trust teachers to make professional decisions (Berry et al., 2020), provide effective professional development opportunities (Kraft & Papay, 2016), and provide sufficient facilities and resources necessary for educational excellence (Center for Teaching Quality, 2004). In Chapter 9, Jackson Smith and Sauls addressed the manifestation of recent teacher effectiveness and accountability policies and their influence on teacher working conditions. Significant attention on these topics arose in the 1980s and has steadily remained as a guidepost for education policy in the subsequent three decades. Recognizing that the typical over-emphasis on "accountability" and "effectiveness" has escalated teacher stress and strain, South Carolina has transitioned the linguistics of policy efforts away from a disciplinary tone and towards a more supportive role. However, policy intentions may differ from practice at the school level, and the way teacher evaluations are executed often misses the mark of both accountability and development (Weisberg et al., 2009). Lastly, in Chapter 10, Buckman investigated the relationship between teacher and principal turnover, demonstrating that high poverty and high minority schools face especially high attrition for both. Teacher retention has specifically been shown to be impacted by a principal's attributes, experience, and disposition.

Part IV: "Moving Forward: How the Teaching Profession Can Ascend and Flourish" is the final section of the book, and it starts with Chapter 11, in which Smith, Tran, and Cain review a series of studies they conducted that aim at understanding teacher recruitment and retention in South Carolina's hard-to-staff rural schools. Several implications are made. First, there is a need to enhance rural-specific training for pre-service and in-service teachers and principals to tackle the pressing needs of rural schools. Additionally, recruitment and retention often center on financial incentives. However, non-monetary needs must also be met through community relationships, administrative support, mentoring, transparency, and communication. While rural communities are often described through a deficit lens, there are many positives associated with rural locales that can be promoted during the recruitment process and used in employer branding initiatives to improve rural teaching recruitment efforts. Finally, similar to other schools, administrative support is critical for teacher retention in rural schools but may look different in the rural contexts relative to other locales. In Chapter 12, Martínez and Tran examine several commonly perpetuated myths about the teaching profession that harm its reputation and ultimately contribute to teacher attrition issues. They dispelled these myths that focused on promoting misperceptions of the relaxing teacher work schedule, adequate teacher compensation, sufficient and comfortable professional resources, and the all too common notion that teaching is an easy job that anyone can do. Lastly, in Chapter 13, Monreal and McCorkle explored the topic of teacher activism and specifically shared reflections from South Carolina teachers concerning their engagement in the historic teacher walkout that occurred in the state, which was part of a larger trend of nationwide walkouts. They argue that a growing number of teachers view political advocacy for education causes as an important element that adds to the traditional pedagogical and curriculum domains in their pursuit of educator excellence. This activism was documented as starting small, building personal connections, redefining what a "good teacher" is, thinking about community impact in choosing political engagements, and understanding/tolerating the professional risk associated with political activity.

In this final chapter, "Looking Ahead: The Future of the Teaching Profession," we draw and expand on what we have learned from the aforementioned chapters and provide implications and recommendations to reconsider the future of the teaching profession.

PREPARING FOR THE FUTURE OF EDUCATIONWORK

The world of work is changing. Workers have traditionally occupied a subservient compliance-oriented role in the employer and employee relationship, being told to be tight-lipped about work complaints, endure poor work environments, and that they should feel lucky to even have a job. However, in recent years, social media activism (such #metoo, #times up, or the nationwide teacher walkouts powered by #RedforED) has provided a platform for employees to increasingly hold their employers accountable for the working conditions provided. Employees have become increasingly vocal about having more humane work environments that include (but are not limited to) safer and more equitable workplaces, compensate fairly, and provide better work–life balance.

While workers have long sought meaning in their work, amidst the COVID-19 pandemic, this search for meaning, coupled with workers' growing resentment towards being exploited or settling for less, has resulted in what Dr. Anthony Klotz termed *the Great Resignation* (Rosalsky, 2021, para. 4). The Great Resignation refers to the record level attrition that has occurred due to "pandemic epiphanies" (Rosalsky, 2021, para. 4), which were influenced by numerous factors, including the lack of daycare for the children of workers, safety concerns, and changes to employee experience resulting from mandatory remote work. These issues affected professionals across industries, including teachers.

While the COVID-19 pandemic exacerbates teacher shortages (Tran et al., 2020), long-standing issues at the state, district, and school levels have sustained the unattractiveness of the teaching profession. These issues are often related to low salaries (with purchasing power declining over time), poor working conditions (with accumulating job responsibilities accumulating over time), lack of career pathways, especially when compared with other professional occupations such as those in medicine and law, and perceptions of inadequate supports (Partelow, 2019). When teachers were not outright ignored when bringing attention to these issues, they were met with empty platitudes about how much they are valued and how they deserve to be paid more, with little substantive evidence to demonstrate things will change for teachers. Instead, teachers were often met with suggestions that they need to be more resilient and practice self care, which could be perceived as a slap in the face given their challenging circumstances.

It is clear change is needed. In the next few sections, we present recommendations for preparing for the future of the work of teaching, based on cutting-edge theory grounded in the latest thinking from the human resources management field. The goals of these recommendations are not just to improve teacher satisfaction, but rather support, engage and inspire the profession.

TALENT CENTERED EDUCATION LEADERSHIP

Drawing on decades of scholarship on educator working conditions and progressive practices and thinking in the human resources management field, Tran (2022) introduced Talent Centered Education Leadership (TCEL) as a new way to reconceptualize the management and treatment of the education workforce. While primarily a human resources management framework for employers, because public educators are primarily prepared by higher education institutions, and ultimately employees of the state, being funded by tax dollars, TCEL has implications not only for school employers but also higher education institutions, the state government, the taxpaying public. These implications will be discussed later, but first, we detail the seven core principles of TCEL, as described by Tran and Jenkins (2022), to better orient us to the framework. They include:

Principle 1: Recognize that employees are the most important asset to the organization; Educator needs and student needs are not mutually exclusive.

Principle 2: Emphasize inclusive talent management; Talent centered education leaders create inclusive work environments and understand the way talent is defined can marginalize or recognize the diversity of talent to leverage innovation.

Principle 3: Focus on the employee experience (EEX).

Principle 4: Utilize data to inform decision making, especially as it relates to designing positive and engaging EEX.

Principle 5: Empathize with employee needs by authentically and regularly listening to their concerns and feedback, providing them workplace autonomy and flexibility.

Principle 6: Focus on employee engagement as a valued organizational outcome.

Principle 7: Consistently show and demonstrate respect for education employees.

Of the seven principles, we will examine Principles 1 and 3 in more detail as they relate directly to the content of this book.

Principle I: Recognize That Employees Are the Most Important Asset to the Organization; Educator Needs and Student Needs Are Not Mutually Exclusive

As it relates to Principle 1, research has consistently found teachers to be the most important "within school" factor affecting student achievement (Rivkin et al., 2005; Hanushek, 2016). Further foundational to TCEL is the encouragement of thinking beyond the common teacher vs. student trope that supports the continued abuse and exploitation of educators for the purported sake of putting "children first." While the teacher walkouts garnered much public support, many publicly opposed them. These individuals often painted a dichotomy between teacher and student needs, as if they were diametrically opposed (especially given that the protesters were also calling for school funding improvements), and claimed that the teacher activism was hurting students (Chapter 1). For example, then-Secretary of Education Betsy DeVos criticized teachers for neglecting student needs and service in pursuit of their own interest (Reilly, 2018), while Arizona state senator Kelly Townsend threatened to engage in a class-action lawsuit against teachers for the "harm" (e.g., extended school year) that their walkout caused (Roberts, 2018). In South Carolina, Superintendent of Education, Molly Spearman, famously no-showed the May 1st teacher rally at the state capitol, prompting protestors at the rally to chant, "Where is Molly? Where is Molly?" In a statement released to the public 2 days before the walkout, Spearman wrote,

> I became a teacher because I love and believe in education and the needs of my students always came first. Now, as State Superintendent, my first responsibility and top priority is to the nearly 800,000 students of our state. That is why on May 1, I will not be joining those teachers who decide to walk out on their classrooms. Instead, I will be walking into the classroom of an absent teacher to serve as a substitute. I am not doing this to help facilitate the walkout, but rather to do all I can to ensure as many students as possible receive the instruction they deserve.
>
> All can agree that areas of South Carolina's education system are in need of improvement. This year, I have worked with the legislature to raise teacher salaries, provide additional mental health and safety resources for all students, and reduce excessive testing that takes valuable time away from teaching. Progress continues to be made but much more needs to be done.
>
> I support teachers using their voice to advocate for needed change and share in their commitment to ensuring reforms become reality. However, I cannot support teachers walking out on their obligations to South Carolina stu-

dents, families, and the thousands of hardworking bus drivers, cafeteria workers, counselors, aides, and custodial staff whose livelihoods depend on our schools being operational.

I pledge to continue fighting to improve the opportunities and resources for all South Carolina students and teachers. (Spearman, 2019, para. 1–3) Unfortunately, this pledge of support rang hollow for many educators in the state as they felt this stance taken by Spearman demonstrated that she did not support teachers despite her claims to the contrary. Understanding that teacher and student needs are not mutually exclusive is important at the school, district, state, and broader levels. Otherwise, the effort will be spent villainizing and blaming teachers for the troubling academic outcomes of our youth, as opposed to dealing with entrenched systemic problems rooting from underfunding (Chapter 4, 5, 6), under-compensation (Chapter 7), racism (Chapters 2, 3, and 4), sexism (Chapter 1), and an overall lack of respect shown to the teaching profession (Chapter 11 and 12).

Principle III: Focus on the Employee Experience

Progressive and modern human resources experts and practitioners have increasingly advocated for the EEX design approach to workforce management (Claus, 2019; Rasca, 2018). Modeled after design thinking and an evaluation of the traditional organizational emphasis on customer experience (Mahadevan & Schmitz, 2020), this approach to talent management is based on the culture of data-informed decision making with iterative testing and learning for the employer based on employee feedback related to their needs. The emphasis is on designing positive, engaging, and supportive EEX for the workforce. It is designed to evolve the organizational culture from unilateral top–down decision-making toward a balance to include bottom-up processes where innovative and diverse ideas are rapidly tested and refined in a human-centered organizational learning culture.

Tran and Smith (2021) relied on design thinking (Plaskoff, 2017) to develop an EEX approach to teacher talent management that views work as more than just employment. Rather, work is viewed as part of a larger life journey with many milestones and interactions. In the process of engaging in strategic talent management to develop an EEX approach, employers should

Step 1: Empathize with employee needs across the teacher career span with organization.
Step 2: Identify potential "solutions" to those needs.
Step 3: Map those solutions to the decision points or "moments that matter" across the teacher career journey (Tran & Smith, 2020, p. 88).

To address these steps, Tran and Smith (2020) leverage career choice theory and Herzberg et al.'s (1957) motivation-hygiene theory to introduce an EEX approach to specifically examine teacher retention in hard-to-staff schools. Much of the teacher talent literature remains focused on the initial decision to pursue teaching and year-to-year retention rather than a holistic perspective of the teacher career span. Many policy efforts to address teacher shortages, particularly in hard-to-staff schools, are reactive and piecemeal, failing to account for how these efforts can work cohesively to address teaching staffing issues (Strunk & Zeehandelaar, 2015).

Career choice theory (Farley-Ripple et al., 2012) emphasizes understanding personal characteristics, environmental conditions, and individual behavior related to the career path and trajectory. Critical to this is collecting, engaging, and analyzing data to inform decision-making. For example, it is important that stakeholders and decision makers authentically listen to feedback provided by teachers about the challenges they face in their work environment and suggestions for improvement. Meanwhile, Herzberg et al.'s (1957) motivation-hygiene theory suggests that job satisfaction and dissatisfaction exist on a dual continuum rather than on the opposite ends of the same continuum. From this perspective, the opposite of job satisfaction is no job satisfaction, and the opposite of job dissatisfaction is no job dissatisfaction instead of the common notion that job satisfaction and job dissatisfaction are opposites. With this, attractive factors (motivators, such as curricular autonomy) affect the degree of job satisfaction (from high satisfaction to no satisfaction), and detracting factors (hygienes, such as low compensation) affect the degree of job dissatisfaction (from high dissatisfaction to no dissatisfaction). Motivator factors represent intrinsic motivations for the job, and hygiene factors represent extrinsic factors in the job context often influenced by the employer or its environment. Tran and Smith (2020) draw from both theories to introduce *the sustaining teacher employment model* (Figure 14.1) to make sense of how to address teachers' EEX for recruitment and retention. The model centers on hygiene factors as a critical focus of recruitment efforts to minimize job dissatisfaction that ultimately contributes to sustaining rural teacher employment. They further postulate that motivator factors can also be critical for initial recruitment, but especially for retention, increasing teacher satisfaction, and engagement.

Based on prior research and scholarship, Tran and Smith (2020) consider the career life cycle needs of teachers in three stages: Beginning (1 to 3 years of experience), mid-career teachers (4 to 18 years of experience), and late-career teachers (19–30+ years of experience). In a "survival" mindset, beginning teachers are still learning to teach and navigate the school employment environment and context. In this beginning stage, teachers can benefit from recognition, realistic expectations, encouragement, clear expectations, actionable feedback, and less uncertainty with their day-to-day

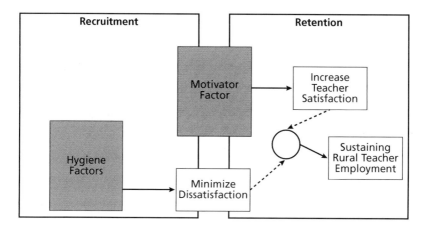

Figure 14.1 Sustaining teacher employment model.

work environment. Teachers in the beginning stage that have more negative attitudes of their principal tend to depart at higher rates, emphasizing
the need for principals to be better trained to recognize individual teacher
needs and differentiate support accordingly (Boyd et al., 2011).

In the stabilization years (4 to 6 years of experience), mid-career teachers
have developed stronger confidence, commitment, and comfort with teaching. It is important to continue to provide early mid-career teachers with
new challenges and opportunities for growth, including continued mentorship. This mentorship can occur through schools, districts, states, and
the broader local community. Mid-career teachers in the experimentation
or activism years (7 to 18 years of experience) often seek new challenges
through experimentation with new teacher strategies, content, becoming
mentors, and assuming school leadership roles. This includes some moving
to administrative appointments (e.g., principal or assistant principal) that
contributes to teacher turnover. Colleges of education specifically are well-
positioned to better support mid-career teachers through improved professional development opportunities, especially non-credit and low-to-no-cost
accessible options.

Late-career teachers (19 to 30+ years of experience) often face little attention in the career lifecycle. They may be asked to become mentors, but
lack mentoring themselves and often are provided with the same professional development opportunities as early and mid-career teachers. District
leaders, state education leaders, and policymakers should focus efforts on
providing space, time, and resources to support the formation of collaborative relationships with late-career teachers that provide opportunities to
share their knowledge and experiences. These relationships also provide

opportunities for school leaders to understand how to better meet the needs and desires specific to late-career teachers.

Tran and Smith (2020) note that the teacher career lifecycle must be considered within the context of the subject matter, level, and location. One must recognize that the sustaining teacher employment model is only as effective as the principal implementing it at the school level and the resources and supports available to principals by district leaders, state leaders, communities, and policymakers. The importance of the principal in providing administrative support, development, and mentoring is of the utmost importance towards teachers' positive experiences with motivation and hygiene factors leading to teacher retention. However, an effective principal alone is not sufficient. Other stakeholders, such as higher education institutions, community leaders, and the general public, are important in supporting teachers and the principal in their work.

It Takes the Village

An old saying argues it takes a village to raise a child. Similarly, it will take the collective efforts of multiple parties, including the school employers, government, and broader public, to repair the damage that has been done to the teaching profession's reputation and once again restore its status as an attractive career option. Tax revenue plays a vital role in funding school resources for public school teachers, including determining their salaries, which has long been cited as critical for teacher recruitment and retention. While tackling inadequate pay is necessary, it is insufficient to improve the attractiveness of the teaching profession. To do so, we must reconceptualize how teachers are treated and what it means to be a teacher and redefine their experiences to ones of support and respect. We have argued that the avenue to do so is through Talent Centered Education Leadership.

Recommendations for the government and public. Governmental entities have a vested interest and responsibility in public schools' oversight, organization, and direction. State government involvement in public education has increased since the 1980s, focusing on student achievement and subsequent accountability measures for teachers. Until recently, government bodies have largely stayed out of recruitment, hiring, and retention practice. However, the state of the current labor market for teachers has necessitated greater governmental involvement in the recruitment and retention of high-quality teachers, especially for schools struggling to manage educator talent.

The U.S. economy has rebounded strongly from the immediate negative economic impacts during the onset of the COVID-19 pandemic. Stock market indexes find themselves at record highs in 2021 (Li et al., 2021), and unemployment figures have rebounded much quicker than previous economic recessions in the United States (Albanesi & Kim, 2021). Many state economies and state tax revenue levels have rallied to pre-pandemic levels, even adjusting for inflation. Tax revenues exceeded pre-pandemic levels in 30 states by the first quarter of 2021 (Rosewicz, 2021). State policymakers need to prioritize K–12 education funding investments as state economies continue to grow. Specifically, attention should focus on new revenues diversion to increasing teacher pay relative to other professions with comparable training within states and regions. Short-term recruitment and retention bonuses may ameliorate some staffing issues in the immediacy, but long-term improvement will necessitate enhancing the minimum base salary of new and continuing teachers. However, we also know that while salary matters, other working conditions are important too. Specifically, teachers often lack administrative support, mentoring, and professional development opportunities. Recognizing that teachers are the most important variable in student achievement, state policymakers should allocate funds for these specific purposes—rather than relying on the general appropriation process to fund all needs. Professional development supports necessary for teacher growth are relatively easy decisions for district leaders to set aside when making budgetary decisions among the range of basic school needs.

Parents, community members, and the general public also have an important role in stemming the tide of resentment and discontent that too often is directed at teachers. First and foremost, the public-at-large must take a more concerted effort at nominating and electing teacher advocates to school boards and state education posts. The public should ask candidates for other state offices that influence state education policy to take a stance on teacher working conditions and quality issues and ask them to specifically support teacher-support-oriented legislative efforts. Beyond these more formal influences, the general public can and should hold one another more accountable in teachers' general treatment, beginning in recognizing the importance of teachers in everyday conversations. We must return to a time when political leaders, communities, and the general public recognize the importance of teachers in preparing our next generation.

Recommendations for higher education institutions. Many issues and challenges facing teachers are multifaceted and require solutions that are often beyond the control of the school district (e.g., housing, community engagement, social opportunities, spousal employment). Therefore, outside non-profit and government agencies and organizations have a significant ability to improve the overall condition of teachers. For example, some school districts have become more active in matching early-career employees with the United States Department of Agriculture's (USDA) income-based housing programs that allow for low-to-no down payment and low-interest mortgages. Given the limited personnel capacity of school districts, state education leaders could take a more engaged role in facilitating collaborations and partnerships with outside agencies and school districts.

Because of its general neglect, college and university-based teacher preparation programs must also focus on rural-specific teacher training and development. Rural school districts that also exhibit hard-to-staff characteristics (e.g., high poverty, low academic achievement) are particularly important to prepare students for. Context-specific training to prepare students for school environments needs turnaround is especially important. Teacher quality, experience, and preparation are exceptionally important to school turnaround efforts. College and university teacher preparation programs can focus on content and experiences (e.g., practicums, internships, observations, paid experiences) that develop pre-service teachers' self-efficacy in working in rural hard-to-staff contexts. Barley (2009) highlighted the lack of rural-specific training available to pre-service teachers. Because rural educators teach across multiple subject areas or out-of-subject at higher rates than peers (Barley, 2009), it is important for college and university teacher preparation programs to focus greater effort on providing multiple endorsement area opportunities to students. At present, few teacher preparation programs include rural-specific curriculum, offer streamlined pathways to multiple-subject certifications, or focus efforts to recruit students to the most critical shortage areas in regional rural schools. Many teachers seek employment within proximity to where they consider home (Boyd et al., 2005). Likewise, community college students enroll in a college within an average of 31 miles of home (Hillman & Weichman, 2016). Therefore, teacher preparation programs must improve community college transfer pathways to 4-year teacher preparation programs by eliminating the loss of credits through transfer articulation and offering more teacher preparation programs at a distance and satellite locations (such as the community college).

Recommendations for school employers. Teachers' perception of supportive working contexts is the strongest in-school factor related to their positional or occupational retention. These supportive working contexts include environments that provide administrative support, teacher collaboration, autonomy, and growth opportunities (Tran & Smith, 2020). Consequently, school districts should provide proactive and formal support and resources in these areas. One recommended way to accomplish this is through the EEX approach via the Talent Centered Education Leadership framework (Tran, 2022). When EEX is emphasized, the principal should have significant time and effort dedicated to leading and organizing these activities within their job duties. School leaders should emphasize inclusive talent management to their workers, cultivating work contexts where the talents of a diverse workforce can not just survive, but thrive.

School districts should also proactively engage future and new teachers with community resources and opportunities outside of the school district, beginning in the recruitment phase and through onboarding and first-year support programs. Rural school districts, in particular, should work diligently to foster stronger relationships with college and university teacher preparation programs to sponsor student teachers in their districts and even work to provide incentives such as housing and stipends. In addition, rural school districts should partner with teacher preparation programs to improve and enhance grow-your-own teacher recruitment efforts within their districts. Continuing to look internally, we must also recognize that the nature of school leadership has changed. Principals report spending more time than ever on accountability, assessment, and school discipline issues (Sebastian et al., 2018). This comes at the expense of providing necessary administrative support to teachers. School districts and building leaders must find a way to regain the time and effort necessary to support, develop, and nurture high-quality teachers—especially in the critical early years, but also throughout their tenure. Furthermore, school leaders should also not neglect their non-teaching staff. In sum, school principals cannot lead effectively if the entirety of their focus is on the students. Instead, they must create the enabling conditions so that teachers can flourish and allow the teachers to focus on the students. School employers should provide principals the necessary support, development and resources so that they can be successful in accomplishing this, without burning themselves out (Chapter 10).

FINAL THOUGHTS

Unfortunately, the general perception of the teaching occupation is riddled with high stress, low pay, and low status. To make matters worse, professionals who work in helping professions such as education are typically more susceptible to burnout (Burke et al., 1996). As a result, the profession has been decaying for quite some time now, with the situation further exacerbated because of teacher treatment during the pandemic. The question for us, then, is how can we redesign and reconceptualize the teaching profession to become revitalized and rejuvenated, with its nobility restored.

As Staiger (2005) explains, schools serve a normalizing function in a society that "creates a more docile, manageable and politically incapacitated human being" (p. 556). This socializing role is similar to the role most employers occupy, so when taken together, school employers become particularly prone to promoting regulation and control by reducing the individuality of the employed (Tran, 2022). In a seminar sponsored by the Center for Innovation in Higher Education at the University of South Carolina, presenter Dave Stovall (2019) discussed how school and education are not the same and that school is designed to coerce individuals into the prescriptive rules of society, education actively rejects that. In K–12 spaces, the coercion takes various forms, most notably through compliance and accountability mechanisms. Stovall explained that if we do not educate ourselves on our terms, we are destined to be dehumanized by the system. These dehumanizations take place in various ways in the education work context. For example, professional development in school districts is often disconnected from the needs of educators because they are based on an economic agreement with firms where the professional development is "done to" educators. When educators speak out against it, they refuse their dehumanization but put themselves at the risk of not being "compliant." Similarly, administrators are often hesitant to take a stand despite the system or "rock the boat," for fear of career retaliation. This fear fosters the perpetuation of the status quo. Yet, a school should not be a place of fear. Not for administrators, not for teachers, not for any staff members, and not for students.

The first step to addressing a problem is to admit that there is a problem. And the data and decades of research are clear. There is a problem with how the teaching profession is viewed and treated. The situation is dire. The status and respectability of the teaching profession are in decay. As we highlighted with our foci state of South Carolina, rural school districts, in particular, face chronic underfunding, overcrowding, staffing shortages.

Similarly, a growing disrespect exists for the education professionals working to cultivate and nurture our next generation. We need politicians, state policymakers, school boards, parents, and community members to make education a top priority. We need more than words and empty promises for improvement, but intentional, substantive, timely and responsive action. High-quality education begins with high-quality teachers. To recruit and retain high-quality teachers to all schools, we must move beyond the growing partisan political narrative aimed at public education and educators and focus on making real improvements for the teacher working conditions. Educators play a vital role in the future of the United States, and they should be acknowledged, supported, respected, and rewarded for the time and effort they dedicate to the development of our youth.

REFERENCES

Albanesi, S., & Kim, J. (2021). Effects of the COVID-19 recession on the US labor market: Occupation, family, and gender. *Journal of Economic Perspectives, 35*(3), 3–24.

Allegretto, S., & Mishel, L. (2020). *Teacher pay penalty dips but persists in 2019: Public school teachers earn about 20% less in weekly wages than nonteacher college graduates.* Economic Policy Institute.

Barley, Z. A. (2009). Preparing teachers for rural appointments. *The Rural Educator, 30*(3), 10–15.

Berry, B. (2011). *Teaching 2030: What we must do for our students and our public schools . . . Now and in the future.* Teachers College Press.

Berry, B., Dickenson, T., Harrist, J., Pomey, K., Zheng, J., Irvin, M., Moon, A., & Hodges, T. (2020). *Teachers and teaching in the midst of a pandemic: Implications for South Carolina's policy leaders.* Research commissioned by The SC Education Association, the Palmetto Teachers Association, and the SC Department of Education. https://sc-teacher.org/wp-content/uploads/2020/08/TG_POLICY _FINAL_AUG5.pdf

Boyd, D., Grossman, P., Ing, M., Langford, H., Loeb, S., & Wyckoff, J. (2011). The influence of school administrators on teacher retention decisions. *American Education Research Journal, 48*(2), 303–333.

Boyd, D., Lankford, H., Loeb, S., & Wyckoff, J. (2005). The draw of home: How teachers' preferences for proximity disadvantage urban schools. *Journal of Policy Analysis and Management: The Journal of the Association for Public Policy Analysis and Management, 24*(1), 113–132.

Brown v. Board of Education of Topeka, 347 U.S. 483 (1954)

Burke, R. J., Greenglass, E. R., & Schwarzer, R. (1996). Predicting teacher burnout over time: Effects of work stress, social support, and self-doubts on burnout and its consequences. *Anxiety, Stress, and Coping, 9*(3), 261–275.

Carver-Thomas, D., & Darling-Hammond, L. (2017). *Teacher turnover: Why it matters and what we can do about it.* Learning Policy Institute.

Center for Educator Recruitment, Retention, & Advancement. (2020). *South Carolina annual educator supply and demand report (2020–21 school year).* https://www.cerra .org/uploads/1/7/6/8/17684955/2020-21_supply___demand_report.pdf

Center for Teaching Quality. (2004). *Listening to the experts: A report on the 2004 South Carolina teacher working conditions survey.* https://nepc.info/sites/default/ files/EPRU-0504-111-OWL.pdf

Chuck, E. (2019, July 11). *School by day, assembly line by night: How teachers in South Carolina make ends meet.* NBC News. https://www.nbcnews.com/news/us-news/ school-day-assembly-line-night-how-teachers-south-carolina-make-n1026381

Claus, L. (2019). H.R. disruption—Time already to reinvent talent management. *BRQ Business Research Quarterly, 22*(3), 207–215.

Cowan, J., Goldhaber, D., Hayes, K., & Theobald, R. (2016). Missing elements in the discussion of teacher shortages. *Educational Researcher, 45*(8), 460–462.

Edelman, A. (2021, June 6). *Biden wants to fix the nation's teacher shortage. Educators say the problem is worsening.* NBC News. https://www.nbcnews.com/politics/joe-biden/ biden-wants-fix-nation-s-teacher-shortage-educators-say-problem-n1269340

Egalite, A. J., Kisida, B., & Winters, M. A. (2015). Representation in the classroom: The effect of own-race teachers on student achievement. *Economics of Education Review, 45*, 44–52.

Etzioni, A. (1969). *The semi-professions and their organization: Teachers, nurses, social workers.* Free Press.

Farley-Ripple, E. N., Raffel, J. A., & Welch, J. C. (2012). Administrator career paths and decision processes. *Journal of Educational Administration, 50*(6), 788–816. https://doi.org/10.1108/09578231211264694

Flannery, M. E. (2020, August 14). *Safety concerns over COVID-19 driving some educators out of the profession.* National Education Association News. https://www

.nea.org/advocating-for-change/new-from-nea/safety-concerns-over-covid-19
-driving-some-educators-out

Fultz, M. (2004). The displacement of Black educators post-Brown: An overview and analysis. *History of Education Quarterly, 44*(1), 11–45.

Garcia, E., Weiss, E., & Economic Policy Institute. (2019). *The teacher shortage is real, large and growing, and worse than we thought.* https://www.epi.org/publication/the
-teacher-shortage-is-real-large-and-growing-and-worse-than-we-thought-the-first
-report-in-the-perfect-storm-in-the-teacher-labor-market-series/

Gershenson, S., Hart, C., Hyman, J., Lindsay, C., & Papageorge, N. W. (2018). *The long-run impacts of same-race teachers* (No. w25254). National Bureau of Economic Research.

Gershenson, S., Holt, S. B., & Papageorge, N. W. (2016). Who believes in me? The effect of student–teacher demographic match on teacher expectations. *Economics of Education Review, 52*, 209–224.

Goldstein, D. (2015). *The teacher wars: A history of America's most embattled profession.* Anchor.

Goldstein, D., & Casselman, B. (2018, May 31). Teachers find public support as campaign for higher pay goes to voters. *The New York Times.* https://www.nytimes.com/2018/05/31/us/politics/teachers-campaign.html

Grooms, A. A., Mahatmya, D., & Johnson, E. T. (2021). The retention of educators of color amidst institutionalized racism. *Educational Policy, 35*(2), 180–212. https://doi.org/10.1177/0895904820986765

Hanushek, E. A. (2016). What matters for student achievement. *Education Next, 16*(2), 18–26.

Herzberg, F., Mausner, B., Peterson, R. O., & Capwell, D. F. (1957). *Job attitudes: Review of research and opinion.* Psychological Service of Pittsburgh.

Hillman, N., & Weichman, T. (2016). *Education deserts: The continued significance of "place" in the twenty-first century.* Viewpoints: Voices from the Field.

Horsford, S. D. (2011). Vestiges of desegregation: Superintendent perspectives on educational inequality and (dis)integration in the post-Civil Rights Era. *Urban Education, 46*(1), 34–54. https://doi.org/10.1177/0042085910391596

Kraft, M., & Papay, J. (2016, April). *Developing workplaces where teachers stay, improve, and succeed.* Albert Shanker Institute. http://www.shankerinstitute.org/blog/developing-workplaces-where-teachers-stay-improve-and-succeed

Ladd, H. F., & Sorensen, L. C. (2017). Returns to teacher experience: Student achievement and motivation in middle school. *Education Finance and Policy, 12*(2), 241–279.

Li, W., Chien, F., Kamran, H. W., Aldeehani, T. M., Sadiq, M., Nguyen, V. C., & Taghizadeh-Hesary, F. (2021). The nexus between COVID-19 fear and stock market volatility. *Economic Research-Ekonomska Istraživanja,* 1–22. https://doi.org/10.1080/1331677X.2021.1914125

Lieberman, M. (2021, October 15). How staff shortages are crushing schools. *Edweek.* https://www.edweek.org/leadership/how-staff-shortages-are-crushing
-schools/2021/10?utm_source=fb&utm_medium=soc&utm_campaign=edit
&fbclid=IwAR02_k1BFPFjwcESeymApqOd2jKXF-ToyGLHRJg-U_iYDM9Rs__
UCu3bhig

Lortie, D. (1975). *Schoolteacher.* University of Chicago Press.

Mahadevan, J., & Schmitz, A. P. (2020). HRM as an ongoing struggle for legitimacy: A critical discourse analysis of H.R. managers as "employee-experience designers." *Baltic Journal of Management, 15*(4), 515–532.

Oakley, D., Stowell, J., & Logan, J. R. (2009). The impact of desegregation on Black teachers in the metropolis, 1970–2000. *Ethnic and racial studies, 32*(9), 1576–1598.

Partelow, L. (2019, December 3). *What to make of declining enrollment in teacher preparation programs.* Center for American Progress. https://www.american progress.org/issues/education-k-12/reports/2019/12/03/477311/make -declining-enrollment-teacher-preparation-programs/

Plaskoff, J. (2017). Employee experience: The new human resource management approach. *Strategic H.R. Review, 16*(3), 136–141.

Rasca, L. (2018). Employee experience-an answer to the deficit of talents, in the fourth industrial revolution. *Calitatea, 19*(S3), 9–14.

Reilly, K. (2018, September 13). I work 3 jobs and donate blood plasma to pay the bills. This is what it's like to be a teacher in America. *Time.* https://time .com/5395001/teacher-in-america

Rivkin, S. G., Hanushek, E. A., & Kain, J. F. (2005). Teachers, schools, and academic achievement. *Econometrica, 73*(2), 417–458. https://doi.org/10.1111/ J.1468-0262.2005.00584.X

Roberts, L. (2018). *Roberts: Arizona legislator threatens to sue over teachers' strike. But sue who?* AZcentral. https://www.azcentral.com/story/opinion/op-ed/laurie roberts/2018/04/24/roberts-arizona-legislator-threatens-sue-over-teachers -strike-but-sue-who/548103002/

Rosalsky, G. (2021, October 19). *Why are so many Americans quitting their jobs?* NPR. https://www.npr.org/sections/money/2021/10/19/1047032996/why-are -so-many-americans-quitting-their-jobs

Rosewicz, B., Theal, J., & Fall, A. (October 14, 2021). *State' tax revenue recovery improves at start of 2021.* Pew Charitable Trust. https://www.pewtrusts .org/en/research-and-analysis/articles/2021/10/15/states-tax-revenue -recovery-improves-at-start-of-2021

Rousmaniere, K. (2005). In search of a profession: A history of American teachers. In D. Moss, W. Glenn, & R. Schwab (Eds.), *Portraits of a profession: Teaching and teachers in the 21st century* (pp. 1–26). Praeger.

Sebastian, J., Camburn, E. M., & Spillane, J. P. (2018). Portraits of principal practice: Time allocation and school principal work. *Educational Administration Quarterly, 54*(1), 47–84.

Siddle-Walker, V. (2009). Second-class integration: A historical perspective for a contemporary agenda. *Harvard Educational Review, 79*(2), 269–284. https:// doi.org/10.17763/haer.79.2.b1637p4u4093484m

Spearman, M. (2019, April 19). *Facebook update.* https://www.facebook.com/Spearman Molly/posts/i-became-a-teacher-because-i-love-and-believe-in-education-and -the-needs-of-my-s/2229492650451991/

Staiger, A. (2005). School walls as battle grounds: Technologies of power, space and identity. *Paedagogica Historica, 41*(4–5), 555–569.

Starr, J. P. (2021, September). *PDK poll of the public's attitude toward the public schools.* PDK. https://pdkpoll.org/wp-content/uploads/2021/09/Poll53_final.pdf

Stovall, D. (2019, November 5). *Staying in trouble for all the right reasons: Leadership and justice in the face of adversity* [Seminar presentation]. Center for Innovation in Higher Education, University of South Carolina, Columbia.

Stringer, K. (2018, August, 27). *New poll: For first time ever, a majority of American parents do not want their children to become public school teachers.* The74. https://www.the74million.org/new-poll-for-first-time-ever-a-majority-of-american-parents-do-not-want-their-children-to-become-public-school-teachers

Strunk, K. O., & Zeehandelaar, D. B. (2015). Added bonus? The relationship between California school districts' specialized teacher staffing needs and the use of economic incentive policies. *Educational Policy, 29*(2), 283–315.

Szczesiul, S. A., & Huizenga, J. L. (2015). Bridging structure and agency: Exploring the riddle of teacher leadership in teacher collaboration. *Journal of School Leadership, 25*(2), 368–410.

Tillman, L. C. (2004). (Un)intended consequences? The impact of the *Brown v. Board of Education* decision on the employment status of Black educators. *Education and Urban Society, 36*(3), 280–303. https://doi.org/10.1177/0013124504264360

Tran, H. (2018). *Taking the mystery out of South Carolina school finance* (2nd ed.). ICPEL Publications.

Tran, H. (2022). Revolutionizing school HR strategies and practices to reflect talent centered education leadership. *Leadership and Policy in Schools, 21*(2), 238–252.

Tran, H., Hardie, S., & Cunningham, K. M. (2020). Leading with empathy and humanity: Why talent-centred education leadership is especially critical amidst the pandemic crisis. *International Studies in Educational Administration (Commonwealth Council for Educational Administration & Management [CCEAM]), 48*(1), 39–45.

Tran, H., & Jenkins, Z. (2022). Embracing the future of education work with talent centered education leadership. *Journal of Education Human Resources, 40*(2), 266–276.

Tran, H., & Smith, D. (2019). Insufficient money and inadequate respect: What obstructs the recruitment of college students to teach in hard-to-staff schools. *Journal of Educational Administration, 57*(2), 152–166.

Tran, H., & Smith, D. A. (2020). Designing an employee experience approach to teacher recruitment in hard-to-staff schools. *NASSP Bulletin, 104*(2), 85–109.

Tran, H., & Smith, D. (2021). Talent-centered education leadership: Using the employee experience to improve teacher-school relations. *Journal of Cases in Educational Leadership, 24*(1), 42–54.

U.S. Bureau of Labor Statistics. (2017). *Labor force characteristics by race and ethnicity.* https://www.bls.gov/opub/reports/race-and-ethnicity/2017/home.htm

U.S. Department of Education. (2016). *The state of racial diversity in the educator workforce.* Department of Education.

Weisberg, D., Sexton, S., Mulhern, J., Keeling, D., Schunck, J., Palcisco, A., & Morgan, K. (2009). *The widget effect: Our national failure to acknowledge and act on differences in teacher effectiveness.* New Teacher Project.

ABOUT THE EDITORS

Henry Tran is an associate professor at the University of South Carolina's Department of Educational Leadership and Policies who studies issues related to education human resources (HR) and finance. He has published numerous articles on the topics that have appeared in journals such as *The Journal of School Leadership, The Journal of Education Finance, Educational Management Administration and Leadership, Leadership and Policies in School, Journal of Student Financial Aid,* and more. He holds two national HR certifications and serves on the Board of Advisors and Board of Trustees for the National Education Finance Academy. He is also the editor of the *Journal of Education Human Resources* and the director of the Talent Centered Education Leadership Initiative. Prior to his professorship, Tran served as an HR practitioner in both the private sector and in public education. He draws from both experiences in his research and teaching.

Douglas A. Smith is an associate professor in the School of Education at Iowa State University. He is an associate editor of the *Journal of Education Human Resources.* He studies leadership development, talent recruitment, and issues around rural education across the P–20 spectrum. He has published frequently on these topics, emphasizing community colleges and rural K–12 settings. Most recently he has been conducted research on the leadership and ethical preparation of next generation practitioners and leaders to meet academic and workforce needs.

How Did We Get Here?, page 353
Copyright © 2022 by Information Age Publishing
www.infoagepub.com
All rights of reproduction in any form reserved.

Made in the USA
Middletown, DE
27 February 2023

25769381R00201